Taking the Mask Off

*Destroying the Stigmatic Barriers
of Mental Health and Addiction
Using a Spiritual Solution*

Cortland Pfeffer
Irwin Ozborne

BALBOA
PRESS
A DIVISION OF HAY HOUSE

Copyright © 2016 Cortland Pfeffer; Irwin Ozborne.

All rights reserved. No part of this book may be used or reproduced by any means, graphic, electronic, or mechanical, including photocopying, recording, taping or by any information storage retrieval system without the written permission of the author except in the case of brief quotations embodied in critical articles and reviews.

Balboa Press books may be ordered through booksellers or by contacting:

Balboa Press
A Division of Hay House
1663 Liberty Drive
Bloomington, IN 47403
www.balboapress.com
1 (877) 407-4847

Because of the dynamic nature of the Internet, any web addresses or links contained in this book may have changed since publication and may no longer be valid. The views expressed in this work are solely those of the author and do not necessarily reflect the views of the publisher, and the publisher hereby disclaims any responsibility for them.

The author of this book does not dispense medical advice or prescribe the use of any technique as a form of treatment for physical, emotional, or medical problems without the advice of a physician, either directly or indirectly. The intent of the author is only to offer information of a general nature to help you in your quest for emotional and spiritual well-being. In the event you use any of the information in this book for yourself, which is your constitutional right, the author and the publisher assume no responsibility for your actions.

Any people depicted in stock imagery provided by Thinkstock are models, and such images are being used for illustrative purposes only. Certain stock imagery © Thinkstock.

Print information available on the last page.

ISBN: 978-1-5043-6661-8 (sc)
ISBN: 978-1-5043-6663-2 (hc)
ISBN: 978-1-5043-6662-5 (e)

Library of Congress Control Number: 2016915998

Balboa Press rev. date: 09/22/2016

TABLE OF CONTENTS

Preface: *The Masks We Wear* ix

The Book of Hope: *The Gifts of Madness* 1

Introduction:	Suicide through the Cracks	3
Chapter I:	My Name is Tim	23
Chapter II:	State of the Psychiatry Industry Address	39
Chapter III:	Love and Fear	61
Chapter IV:	Love Addiction	79

The Book of Purpose: *Connection* 93

Chapter V:	Psychological Tsunami	95
Chapter VI:	Alien Encounters	115
Chapter VII:	Love Revolutionaries	139
Chapter VIII:	The 危機 Theory	167
Chapter IX:	Vulnerability Removes the Mask	193

The Book of Obstacle: *Addiction* — 209

Chapter X:	The Phantom of Society	211
Chapter XI:	The Ego Has Landed	235
Chapter XII:	Down the Rabbit Hole	261
Chapter XIII:	Soul Contracts	283
Chapter XIV:	It's All Synchronicity	297
Chapter XV:	The Dark Night of the Soul	315

The Book of Wisdom: *Recovery* — 333

Chapter XVI:	Recovery	335
Chapter XVII:	Freedom to Be Me	355
Chapter XVIII:	Relapse	369
Chapter XIX:	Forced Surrender	387
Chapter XX:	The Lunatic is on the Grass	405
Chapter XXI:	Disillusionment	425

The Book of Love: *Enlightenment* — 449

Chapter XXII:	A Perfect Third Step	451
Chapter XXIII:	Ego Traps	465
Chapter XXIV:	Shadow Work	487
Chapter XXV:	The Revolution Has Begun	505
Chapter XXVI:	Taking the Mask Off	521

PREFACE: THE MASKS WE WEAR

> *"Did you hear about the rose that grew from a crack in the concrete? Funny, it seems to be keeping its dreams; it learned to breathe fresh air. You see, you wouldn't ask why the rose that grew from the concrete had damaged petals. On the contrary, we would all celebrate its tenacity. We would all love its will to reach the sun. Well, we are the rose – this is the concrete – and these are my damaged petals."*
> - Tupac Shakur

One summer in a small village, all the people gathered for a picnic. As they shared food and conversation, someone noticed a baby in the river which was struggling and crying. It was clear the baby was on the verge of drowning and facing imminent death if someone did not act swiftly.

Without thinking twice, someone promptly aborts everything to jump into the river and save the baby. Everyone's heart had been racing in panic and confusion, rush to ensure the baby is safe. Just as things start to calm down, they notice another screaming baby in the river. Again, someone jumps in to pull the baby to safety.

Soon, more babies were seen drowning in the river and all the townspeople were pulling them out and the entire village was involved in many tasks of rescue work: pulling the poor children from the stream, ensuring they were properly fed, clothed, housed, and integrated into life of the village. While not every baby could be saved, the entire village spent all their day trying to save as many as possible. As everyone kept busy in the recovery efforts, two townspeople started to run along the shore of the river.

"Where are you going!?" shouted one of the rescuers, "We need you here to help us save these babies!"

"Don't you see?" They cried, "If we find out how they are getting into the river, we can stop the problem and no babies will drown! By going upstream we can eliminate the cause of the problem."

"But it is too risky," said the village elders, "It might fail. It is not for us to change the system. And besides, how would we occupy ourselves if we no longer had this to do all day?"

This parable explains the modern industry of human services. Another version would include someone jumping into the river and teaching the babies to swim. While it is fair to say that everyone in this situation is doing their absolute best to fight the problem, real change is only going to happen once we find out the core problem to eliminate more from falling into the river.

Is there some mysterious illness in these children? Had the shoreline been made unsafe by a natural disaster? Was some hateful person throwing them in deliberately? Or was there an even more exhausted village upstream that had been abandoning them out of hopelessness?

Just like with addiction and mental health, we can fix all the presenting symptoms, but there will never be long-lasting change until we can get to the root of the problem. Everyone is innocent and pure at their core.

The Masks We Wear

Humans have been donning masks for as long back as the Stone Age. While the material and designs change, the reasons remain the same. Humans have always worn masks primarily to hide their identity and create a new one; they wear masks for protection; part of spiritual rituals; or in theatre – again to create a false identity.

We still put on physical masks for special occasions such as Halloween and Mardi Gras. These nights are a huge success because it allows adults to hide their identity, let go of feelings of self-consciousness, and truly be themselves for one night. But the irony of it all is that we are putting on a temporary physical mask to cover up a permanent psychological mask in which we have created through our lifetimes.

Just as ancient warriors would put on masks to prevent attacks from enemies, we put on masks daily for the same reasons – to prevent others from hurting us on an emotional level. There are times when we need to put on these masks for safety, but the danger lies when we begin to rely on the mask to go through everyday life.[1]

Our masks are created daily by the way society teaches us how we are supposed to be, when we are supposed to eat, how to talk to each

---

[1] Nunley, J., & McCarty, C. (1999). *Masks: Faces of culture*. New York: Abrams in association with the Saint Louis Art Museum.

other, what are interests are, what are goals should be, and what we need to know about life.

And most importantly, society teaches us to lie.

"I'm fine" is the most common lie told in modern society. We say it daily without thinking twice as it has become such common practice, and we know it is not true. It is the safe way of protecting ourselves but it also blocks us from real connection, depletes our consciousness, and hinders our spirit.

About the Book

The purpose of this book is to battle the stigma of mental health and addiction in society by empowering the individual. All equal rights movements gained true power when the oppressed group realized that they were already perfect beings, in an imperfect society.

We have seen it with the Civil Rights movements as African-Americans embraced their heritage and being proud, the rise of feminism allowed women to feel free to be themselves and not fit the mask that society created, many Native Americans find peace by returning to their traditional lifestyle, and most recently the gay rights movement has been catapulted by one word – pride.

The Mad Pride movement is attempting to do the same, being proud of the spiritual gifts that are found in each "mental illness." This book aims to show that there is no mental illness, only spiritually gifted individuals that are being oppressed by a society that does not fully understand. It also aims to explain addiction as a medical disease that requires a spiritual solution.

I have a unique journey and perspective in that I have a personal history on both sides of the desk. I have been a patient in psychiatric hospitals, an inmate in jail, and a number of treatment centers. Additionally, I've worked as an RN supervisor and staff in the same locations – psychiatric wards, jails, and treatment centers.

On March 4, 1994, I was committed as mentally ill. Twenty-one years later to the date – March 4, 2015 – I was the charge nurse at the exact same facility.

In June of 2014, I started a blog (www.takingthemaskoff.com) which shared some of my personal experiences as a patient, staff, and supervisor. I was gratefully overwhelmed with the positive response to my writings. This incredible shared passion of lifting the stigma has prompted me to putting together this book, knowing there are so many people just as eager to break the stigma.

This book is divided into five sections – Hope, Purpose, Growth, Wisdom, and Enlightenment. The book follows my life journey from an attempted suicide to inner peace which correlates with these five concepts. Each section also has a theme in regards to the mental health/addiction industry, and parallels with the Four Noble Truths of the Buddhist philosophy.

It also utilizes angles from all spectrums – science, personal experience, spirituality, and philosophy. It shares information that agrees with all fields. It is not about religion, spirituality, science, philosophy, or even about my journey – but rather, it is about all of the above and only when they are all in agreement. This approach ensures the most accurate information from all points of view.

Birth of the Mask

We can learn a lot by watching our children at play. Toddlers are free of shame and embarrassment and enjoy pure psychological freedom. They can walk up to a stranger and ask to be their friend, cry when they are sad, not afraid of what others think of them, live in the moment, show curiosity about the world around them, and live in peace, harmony, and nirvana.

While this is going on, children are constantly told what is "right" and what is "wrong" based on whatever is the cultural norm of their time and place. As these messages get repeated over and over, slowly the first part of the mask starts to be put in place.

Eventually, the children go to school and someone will point out one of their flaws and the mask gets stronger. Suddenly, it is no longer OK for a boy to wear pink or for a girl to burp after a meal. This continues to get reinforced over-and-over from teachers, siblings, friends, parents, and the media until we have all put on protective masks to prevent us from getting psychologically hurt.

We have been trained not to share what is really going on, we have been trained to act and that the entire world is a stage.

We start putting young girls in beauty pageants, on diets, and wearing makeup before they even enter their teenage years; thus putting a strong emphasis on our image over who we are as a person. We are teaching young women that their value only lies in their mask they wear, literally.

And it doesn't work.

Americans rank number one in beauty product consumption and rank 23rd in overall life satisfaction according to the 2012 Satisfaction with Life Index (SWLI)[2]. Brazil citizens spend the second most amount of money on cosmetic surgery, only behind the United States, and rank 81st in the SWLI. Whereas, the two countries that spend the least – Sweden and Netherlands – rank at the top of the charts for satisfaction with life.

In this country, we spend more than 12 billion dollars on cosmetic surgery annually, including over one billion dollars on breast augmentation alone. And these numbers have skyrocketed in the past 20 years with sales up 471-percent since 1997.[3]

Men also wear masks to hide their true selves. From the time they are children, they are not allowed to show any signs of weakness. They are not allowed to cry, to show love, or compassion. And we teach them that not only is anger and aggression ok, but that it is the only emotion that is acceptable for them.

Hence, each gender has their societal mask.

Taking the Mask Off:

In 1994, Jim Carrey starred in the movie *"The Mask"* in which he plays a shy bank teller who gets pushed around by everyone. One day he encounters a mask which transforms him and gives him super powers. He soon relies on this mask to get through the everyday concerns of life.

In Pink Floyd's *"The Wall,"* the character is born during the end of World War II and has his father killed in battle, has an overbearing mother that pushes her insecurities on to him, part of an outdated

---

[2] Satisfaction with Life Index (2012): Compiles data from a range of sources in order to provide a measure of overall national happiness.
[3] American Society for Aesthetic Plastic Surgery (2013)

education system that teaches people what to think rather than how to think, an estranged wife, and all these things push him further away. He begins to build a proverbial wall around himself to isolate from the real world rather than facing his fears. The album ends as he is forced to "tear down his wall."

This happens when we become enlightened. Which is a process, it typically does not happen overnight. Although Bill W., founder of AA, was able to have an instant spiritual awakening and the Buddha had one after sitting under a tree for three days – but these are not likely. Spiritual awakenings are a process that happens slowly over time.

In a powerful TED Talks video, Glennon Doyle Melton perfectly describes this phenomenon in using the analogy of super-hero capes. She goes on to state that everything she learned about life is what she learned in a mental hospital. While in treatment, everyone was included, you were encouraged to talk about how you felt, you talked about real things going on, there were no cliques, and people took off their masks for the first time.[4]

Imagine all the good that could be done in the world if we offered treatment services – people getting real, talking about feelings, everyone included no cliques – and encouraging adolescents to take off their masks, rather than teach them how to build one and wear for the rest of their lives.

---

[4] Melton, G. D. (2013, January 1). Lessons from the Mental Hospital. *TEDx: Traverse City*. Lecture conducted from, Traverse City.

Lost and Never Found:
An Alcoholic's Unknown Story:

The first time we see beyond the mask is done so without a conscious effort – it just happens and we observe. I want to share a story about the first time I saw behind the mask.

The story is of a woman who just had her eight children taken away from her for neglect and abandonment. Emotional and physical abuse was a part of the daily routine. The children would be forced to kneel down in prayer, before she threatened to beat them if they told anyone she had been drinking that day.

"It's just a little cut, get over it!" she once yelled at her two-year-old that recently fell on an empty beer bottle. Unable and unwilling to do anything for the child, her 14-year-old daughter had to drive the toddler to the ER for surgery.

In another incident, the woman fell and passed out on top of one of the kids. The other seven children all worked together to get her off, preventing the infant from suffocating.

The oldest daughter took care of the children with what she had to offer. She cooked ramen noodles on the grill in the freezing temperature as it was all they had to eat. The kids rarely attended school and when they did make it, they were usually welcomed to harassment, beatings, ridicule, and bullying.

Where was their father during this time?

Well, he was actually a doctor and a well-respected man in the community. But behind closed doors, he was an abusive alcoholic that lashed out daily beatings to her. While she was pregnant, he once dragged her across the room with a belt leading to a miscarriage – with the children burying the dead fetus in their back yard.

Around age 40, the father died of a heart attack, leaving the family in the hands of their alcoholic mother and eight children – most of them under the age of 10. This woman was left with a healthy inheritance but spent it primarily on booze. And when the money train stopped, the next train that came in was by the state department taking away her children to foster care.

She would call and harass the foster parents, but never took time to see them or get to know them. The kids moved on with their lives not giving her any sympathy as she was the monster who destroyed their childhoods. However, the oldest daughter continued to see beyond the mask. She continued to go back to the house and help her mother. She chose to believe there was more to this monster than what was being presented. In turn, the oldest daughter received the most abuse, but continued to care for her and spend her young adulthood by showing love.

The drunken woman continued the emotional abuse, creating permanent psychological damage to her daughter – even though, her daughter was the only one who ever showed her love.

Unknowingly, this unconditional love and compassion of this child is what recovery is all about. People do not need to be kicked when they are down; they need someone to see beyond the behaviors. They need someone to tell them "you are a good person, but this disease is preventing you from being that beautiful soul. We just need to remove this barrier."

What you could not know by reading this woman's story, is what is behind her mask, her untold story. The part of our lives that no one knows.

For this case, it is that when this drunken woman was seven years old, she was babysitting her five-year-old brother before watching him get hit by a truck and killed. From this point on, she was blamed for his death. A seven-year-old does not have the mental capacity to understand this is not true. A seven-year-old cannot tell if Santa Clause is real or not, how is she supposed to know it is not true when her parents label her as a killer, irresponsible, and bad person. On top of that, both her parents were alcoholics that emigrated from Ireland and faced immense discrimination during the 1920's on the east coast.

So beyond her mask is a pair of alcoholic parents that were verbally and physically abusive to her. She was blamed for the death of her sibling since she was seven. She married a well-respected man whom was loved and adored by the community, only to have this same man beat her within an inch of her life when he comes home from work.

Her husband was glamorized in public, while she was ridiculed. Her upbringing had trained her that you do not mention these things, so she buried it away, put on her mask, and turned to alcohol. She began to believe all these things about her to be true, turned people away from her, and "chose" booze instead of her kids.

At seven years old, we are innocent. Imagine back to a happy time when you were around that age. Getting ready to do something you love to do (in her case, dance class) and then to watch your five-year-old brother wander into the street and get hit by a truck and killed. Life changes just like that. And then to be blamed your entire life for this without anyone ever letting you know the truth. Then the trauma continues to come in waves and waves, while others stand by at the dock pointing and ask:

"Well why doesn't she just get out of the ocean? Those waves are too high. She is going to drown."

So she lost her way, but how does the story end? When did she get out of that mess? The popular feel-good stories tell us the incredible journeys of those who overcome, get better, and find their way in the world. So, how does this one end?

The truth was for this woman as it is for many of us with mental illness and addiction. We suffer until we die. We die thinking we are monsters. We are all lost, but rarely found.

This story is not unique, but unfortunately, the norm in mental health and addiction. We observe and judge the behavior without taking a look beyond the mask. The behavior (mask) is going to stand out.

And the uglier the mask, the longer-lasting impact it will have on us. We treat those with the ugliest masks, the worst. We use it as a guide as to determine the evilness of the person inside. And until we can consciously look beyond the mask of each person affected by mental health or addiction, the situation will never improve.

I remember this woman's funeral quite well. Her adult children all arrived from out of town, had not been around for years, but made their grand entrance for the spectacle. You could sense the anger and negative energy in the room.

"She is going to burn in hell," was the common theme among these kids who had not seen her in years and never really took a peek behind the mask. They never really knew their own mother. They were all in foster care before they were five years old, but made an appearance at her funeral to wish her well spending eternity in flames.

But the oldest daughter always stuck around, caring for her mother as she watched her slowly drink herself to death. Continuing to care for her mother, no one quite understood what made her return day-after-day and take on the abuse. They questioned her mental stability, courage, and strength.

While they thought she was weak and pathetic, they missed out on experiencing the strongest and most courageous person in their lives. This level of unconditional love could not be broken. She did not listen to what others said about her, no one could prevent her from loving this "monster."

Every day, people would expect her to stop showing up, stop caring, stop loving, and stop trying. She saw something no one else saw. And if you haven't been there before, there are no words in the world that can be said to make you understand. And if you have been there before, no words are needed and you already fully understand everything.

The daughter never heard the words, "I love you," or "I'm sorry."

There is no storybook ending. The woman died without ever saying goodbye. But, this woman did get what she always desired – to believe she was a good, worthwhile human. She had finally received her life, liberty, and pursuit of happiness. This woman finally felt loved for the first time in her life during the last few years.

While the daughter may not have noticed this new unconditional love was reciprocal, I did notice. And it changed me forever.

I know because I saw it in the mother's eyes and I know the daughter was right all along.

I know so because the drunk lady is my grandmother.

When I was nine-years-old and visiting, I was begging for a football. It's all that mattered to me. I had to have it, I was impulsive, and I needed it. Now, remember, my grandmother is this same nasty-old drunk I've been talking about for the past few pages, but she saw that I truly needed to have this football.

My grandma saw I needed it and she understood. She didn't drink that day for the first time in nearly 45 years, because she gave me her last seven dollars to buy that football, which I still have today.

That was my Grandma. And the oldest daughter was my mother. This is how I first saw the truth and to see behind the mask.

Section I:
THE BOOK OF HOPE

Introduction:	Suicide through the Cracks	3
Chapter I:	My Name is Tim	23
Chapter II:	State of the Psychiatry Industry Address	39
Chapter III:	Love and Fear	61
Chapter IV:	Love Addiction	79

INTRODUCTION

Suicide through the Cracks
The one the system missed.

Introduction
Suicide through the Cracks: The One the System Missed

"Jim is dead."

That was the subject line of an email I received on February 26, 2010. One day earlier, my best friend took his own life.

"He hung himself in the garage. I found him this morning."

These words froze me and still do to this day. There may not be a worse feeling in the world to hear the news of a loved-one committing suicide; it leaves many unanswered questions along with mixed feelings of confusion, grief, guilt, and sadness.

I had attempted suicide years ago, which is where my story begins in Chapter One. But Jim's death was the moment in which my awareness shifted and became the foundation for writing this book. It was not some magic, inspirational moment; rather, it led me down a path of destruction to the darkest nights of my days, before a collection of events resurrected my soul.

Jim's death opened my eyes to the flaws in the mental health, chemical dependency, and psychiatric industries. As I lied in my bed, heart-pounding, mind-racing, and emotions pouring, I could not begin to comprehend that my best friend took his own life.

"He shouldn't have died," I thought to myself, "It should have been me."

As both of our life stories played before my eyes, I felt a sharp pain in my abdomen and I couldn't move. How could this happen? It didn't have to end this way and have his life just slip through the cracks of an unjust system.

I have attempted suicide; Jim committed suicide.

I also spent years receiving treatment in rehab centers and psychiatric hospitals. However, Jim, spent many years on the streets and in jails before his story ended on February 25, 2010.

Trying to put the pieces of this puzzle together, it only led to more questions as to how this had transpired. In reality, it is quite transparent – the system is not flawed, it was designed this way. It was designed by the elite class to favor those with resources, while those at the bottom are literally left for dead.

There is no difference between Jim and me besides our resources and the subsequent treatment we were provided. He grew up in a rough environment including his home, neighborhood, school, friends, and life experiences. I grew up in a family that had money, offered support, and always knowing I had a security blanket if things went astray.

That is how our stories began and unfortunately how one of our stories end. But did it have to end this way?

Suicide versus Suicidal

There is enormous stigma associated with the word "suicide." People cringe when you even mention the word and immediately change the subject. If we are afraid to talk about it, how on earth do we think we are going to prevent it? According to the Centers for Disease

Control and Prevention, suicide is the tenth leading cause of death in the United States, taking nearly 40,000 per year.[5] At this rate, in one decade, we lose 400,000 people to suicide – equivalent to the entire population of Oakland, California.

When someone is suicidal, the typical reaction is "don't talk like that!" or "that's not even funny." Or it turns to simplifying the situation such as, "other people have it worse than you," or "just snap out of it, things will get better." Nobody wants to "deal with it" and most people will adamantly refuse to even discuss it. You may even be considered selfish for having those thoughts of leaving close ones behind.

But when suicide does occur, the response is reaches the opposite end of the spectrum. Suddenly, everyone becomes available for the person and feels terrible. They did not see the signs, never saw it coming, and can only talk about all the amazing qualities of the deceased. It even goes as far as to hear people saying, "Why didn't they just reach out?"

If anyone has ever lost someone to suicide, they know the tremendous amount of pain associated. There may not be a worse feeling in the world. There are so many unanswered questions, "what ifs", and "should haves". In the end, nobody commits suicide because they want to die; they commit suicide because they want the pain to go away.

I was suicidal, Jim committed suicide.

Part of the reason Jim is dead is because of the stigma associated with suicide along with the professionals he worked with that neglected and labeled him. He did not get treated as he deserved.

---

[5] Center for Disease Control and Prevention (2012). Suicide Fact Sheet.

Jim didn't have money, my family did. He went to jail with long-term stays; I went to jail and got bailed out. He remained locked behind bars, while I was offered treatment instead. His crimes were all non-violent drug possessions, mine were DUI, assault, and disorderly.

The difference? I had money and resources. Based on the information in the paragraph above, is there any other reason for the difference in penalties?

From the same temperament:

There are four main temperaments – sanguine, choleric, melancholy, and phlegmatic. We are each born into one of these, which ultimately will determine the person we are to become. In fact, there may not be a greater influence in personality than that of your innate temperament. The temperament determines everything you do. It determines how you communicate, learn, activities we enjoy, people we marry, and how we raise the next generation.

Sanguines (the talker) like to be heard, they are pleasure-seeking, optimistic, social, and likes to talk a lot. They struggle finishing projects, tend to be late, forget things and make decisions based on emotions. The downside is they struggle to control cravings, do not handle boredom, and need to be absorbed by something meaningful.

Cholerics (the doer) are ambition and leader-like. This is the "type A" personality in which the person is task-oriented and known for accomplishing goals. They tend to care less about the feelings of others, they compulsively want to change things, and like to be in charge of everything. Their trouble lies in dealing with anger, intolerance, and relying on facts over emotions. They tend to not have as many close friends.

Melancholies (the thinker) are more introverted and thoughtful. They are analytical and use caution and restraint. Because of their deep-thinking, they tend to see the negative aspects in life and become preoccupied with the tragedy and cruelty in the world. They long to make a lasting difference in the world and are very loyal. They often hold themselves to a high standard in which they can never achieve leading to depression and moodiness. They tend to have lower self-esteem and notoriously feel guilty.

Phlegmatics (the watcher) are usually relaxed and quiet. They seek quiet and peaceful atmospheres, desire steadiness, and consistency. They tend to be shy and prefer stability to change. They seek cooperation and interpersonal harmony. On the downside, they can be selfish, judgmental, resist change, and passive aggressive.

And we do not have a choice, we are all born into this. None of them are better than another, it is just part of our genetic makeup.

Jim was born into the sanguine temperament. Undoubtedly you know many others born into this temperament as characterized by talkative, outgoing, compassionate, and enthusiastic. On the flip side, the sanguine temperament also tends to be undisciplined, scattered, and viewed as emotionally unstable. Because of the compassionate aspect of this temperament, the sanguine is also more in tune with others emotions and carries greater sensitivity. This is neither good nor bad, just the way we were born.

Within the temperament, there is also a spectrum in which each of us is placed. Jim was on the high end of the sanguine spectrum and these traits were quite prevalent. His innate elevated temperament made him the loving, caring person that everyone came to love. It was easy to love him. To be on this far end of the spectrum combined with lack of a healthy living environment and continuously being denied support and connection – it is a formula for addiction.

This is referred to this as the biopsychosocial model. In Jim's case the biological component lies in his genetic makeup; the psychological aspect refers to the emotional neglect and trauma; and the sociological element refers to growing up in a difficult home, overpopulated schools with minimal resources, poverty, and lack of positive role models.

Some people are born more sensitive than others, meaning they are going to get hurt more easily. Being an extremely sensitive male is vastly unacceptable in this society. It results in repeated invalidation such as "you are overreacting," "you shouldn't be feeling that way," "men don't cry," "tough it out," or "what's wrong with you?" It also leads to being greatly misunderstood and isolation – the opposite of what the sanguine needs. The only way to gain acceptance is to create a mask, or a false self, to find a sense of belonging or purpose. People accept you when you wear your mask which is why it becomes so difficult to remove. But deep inside, we know it is not our true self.

For example, the mask teaches us that men are supposed to act out in anger when they are hurt. When we respond in anger, it is accepted. When we misbehave, we are accepted.

The mask brings us great power to finally feel alive. The more acceptance and connection the mask gains for us, the more we try to fill these roles. In fact, we start to believe that we are the mask we wear.

Then something bizarre happens. People turn on us for that exact same mask that they once praised. Suddenly "you took things too far" and you get labeled and judged for the same behaviors that were once glamorized.

This leads to addiction. It can be any substance or activity outside of ourselves that allow an escape from the pain. This can take the form of alcohol, drugs, sex, gambling, co-dependency, anger, or any compulsive behavior that lets our soul temporarily come through the cracks in our mask.

Each culture and society has their own version of acceptable masks. But they all serve the same purpose, to escape the pain and hide from any difficult emotion. It grants us temporary relief, which is highly reinforcing. It becomes quite simple to take a pill, smoke a joint, or drink a beer and the pain instantly vanishes. This creates a pattern of depending on our substance/behavior, believing that we are killing the pain, but in essence we are only adding fuel to the fire. The need for the substance/behavior becomes a matter of life-or-death and we start doing things we normally would never have imagined.

All of this is as an effort to temporarily ease the pain.

A Mask that Kills

Take all the above into consideration. Born into a situation where it is unacceptable to be your true self, so you put on a mask that is more accepted. In using drugs, it allowed Jim to remove his mask and let his spirit come through. But with addiction there will always be some level of consequences in different areas of your life.

Then these new behaviors get judged and labeled as being a "bad person." Now, we have a situation in which the person created a mask to be accepted, and in turn, ends up hating the monster they have created.

And that is just it! We hate the monster / the false-self / the mask. We don't hate ourselves. We hate the mask that we have been wearing.

I saw an episode of the kid's television series "Goosebumps" in which a girl was trying to find a costume that would allow her to be "scarier." She found a mask which worked to scare all her friends, and soon she started to love it and didn't want to take it off. Her friends told her to take it off, but she refused because she loved that she was finally able to scare people. Then suddenly, she started becoming more mean and turning into a bully of sorts. Once she realized that this was no longer her true self, she tried to take the mask off, but it had grown into her skin. She had become the mask and she knew it, but there was nothing she could do.

Little did R.L. Stine (creator of "Goosebumps") know, he had actually been describing the process of addiction in this story.

So, the truth is when someone says, "I want to kill myself," they have it reversed. It is not the "self" that needs to die, it is the "I". The "I" refers to the ego / false self / the mask. We need to kill our false self and then the healing can begin.

As Eckhart Tolle states, *"The secret of life is to die before you die, and find that there is no death."* He is referring to the death of the ego, the self-righteous suicide.

No health professional ever reached out to Jim, no one even talked to him, nor did they even know how to approach him. Instead they saw a "criminal" who was "angry" and was misjudged and mislabeled. While I went through the same difficulties, I was referred to as the "patient" that had a "disorder" and only needed proper treatment.

They never got to see beyond his mask. Jim was the most sensitive, caring, loving, and loyal person you could ever meet. However, that was not accepted in his culture so he became the angry, arrogant, drug addict – which sadly, is more acceptable. He wore this mask his entire life, hiding his true self which led to more drugs, crimes, and erratic behavior.

No one in the field ever even dared to think, "This is a genuinely good kid who has never gotten a chance to show himself." Because once the label is created, everything you do is attached to that label. They read your chart and a decision is made before the first encounter.

While my rap sheet was for more horrendous, I was considered "a poor sensitive kid that needs someone to love him." Whereas Jim, was considered "unreachable."

The difference in outcomes is related to how the patients are treated. The quote above is one of my favorite sayings as it explains so much of what the system is missing. Yet, in this field we are told to get the deepest secrets of the client, but not *too close*. It doesn't work that way. I won't show you what is behind my mask until you show me what is behind yours.

Jim let me see behind his mask and I let him see behind mine. And that is how true connections and relationships are built. I know the real Jim, something the "professionals" never took time to do.

Although I received better treatment, Jim was the better man. We shared a special bond and he would always reach out to me at times of need. One time he ended up in jail and had no place to go once released. He called me and we let him stay in our home for a while. On the first night at dinner, he looked to my ex-wife and said, "This is the best food I've ever had." And he meant it, to him it was everything, while I had grown so accustom to these little things I had taken them for granted.

Jim had a unique following of people. He loved to love. If he had two dollars to his name, he would spend it on others. He gave just to give, never expecting anything in return. This is what attracted people to Jim, he was pure once you got to see behind his mask.

He also had a son, Timmy, who he loved more than anything. You could see and sense the love these two had for one another. Jim would always say, "I love you buddy" and kiss Timmy. I never saw a man kiss his little boy before, it was admirable. I make sure that I do that with my three-year-old son now and I think of Jim every time.

Timmy never saw the labels of "drug addict," "bipolar," or "criminal." That is the beauty and genius of children, they do not see masks or labels. Timmy only saw him as I did, as an angel. A kind, beautiful human with so much severe pain that nobody knew existed.

As time went on, more-and-more of his friends started showing up at the house, and I started coming home to see my 10-year-old daughter sitting at home with a bunch of strange men I've never met.

After a few warnings we told Jim he couldn't stay with us if these random people continued to show up at our home without notice. He told his friends to wait until he was home, but they refused to listen. That's the downfall of being so pure is that people will take advantage of you. It broke my heart, but we had to remove him from our home for safety of our daughter.

A few months later I received an email that gives me chills just thinking about.

"Jim is dead. He hung himself."

He didn't call me this time. Perhaps the pain grew too great that he didn't want someone to talk him out of it one more time. I had kicked him out, I was his support, and the guilt I carry with me is insurmountable at times.

So, when people ask me why I fight so hard for patients, this is one of the main reasons.

If we lived in a just world, Jim would have received the treatment I received and he would be with us today. If we lived in a world guided with love, somebody would have built trust with him, got to know him, and offer the services he needed. But in a world guided by fear, we judge, label, and allow 40,000 cases like Jim happen each year.

You Are Not Your Body

Although Jim is dead, he is not gone. Only the false self and our human body vanish, but the spirit is eternal. The things Jim passed on to me, I still carry and pass along to my children. He is with all of us that remember him. He is here right now as long as we let him in.

We are not a body that has a spirit, but rather, a spirit that has a body in a human experience.

I remember when I was in second grade and looking in the mirror, suddenly I asked my reflection "Who am I?" I could clearly see my body and I knew of all my experiences, but I was wondering who is inside running this operation? Then, I looked around at my classmates and teacher and wondered the same thing about each of them.

What is this entire experience? It was quite confusing and I had a hard time shaking this heightened consciousness. I saw everyone running around and going about the day and it no longer made any sense. Why are we doing all of this? Why am I responsible for this human body? Who am I?

Looking back, I now see that this was my first spiritual experience and ability to detach from the human realm. My true self was shining through and I was curious as to why I was wearing this mask.

While I understand the term "spirituality" has tendency to turn a lot of people off, which is why it is essential to define the term early in this book. Spirituality is not religion. However, religion is a *type* of spirituality. Spirituality refers to finding a sense of purpose, meaning, and connection outside of our self in this life. People can find this in nature, support groups, sports teams, the universe, and of course their religious practice. This is not a religious book, nor does this book slam religion. It is a book that defines a problem with a spiritual solution; and however you choose to find your spirituality – or sense of purpose in life – is how you should refer to it as it is mentioned throughout this book.

Simply put, spirituality is about discovering our true self – or *Taking the Mask Off.*

When we are young, we are born without a mask but we do not have the mental capability to realize this. As we grow up during the first few years our brains are wired and trained to behave like the agreed upon norms of the given society of that time and place. Soon, all the rules and lessons we are taught create a civilized person and we go along with these norms without questioning them.

But, I remember this feeling in second grade and I often went back to it. Whenever I wanted to feel it, I would say to myself, "I am a human, but who am I?"

Since then, science has backed up my belief that we are not our body. Jonas Frisen, stem cell biologist at Karolinska Institute in Stockholm, has been able to determine the age of the cells in our body.

All the cells that make up our body are constantly dividing, dying, and regenerating. Our skin is completely replaced every two weeks by dying off and regeneration of cells due to constantly being attacked by external elements. Your red blood cells last about 120 days, your liver regenerates every 300 to 500 days, and your entire skeleton replaces once every ten years.[6]

But, if we are not our body, the question still remains – Who Am I?

In using the finest tools of science, spirituality, and ancient philosophy it is apparent that we are all one interconnected being experiencing life from different perspectives. While that sounds like some type of science fiction film, the science backs this up and this is just the tip of the iceberg.

The irrefutable evidence of today tells us that the universe was created by the Big Bang. This means that all matter came from one source of energy. Fourteen billion years ago, space expanded very rapidly resulting in the formation of atom's, then stars, galaxies, etc. It is still expanding today.

This reaffirms what ancient myths, traditions, beliefs, and texts have always told us: We are not separate. All elements are interconnected and we come from the same source. Hence, we are One.

Furthermore, once things are connected they will always be connected. A couple different experiments have also proved this to be true. Scientists have split photons and separated them miles

---

[6] Wade, N. (2005, August 2). Your Body Is Younger Than You Think. *New York Times*.

apart. When one of the photons was forced to choose between two pathways, the second photon always made the same choice as if it "knew" what its twin was doing.

A second study, which seemed more fascinating, is researchers took a swab of tissue and DNA from inside a volunteer's mouth to see if it would react once removed from the body. The DNA was taken to another room and measured eclectically to see if it would respond to the emotions of the person it came from with the donor hundreds of feet away. The person was shown different images which would spark emotions – ranging from war movies, to erotic images, and humor. When he experienced emotional peaks and dips, his cells and DNA had a powerful reaction at the same instance. However, they took this study to another level and separated the DNA more than 350 miles from the volunteer and still had the same results![7]

This explains that once things are connected, they are always connected. And if we all came from the same source – we will always be connected to everything in the universe!

Another simple understanding of this interconnection is to go back to our seventh grade science homework. Plants use photosynthesis to "breathe in" carbon dioxide and "breathe out" oxygen; whereas, humans inhale oxygen and exhale carbon dioxide.

One of the greatest scientific minds of the history of humanity, Albert Einstein, confirmed what indigenous cultures have been teaching for thousands of years. Einstein stated:

> "A human being is part of the whole called by us universe, a part limited in time and space. We experience ourselves, our thoughts and feelings as something separate from the rest. A kind of optical delusion from consciousness. This

---

[7] Braden, G. (n.d.). *The divine matrix: Bridging time, space, miracles, and belief.*

> *delusion is kind of prison for us, restricting us to our personal desires and affection for a few persons nearest to us. Our task must be to free ourselves from the prison by widening our circle of compassion to embrace all living creatures and the whole of nature in its beauty. The true value of a human being is determined by the measure and the sense in which they have obtained liberation from the self. We shall require a substantially new manner of thinking if humanity is to survive."*

While the Big Bang is the most scientifically likely theory to hold true as the creation of the universe, it is certainly not the most appealing. Different cultures have used different stories and tales but it always comes down to the same concept of interconnection, loving each other, and returning to the source which is paradise/heaven/nirvana.

In India, there is an ancient Hindu story regarding creation which is scientifically accurate and gives an image and understanding of the "Who Am I?" question.

Brahma is the Supreme Being, or God, and in the beginning nothing existed. Out of boredom, he decided to create a game to play. Needing a partner to play, he first creates Maya, the goddess of illusion. Maya comes up with the idea for the game and tells Brahma to create the entire universe, the stars, planets, oceans, plants, and animals.

Next, Maya suggests that Brahma creates an animal that is so intelligent that it can appreciate all of his creation – and humans were created.

"What a beautiful world of illusion you have created," said Maya, "OK, now let's play the most wonderful game."

Maya then cut Brahma up into thousands of tiny little pieces and put one in every human.

"Now the game begins," Maya said, "I am going to make you forget what you are and you are going to try to find yourself!"

This continues to go on today as Brahma is inside of each of us, and Maya continues to stop us from remembering who we are. Once you awake from the dream, you realize that you are Brahma again and reclaim your divinity. Each one of us is part of the divine trying to remember and each one of us is the universe that wanted to experience it subjectively.

This is your true self. It is hidden behind loads and loads of masks that we wear each day. The book is titled "Taking the Mask Off" as that is the secret to returning home to the true self. This is the reason the book takes a spiritual solution to the problems, because it is a spiritual problem. We have forgotten who we are and it is only until we can realize this that the problems will be alleviated.

It is quite often that people that are more spiritually-minded tend to be more anxious, depressed, feel homesick, or have is described as being "mentally ill." The closer we come to discovering our true self, the tougher the ego fights back. The reason is because it is scary without our mask, we become vulnerable and we do not know what to expect. The ego convinces us that we are in need of the mask for protection which creates inner turmoil.

False Self versus True Self

I use the terms "false self," "ego," and "mask" interchangeably throughout the text. The ego basically refers to an idea that we have about ourselves, which creates the "false self." We refer to ourselves by descriptors of age, race, nationality, political party, gender, personality traits, etc. Once we start to identify with each of these we start to say "I am a …." This is all part of the false self, we create a personality based on this idea we have about ourselves which has been built as a reflection of how society feels. We soon start to believe this and it is very hard to detach from these things.

You can tell when the ego is in control as the person becomes more *me-centered*, focusing on the individual needs, along with greed, craving, impatient, inflexible, jealousy, narrow-minded, comparing to others, blaming, self-centered, and guided by fear and hate.

The terms "true self" and "spirit/soul" are also used interchangeably. This is who you are behind the mask. Think of a time you are in your flow of life. You do not know of the past or future, only the present moment. You feel inner peace, all worries and stress have vanished, and you experience euphoria. That is your soul shining through without the mask. That is the state we all strive to find on a daily basis. This is what is meant by "taking the mask off."

The person's soul is the guiding force when they are more focused on "we" as opposed to "me," they are peaceful, patient, generous, happy, confident, self-accepting, non-judgmental, compassionate, simplistic, and guided by love.

This is an everyday struggle for all of humanity. We are all lost and trying to be found, which is the essence of spirituality.

We have built this false self as a guide to tell us how to act, dress, behave, make decisions, and go about life. Then, as a society, we begin to reward people who live up to this false self the best. If you can conform and be a part of what everyone agrees is normal you are rewarded, while if you question the way we do things you will face punishment and isolation.

Just like the physical masks of the ancient times, these psychological masks provide safety and security. The process of enlightenment is not only to remove the mask, but to be able to pass through moment-by-moment and let the events happen to you, but also to know that they do not define you.

In terms of mental health and addiction, there is a highly spiritual connection. People with mental illness have high spiritual insight and are being misguided by a corrupt industry that profits off their "sickness." Addiction is a spiritual disease as well; people with a high craving for spirituality find that drugs give a glimpse of a spiritual connection which makes it highly reinforcing for the person to use, eventually leading to consequences and destruction.

This book is created to break down the stigma of mental illness and addiction, spark changes in a corrupt industry, and allow others to free their soul and discover their true selves.

This book is for you Jim. You died so others could know what it was like to be alive.

CHAPTER I

My Name is Tim
Soul Retrieval

Chapter 1
My Name is Tim: Soul Retrieval

Wait! Why am I waking up? This isn't how it is supposed to go. The room is spinning, my body shaking, my mind foggy, and physically Debilitated. As I stumble through the over-crowded living room my cousin Little Bill asks, "What the hell is wrong with you?"

This is where my journey begins.

As my discomfort grows with each waking second, I attempt to make it into work but the agony is far too overwhelming and I am literally forced into the fetal position in an effort to ease the increasing pain. My mom stops and I told her what had happened.

Immediately rushed to the hospital via ambulance, they begin feeding me activated charcoal to reduce some of the drug absorption. They start pumping my stomach and all I can recall is more charcoal, more charcoal, followed by violent projectile vomiting. I am exhausted. Emotionally and physically drained and beat down.

As I start to regain consciousness, the room is cloudy, hectic, and endless chatter seeming to come from every direction. The mood of the room changes as everyone grows aware that I am waking up. I start to recognize people and see my mother. She is bawling as she watches and talking to her sister, Keena, and Dr. P (a family friend).

"What the fuck? Why did I tell them? I should be dead," I recall thinking this to myself. I had just overdosed on a plethora of pills. I was the human garbage disposal the previous night, taking anything I could get my hands on with the intent to make the pain permanently vanish.

While Keena and my mom sat there, I could only watch in shame, embarrassment, and humiliation. No one was really talking about what had just taken place, but that is how my family had always operated – put on a mask and avoid the elephant in the room.

Diagnostic Labeling

My mother is severely depressed. My father, although never diagnosed, has many symptoms of Asperger's Syndrome. Still today he will ask me, "Where do you come up with these things?" It's as if he is embarrassed. There is nothing "bad" about Asperger's. In fact, this entire notion on "diagnosing" people is extremely detrimental to providing care. This system has us seeking what is "wrong" with people instead of valuing the positive and unique qualities that make us shine as individuals.

Take Asperger's for example; we give the formal diagnosis and describe the person as having poor social skills, isolative, weird, etc. Instead, what if we were to look at this same person and say that they are smart, focused, speak the truth, and do not play childish games. There are many incredible qualities about this so-called "disorder."

This is how Western cultures "treat" people in the industry known as "health care."

They create diagnoses, which comes with negative connotations and labels. Such as Borderline Personality Disorder (BPD), in which the person is considered overly emotional, manipulative, and play games. Instead, we could refer to emotional as a positive trait because they are passionate and caring, they feel connected to the world and people around them. Neuroscientists around the world continue to prove that our brains our wired to connect with others, help those suffering, and provide love and compassion.[8]

And if emotionally connecting with others, love, and compassion are innate human characteristics, wouldn't it make more sense to cherish the advancement of those who are overly-emotional?

Furthermore, a feeling of connectedness is a sign of being awakened. As you awaken, you are aware of this wondrous interconnection of all living things. But instead of celebrating their deeper understanding and gift in these areas, we attach labels and focus only on that specific label.

Sticking with the example of a person diagnosed with BPD, if they do something loving, caring, or extraordinary it is quickly shrugged off and discarded. But if they attempt to manipulate, we are quick to point out that it is a sign and symptom of BPD. Once this diagnosis is in place, we seek out these symptoms and behaviors. We become narrow-minded as we interact and observe people and become more and more judgmental.

In reality, manipulation is not a symptom or a sign of a disorder. It is a pretty standard human trait. It is simply a method of getting one's needs met. We all do this to some extent from the time we are infants. Although it is unhealthy, it is natural. Rather than scold, shake our heads, label, and judge those for manipulating, it would be more beneficial to understand that they are in need of something and not sure how to ask. This is a teaching opportunity and we can help them grow rather than kick them while they are down.

The problem lies when the person grows addicted to the drama, it becomes their drug, their altered state of consciousness and they begin to seek it out. This does not make them ill, it is human

---

[8] Keltner, D. (2004, March 1). The Compassionate Instinct. *Greater Good.*

nature to want to change our level of consciousness and we all seek it through different avenues. Instead we should be highlighting their superior qualities and embracing those so that the dramatic behavior is no longer appealing – the same way we would entice a recovering drug addict to find a spiritual connection to replace the drugs and alcohol.

The attitude towards mental illness needs to change, along with the actions of those diagnosing and treating the affected person. If we are to continue to progress, we need to evaluate the way we treat people. In awakening our souls, our perspectives change, and we begin to save lives.

Imagine that you are coaching a youth baseball team and a kid continues to drop the ball. Each time he drops the ball, you yell at him to "catch the ball." And that is your only coaching that you provide. Then when you analyze the team at night, you continue to keep that kid out of the lineup because he "cannot catch the ball." Like everyone else on the team, he catches the ball far more often than he drops it, but you have created in your mind that this kid cannot catch the ball.

You only point out when he drops it, never instruct him on how to catch the ball, and dismiss anytime he actually does catch it. How is this kid to ever improve? How is this kid ever to learn? Then when he quits the team, or lies about catching the ball, or doesn't listen to other instruction, who is really to blame?

My parents did many wonderful things while I was growing up. They tried their best and made the most of what they had to offer. I was confused during this dark period of my journey and was never sure where to turn. Not having my father there in times like this was normal to me and my mother would never confront me or discuss things with me.

This is not their fault. They each have their own journey and these personality traits have been passed down from generation-to-generation. My father's ancestors are rich in English tradition which historically involves not expressing emotions, incredibly private people, strictly maintain standard protocol in most situations, typically come off as non-friendly, avoid prolonged eye-contact, takes a long time to build friendships but once formed usually last throughout time and distance.

Asperger's "symptoms" include: routines, difficult in social situations, formal and distinct speech, and social isolation. However, these seem like traditional English lifestyles. Routines are simply following protocol; unease in social situations could be mistaken for not making eye-contact; isolation could be about privacy needs; and not expressing emotions has been the norm for this culture for centuries.

My mother's ancestors come from the isle west of England, Ireland. The Irish also have very distinct cultural traditions that date back hundreds of years. Ironically, the Irish traditions are nearly opposite of every English norm. The Irish have turned speaking into an art form with quick wit, using humor in everything (including at themselves), they are great story-tellers and that is their primary way of communicating information, it is common to insult those in which they have close ties, eye-contact is maintained, shaking hands with children is normal, greetings turn into long conversations, in business they use first names and are more casual, the social classes mingle together and they do not use business cards, and always have good manners.

In fact, it is more important in Irish tradition to be polite than to tell the truth. They have a very non-committal response, because they feel that saying "no" is impolite. If there is a disagreement, it is often that this will be indirectly communicated rather than confront the other person. The Irish do not like confrontation and tend to avoid them at all costs, many times by using humor to change the subject. They tend to talk and banter and pride themselves on seeking all sides of a problem.

With the two conflicting cultures, it is no wonder that the communication in the household was often difficult. As my mother's emptiness in her marriage continued, she sought out connection with her sisters. Also, Irish tradition has incredibly deep ties in extended family. Even after members move away, there is always a deep closeness and connection.

Returning Love for Hate

Back in the hospital, this explains why this situation was nothing abnormal to me. My mother was there with her sister with nothing being discussed and my father was absent. Perhaps it had to do with undiagnosed "mental disorders" or maybe it just had to do with their heritage/culture and conflicting views on the world. Either way, this just added to my permanent state of confusion.

Who am I? Why am I different? What is wrong with me? What is normal? How am I supposed to act? What the hell is all this about anyway?

I have always known I was different. But, it was difficult to keep it all inside all the time. The only emotions that I knew were anger and hostility.

This was the moment I tried to literally kill myself. At this time, I did not know there was a way to kill yourself without losing your body; a way to liberate your soul, find inner peace and freedom. But I was on the right track. I knew it was all phoniness and lies, and all I wanted was liberty.

And the paradox is that you have to die before you can get all of this. Figuratively, not literally; kill the false self to redeem the true self.

As the confusion settled, my only emotion – anger – began to intensify. Anger is a real emotion, but it is a secondary one. Anger is actually an emotional response to a perceived injustice. It is a lot of different emotions bundled together and they release to the outside world as anger.

Our brains develop from the back to the front, starting with the most primitive parts. Every animal alive has the limbic system and the subsequent autonomic nervous system - which is most recognizable as the "flight or fight" response system. It is a built-in survival tool that helps us escape danger. Its primary products are fear and stress. It works like this:

If you are in the woods and being chased by a bear, you are going to feel fear. That is a normal emotion. It is put in place to let you know there is a threat. Stress is the physical reactions to fear, your heart races, muscles tense, focus increases, and perspiration occurs. This is done to help your body fight or flight in the scenario – by increasing focus, strength, and stamina. Now, say you run away to safety and hide in a car. Your heart rate slowly comes down, muscles relax, your breathing slows down, and your fear subsides.

This is the beauty of how our body was created. We do not have to do anything and this is in place. Heart pumps blood to the big muscles to "fight" or "flight", our skin vesicles constrict to limit bleeding, our senses heighten, and parts of our body that are not needed for survival shut down. But the problem is, when this system stays turned on.

The next day, you walk down the same path and you start experiencing these symptoms of stress again – racing heart, rapid breathing, etc.

This is called anxiety. It is a stress response to a threat that may, or may not, be real. It is the anticipation of danger. Then anger comes out as a secondary emotion. We get upset with the park ranger for not taking care of the bear population, we get upset we can't walk down this path anymore, or maybe we get frustrated and take it out on the people at home for not getting a job so we can get a second car. Either way, none of these are the real problems. The real problem is that a bear was chasing us the other day and we experienced fear.

And that is how anger works in all cases. It is a secondary emotion that typically comes after fear, hurt, or betrayal. Anger also works on the stress response system and actually puts us into an altered state of mind. When we are in a rage, we cannot think clearly, cannot possibly make good decisions, and this state-of-mind can be attractive – it is mood-altering.

There have been studies done that have shown police officers make poor decisions when they get too stressed, due to increased heart rates. In turn, they have worked with them to manage their heart rate so their stress-response system does not get overacted too easily to prevent fatal mistakes.

Just as I previously explained with the addiction to drama for those with BPD; the same can be true for men or women with an addiction to anger. This becomes the altered state of consciousness that they desire, crave, and makes them (or me) come alive.

One of the problems with American society is that we raise our men to only show one emotion – anger. It is not OK for men to show fear, sadness, or even love. The only emotion men are accepted to show is one that is secondary, one that only arises when we perceiving an injustice somewhere.

So, I lash out at my mother in the hospital because anger is the only thing I know. Plus, I know she will not fight back, so there is no risk involved. I tear her apart emotionally and scream at her to get out of my room immediately.

I remember Dr. P telling me, "Don't do that to your mother, she cares about you."

"You stupid motherfucker! Don't talk to me!" I had to shout back in defending myself.

The doctors told me that I had a third degree heart block in the night and would have to stay in the ICU for a few days. My mom kept coming back and let me rip into her moment-after-moment. She just sat there and took the abuse. And that is what she has done her whole life – just took abuse and return it with love. That is a gift.

Spiritual guru, Dr. Wayne Dyer, describes this as one of the most difficult tasks in the human experience – to return love for hate. My mother showed me this daily, she gave me unconditional love. It is one of the amazing wonders of my universe. This woman never received love, all she ever received was abuse, but somehow she always returned the hate with unconditional love. Her only goal was to love her children, and she did that better than anyone could imagine. She knew nothing about boundaries, nor did she care to know.

And this is what made her an easy target for me. I could release my anger without any threat of anything being reciprocated.

As the days passed in the hospital, I wanted to leave, I needed to leave.

This is when I first learned of a term called "psychiatry hold." What is this? They can just keep me in here? This was unfamiliar territory for me. I have been in complete power and control since I was seven years old. I ran the family, they gave into my demands, and I got what I wanted.

I called their bluff. They cannot keep me here against my will. All I need to do is throw a tantrum, create some problems, and they will let me go.

But, it didn't work this time. For the first time in my life, I was experiencing loss of control and loss of power.

A few hours later, in walks some bearded man to introduce himself to me.

Soul Retrieval

"Hi Cortland. I'm Tim."

"Hi Tim, go fuck yourself!" I respond.

"How are you feeling? What is going on?" Tim responded kindly as if he did not hear what I just said.

"Go fuck yourself!" I shouted louder.

He just kept coming into my room, smiling, and trying to see how I was doing. He was talking to me about an array of topics that had nothing to do with why I was there, mental disorders, behavior, or anything related to the hospital.

Finally, I caved. Cussing him out received no reaction, he continued to just try to talk to me, so there was no use fighting it anymore since I had not control or power.

"I like baseball," I said quietly.

Then Tim starts talking about baseball non-stop. It doesn't take long before Tim brings in Tony Oliva, Minnesota Twins Hall of Famer, to come visit me and give me an autographed bat.

"Maybe this 'Tim' guy ain't so bad," I remember thinking to myself. Maybe I like Tim, he is actually pretty cool. He never lectured me, never said I was bad, never talked down to me. He just talked to me and suddenly his stupid smile stopped bothering me.

As I look back on everything, I was ready to bolt somehow. I was planning on finding a way out, which would have resulted in being placed on a hold. But Tim, who I now view as my friend, tells me that if I am OK that they will let me out. He tells me to not force anything on them and I trusted Tim. He seemed to really care about me and would always come and visit during the day. I don't really remember anything we talked about, but I just remember how I felt when he was working – I felt content and safe. I started to anticipate his visits and I always knew that I was going to miss him.

I now realize, this is the key to mental health treatment. Actually, this is the key to all human relationships – empathy and compassion. Because people do not care how much you know until they know how much you care. In talking down to people, judging, or quickly jumping to give advice we have no chance to make a difference – especially if we haven't taken the time to get to know them personally. This goes for all human relationships, but in the mental health industry this is only intensified exponentially.

When you are working with people with trust issues, in a hospital setting, or other trauma, the first step has to be forming a relationship that goes beyond worker-patient. How would you expect a 16-year-old girl that has been sexually abused to share anything with someone that only sees her behavior of cutting as "bad," or "attention-seeking."

Trust takes a long time to build and even more-so in the aforementioned settings. But it is also a simple formula. Like, Tim did for me, it starts with a simple "hello," not judging or pushing beliefs, and just getting to know each person individually.

And then the healing can take place. It does not always have to be some Hollywood-esque interaction with the person to help them recover. Too many times, we try to make the big splash and everything goes overboard. We try to rush into this person's lifetime of trauma and cure it with quick advice. This creates resistance and the person pushes back which gets charted as "they are not ready to get better."

Sometimes the best thing you can do is just say "hello." The next day, do it again. Then ask, "How are you doing?" There is nothing magical here. This is how children build relationships on the playground in elementary school. Eventually ask, "What is it you like to do?"

Remember, it is not about us and that the focus should always remain on the client. Let the client guide the conversation, let them do the talking. And when they talk, all we need to do is listen. Actively listen, without running our mind and thinking of what to say, but to just drop all thoughts and give our undivided attention.

That is what all humans want and desire. In Mark Laaser's book "Seven Desires of Every Heart," he begins by describing being heard and understood as the first desire of every human. In actively listening, we begin to seek out curiosity of the person speaking – and this is the key to true empathy. To be truly invested, interested, and curious about this person's life, thoughts, and ambitions is what makes empathy and building a relationship possible.

How active do you listen to others? Do you get caught up thinking about what you want to say first? Do you "space out" and miss out on important comments? Do you tend to interrupt?

In doing so, the other person picks up on this on a subconscious level. This term is coined "neuroception," which is the human's ability to subconsciously read other people for safety, communication, and engagement. This is necessary for humans to build positive relationships. It starts in our infant years as we are unable to communicate verbally and we need to rely on this system for safety.[9]

This is all a process. If someone is abused as a child, they never got past the "safety" phase of neuroception. This could be why it is difficult to communicate and engage, but more noteworthy in this sense, they are constantly trying to read people as they have been trained to not trust the world. There are also a number of studies that show that children from orphanages lack key areas of development, less gray matter, and smaller brains, due to the lack of connection, love, and care-giving we are to receive as infants.[10]

This only enhances the incredible need and opportunity to shut down our mind and listen to each other. You will not miss anything, in fact, you will gain everything. This is what awakening and awareness is all about. Tim was awakened and enlightened, his actions altered

---

[9] Porges, S. (2004). Neuroception: A Subconscious System for Detecting Threats and Safety. *Zero to Three, 24*(5), 19-24.
[10] Adler, I. (2014). How Childhood Neglect Harms The Brain. In *Common Health Reform and Reality*. Boston:

my world forever. If it were not for his actions and attitude towards me, I would have attempted to escape that day. And maybe I would have escaped only to be arrested, or take another attempt at suicide.

I realized that every one of our actions have a profound impact on the universe. If Tim had been bothered by his thoughts, or believed his thoughts to be true, he would have treated me different which would have drastically changed my path in life.

Tim sensed that I was in fear of the unknown and uncertain what to do without any control over my future. So he walked me to the psych ward and told me that he would visit me. I got up with him and walked over to the Divine Redeemer adolescent psych ward with Tim and my autographed Tony Oliva baseball bat.

As I walk in, I realize that this place is familiar. I have been here before. I fooled everyone here once before and I can do it again. This should take about a week and I'll be out of this hell.

I was wrong.

CHAPTER II

State of the Psychiatry Industry Address
We Are Not the Sick Ones

Chapter 2
State of the Psychiatry Industry Address: We Are Not the Sick Ones

As my first experience in the psychiatry industry is about to unfold, I really knew nothing of what takes place behind closed doors. Just like anyone else, I trusted that those in charge were providing what was best for me in a well-respected profession.

Psychiatry is defined as the study and treatment of mental illness, emotional disturbance, and abnormal behavior. It is a field that sounds quite fascinating and wonderful to be able to shine light on those who are struggling and help them flourish.

But, it doesn't quite work that way in real life as I would soon find out.

How did it get to be this way? Well, just like we dove deep into my personal and family history to find out why things are as they are in the present – we need to do the same for the entire industry. This chapter goes away from my personal story and more into the history of psychiatry and what made it what it is today.

> "Who controls the past controls the future; who controls the present controls the past." – George Orwell

The quote above by George Orwell in his book, *1984*, is the political ideology of the totalitarian government in his novel. Yet, the words are so true in all of history in every single realm. Psychiatry is no different. Presently, psychiatry is owned by drug companies and in turn they can eliminate the past horrendous acts by trying to change history. This had led to them controlling the future as the state of psychiatry is heading in a direction in which every single person will soon be on some type of pharmaceutical drug. Again, how did it get this way?

In the previous chapter, I spoke about having a lot of anger as a young man. Anger is a natural emotion, which is a response to an injustice which may or may not be real. However, it jacks up our stress-response system to the point we cannot think clearly. Yet, this emotional is trying to tell us something – that there is an injustice in the world. This is the emotion that sparked movements by Martin Luther King Jr., Ghandi, Nelson Mandella, etc. You better believe they were angry about the unjust system they lived, but instead of yelling, screaming, complaining, and blaming, they funneled their anger for something positive.

It may have taken me nearly twenty years to recognize all the injustice in the psychiatry system and I have felt anger throughout my journey. Today, I am able to finally use this emotion to fight back in a meaningful manner.

Psychiatry has long-held a dark history of mistreatment and failures. In ancient times, they would drill holes in the skull of the person with symptoms as a means to release their demons. The middle-ages led to burning people at the stake, claiming they were witches. In recently modern times, the age of asylums included inhumane torture, isolation, abuse, and cruelty.

Today, psychiatry drugs the mentally ill in a multi-billion dollar pharmaceutical industry. What makes us think that we have it right this time? Are we really working to help those in need or is this a way to secretly profit?

History of Psychiatry

Since the beginning of humanity, there have been people with so-called mental health disorders. Of which, they have also been the most highly discriminated against people in the history of the world. They have been discriminated against, because there is no basis for understanding. The ancient disorders involved emotional distress, melancholia, and hysteria/mania.

Starting about 35,000 years ago, Humans relied mostly on intuition and cohabited with other animals. After some time, humans started to see themselves as separate. Not until recently modern times has the age of science and reason put a stronger emphasis on logic rather than "feeling." There are plenty of examples in the Old Testament that would concur that ancient times relied on "knowing," as well as "hearing voices" and "having visions" all of which guided decision-making. In fact, most of the world would have been diagnosed with schizophrenia during some of the biblical eras.

Moses, Abraham, Ezekiel, King Saul, and Jesus himself very likely could have and would have been diagnosed with mental disorders. But were they sick, or were they spiritually gifted?

Shamanism is humanity's oldest form of healing, dating back to the Paleolithic era. A shaman is a person who has access to, and influence in, the spiritual world. They practice healing by entering into a trance to practice divination and healing. Many traditional cultures viewed psychotic breaks as an initiation into Shamanism. Mircea Eliade explains in *Myths, Dreams, and Mysteries*:

> *"The future shaman sometimes takes the risk of being mistaken for a "madman"...but his "madness" fulfills a mystic function; it reveals certain aspects of reality to him that are inaccessible to other mortals, and it is only after*

> *having experienced and entered into these hidden dimensions of reality that the "madman" becomes a shaman."*

In later prehistoric times, it was believed that mental illness stemmed from magical beings that had hijacked the mind. Different tribes treated these conditions in their own manner, with most believing that they had to get the "evil spirit" out of the mind. Archeological evidence has shown cases of trepanation – or drilling holes in the skull – as an effort to free the spirits. While this seems barbarous, the belief was that it was not actually harming the brain and was the only way to bring about a cure.

The idea of demonic possession continued into the ancient Babylonian times, but instead the mentally ill were treated by priest-doctors with less-brutal tactics such as exorcisms, prayer, and other mystic rituals to drive the spirit out. If none of these were to work, they would use threats, punishment, or even submission.

In early times of Egypt it was believed that mental illness resulted from a loss of money and/or status. They were the first of cultures to use talk therapy as a cure. Also, the Egyptians recommended turning to religion, faith, and prayer as a remedy.

Ancient Egyptians later viewed mental illness and physical illness as one in the same. They believed the majority of illnesses were a result of body etiology.[11] Treatment involved a variety of methods such as bringing about more recreational activities such as singing, painting and dancing to return the person to "normalcy," or they were one of the first cultures to use opium as medication for sleep, ease pain, and

---

[11] Okasha, A. (1999). Mental health in the Middle East: An Egyptian perspective. *Pergamon, 19,* 917-933.

quiet the nerves.[12] The Egyptians were the most forward-thinking in terms of placing mental illness as more of a priority for their society.

All of these ancient cultures shared the belief that mental illness was created by a supernatural force interfering with the person's psyche. Almost always it was believed to be an angered deity, whom had to be removed and the cause of this phenomenon was typically assumed to be a punishment of the individual.

In Europe, starting with Homer – lived sometime between 12th and 8th century B.C. – still believed in the spiritual connection to mental illness, believing it resulted from God taking away one's mind and he offered no cure. This was followed by Aeschylus in the fifth century B.C., whom continued to believe demon possession created mental illness and that exorcism was the only cure.

Socrates, the father of modern philosophy, was the first to break the mold. He believed that mental illness was "heaven sent" and therefore no cure was needed, but rather to embrace it as a gift from the Gods. Socrates teachings were so profound at the time and so meaningful, in which philosophy is broken down into two periods: before Socrates and after Socrates. Similar to the teachings of Jesus Christ and how we organize our calendar before Christ and after Christ.

Socrates asked the demon for divine inspiration, stating that great creativity came from these altered states of consciousness and should be strived to achieve. Madness was viewed more as a virtue, in which the term mad-genius is derived.

His greatest student, Plato, argued there were two types of mental illness: divinely inspired and giving the person prophetic powers;

---

[12] Rosso, A. (2010). Poppy and Opium in Ancient Times: Remedy or Narcotic? *Biomedicine International*, 81-87.

and others that were caused by physical illness. Plato also shared the connection between creativity and mental illness. While Plato's prized student of his own, Aristotle, asks the question,

> *"Why is it that all those who have become eminent in philosophy or politics or the arts are clearly melancholics and some of them to such an extent as to be affected by diseases caused by black bile?"*

Hippocrates, the father of medicine, went along with the Egyptian belief that mental illness derived from physical dysfunction. He presented the humoral theory, stating that illness was created by an imbalance in the different fluids in the human body. The theory states there were four basic humors (fluids): blood, black bile, yellow bile, and phlegm. When these fluids were in balance the person was healthy, but when they were imbalanced is when illness arose. He was the first to dismiss the supernatural explanation of the disease. Hippocrates believed the cure was natural diet and exercise.

The later philosophers of the 2nd century, such as Celsus and Galen, were of the belief that mental illness could be treated with entertaining stories, diversion, humor, confrontation, and exercise. Galen, followed the work of Hippocrates, and emphasized data of experience over primitive and philosophical hypotheses. He believed mental disorders were a result of psychic dysfunction in neurological structures.

While the belief that mental illness stemmed from the mind was the most prevalent belief, other suggestions of morality, demon possession, magical, punishment for sin, or test of faith continued to persist throughout the dark and middle ages.

The most severely ill were chained to walls in institutions for the rest of society to forget they existed. The conditions of these asylums were horrendous – sleeping five to a mattress in a dark, wet, floor, while being chained to the walls – while being whipped and beaten and treated like animals.

The victims were actually blamed and there immoral behavior was the cause of their illness. Yet, they did not refer to it as "illness" or "sick" because they wanted to dehumanize them. If doctors or professionals were to speak out against the inhumane treatment they were threatened themselves.

During the middle Ages, the care for the mentally ill generally took place in their own home. However, the mentally ill were typically widely abused, particularly in Christian Europe due the shame and stigma that surrounded mental illness. Other "humane" approaches were that the belief was because of a humoral imbalance in which they would try to "naturally" balance the humors by intentionally vomiting or drawing blood.

During the 16th and 17th centuries, the infamous "witch hunts" took place in which the mentally ill were tracked down, tried as witches, and then burnt at the stake. By the end of the 17th century were the first forms of "treatment" of the mentally ill. This treatment was just a different form of punishment but the mentally ill were viewed as being immoral or demonized souls, but rather insensitive wild animals. The restraint chains were still used and viewed as therapeutic to tame the wild animals. Or they would be branded with a red hot iron to be brought to their senses.

In the 18th century, the rise of institutions for the mentally ill started to develop. The notorious Bedlam institute is the first of its kind to specialize in treating the mentally ill, opened in 1677. Visitors arrived, like at a zoo, to watch the lunatics in their cell. They were allowed to bring sticks to poke into the cell at the inmates.

The first mental asylum in America opened in 1769 under the guidance of Benjamin Rush, who became known as "America's First Psychiatrist." Rush actually disapproved of whips, straitjackets, and any type of restraints. The tactics he used were still inhumane, but less barbaric than his predecessors.

It took another 100 years for people to recognize the appalling treatment of the mentally ill before less-torturous treatment took place. Due to industrialization and population growth in the 19th century, there was also a rise in mental asylums.

The asylum superintendents, which were initially called "alienists" because they were believed to deal with people who alienated themselves, were to be known as "psychiatrists." Psychiatry was then coined a medical specialty and was more academically established. However, the rest of the medical field did not take them too seriously.

Psychiatrists first stated they just needed to attend the asylums to cure mental illness, but that proved to be unsuccessful. They were not regarded as real doctors because they were not doing anything medical. They needed to be more scientific to prove it was a real medical field.

And psycho pharmacy was born.

Psychiatry and Pharmaceuticals

The marriage between psychiatry and pharmaceuticals is about 100 years old, but only recently has it exploded into this billion-dollar industry.

In the late 19th century, the first magical drugs were morphine and opium – to alleviate symptoms of mental illness. Quickly it was discovered these drugs solved nothing and only created more problems with addiction. Then it was Sigmund Freud, "the father of psychotherapy," introduced the world to the new magic drug – cocaine. He spoke candidly of the drug for its effects of creating joy, excitement, motivation, and euphoria despite his patients overdosing on the "medicine."

While it has been well-documented of Freud's love and addiction with cocaine, it is not as well known that his persistent promotion of the drug was a result of his hefty payments from the newly formed pharmaceutical companies Merck and Park Davies to endorse their rival drugs.

This has been the pattern of pharmaceutical drugs ever since. There is some type of scientific-medical breakthrough, a new drug is deemed the miracle drug with no side effects, eventually the side effects become glaringly obvious, and the search for a new drug begins.

During World War II, the first systematic killings of the holocaust were part of a euthanasia program to wipe out the mentally ill. It was believed that the mentally ill were a financial burden to the German society and state. In 1934, the first forced killings of citizens began under the secretive Trogram. Hitler believed that during war-time it would be easier to cover up the killings and would also free up hospital beds and medical personnel.

Though this was not Hitler's original idea, he actually gives full credit to the United States in their program which has sterilized more than 60,000 citizens – all of which it was unbeknownst to them. In his book, *Mein Kampf,* Hitler states,

> *"I have studied with great interest the laws of several American states concerning prevention of reproduction*

*by people whose progeny would, in all probability, be
of no value or be injurious to the racial stock."*

In the post-war era, psychiatry was still trying to prove itself as a true medical profession. On March 26, 1954, they claimed to have a medical breakthrough with the introduction of the FDA approved first psychiatric drug – Thorazine. Prior to this "breakthrough," mental illness had been treated with psycho and electroshock therapies and institutionalization. In fact, Egaz Mozine – inventor of the lobotomy – won the Nobel Prize in 1941 in Medicine for finding a way to shut down the frontal lobe.

Thorazine was the first of the magical drugs. It was considered a chemical lobotomy. Psychiatrists no longer needed to do a medical procedure; they could just prescribe a pill to shut off the frontal lobe of their patients. The breakthrough was the latest of attempts of a corrupt profession to gain credibility.

Thorazine was also an enormous money-maker and the profession was changed forever. This allowed psychiatrists to empty their facilities and bring their "services" out in the community. It was the death of psychotherapy and the birth of treating every difficulty in life with a pill. This put hundreds of thousands of mentally ill on the streets – most of which ended up homeless or incarcerated.

One year later, the new magic drug Milltown was created with high endorsements of notable psychiatrists at the time. This was also the beginning of the free sample marketing scheme in which sales reps give free samples of their drugs to the doctors. If the doctors have free samples, they are willing to give them out. If the patient likes them, it only makes sense to continue to supply. It would take more than a decade until the public found out that Milltown was more dangerous and addictive than methamphetamine or cocaine.

But psychiatry had arrived as a real medical profession, prescribing real medicine, and nothing could stop the gravy train. Valium was known as "momma's little helper" and prescribed to stressed-out housewives to the tune of 2.3 billion tablets sold in 1978. The next miracle drug was Prozac, used to cure depression and as soon as it hit the market, instantly the number of depression diagnoses skyrocketed. Prior to the invention of SSRI drugs, it was estimated that 100 out of every one million people were diagnosed with depression. Since SSRI drugs, the numbers now indicate that 100,000 out of every one million have depression – a one-thousand fold increase!

They receive a patent on their drug for seven years, which allows them to charge monopoly prices. Once that patent expires, a new breakthrough is created. This happened in the 1990s as Paxil was created to treat bipolar, which followed with thousands more diagnosed with bipolar disorder. In the DSM-3, about one-tenth of one percent of people had bipolar disorder. Now that number has jumped to 10-percent (100-percent increase)? Are there this many more people getting sick, or is it just a great marketing campaign?[13]

DSM: The Devil's Dictionary

Coinciding with the pharmaceutical boom was the creation of the Diagnostic Statistical Manual for Mental Disorders (DSM). In 1952, the first DSM was published in a 130-page packet which included 112 disorders. These were not based on science, but rather voted in on a mail-in ballot that was sent to 10-percent of APA member psychiatrists.

By 1994, the fourth edition of the DSM was published in an 860-page book with 374 diagnoses. In 42 years, we had tripled the

---

[13] *The Marketing of Madness: Are We All Insane?* [Film]. (2010).

number of diagnoses? And they weren't being discovered, they were simply being created and voted in at psychiatry conventions. And with each new diagnosis, another medication could be prescribed.

To show how fraudulent the system is, homosexuality was listed in the first two versions of the DSM. It wasn't until 1980 that it was removed in the third edition. Not because that they realized it was not a mental disorder, but because of political pressure to remove it.

The DSM-V was released in 2013 with 19 of the 27 planners of the committee having significant financial ties to pharmaceutical companies. It is estimated that 450 million people are diagnosed with mental disorder – for perspective, there are only about 320 million people in the United States.

And the criteria for the diagnosis are so subjective that any person could be diagnosed with any disorder at any time. The 1972 Rosenham Experiment demonstrated this when eight volunteers were presented to an institution stating they heard voices in their head claiming to only hear the words "empty," "hollow," or "thud." All eight were committed.

Once they were admitted, they abandoned all their symptoms but would not be released. They were all diagnosed with schizophrenia and were only released after they admitted they were mentally ill and in remission. The psychiatry industry was furious and another hospital told Rosenham to send patients to their hospital and they claimed they would be able to spot the actors.

Of the next 193 patients, that hospital turned away 41 clients and suspected another 42 as imposters. The problem was that Rosenham had not sent anyone.

Another experiment by the BBC in England had a reality TV show in which the most prominent psychiatrists had one week of examining clients and were to guess what their past diagnosis. After one week, they guessed wrong on three of the five participants! The best psychiatrists were wrong 60-percent of the time when given a week to diagnosis a client, how can they do so in a one hour evaluation?

Then the money-hungry pigs are always seeking for the next way to expand their enterprise. They look for new markets and find it in the elderly and the children. At first, we were told that no one under 18 can be diagnosed with bipolar disorder only to later have five and six-year-olds receiving this diagnosis, and in some cases as young as two-years-old diagnosed with bipolar disorder.

Today, more than one million children are diagnosed with bipolar disorder in America. That is more than diabetes and autism combined. The sickness continues as they expand to the most vulnerable markets possible, foster children. It is estimated that nine out of 10 children in foster care have a mental health diagnosis to begin with, and with that usually comes a prescription.

Let me explain the famous Paxil 329 Study to emphasize the sickness of those in power. Martin Keller ran this study and tested 100 children on the drug and stated that it went well. There were 22 co-authors of this study of important psychiatrists. The FDA granted their blessing on the faulty study and within the next year more than 55 million were on Paxil. [14] [15]

However, seven of those in the study were hospitalized and another 11 had serious side effects. Keller admitted no fault and did not count those in the study and labeled them as noncompliant or that

---

[14] *Paxil, Lies, and the Lying Researchers Who Tell Them.* (2008).
[15] Grohol, John (2008). PsychCentral. *More on Infamous Paxil Study 329*

they had "dropped out." He settled out of court for $2.5 million dollars – less than what they make on sales in one hour. In the same year, Paxil $3.1 billion in sales. In 2012, Paxil's bill increased to $3 billion for fraud allegations in which they plead guilty to unlawfully promoting their drug.[16]

In their guilty plea, GlaxoSmithKline states:

> *"In the criminal information, the government alleges that, from April 1998 to August 2003, GSK unlawfully promoted Paxil for treating depression in patients under age 18, even though the FDA has never approved it for pediatric use. The United States alleges that, among other things, GSK participated in preparing, publishing and distributing a misleading medical journal article that misreported that a clinical trial of Paxil demonstrated efficacy in the treatment of depression in patients under age 18, when the study failed to demonstrate efficacy. At the same time, the United States alleges, GSK did not make available data from two other studies in which Paxil also failed to demonstrate efficacy in treating depression in patients under 18. The United States further alleges that GSK sponsored dinner programs, lunch programs, spa programs and similar activities to promote the use of Paxil in children and adolescents. GSK paid a speaker to talk to an audience of doctors and paid for the meal or spa treatment for the doctors who attended. Since 2004, Paxil, like other antidepressants, included on its label a "black box warning" stating that antidepressants may increase the risk of suicidal thinking and behavior in short-term studies in patients under age 18. GSK agreed to plead guilty to misbranding Paxil in that its labeling*

---

[16] United States Department of Justice (2012, July 2) GlaxoSmithKline to Plead Guilty and Pay $3 Billion to Resolve Fraud Allegations and Failure to Report Safety Data.

> *was false and misleading regarding the use of Paxil for patients under 18....* GSK has agreed to plead guilty to misbranding Wellbutrin in that its labeling did not bear adequate directions for these off-label uses. For the Paxil and Wellbutrin misbranding offenses, GSK has agreed to pay a criminal fine and forfeiture of $757,387,200."

And of course, the Cymbalta clinical testing that resulted in five suicides still found a way to pass through FDA Approval. Nineteen-year-old, Traci Johnson, had no history of depression, suicidal ideation, or any mental illness. Yet, after being involved in this clinical study she ended her life – one of five suicides in clinical testing of Cymbalta. After her death, twenty-percent of the volunteer withdrew from the study, in which the numbers of dropouts simply are not accounted.[17] In 2013, Cymbalta delivered more than $5.1 billion in sales.

Drug companies are profiting more than $80 billion each year as a result of this disease mongering as well as ludicrous markup prices. These medications are incredibly cheap to manufacture – i.e. the cost to produce 100 Xanax pills is about $0.025 (yes that is 2.5 cents). Yet, they sell for $136 in the pharmacy – a 500,000-percent profit margin.[18]

Which leads back to the opening comments of this chapter, are we really doing the right thing this time with the over-medication? The United States holds only five percent of the world's population, but we consume over 80-percent of the world's pharmaceutical drugs. Are we that sick? Or is it the drug companies that are the sick ones?

---

[17] Lender, Jeanne (2005). Slate.com. *Drug Secrets: What the FDA isn't Telling.*
[18] Davis, ShaRon; Palmer, Mary. US Department of Commerce. *The True Costs of Your Prescriptions.*

All of this keeps the lower rings of society down. The rules have been created this way to favor those in power. And all of this has to do with the love, infatuation, and addiction to money and wealth. We are knowingly killing people for the benefit of a few. This is the real mental illness; allowing the true psychopaths to continue this abnormal behavior.

Chemical Imbalance Theory

The chemical imbalance theory states that mental illness is created by an imbalance in neurotransmitters in the brain. Naturally, to fix such an imbalance is to discover a method of increasing /balancing the neurotransmitters and the symptoms will disappear.

There is just one problem with that theory – it is not true.

Not too far off from the ancient Greek's humor theory in which an imbalance in fluids led to the mental disorders, the chemical imbalance theory is also just a theory that has never been proven to be true.

This concept has grown so popular because it sounds good and we are bombarded with continuous advertisements that tell us "this may be caused by a chemical imbalance in your brain…". The advertisements are trying to sell us pharmaceutical drugs that will fix the imbalance in the brain and bring about a cure in the mental illness.

This theory started by accident in 1952 when a group of tubercular patients became euphoric when treated with the medication Iproniazid. It was established that this drug raised levels of epinephrine and norepinephrine in the brain. Then in 1955, it was discovered that reserpine depleted the brain of 5-Hydroxytryptophan, a precursor in the biosynthesis of the neurotransmitters serotonin and melatonin, therefore decreasing levels of serotonin, dopamine, and norepinephrine in animal studies. The animal subjects showed signs of catatonic symptoms, such as inactivity and hunched over posture etc. Scientists concluded that depression was therefore a cause of chemical imbalance.

However, this theory has never been proved in humans. Furthermore, it has not been demonstrated why common depression drugs do not alleviate depression almost immediately, since they create a maximum increase in serotonin and dopamine within two days. The fact is, most depressive patients do not have low levels of serotonin; some drugs that have nothing to do with serotonin or norepinephrine can alleviate depressive symptoms; stimulants that work on increasing dopamine and serotonin do not work for depression; some patients diagnosed with depressions actually have high extremely high levels of serotonin; and there is not one single peer reviewed article that can support claim of a neurotransmitter deficiency in *any* mental disorder.

If such an imbalance existed, how can you know that just by asking questions? Diagnosing mental disorders really comes down to a matter of *opinion*, as there is no physical test in common usage that can pinpoint the condition.

As highly published psychiatrist Ronald Pies stated:

> *"I am not aware of any concerted effort by academic psychiatrists, psychiatric textbooks, or official psychiatric organizations to promote a simplistic chemical imbalance hypothesis of mental illness."*

This has all been a part of a giant marketing scheme as a result of the marriage between psychiatry and the pharmaceutical industry. But the question remains, what makes us think we got it right this time?

This is the history of the psychiatry industry, along with the state of the industry today.

Mental Illness is a Spiritual Gift

While there is no doubt that many people suffer from what is considered "mental illness," I would argue along the lines of the shamanic cultures and the teachings of Socrates – that they are not ill at all, but rather they are spiritually gifted.

People with bipolar disorder and schizophrenia are among the most discriminated against people in the history of the world. It is still socially acceptable to call someone a "schizo" and mock people who hear voices in their head. But when you look closer at the symptoms of mania and psychosis, you soon discover they are the exact same as a spiritual awakening:

- Intense rush of energy that creates a break in reality
- All senses are incredibly heightened to the point can sense emotions of those around you
- You feel that you are everyone and everything – interconnectedness or oneness
- Incredible level of understanding, everything makes sense
- Sense of time vanishes
- Everything becomes sacred, overwhelming sense of love and euphoria

Now, clearly this is the more positive side of things, in which the person is guided by love. When guided by fear, usually a result of traumatic experiences, the symptoms of psychosis and mania can be far more terrifying with voices instructing terrible actions.

But for the most part, people in psychosis are not violent. They are experiencing a break in reality. The same break in reality we seek out through meditation and prayer.

With ADHD, we have a generation of children that are too intelligent to want to sit in a classroom all day and repeat materials. They need a different approach to learning. People with the phony disorder of ADHD tend to be much more creative, energetic, and can focus greater than others when it is a subject they find interesting that intrigues their soul. But, instead, we drug them up with amphetamines to make classroom life seem normal.

Dr. Marianne Kuzujanakis also asserts that giftedness does not always equate to what our society deems "positive" experiences. In fact, up to 20% of gifted adolescents drop out of the school system, displaying such "symptoms" as talking a lot, high energy levels, and impulsive, inattentive, or distractible behaviors [19] - Quite similar to that of ADHD or Bipolar Disorder.

Dr. Jack Wiggins, former president of the American Psychological Association, stated in the same Huffington Post article,

> *"This is a widespread and serious problem – the wasting of lives from the misdiagnosis of gifted children and adults and the inappropriate treatment that often follows."*

This is not to say people do not have these symptoms of these disorders, but instead, we need to focus on how they can use these disorders to unlock their spiritual gifts and change the world. We

---

[19] *Kuzujanakis, M. The Misunderstood Face of Giftedness. The Huffington Post* (Apr. 10, 2013).

are drugging up our future Albert Einsteins, John Lennons, and Gandhis, all because they are "different" than the norm.

Because it is always those who are crazy enough to think they can change the world are usually the ones that do.

CHAPTER III

Love and Fear

The Story of Marty and Donald

Chapter 3
Love and Fear: The Story of Marty and Donald

I'm locked up in the psychiatric ward for the second time this year – not exactly the ideal way to begin my eighteenth year on this earth, and my first year of adulthood. Dressed in an all-white type of gown, the room is unbearably cold, and I am completely grounded to this room. I have been in this situation before and I know the way to get out. My entire life I have lied, conned, and manipulated my way out of things.

Lying awake, I'm contemplating my plan-of-action, in walks the janitor wearing blue shirt and blue jeans. He walks around the room leaning over and basically checks everything in the room.

"Hi. I'm Donald," he says with a smile, "I'll be your nurse tonight."

"OK. Whatever, you look like a janitor," I think to myself. I was always on-edge, ready for a fight. It must have been some type of defense mechanism to avoid any sort of rejection. At this point in my life, my brain had been trained this way and it is important to remember this when working with clients.

All that has taken place is this man walked in and introduced himself, but in my mind I had already decided how I am going to attack him. This all stems from fear.

We are all born into the world with a clean slate. Our first few years are so paramount because everything is new to us. This is when we figure out if the world is safe or unsafe. Our brains are full of gray matter, which refers to the part of the brain that is adjustable and creates the way we think and turns into our personality.

When there is early childhood trauma, this limbic system is overactive and far too much for a child to take on at this stage of development. This leads to the brain shooting out far more stress signals as a child, because they are always in survival mode. Research has shown there is also a break-down in the connectivity between the amygdale and the prefrontal cortex in traumatized brains meaning that the emotional learning is disrupted and the traumatized client continues to be on-edge, overly defensive, or in "survival mode."[20]

The human mind is guided by two primary emotions: fear and love. As the John Lennon quote that opens this chapter indicates, when motivated by love we are open to endless possibilities. But when fear is the primary force guiding us, we hold back and resist life.

I was raised in a Catholic home which is one of the fear-based religions. I always find it ironic that any religion is to be based on fear, rather than love. The most prevalent theme in the Old Testament is "holy fear of the Lord." In Proverbs 9:10 we are told, "The beginning of wisdom is fear of the Lord."

Albert Einstein believed this derived from the primitive man having numerous fears such as hunger, wild beasts, sickness, and death. And more modernly, became an institution for morality such as how a parent raises a child – if you are good you are rewarded and if you are bad you are punished. He believes that this adjustment from fear to morality correlates with the Old Testament to the New Testament.[21]

---

[20] Dong Hoon Oh (2012). Traumatic Experiences Disrupt Amygdala – Prefrontal Connectivity, The Amygdala - A Discrete Multitasking Manager, Dr. Barbara Ferry (Ed.), ISBN: 978-953-51-0908-2, InTech, DOI: 10.5772/48691.

[21] Einstein, A., & Calaprice, A. (1996). *The quotable Einstein*. Princeton, N.J.: Princeton University Press.

But it is not just religion, it is a fear-based society. Western society has been built on installing fear. For example, the police force is put in place to serve and protect us. We pay taxes to ensure safety, but when a police officer is behind you on the freeway, what is the automatic instinctual feeling? The majority of us feel fear. Even if we are not doing anything wrong, we fear the consequences and penalties.

Fear, like anger, also serves its purpose. It is an emotional response to imminent danger or a threat. The problem is when it consumes our life. It can also be used as a great motivator to get us going in the right direction; the problem is when we carry the fear with us everywhere we go.

> *"Fear is your best friend or your worst enemy. It's like fire. If you can control it, it can cook for you; it can heat your house. If you can't control it, it will burn everything around you and destroy you." – Mike Tyson*

When fear is installed in us at a young age, the amygdale is overactive in sending warning signals. This is part of the emotional learning process, we learn the world is not a safe place and we view people as a threat to our safety and our defense mechanisms are put in place to protect us. If I can push people away from me, there is no chance they can get close to me and hurt me. If my emotional learning stems from fear and mistrust, I am not going to let random hospital staff into my life.

The Power of Empathy

But the staff just kept coming into my room and introducing themselves to me and I couldn't push them away. Some would ask to talk to me, but I adamantly refused for about two days. But the most significant element of this story is that they never forced me to talk. No one pushed me, engaged in some type of power struggle, or made me uncomfortable.

Unaware at the time, this is the quintessential profile of a quality treatment staff and healing environment. The field of psychiatry has done quite a few makeovers throughout the history of civilization dating back to ancient times. Initially viewed as a gift from the Divine, to being prosecuted as witches in the 16th centuries, to being tortured in "looney bins" in the 19th century, and eventually we are progressing towards this model of empathy and understanding that I fortunately experienced in 1994.[22]

With such strong tradition in forcing treatment on clients, abusing their human rights, and dehumanization inside the asylum walls, it has been a process to reinvent an industry that has thousands of years of abuse and neglect.

Still today there are clinicians and staff that will force treatment, neglect clients, and push beliefs on them. While it may be very well-intentioned, pushing beliefs on someone who is not ready can be for more detrimental than beneficial to the person's well-being.

There is an old story that describes perception. In a small village, six blind men are introduced to an elephant for the first time. They were invited one-by-one to touch the elephant and explain what an elephant is like. The first man touched the trunk and explained it was like a snake; the second touched its side and described it as a wall; the next man touched its leg and thought it was like a tree; the fourth man touched its tail and described it like a rope; the fifth man touched its tusk and said an elephant is like a spear; and the sixth

---

[22] Foerschner, A. (2010). The History of Mental Illness: From "Skull Drills" to "Happy Pills" *Student Pulse, 2*(9), 1-4.

man touched its ear and flapped it back-and-forth and described it as a fan.

So who was telling the truth? Who was lying? They were all telling the truth from their experience. The same is true whenever we communicate with other people. If a client in a psychiatry ward explains an experience - it is true to them. A clinician's perception is also true to them, but the key remains to actively listen to the other person without preconceived

This is what makes Donald and the rest of the staff different. They understood the power of empathy before it was being taught in universities. They just kept stopping by and saying "hello." They waited for me to be ready and never pressured me to do anything. Eventually, I came out and went to the group. I sat there and listened to how the other kids talked. It was weird, they were just sharing their innermost feelings and no one was laughing or teasing.

Honestly, I was a bit creeped out by it all. Seriously, where am I? They just let me listen and I don't have to participate? Then we get recreation time to play ping pong? And everyone just treats each other kindly? There are not cliques, groups, gossip, or hatred. Everyone just genuinely cares for each other.

Transformation from Trust

And day-after-day, a slow transformation is taking place in which I am unaware. I am starting to trust people and care about them. Evening comes around and Donald asks me to play cards and teaches me how to play Spades. While we are playing, kids start to talk about their lives with no filters.

Groups, groups, and more groups of talking about our feelings and I am starting to get into it and want to participate – but still a little bashful. Feeling a little more at ease, I start small by sharing how my day went, but at least taking a step outside of my comfort zone. I even opened up to Donald and shared with him about my life from my perspective.

But nothing was ever forced. They waited for me to get comfortable, allowed me to sit and listen, and got to know me.

Anyone who has been to treatment understands the significant role this plays in your life. All emotional events have stronger memories because we store it in two parts of the brain. We use our left brain to record all the details such as dates, times, and other information. But when we are emotionally attached we remember how we felt throughout the experience. This can include positive memories such as celebrations, achievements and weddings. And also negative events such as an accident. [23]

This is why every moment in a treatment setting is an opportunity to make an everlasting impact. The moment may seem "just part of the job," for a clinician, but the person receiving the care is creating intense emotional memories.

Although my stay at Divine Redeemer was 20 years ago, the memories are so vivid that I can replay nearly every day in mind with complete clarity.

My case manager, Sam, seemed to be a cool guy that works with my family. Ron the boss, is a no-nonsense tough-guy. His intelligence and mental toughness intimidate people and he is the clear leader of the organization. And then there was Marty, the soft, warm, and

---

[23] Ledoux, J. (1993). Emotional memory systems in the brain. *Behavioural Brain Research, 58*(1-2), 69-79.

loving one. She carries such confidence that she can just be herself and does not have the need to try to impress anyone. And of course, Dr. Housefield, was the one that gave me my medication. I never saw him for more than 10 minutes, he just gave us pills.

I started to get to know all of the kids personally, too. Kirsten and Jodi were the two that had been there for quite some time before me and they were getting ready to be discharged. They would work on treatment packets and kept asking for "puppy uppers," – still unsure what that meant.

Falling Apart so things can Fall Into Place

Wait, have I gone mad? Is any of this even real? People ask for compliments and we just give them? At the same time, all of this seems to make sense at some level. I start wondering if I actually died in that overdose and I ended up in heaven.

But three weeks into this place and I am ready to leave. I am fighting, begging, screaming, and pleading to get out of there. After reading through some pamphlet on rules and rights, I found my loophole. If I am 18, I can sign myself out since I am an adult and it is an adolescent unit.

As I proudly walk up to the desk to present my case, I get knocked off my feet when they tell me that they can keep me and I'll have to take the case to court. The confusion sets in, which comes out as furious anger.

I hit the Plexiglas at the desk and it doesn't break. I am sent to my room by myself and throw another tantrum and this doesn't work either. My last resort is to call my mom and beg her to get me out of here, clearly manipulating the situation.

But she said "no."

For the first time in my life she said "no." I didn't know what to do. My rage and fury continued as I remember she came up for her birthday to visit me and I smashed some cupcakes in her face before spitting on her. This woman, who did everything for me, was abused her entire life and this was my response!?

The staff all saw this, but no one judged me. They try to talk to me, but I had already disconnected from everyone. I had my court hearing Tomorrow and all of this will be behind me.

On the day of the hearing, I am handcuffed and put in the back of a squad car with two older guys. Upon getting to the courthouse, we are sent in some time of waiting room. One of the guys keeps ripping up paper and then he will shut off the lights, which has me terrified.

My Mom was in a different room waiting. All I could think about was how she did this to me and that she, and everyone else, was going to pay for this somehow. I had no idea what this hearing was about at the time, I just knew it was part of the process to get me out of the hospital. However, it turns out this was actually my commitment hearing. My Mom had signed a petition to have me committed and those other two guys were from the adult unit being committed to the state hospital.

> *It was March 2, 1994. At age 18, I am committed to the state as mentally ill. I am now a danger to society. I am unable to care for myself and the state must step in. The ruling allowed for me to stay at Divine Redeemer, stating that if I break the rules of the program I would be sent to the State Hospital.*

I didn't get it. Throwing tantrums and being a jerk had always worked for me. I always got my way. Now, this time I end up stuck in this land of feelings? I felt like everything was just falling apart in front of me.

The bad news is that everything was falling apart, but that was also the good news. Falling apart and having nowhere to run is precisely the conditions needed for someone to experience the spirit and the awakened state.

As time went by, I became the senior member of the unit. The older members started to get discharged and we would have emotional goodbyes with everyone crying and wishing them well. Such strong bonds are created within the walls of a psych ward as you have a group of people making such emotional connections because we are being taught how to live for the first time, which makes goodbyes so difficult.

Feeling Good

Being a senior member brought a sense of power and control. And with this power, there was bound to be some sort of abuse. I remember we got a new admit one day, Taylor, a heavy-set girl that recently attempted suicide.

"What are you in here for?" I asked.

"I tried to kill myself," she stated, "I took a whole bunch of Tylenol."

"Woah, big shot!" I said with a snarky tone of voice. "Took 12 Tylenols!? What is that going to do?"

I was confronted about this behavior as this is the first impression she had of the unit. A senior member questioning her "level of craziness," was her first interaction. Aside from that, who am I to question anyone else's journey? With suicide, if someone has intent to die, no matter how minor the method may seem, it is just as real as any other attempt. And even if she clearly knew that she would not die and it was a cry out for help, there is clearly something significant going on in her life in which she is going to extreme lengths to make her pain disappear.

And that is the most important thing about suicide. Nobody commits suicide or attempts to commit suicide because they want to die. I repeat, nobody actually wants to die. People who are suicidal only want the pain to go away. Those who carry through come to a point in their lives where the pain is so incredibly strong that the person has decided that ending their own life is the only way to escape the pain.

The confrontation came from a good place, was about concern, and actually was beneficial for me. Then miraculously, I started feeling pretty good. The staff was happy with my improvements, I am becoming a leader and working on the same pink packets that Kirsten and Jodi did before they left. I am not sure if it is the pills, the group, the feelings, or the structure. It was likely a combination, but whatever it was, it felt good.

New kids started coming in and it seemed that each one came with a story more horrific than the last. There was Jordan, age 12, with the bad temper; Leah, 13, that came from an abusive household with a drug-addicted mother; and a couple of other guys Dustin and Don. I also remember a weird girl that left after just 12 days. The unit really took it hard because we all felt that she was "crazier" than any of us and really needed the help. It turns out it had to do with her insurance not covering the stay and that moment sticks with me as breaking my heart seeing this girl who needed help was not allowed treatment.

Also, this was my first taste of the corrupt marriage between the health care and insurance industry. As a patient, especially an adolescent, you want to believe that everyone is being held as part of their treatment plan and what is best for them. But, here we discovered our length of stay was primarily based on how much our insurance would cover.

Hearing their stories made me feel guilty in a way. I felt bad for complaining about my simple life and I felt the need to help lead them. We learned and benefited from each other and I really didn't want to leave this situation.

Gorillas in the Mist

The 1988 film *"Gorillas in the Mist"* chronicles the journey of field biologist, Dian Fossey, as she befriends a tribe of gorillas. She did so to continue the work or her mentor, George Schaller, a renowned primatologist who had collected more information on the intimate life of gorillas than all other scientists combined.

When colleagues asked how he was able to get such information from these creatures, his simple response was that he didn't carry a gun. Loving kindness, and togetherness, is also what I experienced at Divine Redeemer. The staff didn't carry any proverbial guns and were able to get to know the person behind the mask.

This is how all interactions in the world work. We feed off the energy of those around us. As an experiment, take a look in the mirror and what do you see? Once you change your posture, your reflection also will change. If you are friendly, it is friendly in return. If you are angry, it will get angry too. This also works with human interactions. People will sense your anxiety, fear, love, arrogance, genuineness, etc. This is how you change the world, but smiling at the next person you see and brightening their mood and having them pass along the chain of love.

Once I started to have family meetings, I would break doors, fight and create as much havoc and chaos as humanly possible. Eventually, I had to come clean and tell them everything. I didn't want to leave because I felt so safe and comfortable. I shared all of this with Marty and Sam. They didn't judge me; they just listened to what was going on inside my head.

This place is the opposite of what my previous life. They were patient with me and allowed me to be comfortable. And when I blew up, they never reacted. They just waited until I was calm before we discussed things. I was validated for positive behavior, I was never judged, teased, bullied, blamed, or criticized. And most importantly, they did everything with love.

Ahh, there it is. The other motivating factor in life: love. As described by Jack Kornfield in *A Wise Heart*,

> "When you love anyone enough,
> they will share their secrets."

I remember one time hearing Ron say, "I'll load the gun if someone will shoot him."

Imagine hearing that as a kid? Especially in a place in which they are supposed to be treating you for mental health! I was devastated, hurt, and broken. I had the courage one day to share this in group with Marty and she told me she was going to bring this up because it "wasn't right."

I pleaded against this! That is the last thing I want is for Ron to know he hurt me. This was the old motivating factor, fear, taking over again. I was afraid of rejection, failure, and of people not liking me.

Marty wouldn't budge. She told me, "No, it is not OK."

After she told him, Ron called me into his office. Terrified, shaking, and looking away from him I slowly made my way into his office only to hear him apologize. He told me that it was wrong of him. He also shared that he has been disappointed in me and expects me to be leading more on the unit.

What? Did an adult just tell me that they were wrong? Then apologize to me? And of all people, Ron?

We just sat in there and talked. This was an essential learning moment of my life. This is stuff that a lot of people learn early on in life. But in the field of mental health and addiction, that is not always the case.

This reminds me of an Oscar Wilde quote in which he states,

> "Education is an admirable thing, but it is well
> to remember from time to time that nothing
> that is worth learning can be taught."

No matter how many times you tell a person about effective communication, it is not truly effective until we experience it firsthand. I experienced it in this moment and it made sense. I saw it in action. If I were to be scolded or lectured about communication, it would not have sunk in as well as when Ron told me, "I was wrong."

From the other perspective of the industry, I've heard staff say, "C'mon, they just need to make better choices." I hear clients ripped on, called names, and antagonized. How is anyone supposed to get better in those conditions? This is not teaching, helping, or caring. This is simply abusing one's power.

This is the power of the stigma of mental health and addiction. People make judgments on the behaviors and actions of individuals and can't see the forest for the trees. We need to build more people like Ron, Donald, and Marty in this industry – and more importantly in this world.

While this interaction with Ron helped move me in the right direction, it also hit me off-guard with an unforeseen fear. I had been progressing well, in fact, so well that they were ready to successfully discharge me.

I wasn't ready for this. I had just met Christine on the unit. She was gone, lost, and a little bit crazy, you could see it in her eyes. She was likely sexually abused as a child and carried a feeling of emptiness in her. She was my new girlfriend. I finally had things going well for me.

So how could I possibly leave? No Christine, Donald, Marty, Ron, or Micky? I got upset and couldn't handle the thought of leaving and began damaging hospital property. This was not well-received as I had become the peer leader at this time and had higher expectations. Next, they separate the genders because of my relationship with Christine on the unit.

Everything was getting taken away from me again. I started causing problems on the unit by mocking new clients, more tantrums, dominating others, and always in an angry mood. At one point I smashed a trash can and got a group of the younger kids riled up. We caused chaos all over the unit. This is my way of communicating, it always has been.

After the riot settled, I was thrown into a room and unleashed uncontrollable bawling and crying in front of Micky, a staff from the CD unit. Anger is always easier to display than the true emotion. Just as I described the person being chased by the bear in Chapter I, I was not really angry at the staff. It was the opposite, I was sad that I would have to leave them.

But when we are in a rage, the last thing we are going to do is try to figure out the underlying emotion. This is why they put me in a room, let the anger settle, and see what the true emotion was that was masking as anger.

This is not uncommon, especially in adolescent units. Whenever kids are close to a discharge date, they begin to "self-destruct" and sabotage their own discharge date in order to stay in a place that is comfortable. Then when asked about the behavior change it comes back as anger towards the hospital or facility – just as I had demonstrated.

Now, I cannot tell you one word that Micky said to me that day. But I remember vividly how she made me feel. I just remember feeling so much better, calmer, relaxed, and with someone who understood.

In any teaching environment – school, church, athletics, or treatment – the student will never remember the words that you said, but they'll never forget the way you make them feel. Again, this is because we are motivated by emotions. Think of your best teachers and coaches throughout the years, do you remember what they told you specifically? Or are the memories stronger with your emotions and how they made you feel?

So here I was in a room with no bed, out of control both inside my mind and in my external environment. As I reflect back on that moment, that may have been the darkest and coldest room in the hospital but my memories seem to play back a place of bright light, warmth, and hope.

However, it was too late. I had been causing too much chaos for too long. I violated the agreement and they were going to send me to the state hospital. I was an 18-year-old on an adolescent unit, destroying property, and infringing on other's ability to succeed and recover. They needed to protect the unit and the rest of the kids and I had my epiphany one riot too late.

The meeting was set for 3:30 p.m. I plead my case to Marty, Micky, and Donald. I cry and beg for one final chance and promise a change in behavior.

"Don't send me away," I remember crying to them as they walked into the meeting. I sat in the hallway outside my room unsure of my future once again. My life's journey was out of my control once again and I needed at least one person in that room to believe in me.

As they walked out, Micky came up to me and said, "Marty fought for you, all by herself. She went against everyone else…and she won."

I was given a final chance all because one woman believed in me when nobody else did. My family had given up on me and even those who thought they could handle me had seen enough. But not Marty, she saw a different side. She put herself on the line, the same way my mother stood up against others when my grandmother died. When you fight with pure love, fear and hate stand no chance.

And, in that very instance, my life turned around. That is not to say that I have not had problems and difficulties. But for the first time in my life, I was headed in a right direction.

Like in Alice in Wonderland, when she encounters a fork in the road, Alice asks the Cheshire Cat which road she shall take. The Cheshire Cat asks where she is going and Alice responds, "I'm not sure." To which the cat smiles and laughs, "Then it doesn't matter which path you take."

Similarly, I was not sure where I was going the first 18 years of my life. I was just wandering endlessly, until that moment when Marty stopped me in my tracks and put me on the right path. It may have seemed like another mundane moment, typical afternoon discharge meeting among clinician staff, and just another day to those involved. But, it forever changed my life. I wish I could take the time to thank them for what they did to me. We never know the impact we have on people and the significance of each small moment has the capability of being a life-changer.

Two weeks later, I was successfully discharged. It only took one person to see a different side of me and a different perspective. Marty doesn't wear a mask because she doesn't need one. She is courageous and confident enough to go through life without the need to pretend to be someone else.

She is a quiet and reserved woman, but she knows what she believes in and when needed she will put on a different mask and go to battle for her beliefs. She stood up to Ron and risked her job for me and then challenged the entire staff on my behalf.

And while she put on a temporary mask to meet the demands of the situation, her courage showed me that it is OK to take off my permanent psychological mask that I had been wearing my entire life.

CHAPTER IV

Love Addiction
The Great Escape

Chapter 4
Love Addiction: The Great Escape

Seventy-Five days later, I was discharged from the hospital, apparently shattering the previous record for longest inpatient stay. But it had worked. I was a different person with healthy ways of living and healthy friends.

Finally, I was a free man. Well, kind of. I was given a provisional discharge, meaning that I was granted a discharge while on commitment. If I was able to follow specific rules and guidelines, I could go about my life and be a "normal" citizen.

There are three typical phases that everyone in treatment must go through if true change is going to take place:

1) ***Resistance*** – This can mean physically resisting by trying to fight the system, or run away from the actual facility. It also means mental resistance, but denying there is a problem, not participating in groups, and rebelling against those trying to offer any assistance.

2) ***Adoration*** – You begin to love everything about the program. After breaking down the old ways of living, you there is a different way to living. You begin to feel safe, don't want to leave, provide leadership, and start to focus your efforts on watching others flourish.

3) ***Ready*** – Understand the reason for the treatment, appreciate the tools that you have developed, and no longer afraid to return to the outside world and apply your new personality to the world.

Although I was in the "Ready" phase, due to my home environment, I was sent to a place for adults with mental illness called "Gills Place." I lasted until all of about 6:00 a.m. on the first day before going back to my mother's house.

This could have easily been justified as grounds for revoking my provisional discharge. No one would have argued if they reviewed my case and sent me to the state hospital. I bring this up only to point out the enormous power in the hands of the social workers. The social workers are put into difficult situations in which their decisions have life-lasting impacts on individuals and their family.

They work 50-plus hours each week, overwhelmed with the number of clients on their caseload, and deal with conflicting opinions on how to handle each client. While they are in an unfair position, even more unfair is the client's they serve. Your entire life depends on who is in charge of your case.

Anyone who goes into the field of social work typically has some type of personal reason to join this industry. College-aged students have been somehow affected by addiction, mental illness, or some significant event in which they want to give back. A common reason for entering the field is, "I want to help people."

This is a natural human trait. Our brains are wired to connect with each other and we all carry the compassionate instinct. Connecting with others in a compassionate way not only heal our minds, but research continues to show the effects it has on curing physical diseases, and even increase our lifespan.[24]

Plus with the "career-outlook" planners estimate a 19-percent growth in the field for the next 10 years, it is appealing knowing that there will always be available work. It has glamorous appeal to

---

[24] Seppala, E. (May/June 2013). The Compassionate Mind. *Observer, 26*(5).

young-adults seeking to stamp their mark on the universe – they get to help people and there will always be jobs available.

The problem is, you end up with a vast number of unqualified – albeit, well-intentioned – young adults that are granted the power to alter the life of another human-being. The glamour of the job fades away the first time you get cussed out or realize that the reason the people "need help," is because they come from pretty disastrous backgrounds.

Another issue is that when you have an industry flooded with interested people to work, you get away with lower salary. It is simple supply-and-demand. The irony of it all is that while trying to save expenses with cheap labor, you end up with lower-quality service. In this industry, if the quality of care is poor, the client likely will end up back in the hospital at some point in their lifetime – which is far more costly than if we were to invest in higher-paying social workers.

For example, it is clear that junk food in America is far cheaper than eating healthy, with one study showing as much as $1.50 per day cheaper![25] This makes the cheaper, unhealthy choice, the attractive bargain. But with all bargain shopping, you get what you pay for in the end. Although it doesn't show up right away, choosing the cheaper unhealthy food leads to far more substantial long-term costs in terms of diabetes, heart disease, obesity, and other lower quality of life.

Back at Home

I fully admit that I was quite fortunate to have a social worker that took time to understand what I was going through, because I was

---

[25] Polis, C. (2013, December 4). Eating Healthy vs. Unhealthy Will Cost You $550 More Per Year, Study Reveals. *Huffington Post*.

never sent to the state hospital. I continued to take my medications and had daily conversations with my healthy friends via the telephone. However, I went back to the same home environment.

Back at home, nothing had changed and I was feeling abandoned. One day, my mom was gone all day and she returned with my older brother Reggie and a couple of pizzas. I was irritated with her already and things quickly escalated. I do not remember any of the circumstances around this event, only that I felt alone and did not know how to handle it.

She yelled at me and I responded without thinking by knocking the pizzas out of her hands. There is the impulsivity again, which I have carried my entire life. Back to the developing brain, when the stress response system (fight of flight) in constantly turned on from a young age, the long term affects are going to be impulsivity, depression, hostility, suicidal ideation, and substance use. This was my first test outside of a controlled environment, and I failed.

After she slapped me, I grabbed her and started screaming. At this point, Reggie intervened in an attempt to be the family hero. This had nothing to do with this isolated incident, but was a build-up of anger and tension and there had been a sibling rivalry between us since we were young.

He charged at me as if he were a guard protecting the kingdom from an invasion. After throwing him to the ground, he laid on the ground faking injuries which turned everyone against me as always. It was the same ole story. My mom crying, Reggie was the victim, I was the bad guy, again.

It was all too much, too fast. Back into this same environment and everything resurfaced immediately. We all need time to ourselves, alone, in solace, and meditation to replenish our mind, body, and spirit.

All the spiritual masters have done this for thousands of years including Buddha and Jesus.

While I didn't know this at the time, in fact, all I knew is that I had to escape the situation. I needed to remove myself from this environment. I went to call all my friends from the hospital, but this time nobody was available. As I kept going down the list, I came to the very last name…Taylor.

Yep, same big, heavy, "12-Tylenol Taylor" was my last option.

Understanding Karma

She answered the phone and I immediately left to hang out with her. And this moment in my life, that day, that fight, nobody available besides Taylor, that phone call changed everything. I spent the entire day together with Taylor and finally we go to meet up with her best friend, Adrianne.

We met for the first time and it was my first true synchronistic connection. We caught eyes for the first time and it was apparent that this meeting was supposed to take place, it was prearranged by some force greater than ourselves. Look at all the factors that had to add up for this encounter: extended-stay at the hospital, Taylor's "suicide attempt", the impulsive lashing out and fight with family, and then the first fifteen people on my phone list not answering their phone. If one other person answered their phone, I would be telling a far different story.

As an 18-year-old kid, dying for acceptance, I was quite unaware of the spirituality of this moment. It appeared that my life had been falling apart, but this had to take place for this moment to come together. In a larger picture, this moment also changed the course of history for everyone in my family as well – although I am not certain on the path it led them, it put them in line with their journey.

This is Karma. People believe that Karma works as some sort of spiritual currency and that if you do good things, good things happen in return; and if you do evil, then you will be punished.

Karma is a Sanskirt word that means "to do" or "action." It has less to do with fate than we commonly associate. It means that each action we take (thought, word, or action) sets in motion forces that produce a new condition in which we have to respond. It is the essential piece of "living in the moment" or "one step at a time."

This altercation with my brother sent into motion forces that would continue to strain our relationship to this day. At any point, we have the ability to change it with another action. It also led to me responding to seek refuge and out of desperation I contacted the last person I wanted to speak with on my list and I had a choice and my inner knowledge told me it was in my best interest to call Taylor in that moment which was Karma – leading me to meet Adrianne.

Adrianne was wearing a yellow shirt, with blue horizontal stripes, long blonde hair, with a flirtatious smile towards me. We drove around all day in my car, Taylor was driving, when she lost control of the vehicle and sent us over the curb. There was a brief panic as Taylor did not have her driver's license. This was another one of those moments, in which Karma instincts took over. For once, impulsivity worked to my advantage.

I had to quickly jump into the driver's seat at take the fall to protect my friend. And I mean it, Taylor, was a true friend. I teased her when we first met, I judged her, but despite all that she was the one who was there for me when I needed someone the most. So, in return, I was there for her when she was in need – another Karma intervention. Her friend, Adrianne, saw this genuineness in me and she started to rub my back and we exchanged numbers.

I call her up the next day and go over to visit. And just like that, she is my new girlfriend.

The Love Addiction

Adrianne comes from a far worse situation than me. She has already been to a Treatment Center and is trying to get clean from drugs and alcohol. We were two truth-seekers that were empty and lost with nowhere to go and we became each other's escape from a phony world.

We are absolutely certain we are going to save each other from the cruelty of the world. We have talks daily, spend every minute together, and share things that we have never shared with another human – hence, taking off our masks.

I grow completely invested to give her anything and everything. I thought I was truly in love, even though I had no idea what this was, except for in my imagination. I spent every second of every day with her. I felt what I thought was love and the new addiction had formed.

When we live within our own mind, or ego, we know that there is more out there – we become truth-seekers. We feel this emptiness in our lives and try to fill that void by cramming it with things from outside ourselves.

And you can physically feel it when you find something to fill that emptiness. It is no different than when an athlete reaches for water or Gatorade to quench their thirst and replenish the fluids that are lost during competition. Humans also reach to quench their spiritual thirst with things outside of ourselves.

For me, first it was anger. Lashing out in a rage, altered my level of consciousness to the point it gave me the boost I thought I needed. Anyone who has ever been in a physical fight knows this feeling. Senses heighten, you don't even feel the pain of getting hit, the intensity, the rush, and then it is over. It is a drug. I used to have a friend that would go out each night seeking fights. I did not get it at the time, I thought he was just a bully and a punk, but looking back, that was his drug.

Then I turned to gambling as it also creates a dopamine rush that made me feel alive by taking risks and enjoying the thrill of anticipation. Knowing that the next card being turned over on the table was beyond our control, yet it could mean we wouldn't have a ride home or we would be living the high life for one night. Again, senses heighten; we live in the moment, and feel alive.

Now, I have a new drug, or addiction, in which society accepts and rewards – love for another person. My new cure to this emptiness was another person, my drug of being loved. Truth be told, love is not the problem. In fact, love is the answer. It answers everything and it is the only truth in this world. But, the addiction to love from another person can get complicating when we rely on this person to fill our emptiness. The healing love I speak of, is love that comes from within, not from without.

We were only together for four months and we had already moved in together. Neither of us were going to school, she was 16-years-old and I was 18 at the time. We really did not have a clue as to what we were doing, where we were headed, or what life was really about. All we knew was that we were happy and filling that void for each other. Two empty souls finally being filled with what had been missing.

Then it was time to meet my mom. For once, I got to be the good guy. My mom was ecstatic! She finally had a "normal" child. There are five kids in my family and at this time four of us were in our teenage or young adult years – and not one had ever introduced a member of the opposite sex to the family.

All the love and attention that all the kids in the family crave, is now geared towards me – the bad guy. As expected, this creates huge backlash in the family and the resentments escalate quickly.

"You two get cracking," my mom tells us one day, "I need grandchildren and you will probably be the only one who has them."

So, we oblige. We had talked about it and we wanted kids. Adrianne ran away from home and my mom supported us by furnishing us with an apartment. We invite all our friends over, it is a daily party, and life is great. I was basically being paid by my mother to get this girl pregnant.

That is how desperately my mother wanted to have more children around. This was her way to fill her own void, emptiness, and lack of love. She knew that children have always brought love, acceptance, and joy and this was her ticket to happiness.

Just like the athlete reaching for that Gatorade, someone who is spiritually empty turns to alcohol, drugs, gambling, sex, shopping, food, or people. Behavioral addictions are deceiving, but they work the same as a drug or alcohol addiction. Sex addiction or pornography addiction is easy to label the person as a "creep," or "weirdo." But, it really is not about the actions, it is about filling that emptiness and feeling that sense of control over our emotions and bringing a rush of pleasure into our lives.

All addictions start with pain and end with pain. Emotional pain is inevitable. We all go through pain in our lives. Suffering happens when we hold onto that pain. To stop the suffering, the person reaches for something external (a proverbial band-aid), but the more we grasp to things externally, the less we receive. Such as squeezing your hand to catch as much water as possible, we soon see that it all rushes out of our hands. Whereas, if we were to just cusp our hands and let the water flow, we recognize we actually preserve more water.

The first Noble Truth of Buddhism refers to all of life has inevitable, unavoidable suffering. The problem is we try to cover up the suffering, hide from it, or run from it. But it is unavoidable and this strong desire to prevent suffering only creates further damage.

Vietnamese Zen Master Thich Nhat Hanh states:

> *"We have a tendency to run away from all suffering. But the fact is that without suffering, there is no way to cultivate understanding and compassion. I don't want to send my friends and children to a place without suffering because a place without suffering is a place without understanding and compassion. Without understanding and compassion there can be no happiness."*[26]

When the escape from suffering, or addiction, involves another person then the destruction and long-term pain can be detrimental. This is due to the society's approval of relationship addiction which allows for these patterns to continue. Any relationship that begins with this intense clinging and attachment creates a sense of need.

---

[26] Thich Nhat Hanh, *Breathe, You Are Alive!* (Berkely, CA; Parralax Press, 2008)

This soon turns into jealousy, possessiveness, control, rage, and despair.

The Story of Adrianne

This describes the beginning of my relationship with Adrianne to a tee. We are clinging to each other, fully attached, and no idea about the trap we built around ourselves. We start fighting, throwing objects, verbal, emotional, and psychological abuse takes place daily.

Until she cheats on me, actually, she does this a number of times.

My heart was shattered into pieces. I felt an intense pain in my stomach like I've never felt before as if someone just shoved a knife into my abdomen and all I could do was kneel over and hope the pain would stop.

I was physically ill, physically in pain, and felt the life had been taken out of my body. I have never felt anything like this in my life. Of course, I took her back at the first opportunity that arose but it didn't come without retaliation. My innocence was gone and all hell broke loose daily in that apartment. We were just two fucked up kids with no guidance and we clung to each other for something that we could never get from each other.

Then came the big news: *Adrianne was pregnant.*

Oh, and the reaction was that only comparable to a king conquering a country or an athlete winning a gold medal for his country. Hugs, pats on the back, congratulations, and even a hand shake from my father.

Behind closed doors, our relationship has not improved – probably worsened, if anything. When we argue, Adrianne hits herself in the stomach when upset with me – Wow, I've truly met my match! She is worse than me, more depressed, more self-hatred, and more destructive than I could ever imagine.

I despise this girl, but I cannot leave her because in my mind she is the only one who will ever love me. And the feeling with her is mutual.

My jealousy spirals out-of-control to the point that I am so afraid of losing her that I do not allow her to leave the house. When she is late, I completely lose control and damage the house.

This control is just an illusion. We never have control of anyone or anything. Anytime we try to control situations, it increases the level of suffering. When we completely surrender and "let go" of everything, we realize that we never had any control in the first place.

The serenity prayer of Alcoholics Anonymous states:

> *God, grant me the serenity to accept*
> *the things I cannot change;*
> *The courage to change the things that I can;*
> *And the wisdom to know the difference.*

This is the foundation of any Twelve-Step program; the art of surrendering control. The First Step tells us that we need to first admit we have no control; the Second Step tells us that we can be restored to our true self without our mask by releasing control to a power greater than ourselves; and the Third Step is the action of letting go and surrendering. That is the heart-and-soul of any recovery program.

You cannot change other people, despite what popular movies try to teach us at a young age. The movies teach young women to find the "bad boy" and then change him, because there is a soft side underneath. But, in real life, it doesn't work that way, ever.

Here was this young girl who grew to be totally in love with me, she was committed and loving. But at this point, I had already been destroyed. I wanted to end my life and I had no skills to deal with this part of life and no self-esteem. In my mind, we had built up something incredible together, our closeness was amazing, but I was so terrified of losing her that I turned into a monster. And it all stemmed from fear; fear of losing something.

She was no angel, herself. She hit me and was just as awful to me. But, as the second line of the serenity prayer states, she *had the courage to change the things she can* – by leaving me. I am glad that she was brave enough to do so, because I was lost, ravaged, and broken.

Through all this pain, came the greatest love that I have ever felt.

On June 28, 1995, our little girl was born. Kylee Ann.

I didn't know how to love, what love was, or what it felt like until that day. All I know is that I had never felt love as strong as the moment that I held my daughter in my arms. My life had been altered once again. My veil had been lifted from my ego and I could see the one truth in this world – pure love.

> *"The ego is a veil between you and God."* -- Rumi

That love that I felt that day still resides within me today. I was experiencing the miracle of life, the meaning of our existence, and seeing the face of God, Buddha, the Great Spirit, or whatever you want to call it. When you feel it, you realize it is nameless.

Section II
THE BOOK OF PURPOSE

Chapter V:	Psychological Tsunami	95
Chapter VI:	Alien Encounters	115
Chapter VII:	Love Revolutionaries	139
Chapter VIII:	The 危機 Theory	167
Chapter IX:	Vulnerability Removes the Mask	193

CHAPTER V

Psychological Tsunami
The House That Withstood It All

Chapter 5
Psychological Tsunami: The House That Withstood It All

Pain is inevitable, but suffering is optional.

I describe it like this, if I were to hold a glass of water and to ask you how much does it weigh? I would get an array of answers including the typical "8 ounces," "12 ounces," or even the more clever answers that add in the weight of the glass holding the water.

But the truth is that the weight of the glass of water does not matter. What matters is how long I hold the glass. If I hold it for an hour straight, it is going to create physical pain and agony. I am going to lash out in anger and have a short fuse. The longer I hold it, the heavier it will get and the longer internal damage it will cause.

But all I need to do is put it down.

This is how psychological pain works, too. I always knew the world we lived in was not real and sought any sort of refuge. I started to look towards external things to escape myself such as anger, control, gambling, suicide, and then Adrianne. But all these things that were outside of myself continuously led to paths of destruction – hence, more pain. I always had the power within me to end this pain, in fact, we all do. But I was blinded and so my journey continued.

After Adrianne left, I was dead on the inside. I was a living corpse with no meaning or purpose, just going through the motions of life.

I met a guy named Jerry, one of Adrianne's ex-boyfriends, and we moved into an apartment together. Jerry liked to smoke pot, have deep conversations, enjoyed spending time with me, and gave me non-stop compliments. He was very outgoing, incredibly intelligent, and genuinely enjoyed the company of others. This is what I needed to keep me alive.

Who knows, maybe he was taking advantage of me to give him rides to the different drug houses and parties we went. But regardless, it got me out of the house and kept me breathing. Perhaps we needed each other in a way.

And I met some incredible people along in our time together. Especially at one house in particular – a dilapidated, run-down home, in a sketchy neighborhood in St. Paul.

As we opened the door, all five of my senses were hit with something they had never experienced to this point in my life. Immediately hit with the stench of smoke – cigarettes and marijuana – covers up the stink from the animal feces on the living room carpet. Bonnie, the mother, sat at the kitchen table smoking pot while all the neighborhood kids ran around drinking and smoking.

Then there were a couple other old-timers, Buddy and Martin. Buddy was a school bus driver and he was always screaming at the top of his lungs about something or other. Martin was always drinking, drunk, or passed out. He would eat bugs off the floor for cash. We couldn't help but to find humor in this at the time and gladly obliged to give this man cash to eat a few bugs; not knowing that he was doing this in order to collect enough money so he could buy some more booze.

> "I hung around with the thugs;
> And even though the sold drugs;
> They showed a young brother love."
> ▪ *Tupac Shakur*

But what always stood out was the kids in this house. They were all incredible people with huge loving hearts, caring, considerate, and love for each other.

Spirituality in Low Places

There appears to be a direct correlation between the less materialistic a group of people, the greater sense of connection and love. I have a friend who adopted a girl from Somalia and he shared with me the amazing spirit of the community, despite living in conditions far worse than we could ever imagine in this country. He told me:

> *"It is quite sad, they having nothing. But at the same time, it is quite precious, because they have everything."*

I also heard a Buddhist monk state that Americans view India as a developing country in terms of materialism and consumerism; yet, India views America as a developing country in terms of spirituality. The same is true for the class-structure in American society. They upper rings practice competition and separation, while the lower class still has that sense of community and belonging. I saw it the instant I walked into that home.

In the suburban schools, when you see kids like this they are immediately judged, criticized, labeled and condemned. We see the exterior only. Wearing the same old raggedy clothes each day, smell like smoke, covered in filth, talk too loud, and lack manners. We never get a chance to get to know them, because we see the exterior and have already made a decision about how we feel about them on the inside.

I remember one day in Junior High School in which I felt quite alone. Lunch time was the worst part of the day because I had no one to sit with. I felt judged and not accepted at every table. So, I decided to sit with the "stoners." The kids who barely made it to class, wore the same Metallica shirt every day, long hair, trouble-makers. They let me sit there, and we just ate and told jokes like any other table. They accepted me.

"What are you doing?" I was asked by one of my teachers as she put her hand on my shoulder, "Why are you sitting here? You don't have to do this."

I looked up at the group of kids who have been abused, pushed away by society, and broken on the inside. They looked at me as if to say, "go ahead, we understand."

"Do you want to sit here?" she asked me directly.

I looked at the kids at the table and said, "Yes, I want to sit here."

She turned away and walked away furious as if she had just "lost one of the good ones." But, what she didn't know, is that the rest were of the students were the ones that were lost and these were the most real people in the school - including the adults.

Beyond the smoke screen, these kids are dealing with an upbringing that no one in the suburban schools could even imagine – specifically the guidance counselors and administrators that help in the process of ostracizing them.

Perhaps this is why these kids were so specially gifted with strong hearts and souls. As the saying goes, *"A smooth sea never made a skilled mariner."* Likewise, I have never met a strong person with an easy past.

When you are given shots of alcohol as punishment when you are eight years old, handed a joint when you are 10, and physically abused on a daily basis – what chance to you have in succeeding in our modern society? Yet, it is so paradoxical that the most beautiful souls in the world were the ones that lived in this cockroach-infested home.

Of all the kids, a couple of them really stood out to me – Donnie and Jim. Donnie had a bigger heart than any of them, a truth seeker himself. The first time I met him, Donnie was probably only nine years old. He looked up to me for some reason. I came over and never smoked pot or drank, so Donnie wouldn't either.

This kid took on all sorts of abuse, but he never let it change his true self.

Donnie could see beyond this false reality that we live in, the mind and the world that we create. This tends to be incredibly confusing to children when they have this ability. They cannot comprehend or verbalize this to anyone, they just know. Donnie was their household's version of my brother, Larry. It was like an alternate universe and it was Larry being raised in poverty.

People take advantage of them, abuse them, and try to harm them but they cannot be reached. They long for escape at a much greater intensity than anybody else because they know that none of this is real. But this longing for freedom and escape, without knowing why, typically leads to severe depression and other mental disorders, addiction, and potentially suicidal ideation.

The other was Jim. He was another with an incredible heart that not many got to see. People tended to see the loud and arrogant kid, but no one saw the hurt soul that was abused daily by his father. I always felt if I was raised in his situation that I would have been exactly like him and vice versa with him being raised in my home.

Jim was their House's version of me; again, the alternate universe of seeing myself raised in poverty. He was their leader and labeled as the "bad guy." All he ever did was give and give to others. He loved more than anyone, but the problem was that he never knew this. He never knew how to love and it came out as hate.

There is No Hate, Only Misguided Love

There is no such thing as hate. Hate is just misguided love. Jim hurt so much that he would tease others, instigate fights, and go into a rage. But he did show me his true self, because I showed him love first. And through this experience, I was starting to understand this is how the path to enlightenment unfolds.

You need to first drop your mask and give love. When I first saw these kids, I knew that they were in dire need of love. My instinctual response was to forget about my own ego, pain, and struggles, and feed their souls what they were craving.

It's no different than if you were to come across a starving child. Even though you may have hunger yourself, you see the need of the child and gladly give up your meal to give them something they desperately need.

I was learning, albeit unknowingly at the time, about enlightenment. Like Jerry had been doing for me, I did for Jim, Donnie, and even Adrianne (over the phone). I started getting a reaction and started seeing things as they really were for the first time.

Jerry was a young man was not afraid to talk about anything to anybody. Everyone loved him when they first met him. He went to my parent's house and helped my siblings with their homework, my parents thought this "stoner" was some sort of saint due to his constantly giving love to everyone.

Then, I started doing the same. Jerry was like some type of guardian angel for me teaching me how to treat others. He showed me how to remove my mask. And it worked with everyone, my relationships were improving and I felt the more love I gave away that the more I received in return.

This helped me grow closer to Adrianne as we started talking more and more over the phone. I dropped my guard (or removed my mask), and things start improving again. Eventually, Adrianne decides to move back in with me.

I had never envisioned this or could have seen this coming in a million lifetimes. Kylee was about 18 months old at the time, I had seen her for visits occasionally and now she was coming back into my life for good. We were finally a family and life was good once again.

This most recent honeymoon phase lasted about four months and came to a screeching halt with Adrianne holding a butcher knife to my throat. She had been partying since she left me and she had no intention to leave that lifestyle. She wanted her freedom; whereas, I was ready for a family. She was gone all the time, always seeking attention of men.

In a final effort to keep her and show her I cared, I emptied my savings account to purchase an airline ticket for Adrianne to fly to Florida to see her mother. Upon arrival, she contacted me only to inform me that she was not coming back – she was going to stay in Florida with Kylee.

It was January in 1996. I had just turned 20 years old and this was the most crushing, devastating blow that I had ever experienced. I felt part of my life sucked out of my soul in this moment as my knees hit the earth and I had to hunch over to try to catch my breath and slow my racing heart.

And she was gone again, nothing to hold on to anymore.

There were many survival stories following the 2004 Tsunami in Thailand that killed more than 300,000 people. One that always stood out to me was that of model Petra Nemcova. As she told her story, she fought a few times while engulfed in water and garbage and eventually she just let go. She told herself *"this is it."* And suddenly she was lifted up above the water and landed in one of the few palm trees that survived the storm. She states that it felt, *"peaceful,"* once she finally just let go, accepted her fate, and went along with the flow of the storm.[27]

While I lay beneath my own psychological tsunami of my own, I also just let go and found a similar type of peace which cannot be described in words. This is what was needed for me to start to take a part my false persona that I had been attached to my entire life.

In the same article, Petra states,

> *"Tragedy gives us the opportunity to put meaning into our lives. It changes our values, gives us the opportunity to think where we want to go."*

I had these brief moments in which I felt good; the hospital, meeting Adrianne, the pregnancy, Kylee's birth. My father shook my hand and was proud of me at one point. I got to be the good guy for a fleeting glimpse. I liked to hold onto those moments.

---

[27] Bennetts, L. (2005, May). Petra's Story. *Vanity Fair*.

But these moments had all passed and I was alone again with nothing to hold onto. This left me empty inside. Empty enough to the point that I was willing to open up.

And this is when I first heard the spirit.

I just sat and listened. That is the only way the divine can enter is when we are silent and listen. For the first time in my life I was thinking about how I had treated other people and the effects that it must have had on them. I thought about all my words and actions and how everything had unfolded.

My ego was disappearing. The blame, anger, revenge, and judgments were fading. Inwardly, my path to enlightenment was unfolding. The breaking away of the destruction had begun.

Addiction as a Spiritual Disease

The classic film, "Wizard of Oz," is highly depicted with symbolism regarding the path to enlightenment. In the beginning of the film, Dorothy sings "Somewhere Over the Rainbow," as she longs to discover the greater meaning of existence. Dorothy is a truth-seeker, she knows that there is more to the black-and-white dull life on the farm in Kansas.

Dorothy is then swept away by a twister that symbolizes the spiral of errors and lessons learned in the material world. The storm brings about old fears, thoughts, and leaving behind everything she knows as she transcends into a higher level of consciousness.

But unlike the fictitious tale of Dorothy, enlightenment doesn't come in one single instance. It is a process, a long-enduring process which includes a great deal of experience and growth. Although I had opened my mind and allowed the spirit to enter, there was still a longing for truth.

Each night I lie awake with my bottle of pills, just waiting to die. I could have ended it all at any minute, but something kept me going. It was probably Jerry and all our fun adventures. He was my best buddy at the time, but I was still broken inside. All my soul-searching has been misguided and I felt a sense of anger turned against me. Everything seems to have backfired.

One night as me and Jerry were talking, I was feeling desperate and I decided to have my first drink of alcohol. I was 21-years-old and had gone my entire life without drinking or smoking pot. I was always the sober one at these fun parties.

But not tonight, tonight I was going to give it a try out of an intensified feeling of hopelessness. At this point, what did I have to lose?

I had never even considered alcohol before due to the horror stories about my Grandmother and the evils of alcohol. But after about half of a beer, all those fears subsided quickly.

It was the most beautiful thing I have ever experienced. It hit me in an instance and suddenly everything made sense.

"Holy Shit!" I shouted, "This is why everyone does this!"

I was truly in heaven. All the pain, fear, and shyness had just vanished from my body. The only thing I could feel was love, my true self, the roadblocks had just been removed. I was fully alive.

But it was also the most terrible thing. As this jumpstarted a three-year binge of alcohol, cocaine, and methamphetamine. This eventually led me down a path of criminal activities to feed my newfound addiction – such as theft and selling narcotics. But this was the path that had to be taken in order to find my way.

First, the insurmountable pain was needed for me to become open to anything. Then the booze gave me a taste of enlightenment, but it would take many more years of destruction before I realized there are no to shortcuts to eternal bliss.

My brother Larry now works as a drug and alcohol counselor and does a couple assessments each day. One of the questions in the assessment is "what are the reasons for using?" It gives a list of responses and he told me that, "100-percent of the time people respond, 'because I like the feeling.'"

Even people who lie their way through the assessment, cannot deny that they "like the feeling" they get from being intoxicated or high.

One day he did an experiment with his group asking everyone to describe this feeling in which they so strongly desire. The group came up with things such as:

- Everything just makes sense – I "get it."
- I just love everyone and everything
- I feel alive; my true self
- I don't worry about any of the small stuff
- I love being around people and feel more connected
- I feel free

They listed all these things on the board and then called in the clinical supervisor to read the board and try to guess what their discussion was about. Without blinking an eye, the supervisor quickly says, "spirituality."

No. They were talking about being high or drunk. So here you have a clinical supervisor of a mental health and addiction treatment center mistaking getting high for spirituality? If 100-percent of the people that are asked why they take drugs or alcohol is because they like the "feeling," and that feeling is easily mistaken for a spiritual connection, it would be safe to assume that 100-percent of these people are actually seeking the feeling (or spiritual connection).

If you were walking through the desert and came to an oasis, you would dive head first into the water to quench your thirst. Likewise, if you have never experienced love and connection and someone offers you a substance, it only makes sense that one would indulge in order to quench their spiritual starvation.

Darkest Before the Dawn

The story above explains the spiritual gifts of recovery, but there is a very dark period that takes place before we reach recovery. Addiction has a very dark side that destroys everything around us. It is quite a paradox; I wish everybody in the world could embrace recovery to reap the spiritual blessings associated, but I would not wish addiction on my worst enemies because of everything it strips away from us.

Unfortunately, this is what was necessary for me. I had to go through addiction in order for my path to enlightenment to unfold, it was the only way for me to rip apart everything in order to discover my true self. There are no stories of addiction that do not include dark nights of the soul and mine is no different.

Addiction starts with pain and ends with pain. As my tolerance grew, I went on to harder drugs like cocaine and meth. We were selling dope, using daily, and slowly wasting away. This was my new escape and I never had to deal with anything. I just came home, got drunk and stoned and forgot about my problems.

Dead broke, brain dead, and burnt out, we were lucky we didn't die. We both got fired from our jobs, so we had to steal and pawn stuff up to get by. Eventually we stooped so low that we stole 400 dollars from Bonnie and blamed someone else. We had sunk that low, that in order to feed our addiction we were robbing from people on welfare, living in a bug-infested home.

These same people that I had shared true love with, I had just stolen from them. Yes, the same people that I told you that were the most genuinely kind people I ever met – I stole from them.

I couldn't do it anymore. But, I also couldn't communicate that I couldn't do it anymore. So I had to just sneak out and run away from my best friend. I had rare moment of clarity amidst an intense addiction, I felt stuck and the only thing I knew to do was run. I gathered some money and got an apartment with a grade-school friend of mine, Bob.

I soon found out that the change in environment didn't change much. The drugs and alcohol continued at the new place. When you try running from yourself you try to change the environment and it works temporarily, but never anything lasting. Sort of the same way that drugs work, they give temporary pleasure – but only true joy comes from within.

There is no escaping yourself. No matter where you go, you are always with yourself. And it is only until we realize this, are able to surrender it all and awaken from the nightmares we create. I was far from any moment of awakening at this point, still running and seeking.

But along our journey, like in the Wizard of Oz, we are presented with signs and symbols along the way. Another one for me was when I was hired at a group home, working with kids. I absolutely loved it. It was one of those moments that just made sense to me. However, I was too enamored in my addiction and couldn't keep pace and lost a job I truly loved.

As my psychological pain and addiction deepens, I find an overnight job at a home for people with mental illness. This seemed like a perfect place for me. I have always been fascinated with the mind and what society deems "mental illness." Their mind falls and we call them "sick," but really they are the ones who are finally free.

My first night there, a guy is up all night just talking to himself. I am so intrigued by it all and love this job. The next night, a 65-year-old transvestite comes up to me at 3:00 a.m. to tell me, "Sir, I just masturbated for the first time in eight years. And it felt absolutely wonderful!"

I was in love with this job and infatuated with these people and how their minds worked. I actually noticed myself drinking less while I was here because I was starting to find myself having some sort of sense of meaning and purpose. I didn't need that escape as often anymore.

Then I get hit with another bombshell from Adrianne: She calls me to tell me she is seeing someone in Florida and wants him to adopt Kylee. She asks me to sign off on this. My psychological pain is excruciating.

I refuse to sign away my daughter's rights and still try to call and talk to her whenever possible and make a few trips to Florida myself. I never know where they are living, but whenever I find out, I make sure to send some cash for Kylee.

Living on such low wages, along with my addiction, I stop drinking for a couple of weeks to save up money so I can fly to Florida to see Kylee. Adrianne has no interest in me and Kylee doesn't even know who I am – my own daughter doesn't recognize me. I wouldn't wish that pain on anyone, there is no physical pain in the world that can come close to the feeling I felt that day. I would see her maybe two times a year and go through this every single time.

Until one day I get a phone call from Kylee herself.

She says, "Hi, my daddy buys me shoes and plays with me."

Yep, Adrianne put her on the phone only to tell me that Kylee calls someone else her father. She knew this was my weak spot and she went after it like a wild animal going after their wounded prey. I had just sent $500 to her and they took the money and spent it as if I never existed.

Then Shawn gets on the phone telling my family that he is Kylee's father.

I was literally paralyzed hearing this. Even to this day, writing this paragraph makes my body go limp and the sensation of razor blades cutting away at every cell of my body emerges just thinking about that phone conversation.

This was the single most devastating blow I have ever been dealt in my entire life. There is no feeling associated with it, I was just broken in every way, shape, and form imaginable. I hurt beyond anything words could ever describe. First, I lost a child which is the gift of true love. This was a gift and a taste of truth and reality. Then it was taken from me.

It was like losing a child to death, but possibly worse, because she was alive. I was just not alive to her. She did not know of my existence and the love that I had for her. I felt like Sisyphus in Greek Mythology being sentenced to forever pushing a rock up a hill and once it gets to the top it falls down the other side and then has to start all over again for eternity.

"My daddy is so great," echoes the voice of my four-year old daughter. But she wasn't referring to me. Another knife wound to my heart.

An innocent four-year-old child, serving as the messenger of her mother's pain, sent me this death blow. Again, there is no hate only misguided love. Her mother, Adrianne, has generations of hand-me-down pain that she was carrying and she only knew how to hurt me and she knew exactly how to do it. I would have rather had her drown me, set me ablaze, or tie me to a train track rather than this slow and painful, horrendous demise she was putting me through.

> *"The wound is where the light enters"*
> - *Rumi*

The Gift of Surrender

My mind just went completely blank and still. But, when your mind goes still like this, it is when you allow answers to enter. This is the main premise of meditation, you intentionally block thoughts and allow the divine to enter. This is when God talks to you, this is when you become God. It is in these dark moments of anguish and despair, you allow the light to enter.

We all must go through a dark night of the soul in order for the light to pass through, in order for enlightenment to occur. I seem to have had more than a few dark nights, weeks, months, and years. But this one has the single most significance.

Many times, people become enlightened through a great leap of faith. However, mine was not courageous at all. I was about to die. I had nothing to live for, and although I knew nothing about death, I did know that it would put an end to the pain. I had no other options and was forced into this moment of spiritual awakening. I am not brave, I continued to avoid it despite the numerous signs.

I had lost my job again, out of money, and then broke my leg during a pickup football game which meant I couldn't even look for new work. I had to have surgery and move back into my parent's house. This meant no more drugs or alcohol, too. All I could do was just sit by myself and deal with my physical and emotional pain, day after painful day.

It was just me and my thoughts for about four months. I was meditating, although I didn't realize it at the time. Praying is when you talk to God and meditation is when you listen. I said that I had been a jerk, a bad person, loser, and destroyed lives. I have lost Kylee and Adrianne forever. Now, I need to just open the wound, listen, and turn my life over and around.

I made a vow to dedicate my life to giving back to people. I was open to listening to what others had to say. The next day, my mom suggested that I try LPN school. It is only a one-year program. I agreed, why not? It is just one year.

I went to orientation, while still on my crutches. I was trying to be a new person. After all, I had nowhere to go, nowhere to run anymore. I had to just let go of my past. I could not fix it, but I am going to try to be a better person. I am going to try to be like Jerry and compliment people, love people the way my mother does, and just be good to everyone.

It was like a rebirth in a sort of way. But like the first birth, it is just a beginning. There are still many stages, obstacles, trials and tribulations, and periods of growth we all must go through.

Like Nemcova in the Tsunami found herself clinging on to a rooftop to try to desperately save her life, it wasn't until she decided to let go and go with the flow of the storm that she felt at peace. Then she miraculously found herself in one of the few surviving trees. She awoke to a shattered pelvis, internal bleeding, and hematoma on her kidney, and couldn't breathe without a tube. She had to learn to live again, like a newborn baby – learn how to turn her side, how to stand up, how to walk, etc.

She states,

> *"It's going to be a completely like a new life. I used to live a lot in the future, in planning, but now at the moment I live day by day."*

Nemcova was also hit with disaster and forced to become reborn. She has turned her life over to philanthropy opening the Happy Hearths Charity. She has used her fortunes from modeling to build more than 100 schools in areas affected by disasters.

Similarly, I surrendered to my situation and let go of my past, which allowed me to be open to being awakened. Healing does not mean that the pain never happened; it just means we are consciously choosing to no longer let it control our lives.

CHAPTER VI

Alien Encounters
Everyone is a Teacher

Chapter 6
Alien Encounters: Everyone is a Teacher

Today is a new day.

Back in school for the umpteenth time, naturally I was filled with fear of the unknown, fear of failure, and fear of falling into old habits again – which meant quitting. I have never finished anything my entire life. I have had some great moments, made progress, only to hit the self-destruct button.

These self-destructing tendencies remind me of a story I heard about Kurt Cobain, the late front man for the 90's grunge band Nirvana. He stated that his wish was to be in a band that was right on the verge of making it big. Each week of his life he wanted to be in a new band right about to make it big and then as soon as they made it big, he would start over in a new band that was on the verge.[28]

I've always felt the same way – that life is about the journey not the destination. And once I feel that destination is near, I panic and hit the self-destruct button.

This stems from the belief that it is the destination we seek that will provide the answers. But there are two problems with this philosophy; 1) you miss out on the journey of life and spend your life living in the future and 2) you never reach any destination, you will always be searching for something extra.

This is not uncommon in Western society, which stems from the perception of time. In the West, the belief is that time is linear – it

---

[28] *Kurt Cobain: About A Son* [Motion picture on DVD]. (2006). USA: Balcony Releasing.

has a beginning and an end. With this belief, we are always in a hurry, in a race, and looking for the next thing to fill our soul before the clock expires. This leads to a society filled with anxiety (spending all our time thinking about the future) and depression (spending all our time regretting the past). Which makes sense, because the belief is that there is only a set number of heart beats to accomplish as many things as possible.

In ancient cultures and traditions, time was always viewed as cyclical – there is no beginning or ending. Life was viewed as an endless cycle of birth and death, like a wheel spinning endlessly. In this view of time, it allows us to understand our true eternal nature, live in the present moment, and creates an inner feeling of bliss. This is still the practice in Eastern philosophies and religions as well as Native American cultures.

Starting with the ancient Judaic tribes, they began to view time as linear – meaning it has a beginning and an end – this belief changed Western cultures. This perception of time was picked up by Christianity, spreading it throughout Europe and into the Americas.[29]

Which is why, along with the incredibly anxious and depressed population, many people in the West are never satisfied. Also, this leads truth-seekers to panic and hit their own self-destruct buttons anytime they near the peak of a journey. They understand that life is more about the journey and they fear if they reach their destination that life will lose some sense of excitement and purpose – and they are right.

---

[29] Cahill, T. (1998). *The gifts of the Jews: How a tribe of desert nomads changed the way everyone thinks and feels.* New York: Nan A. Talese.

Nicole – The Next Great Teacher

My head was filled with thoughts of self-doubt and fear to the point that I felt I was crawling out of my own skin until I was suddenly hit with a sense of calm as Nicole walked into the classroom.

She was clearly not of the human realm – another alien, like myself - and I knew it instantly. In the opening section of this book, I share a quote by Kurt Cobain in which he states that he sometimes feels like an alien from another planet and is just experiencing Earth. At times, he feels "home sick" and once in a while encounters other aliens. I opened up with this quote because it struck me quite profoundly, as I had always felt the exact same way.

I refer to these "aliens" as truth-seekers throughout the book. Alien is defined as 1) a resident born or belonging to another country who has not acquired citizenship by naturalization; 2) a foreigner; **3) a person who has been estranged or excluded**; and 4) a creature from outer space.

The other kids in the treatment center, Adrianne, Jerry, Jim, Donnie, and everybody at that house were all aliens. Which is why it always felt so good to be around people of the same understanding, the connection was natural.

Nicole and I connected instantly. In one quick moment, our eyes and were hooked. Now I had a reason to continue to go to school – albeit an external motivation, it did get me through the first semester.

Not only did I get through the first semester, but I passed all my classes on my own. It seemed like some sort of fluke. I completed something, although only one semester, I stuck with something all the way through until the end.

There was some unexplainable newfound momentous energy inside myself. Everyone in class had aspirations and admirable goals. We all wanted to learn, change the world, and had some magical connection with each other.

Looking back, this is the non-drug induced spiritual connection that my brother was talking about in his groups. There was no drug involved, but the atmosphere inside that classroom made us want to come back. We sensed each other's positive energy and drove us to better ourselves.

And while the entire class was engulfed in this euphoric energy, it was still Nicole that grabbed my attention.

She had a troubled past and a deeper understanding of the universe. She was raped at age 14, never met her father and her mother deserted her. She spent time as an exotic dancer, had a son of her own, and just saw the world through a different lens.

She was my best friend for this time. Here we go again. Like Pema Chodron says,

> *"Nothing ever goes away until it teaches us what we need to know."*

We start spending a lot of time together during, between, and outside of class. The two of us start pouring down the booze, allowing us to drown our emotional pain. But the closer we get, the more Nicole would push away. Perhaps, she too, feared the destination as an end to the journey.

Closeness and intimacy are basic human needs, yet they are warning signs for Nicole. It is a sign to get out of the relationship to avoid further abandonment, hurt, and pain. To the logical mind, this does not make any sense – to end a relationship because of fear of being hurt. But the healing soul, subconsciously seeks out people that will end up reenacting the trauma in hopes of healing the pain.

> *"Your subconscious will continually try and strive to get you to notice and pay attention to it and to integrate it."* – Teal Swan

While this is all done subconsciously, we do not realize that our soul is trying to heal. Instead, we get triggered by emotional cues which bring traumatic memories to our consciousness, leading to irrational behavior and decision-making.[30]

This is why we see so many people self-destruct or develop patterns of re-victimization. In Nicole's case, she never had a caregiver. The ones who were supposed to be there for her abandoned her and when intimacy comes up she chooses to run away before getting hurt again.

While I cannot speak for Nicole's entire journey, only from my perspective. However, she was also filling a void in my life. I was also re-victimizing myself as my subconscious had brought me to her in hopes of healing my past hurts. We had subconsciously been seeking out each other and once we met – we already knew it.

We do not meet people by accident. They are meant to cross our paths for a very specific reason. I did not understand this at the time. But I did see that she was filling some of my emptiness and when she abandoned me, I didn't fall apart this time. I was starting to be able to feel an inner calm and confidence about myself. Perhaps it was because I knew I would still see her in class and could get her back.

---

[30] Wheatley-Crosbie, J. (2006). HEALING TRAUMATIC REENACTMENT:. *The USA Body Psychotherapy Journal, 5*(2), 11-28.

More chasing, attaching, and clinging to the external world. Nicole soon became the new drug and I was addicted. In order to be physically addicted to a substance, it only requires two things: increase of tolerance and withdrawal.

I would argue that you can be addicted to a person. There is no question that our tolerance levels change. As we grow more attached to someone, we may be more tolerant of certain behaviors – such as abuse, infidelities, or abandonment – because of our need to be with that person.

Withdrawal from a substance is when your body develops physical symptoms due to lack of the drug. Your body becomes so accustomed to having the drug, that it is the lack of the substance that makes the body sick. In relationships, the withdrawal works the same way. When we create such a dependency on another human, the lack of that person can create physical problems such as insomnia, stomach ailments, depression, anger, or grief.

My tolerance was growing for Nicole as she continued to have suspect behavior I continued to blow it all off. Just like a chemically-addicted person justifies, hides, denies their drug use, I was doing the same for my drug of choice. As my desperate attempts to chase after this new high intensified, I continued to push her further away. Which is another one of life's paradoxes, the more you push for anything you typically will get the opposite effect.

A Crack in the Mask

But, I started learning this time. I was able to hold back from temptations from time-to-time, able to apply some self-love, and started to understand my true nature. My outer shell was cracking and my true self was starting to shine through.

I must have passed some sort of spiritual test because as this was going on, I received some life-changing news from Florida:

Adrianne and Kylee are moving back from Florida.

It turned out that Adrianne's troubles did not end once she moved away. Shawn had been beating, assaulting, and raping her. He had also been constantly threatening Kylee to the point that they had to leave. Adrianne's battle was similar to mine. She always tried to outrun her problems and tried to fill her emptiness with different things outside herself. But these internal demons follow us, stick with us, grow, and become stronger until we can face them. The relationships, drugs, gambling, shopping, or eating can all temporarily escape that problem but it never truly goes away until we go to battle within.

I used to have a beat-up car that would make loud clicking sounds whenever I made left turns. While I didn't have the money to take it into the shop, I tried to not think about it. Clearly, I knew something was wrong and others would tell me something was wrong. I started to combat this by limiting left turns or turning up the radio so the clicking was not apparent.

While this allowed me to distract myself from the clicking noise, it was still there. And each day that went by, it was growing worse and worse until one day my tire flew off on the interstate and my car ended up in a ditch. Thankfully nobody was hurt, but the overall costs of repair and towing far succeeded if I were to have taken the car into the shop when I first noticed the clicking.

Emotional pain works the same way. We can cover it up, run away, and ignore it. But it is still there, building up, and eventually it will cause a wreck if it is not handled.

So, here I am once again in total shock and disbelief with the Adrianne saga. This stuff actually works. All I had been doing was giving to others, being nice, spreading love and good things start to come around. It seems too simple.

> *The ego is happy when we receive; but*
> *the soul is happy when we give.*

Every time I give up, or surrender, something incredible happens to me. This was less than a year after her last phone call nearly led me to ending my life. The greatest gift I had ever received was my little girl and she was taken away from me.

Then a break in the leg, forced me to sit in my own thoughts and open my mind, put me on the right track and I finally got the positive break from life that I never thought I would receive.

In this moment, I realized a simple truth in life: the more you give, the more you receive. No matter how much you feel you can do with your talents, gifts, and skills; it is dismal in comparison to what can be done when you give them away with total surrender.

Domestication of Children

I got my baby girl back, but she was no longer a baby. She was a person, about four and a half years old.

She had just lost the only Dad she ever knew and is now allowed to call me "father." She is confused, but also very adaptable. This is the beauty of children, they see the world as it is before they are corrupted.

The cycle of life is a strange phenomenon. We come into the world with a clean slate, no shame, hate, or embarrassment. Just love. Love for everyone and free-flowing love. We are in complete awe of the world, desire to be awake all the time, go outside and enjoy nature, explore new things, and soak in the beauty of life. Then we are filled with fears about the world that are passed down from generation-to-generation. We start to attach and cling to anything to protect us from these unreasonable fears and create a mask to protect us from the world. Everyone around us grows these masks and we do everything in our power to never let others see beyond the mask. Then as we start to see the world as it really is, we start to try to pull off these masks and it hurts. In fact, it can be so painful that we might just leave them on. And by the time we reach old age, we start trying to fill our bucket lists, give death-bed confessions, and share regrets o the lives we wish we lived.

The five most common death bed regrets are:

- I wish I'd had the courage to live a life true to myself, not the life others expected of me
- I wish I didn't work so hard
- I wish I'd had the courage to express my feelings
- I wish I had stayed in touch with my friends
- I wish I had let myself been happier

If these are the five most regrets, what if we started teaching people to practice these things now so we can cross these off our lists in our final days.

But we already had it in us as toddlers and we were trained like domesticated animals to act and behave a certain way. Then we buy into this concept of linear time and race against a fictional clock to accumulate as many things from the external world as possible. Then on our deathbeds, our one request or desire is to be with the people we love – not the possessions, awards, money, or power – but the people that have showed us love.

Now, whenever I feel I am losing touch with my true self, I spend a few minute talking to my four-year-old to remind me what life is really about.

And this is what Kylee was teaching me at the time. I see her wanting to spend all day outdoors, making friends with all the neighborhood kids, and running around and enjoying every minute of life. It is the most pure and innocent moment of our lives and this is what we all strive for when we walk the path of enlightenment – to return to ourselves as children.

And Adrianne kept chasing. She slowly disappears from the picture once again. She will drop Kylee off a couple of times to go out partying. Eventually, she leaves Kylee with me for the entire summer. Three months with my daughter, as complete strangers.

I was overwhelmed with emotions which ranged from sadness to euphoria. But, I knew that my life was on that upward swing again. Then, like tidal waves, the good kept pouring into my life. It was one tiny miracle right after the other.

When you change the way you look at things, the things you look at begin to change. Looking at the world with love, gratitude, and kindness – all those things started to come back to me. In the past, I had viewed the world as an untrusting, frightening world and subsequently those things found me, too.

Nicole is back in my life and lets me know about this job at an inner city Hospital in the psych ward. This has been my dream job since the day that I was saved by Marty, Ron, Sam, and Donald at Divine Redeemer.

Halfway into the interview, they give me the job because they sense my excitement and passion.

I had it all. My best friend Nicole, my little girl Kylee, my dream job in a psych ward! Just a year ago I had given up on life and now I had everything I wanted. It was a combination of these angels, or messengers, signposts, and a little pain that had made this possible.

Jerry was an outcast/stoner that most people disregard and consider at the lower end of society. Yet, he gives love to everyone and has no enemies. Because of this, he gave me a chance when no one else wanted to be within a 10-mile radius of me. Then he taught me how to treat people and I learned by just observing.

Nicole is another one that most people will look at with a scowl. They see her and label her as a slut, stripper, prostitute, but they don't realize her full story. She motivated me to go to class and believe in myself at a time of hopelessness. And although she provided only external motivation, which is what I needed before I could start to motivate myself from within.

Life seems to continue to play this optical illusion on all of us. These are not two exceptions, but rather the rule in life. We seem to have an inverted view of what it means to be successful in western society.

We place so much value on celebrity status and material possessions while mocking and ridiculing those less fortunate.

One of my favorite stories is of Pearl Jam's Eddie Vedder talking about how he would wear an old corduroy jacket that he got for $12 along with a rugged Army t-shirt. As his band gained notoriety and fame, he suddenly started seeing the same jacket that intentionally mimicked the grungy look (remember it was only $12) that were being sold in stores for $650.[31]

> *"We have multiplied our possessions, but reduced our values. We talk too much, love too seldom, and hate too often. We've learned how to make a living, but not a life. We've added years to life, not life to years."* -George Carlin

This transformation was all the evidence that I needed to live life this way. The more love you give, the more you receive. It starts by detaching to external pleasures, surrendering to what is in front of us, and letting the river flow.

We can't change the wind, but we can adjust the sails.

Nicole left me again, another change in the wind. To say it didn't brutally crush me each time would be an outright lie. I was always devastated, but each time it got a little bit easier to handle. It is a lot like tolerance, but in this case it has to do with growing.

Growth is necessary for life. All living things are either growing or dying. And growth only occurs when we step outside our comfort zone and take on the challenges that the world presents to us. In the past, when Nicole would leave me and I was devastated, I would act out in anger, depression, shut down, or turn to alcohol. This was my way of handling stress, but it was like turning up the radio to the clicking vehicle.

It wasn't until I started to accept the situation as it was. This was going to keep happening and nothing would change until I could detach and surrender. This cycle continued all throughout school. As we neared the end of our program, she left me and never returned.

---

[31] Modell, Josh. "Eddie Vedder of Pearl Jam". *The A.V. Club*. November 6, 2002.

Likely, I handled it better because I had Kylee with me and I was about to actually finish school. I had healthy and positive things in my life that I no longer had the need to attach to Nicole and had no desire to self-destruct this time. That is the power of love, it broke my habits for the time being.

One semester away from graduation and she was gone forever. No reason, no explanation, just gone. Once she knew I was about to complete, she vanished without a trace. Perhaps this was her pressing her own self-destruct button. But she is what kept me going during my times of darkness.

At the same time, Adrianne was also gone to the point that Kylee said to me, "I think my mom is in heaven."

This little four-year-old girl thought that her mother had died and she believed that my sisters were her mother – in a way, I guess they were as they dedicated their free time to helping her out and giving her unconditional love.

While all this good is coming into my life, there was still a major lesson to be learned: the strength and persistence of the human ego.

The Green Team

I understood this newfound concept that when I surrender and allow myself to be vulnerable that good things flow into my life. But the problem is that I start to believe that it is me that is worthy of the credit – this is the role of the ego.

There is ongoing spiritual warfare between the ego and spirit; and the ego will pull out any trick in the book to win the battle. In this classic ego trap, as good things start to happen, we give ourselves the credit for it. Even though the ego was dormant, it gets the credit for success. It doesn't take long for it to regain control of our life.

While working in the psych ward at the inner city hospital, I quickly discover that things are quite different from the perspective of staff, as opposed to my memories of being a patient. The nurses run the unit and do as they see fit. They run it like a prison. They tell the clients what they can do, when they can do it, and if you do not follow orders you will find yourself restrained and secluded. The patients are treated like animals.

The nurses are addicted to this control they have over the lives of their fellow humans; ironically the same humans in which they are getting compensated to provide care!

There is a "Panic Button" on the unit and when it rings, we all run to that floor, tackle the person and lock them in restraints. My first night, this goes off four times and we rush through the place like a swat team tackling people. We are known as the "Green Team," which consists of male nursing assistants but more like night club bouncers. In actuality, a couple of them were bouncers and aspired to be prison guards.

Remember this is a psychiatric ward and the clients are hospitalized because of severe depression or having hallucinations. They are locked up under the direction of power-hungry nurses and the savages of the green team.

When the clients are not acting "sick" enough, the staff antagonizes to the point that they get so upset that the restraints can be justified. The clients are mocked, tormented, and embarrassed. They are thrown down to the ground, faces shoved in the floor and given injections.

> *Where the hell am I? Who are the*
> *mentally disturbed ones here?*

If a client dares to stand up to the staff and challenge them they get reprimanded, refused supper, and eventually restrained. It was non-stop. Any excuse to hit that panic button and the green team rushed in an abused their power.

The charge nurse, Ronelle, was the absolute worst. She led the gossip circle, bad-mouthed the clients, and genuinely despised them as people. If anyone were to call her out…BUZZZ!...In comes the green team!

It was painfully frustrating to watch her treat people in this manner and then have the audacity to complain about how guilty she felt for having so much money. She told me that she had to do this job to ease her guilt and to do "good." But, what she did not realize was that these clients are in emotional crisis and this is not the profession to enter if you are seeking affirmations.

Instead, she was spreading her pain to the clients. I do believe she thought she could help, but found herself being challenged, insulted, and never received thanks. In psychiatry and chemical dependency units, these people are terribly wounded. They are walking around with proverbial knives if their hearts.

They are the lepers of modern times. Nobody wants to touch them or come near them and is just hoping they could disappear. But we are slowly becoming more and more aware that addiction and mental health are so prevalent that there are very few people that have not been impacted in one way or another.

Mental illness has its roots back to prehistoric societies, in which it typically was theorized over some type of spiritual condition.

Ancient tribes would drill holes through people's skulls in hopes of allowing the demons to escape the mind. Homer believed that God had taken the person's mind away and Aeschylus thought the person to be demonized and exorcism was the only cure. While Socrates believed that mental illness was "heaven sent" and not shameful in the least. He considered it a blessing. And Hippocrates, the father of medicine, naturally believed that mental illness could be cured with the right medicine.[32]

After the fall of the Roman Empire and the rise of Christianity, the church promoted mental illness as a divine punishment. In the 1700s, they were not viewed as sick but as engaging in shameful practices with the devil. This led to being burnt at the stake and the notorious witch hunts, followed by the diabolical treatment provided in asylums for the past 200 years.

Now, they are medicated by multi-billion-dollar pharmaceutical companies that are profiting off of keeping clients locked up for longer and on medications against their will. The medications have such intense withdrawals that it leads people who have never had suicide ideation in their lives to committing suicide. They market these withdrawal symptoms as "side effects," and claim that the people commit suicide because they "stopped taking their medications" and were mentally unstable. In reality, the medication creates such a dependency that the withdrawals are so torturous and Debilitation that it drives people into the category of mentally unstable – leading to more justification for medication.

---

[32] Button, N. (2012, June 2). A History of Madness: Perceptions of mental illness have changed dramatically over time. *Psychology Today*.

Following Orders

So, we have people locked up against their will, forced to take medications that debilitate them, and if they speak their mind they are restraint. Of course they are not going to trust you, they are like wounded animals – but that is how we have been treating them. So who are the sick ones here?

This was a wake-up call to me. I thought these psych wards were all about saving people, but what I walked into was more like a prison camp. There was no treatment taking place, no concern for health, and certainly not an ounce of care. Yet, it was called a healthcare treatment facility.

Then eventually, I became one of them. This is how I was trained on the green team and I started to believe that it was normal. I thought to myself, "This is psychiatry. This is what we do."

It is like the Milgram Experiment in 1963, in which Stanley Milgram hired volunteers to see how far people would go in following orders when it involves harming another person. He paired people up as "teachers" and "learners" and put them in separate rooms. Each time the learner answered a question incorrectly, the teacher was instructed give them an electric shock. It began at 15V and went up to 450V, the teacher was to increase the voltage by 15V each time they answered incorrectly.

The results showed that 65-percent of the teachers went all the way to the 450V of shocking their fellow human despite seeing the person in excruciating physical agony. And 100-percent of the volunteers when up to at least 300V, showing that people are likely to follow orders given by authority even up to the extent of killing another human being.[33]

Deep down, I knew what we were doing was wrong but I continued to go about it and followed how they did things. They had influence and power and I went along with what I was told.

One incident in particular sticks in my mind. We had a client that told me his wife called the police and reported that he was suicidal only so they would take him away and he was then placed on a 72-hour hold. I thought to myself, "OK, here is another crazy one making up a story."

I did not even realize what I was thinking anymore. This is where I learned about all of the commitments, holds, involuntary status, and legal proceedings. He was on the phone and visibly infuriated.

"I am not suicidal. I do not need to be here," he shouted, "She just wanted me out of the house."

Time to call the green team! I had already become one of them. I started working out with them, taking anabolic steroids to increase muscle growth, and thought I was one of the tough guys and keeping people in order.

After that great awakening that I had been through and I fell into this pattern? I gave myself all the credit for the changes in my life, I thought it was all because of me.

"Get off the phone!" I yelled to this innocent man. I was trying to be tough and intimidating as this was the mantra of the unit.

---

[33] Milgram, S. (1974). *Obedience to authority: An experimental view.* Harpercollins.

He turned around and smashed me in the head with the phone before the green unit took him down. As it turns out, he was correct. He was discharged the next day as they discovered that his wife is the one who put him in on the hold. He has never had any suicidal ideation and we roughed him out for no reason. All it would have taken is for one person to listen to this man and everything would have been prevented.

Then it all hit me harder than I was hit the night before with the phone against my head. We are creating these seclusions out of our own sickness and perversion. We are supposed to be preventing these by listening and taking time with the clients.

Jim Ronson describes this phenomenon as he details his journey of understanding the diagnostic tool called the, "Psychopath Test." He then attempts to diagnose people with these criteria and finds himself quickly seeking symptoms that aren't there to justify his preconceived judgment.[34] His isolated experiment portrays exactly how this mental health industry works with the expanding DSM which gives such broad criteria and questioning that you could literally diagnose anybody with anything!

Unfortunately it took a few whacks to my head for me to see what I had become. I became one of the monsters that I despise. We should be taking time to listen to clients and treating them like humans. When we make assumptions, it affects how we provide treatment and care.

To take it a step further, preconceived judgments affect how we treat all our fellow humans. I think back to Nicole and Jerry. What would have happened if I ruled them out based on how I felt about their appearance or past?

---

[34] Ronson, J. (2011). *The psychopath test: A journey through the madness industry.* New York: Riverhead Books.

Redeeming the Divine

Had I forgot what it was like to be on the other end? Did I forget what it was like when the staff at Divine Redeemer just let me be alone until I was ready? And it worked! They waited for me to be ready, then I gained trust, and I was able to open up and they helped me find my way.

Must be why it is called Divine Redeemer. They were able to redeem the divine that was already within me. Yet, here I was turning into a barbarian and just following orders like one of Hitler's Gestapo guards.

At the inner city hospital it was an "Us vs. Them" mentality and it occurred on a nightly basis. That is not a healing relationship, it is a brutal dictatorship. How could another human ever have the answer to another's problems? It is not possible. Instead, we have to find a way to help guide the person to discover it for themselves.

We acted as if they were criminals and they deserved this punishment. They didn't choose these lives; nobody chooses to be severely depressed, schizophrenic, or bipolar. Monsters are not born, they are created by other monsters. Imagine if we treated people with heart disease or diabetes in this manner?

If every time they ate something that might hurt their health, we tackled them and locked them up?

Like people, every situation happens for a reason to teach us something we need to know. This inner city hospital showed me the dark side of psychiatry, and of humanity. Those in power create rules/laws to stay in power. It is not really about helping people and it never was.

This was an awfully painful realization. However, I knew that I needed to continue to work in this field and find a way to create change. It was like being a kid and being told about the way our ancestors treated the Native Americans or African-Americans. It is painful and confusing to think that this was accepted, but also propels us to be the change we wish to see in the world.

During my last semester of school, I resigned from my position on the green team. Nicole was forever gone and I have no idea where she is today. But I do know that if it wasn't for her walking into that classroom that I would have never made it through.

Most people will judge her, look down on her, and disgrace her and I am sure she is somewhere within the system today. But she changed my world by being there for me, giving me motivation and confidence, and of course introducing me to the dark world at this inner city hospital.

We all have this power and we all do this for each other but we never are there to see the results. Oftentimes, it gets discouraging and depressing to never see the difference we make in the world and the people's lives that are forever changed because of our words or actions.

There are no small moments in life. Every interaction is an opportunity to change the course of the universe.

In 2009, professional wrestling legend Hulk Hogan had hit rock bottom and was on the verge of taking his own life before his friend Laila Ali (daughter of Muhammad Ali) called him just to see how he was doing. She had no agenda, just noticed he was feeling down and wanted to see if he was alright. It turns out, he wasn't alright, and her phone call woke Hogan up and showed him that he was still loved.[35]

We all need that phone call once in a while to remind us that we are still loved. Sometimes it is a random call from an old friend, sometimes it a stranger at school, and sometimes it is staff in a psychiatry ward stopping by to say hello. Just like Tim did for me all those years ago.

---

[35] Celizic, M. (2009, October 27). *TODAY.* Hulk Hogan: Laila Ali saved me from suicide

CHAPTER VII

Love Revolutionaries
Modern-Day Socrates

Chapter 7
Love Revolutionaries: Modern-Day Socrates

Shamanism is an ancient spiritual and healing practice that evolved in tribal and gathering communities thousands of years ago. The practice involves a shaman, or spirit-worker, reaching an altered state of consciousness in order to interact with the spiritual realm and bring those healing energies into our material world.

Cave paintings in France and Spain that date back nearly 40,000 years have paintings of these Shamans in trance-like phases which indicate the earliest recorded history of humans intentionally altering their level of consciousness and seeking the spiritual realm. The shamans were viewed as healers, highly creative, intelligent, and right-brain focused.

Today, they would be easily diagnosed with mental illnesses. They experienced visual and auditory hallucinations during these trances, passivity and social withdrawal altered with periods of high agitation or mania, highly obnoxious and antisocial behavior, unusual sleep patterns, and sexual promiscuity were all common among ancient shamans.[36]

David Whitley reports in his book *Cave paintings and the human spirit,* that these paintings done by the Shamans were the first works of artistic genius. He later revels that artistically creative people have always leaned toward the "crazier" side of things giving examples of Vincent Van Gogh cutting off his ear along with the suicide of Ernest Hemmingway.

---

[36] Whitley, D. (2009). *Cave paintings and the human spirit: The origin of creativity and belief.* Amherst, N.Y.: Prometheus Books.

In a *Ted Talks* presentation, Whitley argues that these shamans would have fit the criteria for being diagnosed as mentally ill today, but they changed the history for the better.[37]

And while neuroscientists have discovered the dopamine receptor D4 from the DRD4 gene is linked to many neurological and mood disorders, they have also detailed that this gene was first mutated around 50,000 years ago[38] – about the same time that these paintings were recorded. Only further proving Whitley's theory that this change in the development of the brain was the beginning of breakthrough in human evolution.

Dr. Malidoma Patrice Somé, a modern shaman, came to America in 1980 for graduate study and was shocked at the West's treatment of mental illness. He states in an article in the *Natural Medicine Guide to Schizophrenia* that in the West we focus on what is wrong with the individual and that something needs to be stopped, whereas the shamanic view is that it is the "birth of a healer and good news from the spirit world."[39]

He walked around an institution and saw these future healers in straightjackets, zoned out on medications, screaming and being tortured, and he views this as a waste of a person that is already connected to the spirit world. He tells a story about a teenager in America diagnosed with schizophrenia that is unable to be healed, and deemed insane. After spending four years in a village in Africa,

---

[37] Whitley, D. (Speaker) (2013). How mental illness changed human history . *Ted Talks* . Lecture conducted from, Manhattan Beach.
[38] Ding, Y. C., Chi, H. C., Grady, D. L., Morishima, A., Kidd, J. R., Kidd,K. K., . . . Moyzis, R. K. (2002). Evidence of positive selection acting at the human dopamine receptor D4 gene locus.
[39] Marohn, S. (2014, August 22). What a Shaman Sees in A Mental Hospital. *The Natural Medicine Guide to Schizoph*, 178-189.

his spirits were aligned and returned to America and graduated from Harvard graduate school in Psychology.

Somé explains of this young man's journey, "He was reaching out. It was an emergency call. His job and his purpose was to be a healer. He said no one was paying attention to that."

Following Shamanism, ancient cultures the turned to viewing the mentally ill as demonic and "treated" them by forms of exorcism an execution. In the 16th century, the rise of asylums and institutionalizing the mentally ill became the norm with brutal treatments such as isolation, chaining to walls, and beatings. In America, the past 200 years has included much of the same treatment of dehumanizing those with mental illness, such as Dr. Somé described as recently as 1980, and most recently the rise of psychiatric medication which has leaked into the primary care clinics as a cash crop for the industry.

In 1887, Nelly Bly wrote about faking mental illness to see the inside of the insane asylum and documents her findings in her book, *Ten Days in a Madhouse*. After trying to drop her act of "crazy," that only confirmed her diagnosis, stating, "Strange to say, the more sanely I talked and acted, the crazier I was thought to be."[40]

We are talking 10,000 years of mistreating mental illness and to reverse its course is going to take time and a group of people that are not afraid to stand up to the atrocities we witness daily.

I had to get out of working at this inner city hospital because I was becoming a part of the corruption. Soon after, I finally graduated school. I could not believe it – I'm not really sure anyone believed it. I actually followed through with something all the way until the end.

---

[40] Bly, N. (1887). *Ten Days in a Madhouse*. New York: IAN L. MUNRO, PUBLISHER.

Emotional Restriction

After passing my LPN boards in July, I got my first job at Homer's House – a Rule 36 program for the mentally ill. It was a group home, sort of like an institution, with some residents that had been there for more than three decades.

Enter me - The new graduate, feeling good about life and my accomplishments and all the obstacles that I recently overcame. But, in reality, I had not "overcome" anything. This was just an illusion; rather I had just been too busy and sort of forgot they existed. Just like the car with the clicking noise.

There are a few ways in which we avoid emotions rather than deal with them; I have used all of them at different stages of my journey. In the book, *Radical Acceptance* by Tara Bach, she lists three ways in which we avoid emotions:

1. *"We embark on one self-improvement project after another;*
2. *We hold back and play it safe rather than risking failure;*
3. *We withdraw from the experience of the present moment, we keep busy, we become our own worst critics, and we focus on other people's faults."*[41]

Keeping busy with school, work, increased pay, and improving myself had kept me away from some of the internal pain. However, I was getting healthier myself and with that I was more capable of helping others. I never used to believe that cliché, but it turns out to be true. In an airplane, they instruct you to secure your own oxygen mask before helping others because if you are unable to breathe, what good can you do for others?

---

[41] Brach, T. (2003). *Radical acceptance: Embracing your life with the heart of a Buddha*. New York: Bantam Books.

I had been building a great relationship with my five-year-old daughter, who now calls me "daddy" and has forgotten about this other man. However, Kylee was now losing her mother as she had moved back to her hometown, and moved in with a man named Steve and his three children.

Adrianne, Kylee's mother, is a good person and had a really rough upbringing. She is a loving person, with a huge heart, and strong soul, and I wish I could have been healthier for her while we were together. I wanted to save her, but I was not ready. I had not secured my own oxygen mask and was not in position to try to help someone else from danger.

While she had moved away, I had not given up on her. I just had to let it go and detach. The Buddhism philosophy is founded on four noble truths, which are as follows:

1. Life involves suffering
2. All Suffering comes from attachment
3. Suffering can end with detachment which leads to Nirvana
4. The path to enlightenment can be obtained by following the eightfold path (including correct thought, speech, actions, livelihood, understanding, effort, and mindfulness)

Starting with the first noble truth, life is suffering indicates that even if we are happy it will only be temporarily. The word for this is pleasure, temporary happiness. In my case, I filled my emptiness with Adrianne and soon became attached. I believed that the only way to end my suffering was to fill it with Adrianne, which falls directly into the second noble truth.

While I still deeply cared for her as a person, I had to detach from her. And this formula works for all of life. Again, the more we give away (detach), the more we gain in forms of joy or Nirvana.

But Adrianne was still in the suffering stage and continued to attach to anything to fill these holes in her soul. Along with Steve, she was then introduced into hardcore drugs such as cocaine and methamphetamine. This is not uncommon, this is why Americans have the highest rate of drug use in the entire world. The rise of materialism, along with unregulated advertising and propaganda, we have a couple generations brainwashed into believing that happiness comes from the outside.

When you have someone like Adrianne, who has been beat down and abused her entire life, she is feeling down, hurt, alone, and depressed. Then you hand her a substance and all she has to do is smoke it or snort it and it brings sense, meaning, purpose, and energy to her life – of course she is going to indulge. Who wouldn't?

It's the same way we have brainwashed young girls into believing that they are not valuable to society unless they are beautiful. We have put such a strong emphasis on beauty in this country that 81-percent of 10-year-olds are afraid of being fat.[42] By the time a female reaches 17-years of age, she has seen more than 250,000 advertisements that have shown figures of women that represent a figure that less than two percent of the population ever achieve.

Americans went as far to spend more than $12 billion on cosmetic surgery, including $1.5 billion on breast augmentation alone.[43] The United States has the most money in the world, but rank 17th in the World Happiness Project that ranks countries on terms of overall satisfaction with life. Panama, Costa Rica, and Mexico have surpassed Americans when it comes to enjoying life. Likewise, Japan

---

[42] Mellin, L., McNutt, S., Hu, Y., Schreiber, G.B., Crawford, P., & Obarzanek, E. (1991). A longitudinal study of the dietary practices of black and white girls 9 and 10 years old at enrollment: The NHLBI growth and health study. Journal of Adolescent Health, 23-37.
[43] American Society for Aesthetic Plastic Surgery

has the fourth highest GDP, yet ranks 43rd in happiness as they live in a society that strives itself on work rather than community and love.[44]

Yet, places like Denmark and Norway (rank 57th and 49th in total GDP) consistently rank among the world's happiest places in the world. The Danes have free health care as a right, parents get up to 52 weeks of paternity leave to spend time raising children with full-time pay, free education, and they live in close proximity and share a sense of community. They don't spend their money on big house or big cars, but with socializing with their fellow man and woman.

This has been engrained in our heads that materialism and attachments bring happiness, but it couldn't be further from the truth. It is one big marketing ploy for us to buy more products.

I felt I was starting to understand some of this, but my head was still clouded from years of brainwashing. Awakening has to do with breaking down all these old patterns which takes a great deal of effort, courage, and strength.

I do not have many regrets in my path to enlightenment, but I would like to share one deep one in regards to a missed opportunity I had with Adrianne. At the end of that summer, she came to pick up Kylee for first grade. I was not sure what had happened to her or where she went, but had felt I did a nice job of detaching.

She told me she had gotten into meth, but I am not all that worried about it. At the time, I still dabble in it here-and-there. In fact, when she came to get Kylee that August morning, I happened to have some and I shared it with her.

---

[44] "World Happiness Report 2013 Ranks Happiest Countries Around Globe". Huffingtonpost.com. 2013-09-09. Retrieved 2014-04-25.

While we were driving she cries, "Jesus! Everyone does this stuff! Even You!"

She said it as if her heart were broken. As if she was reaching out telling me she was struggling and knew this was not the way to go about it, and then I enabled her and made it seem like it was normal. I wish I could have that day back, that moment back.

In this moment, I could have been a safe zone for her. But, I still had a huge struggle of my own in which I wasn't even aware. I may have detached from her, but my suffering continued as my new attachment came in the form of drugs and alcohol – still searching for that deeper feeling and connection. Like the shamans, I always wanted to be a healer but just needed to find my healthy / natural way of getting there. I knew there was more to this world, as does Adrianne, and drugs were our new way to escape our current reality.

She told me how she had been selling meth and they are making tons of money and it is making her happy. The meth makes her feel relaxed, enjoys life, and feels alive for the first time in her entire life. She had been abused, neglected, raped and is feeling empty inside. Just like I had for so many years and she continued to use men, sex, and drugs as her escape.

My regret is that I know that she was headed down a wrong path and maybe a different response to her confession would have created some change. But she is on her own journey and it is not easy to awaken someone who doesn't know they are still sleeping.

It is like a group of people sitting inside on a rainy day and complaining about the weather. Once you finally are forced to go outside, you see that the rain is not so bad, and you can see the storm is going to pass soon. You rush in and try to tell the others but they are not convinced and not willing to give it a try. To complicate matters, when people have been hurt repeatedly and lack trust. It increases their fear and they are unwilling to take the risk.

As Vivian Greene notoriously said,

> *"Life is not about waiting for the storm to pass,*
> *it's about learning to dance in the rain."*

When I took my first step in the rain, I started dancing and saw the storm was passing. But, before it passed, it was a pretty heavy storm that I would have to embrace the next six months.

Meeting Socrates

I walked into Homer's House for my first day and noticed it was not too much different from the inner city hospital. They have an intercom system in which staff would scream into patient's rooms to get down and take their medications. It wasn't about the patients being disrespectful or not following rules, but the staff wanted to take a smoke break. This wasn't a "home," this was an institution.

They would wake up, get in line at a window, take medications, eat breakfast, etc. All the while, taking verbal abuse and being bullied by their "providers." Hurry! Hurry! Get your meds! No "good mornings" or "hellos," this is about business! If the client does not get to the window by 9:01 a.m. for their medication, they are just out of luck for the morning and will be charted as non-compliant.

Abuse of power comes at every level of society. Any opportunity people have for power over another human, they jump at that chance. Then new staff, like myself, walk in and are trained to operate this way.

This socialization of mental health and psychiatry has been handed down for the past 10,000 years. This is why it is so difficult to make any sort of changes.

Think back 2,500 years ago when Socrates was roaming the streets of Athens and how radical his views must have been during his time. Athens had just been embarrassed by losing the Peloponnesian War to Sparta and was in a transitional stage as the end of their empire neared. The belief up until that time was "Might is Right," meaning that revenge and militaristic rule was the philosophy – not too different than how the west operates today. People still were clinging on to past world-dominance, beauty, and material wealth. He challenged people to look within themselves and find the answers they already possessed.

Socrates never received any compensation for his teachings, nor did he consider his work teaching, but rather conversation that helped open each other's minds. His approach was to ask people to think logically about their life and help them think for themselves - rather than conform to what they have been taught. He would approach people in the street and ask them what they thought about things like justice, virtue, and to challenge them to think about why they do the things they do. His approach was to never teach anybody anything new, but to have them bring out what they truly already knew within.

He believed that no one desires evil, but it stems from ignorance. He also stated that the mentally ill were heaven-sent and not shameful in the least. He considered it a blessing and should not be treated.

Similarly, Jesus spent his time with the lepers, disabled, prostitutes, tax collectors, and lower end of society. Also like Jesus, Socrates was sentenced to death for his "teachings." Socrates also had a chance to escape but, like Jesus, accepted his punishment as a firm believer in the law.

In Benjamin Franklin's autobiography in 1771, he explains that in practicing humility one must "imitate Socrates and Jesus." Putting Socrates in the category of Jesus emphasizes the importance he had on the rise of Western society and the school of thought.

We are starting to use these methods today, now called "Motivational Interviewing" and "positive psychology." Likewise, teachings of the Buddha are starting to be proven scientifically and psychology is starting to see the wisdom of Socrates, Buddha, and Jesus from thousands of years ago is still the most accurate methods.

But progress is slow for an industry that has spent thousands of years in literal and proverbial darkness.

And to further the corruption of an already corrupt field, came the rise of for-profit health care.

Institutions started to rise in the for-profit sector, which only helped increase the dehumanization of clients as they now were viewed as monetary assets. The more clients in a facility, meant more money. The longer they stay in the facility, the more security of income.

> *"The insane asylum on Blackwell's Island is a human rat-trap. It is easy to get in, but once there it is impossible to get out."* – Nellie Bly

In Jim Ronson's lecture entitled "Weird Answers to the Psychopath Test," he shares his trip to Broadmoor Asylum and his encounter with a man named Tony. Tony had faked insanity to get out of a prison sentence, but faked it too well. He states instead of serving a five year prison sentence, he ended up serving 12 at Broadmoor. Echoing the words of Bly from over 100 years ago, he states,

> *"It's a lot harder to convince people you are sane, than that you are crazy."*

He talks about how he was trying to act normal and thing would get charted on him that stated otherwise. He wanted to stay in his room rather than mingle with a strangler and rapist, which led them to chart that he was "isolating."

When talking to the psychiatrists, they knew that he faked insanity because his hallucinations were too basic. But, then concluded, that only a psychopath would fake being insane and fit the criteria of being manipulative, high self-worth, and faking the brain went wrong was a clear indication that – his brain went wrong.

And I was seeing all of this unfold before my eyes at the Homer's House. If a client says that there medications are causing problems, you are considered non-compliant and fits the criteria of being "crazy."

The building had a disgusting stench, rats dwelling outside the building, no air-conditioning in a disgusting living environment with the added hostility of the staff. But it was fitting, because the clients were not treated like humans. They were being treated like the living arrangement suggested – animals or rodents.

The owners, the Homer's, enjoyed this nice for-profit business with a lot of land and money to spare. They hired their kids to work, with no formal education or training in the field to further damage more lives of the "sick."

Here is how the process works: They grab people with run-down lives and nothing to their name, put them in this dungeon, and charged them everything they had. They took every last bit from these tortured souls, including their dignity. Then, they hired the lowest possible licensed staff allowed by state regulations – TMA and LPNs that had no education or training.

Because it was no longer about caring for the health of patients, it was about making a profit and running a business. It is basic economics: (Long-Term Stable Income) – (Low Overhead Costs) = Higher Profit Margin. Keep the clients there as long as possible while providing the minimal amount of care and services required will return the most on their investment.

And who is going to complain? The clients that have nothing? Certainly not the tax-payers, because they have no clue what is going on and on paper it sounds like they are offering services to those in need.

But this is not how it started. The foundations of the Homer's House started with a man giving old veterans a place to stay. Eventually, someone complained and said that you cannot provide this kind of service without a license.

In other terms, the bullies of the government were not getting their piece of the pie.

How many times do we see this? A great service offered and then others get involved, it becomes a money-making idea and the governments, schools, corporations, and doctors get involved so they can increase their wealth.

In order to work as a drug and alcohol counselor you need to be licensed by the state. To be licensed by the state, you need to take college courses – for the most part, state-run colleges. In school, you do not really learn anything that you can't learn while on the job, in fact, there are people that know more about addiction by going to 12-step meetings, in recovery themselves, and have volunteered in the industry than people fresh out of school. But that is capitalism. If there is money to be made, a system will become corrupt.

That is why Alcoholics Anonymous continues to survive without corruption. They have never had leaders or officials, they have never accepted cash donations (other than to pay utilities on the buildings they rent), they refuse to be affiliated with any religion or political party, and only purpose they serve is to help people recover.

Ironically, the schools are trying to steer people away from 12-step programs. You have a program that has been proven effective for nearly 80 years, but we are teaching other methods because that allows for more licensing, more facilities, and more money to be spread around to the elite.

I worked there with about six other kids, all in our early 20s, with no idea what we were doing. But, we were cheap labor and the Homer's bank account grew. It was a lot like the inner city hospital, all the older ladies taking out their frustrations on the clients. And the young people getting their first taste at what it feels like to abuse their power over another human.

But there were two ladies that I enjoyed listening to when they spoke in which the title of this chapter is named after. One was the RN supervisor and the other ran the place. They were like Socrates in ancient Greece. They thought, "Hey, let's treat the patients with kindness and stop the abuse."

I really idolized them and wanted to be like them, the non-conformists in an industry in dire need of change. It was time to start yelling for people to be more compassionate and come down on those who were not – like a positive police force inside the home.

In talking to the residents, I learned their stories. They were all incredibly smart, gifted, kind hearts, and souls. Not one of them had an even decent childhood, all had troubled pasts with abuse, neglect, and trauma. In fact, it was the one thing that everyone had in common was they grew up in these deplorable conditions.

Then they arrive at the Homer's House, but the tormenting and abuse continues. Maybe they have given up on fighting. Maybe this is what they have come to expect. Like in Viktor Frankl's book, *A Man's Search for Meaning,* he describes how many can adapt to anything as he gives his account of surviving in the prison camps of the Holocaust in World War II.

Their feelings, thoughts, and beliefs are invalidated; they are emotionally abused; doped up on drugs (pharmaceuticals)…and all this is happening inside the house! Then if they do not wake up on time, we yell at them, blame them, and increase their pain and suffering.

But like Socrates said, no one desires evil. It comes from ignorance. The staff did not know any better, this is what they have been taught and they are simply following orders.

Imprisoning the Healers

In 1955, there were 558, 239 severely mentally ill patients in the nation's publicly funded psychiatric hospitals. In 1965, the Medicare and Medicaid Act excluded payments to patients in state run psychiatric hospitals and other "institutions for the treatment of mental illness."

This act along with widespread criticism, the number of patients decreased to 71, 619 by 1994 – an 87-percent decrease! But that is only part of the true deinstitutionalization story in America. We also need to figure in population increase in general. In 1955 there were 164 million Americans and 250 million in 1994.

When factoring in population growth, it actually comes down to about 92-percent of people that were living in public psychiatric hospitals in 1955 were no longer living there by 1994.

With this also came the rise of psychiatric medications. In 1997, the United States became just the second country in the world to allow Direct-To-Consumer marketing of pharmaceutical drugs. This led to an overload of psychotropic medications being advertised directly on our television sets, in magazines, and billboards. Only two countries in the world allow this!

These medications were meant for the severely mentally ill and now they trickled down into primary clinics. With the DTC advertising, people walk into a clinic and ask for these medications by name. If the doctor says no, they lose a customer.

This leads to less people in need of institutionalized care being medicated without treatment, a higher number of the general population being diagnosed and medicated to these same psychotropic drugs, leading to a new epidemic in drug addiction – prescription pills.

With less hospital beds, more drugs and more widely available, we are prone to see more atrocious acts in the public such as the increase in school shootings – a term that didn't really exist prior to 1999.

Now the issue becomes "keep the freaks away from my school," "Not in my neighborhood." There is a huge misunderstanding in mental health. I am not pardoning the acts of those who shoot up schools, but trying to look at the bigger picture at how we have created this situation as a society and this is the end-result.

This is always the end result in a capitalist society. We try to cut corners to save money and increase profit, and it always ends up with a less-than-desired product. Then a competitor comes up with a cheaper price and we need to find alternative ways to compete. In America this has meant launching the "War on Drugs" and the "War on Terror" which has been a smokescreen to invade third world countries for natural resources, to get cheaper materials, and increase profit margins.

In the mental health industry, it meant cutting the number of beds to save money. Then to keep people medicated, we allowed psychotropic drugs into the general population. This created a demand and the drug companies and health insurance corporations wanted to get involved. As the need for drugs soared, we found cheaper alternatives in Afghanistan and Pakistan opium fields and keep troops stationed there under the disguise of the War on Terror.

This is why capitalism always fails humanity. This is why we have such a distinguished income gap in our nation because the rich get richer and the poor get poorer. But we are all connected and responsible for each other and everything that happens around us.

When we label and judge it separate us from each other and our divine nature. Like Socrates would spend his days speaking to everyone and trying to get them to open their minds and see their true essence, the Athenians locked him up and sentenced him to death. The Romans did the same to Jesus.

We did the same to John Lennon, Martin Luther King Jr., Malcolm X, and John F Kennedy.

All the labeling, judging, classification, and compartmentalizing is only creating further separation. When the truth is that we are all interconnected in everything we do.

> *"Researchers have proven, scientifically, that humans are all one people. The color of our ancestor's skin and ultimately my skin and your skin is a consequence of ultra-violet light, of latitude and climate. Despite our recent sad conflicts in the U.S. there is really no such thing, scientifically, as race. We are one species. Each of us is much more alike than we are different. We all came from Africa. We're all made of the same star dust. We're all going to live and die on the same planet – a pale blue dot in the vastness of space. We have to work together." – Bill Nye*

Every moment we have an opportunity to make a decision. Each one of those decisions is what creates Karma and presents a new set of circumstances. Each moment gives us an opportunity to expand the overall love of the universe or restrict it.

Which is why when there are concerns and issues as a society, it is everyone who is at fault as we are all one organism. We are all part of the problem, and all part of the solution. While it may not seem like one person can effectively change a mental health stigma that has existed for thousands of years, it can change with one person standing up for what they believe.

The Hundredth Monkey

In the 1950s, on some islands near Japan, scientists had been observing the behavior on monkeys for three decades. They started dropping sweet potatoes in the sand, in which the monkeys enjoyed the taste of the sweet potato – but not so much the sand. One day, a young female monkey realized you could wash the potatoes in the nearby stream and she soon taught this to her mother.

Over time, the monkeys that were taught this started to imitate it. Then one day, after a certain number of monkeys were doing this – let's say 100 of them –suddenly, every monkey on the island began to do so as it had become common practice.

But furthermore, it was observed that monkeys on other islands that had no contact or knowledge started to do the same behavior. The belief is that when a behavior is created over and over gets entered into a memory bank, or morphogenetic field and is accessible to all. Carl Jung refers to this as the collective consciousness, whereas David Wilcox would call it source field.

The morphogenetic field is one of the most important and least understood factors of influence within our society. With every thought, action, and emotion we strengthen this mass consciousness and it becomes available for all. Global fear, judgment, peace, and love are all notions of these fields.

This is what took place in the hundredth monkey observation. This is also why similar inventions are created nearly simultaneously, also explains the power of mass prayer/meditation leading to miracles. You can even feel this at a major sporting event, concert, or political speech.

If this sounds too science fiction for you, quantum physics backs it up.

A study from Princeton University constantly collects data from random number generators collected all over the planet. The information is transmitted to a home base, which has been collected over a period of twenty years.

These random number generators are basically a digital coin-flip; they randomly select a "1" or a "0" about 200-times per second. Typically these charts are as expected, about 50-50. However, every time there is a major event starting with Princess Diana's death in 1997, 9/11, Madrid Bombings,, and Pope's funeral there was more of a recognizable pattern. They chances of this happening randomly each time is around one in a trillion. [45]

Profits over People

All animals are born with telepathy. It is the primary mode of communicating with animals. Humans had this too, until we became civilized and left-brain dominant. Our communication, reason, and logic, has diminished the use of the telepathic nature. But it is still there, as proven above, and we still have the ability to make changes. But we are up against a culture that is doing its best to keep profits over people.

In the western world, we live in excess. This is the cause of a great deal of pain both directly and indirectly. When we chase after material gains, we never are truly satisfied. The external possessions we acquire only bring temporary pleasure, but not true internal joy. Indirectly, the excess we live in takes away from others who are suffering, starving, and being abused.

The United States military budget is the largest in the world at $737 billion. The next closest is China at $188 billion. If you took the combined military budgets of the top 25 countries (besides the United States), it still would not equal the $737 billion per year that the United States spends.

---

[45] Kiger, Patron. 9/11 and Global Consciousness. National Geographic (Sept. 6, 2011).

The United Nations has determined it would cost about $30 billion per year to end world hunger. If the United States really wanted to make a difference and help those in need, it would only need to cut an incredibly small portion of their astronomical military expenditures and they could end world hunger forever.

If you have the money to kill people, you have the money to help people.

> *"The world will not be destroyed by those who do evil, but by those who watch them without doing anything."* – Albert Einstein

The natural reaction to hearing this is to get defensive and angry. Nobody wants to hear that the way we are living is creating pain in the world. But that is what enlightenment is about. It is not about sitting under a tree and having a vision, it is about breaking away all the untruths that you have forever believed to be true.

Most mentally ill people today will be found in jails and prisons because it is cheaper to house them than in a hospital. The Minneapolis Star-Tribune produced a study in 2013 that showed that on average it costs $110 per night to put someone in jail as opposed to $1000 in a hospital. While put in jail, they are treated like criminals before being released without any treatment. This allows the cycle to continue.

America is home to only five percent of the world's population, yet we hold 25-percent of the world's prison population. The United States is the most incarcerated population in the history of the world, yet we pride ourselves on being the self-proclaimed "Land of the Free."

And to top it off, the private sector has gotten their hands into the prison industry as well. As jails became overcrowded, corporations started building prisons for-profit. In order for a business to be profitable, it needs income. The private prison industry generates income by the government setting up contracts which guarantee occupancy rates at 95-100 percent for 20 or more years. In order to sustain these rates, we lock up more people and keep them longer than ever before. The private prisons spent more than $21 million in lobbying last year to lawmakers to hand out tougher sentences which keep the beds full. And ironically, all the good ole boys on Wall Street benefit as a large number of members of congress have stock in these private prisons.

Simply put, lock up more people for a longer period of time equates to more money. Then lobby for tougher laws to lock up even more people and increase prison populations. And to top it off, you can buy stock and profit off all the corruption while in office.

The same is true for the military industrial complex in which congressmen (the law makers of the country) profit of investments in defense contractors such as General Electric and Raytheon. John Kerry, our secretary of state, has profited more than $26 million in his investments in defense contractors in the past 10 years. The same guy that keeps telling us we need to go to war gets a bigger paycheck each time we pull the trigger. It is not a coincidence.

In regards to jail and mentally ill, we see the same people recycle through the doors because of the inadequate care inside the facilities. This is the culture that has been created thousands of years ago and it continues to this day.

The Homer's House is just a microcosm of this entire picture of society. We brought people in off the streets, mistreated them, sent them on their way and watched them dwindle back into the homes.

The for-profit agency hired the cheapest staff, offered no training, and wanted the patients there as long as possible for guaranteed revenue.

Love Revolutionaries

Joanie Frank and Jessie Madder are the ones who stood up to the bullies at Homer's House. They asked us to be kind, caring, and compassionate to those in need. They were the Martin Luther King's of the mental health industry. And they got to me. I wish I could thank them today.

They were visionaries who were far ahead of their time that helped inspire this movement.

Our staff was young and untrained. We fell into the model of judging and labeling, which essentially led to separation from the clients. We went out partying, called in sick, or showed up hungover when we were supposed to be providing care to those in need. The cycle of pain just continued for these people.

But, I had enough at this point. I went in to talk to my boss, Jessie Madder l. She was my idol at the time. A strong, assertive, and fearless leader that was not afraid to take on anyone if it meant doing the right thing.

I told her how all this abusive actions in the house is very hard on me. It doesn't seem right. I told her that I cannot stand watching people treat other people in this way.

Then, one-by-one, staff members were being fired. Dropping out of the house like dead flies. I really felt that Jessie and the director, Joanie Frank, were making something special happen here. We were the Birmingham, Alabama, of the 1960s. I was so inspired by these two because I knew they were risking their careers as others were trying to take them down.

I started to take on a leadership position with the younger staff to help spread the mission. I had already built some rapport with the staff as we went out drinking and now they were starting to get on board with this new approach of actually providing care to those in need. It seems so simple looking back – just treat people kindly. It is not different than how we have treated different cultures, ethnicities, or with different sexual orientations since the birth of this country. Why does it always need to have some revolution just to treat people with compassion?

There was on patient in particular that I remember vividly. She would go to McDonalds and sit by herself all day long. When she returned she would come back and get her peanut butter sandwiches.

"Don't give them to her, Cortland!" I was scolded, "She doesn't get one! They are for the diabetics!"

But there were two extra sandwiches each night and we would just throw them away. It didn't make sense. She wanted one, we were going to toss it anyway, so I would give one to her.

"That's not right!" The older staff would yell at me, "Now everyone is going to ask for them. You have poor boundaries!"

"Boundaries" is a term that gets thrown around a lot in psych, mostly by people that cannot build relationships. They use this as an excuse to try to hold back those who are able to build relationships with clients.

If you are going to go to hell with someone and attempt to bring them back, you are going to need to build some level of trust first. This includes self-disclosure – another controversial practice in mental health. Now it should never be about you as a staff member, but you need to be willing to share a little if you expect anything in return.

This battle was never really about the sandwiches, it was much bigger than that. I refused to throw away sandwiches because I am not above this patient. I am going to give her the sandwich if she wants one.

Eventually, Jessie and Joanie were ousted by a group of people who were not ready for change and were fearful of what was to come. When they walked out, I cried. I cried because I really believed in what they were doing, in what we were doing.

But part of the awakening process includes being persecuted by others trying to destroy you. Not because they know any better, but because you start to challenge structures, organizations, and cultures that have stood in place for many years.

Jesus fought the churches, he did not follow their rules or regulations. He challenged everything they were doing. The Romans got together and eventually executed him by crucifixion. Five-hundred years earlier, the Greeks executed Socrates for "corrupting the youth" for the same reason – encouraging people to think freely and not just blindly conform.

Jessie and Joanie were ahead of their time. The world was not ready for them, but rarely is the world ever ready for radical change. We are prisoners to our own habits that have been created for us by our ancestors. In Erich Fromm's *Escape from Freedom,* he states that once people are freed from authorities that we often feel hopeless and often cling and attach to a new form of order in which it is safer to go along with the crowd than to stand alone.

Eventually, Homer's House would come crashing down within months of firing Jessie Madder and the resignation of Joanie Frank. But, I was still devastated. In tears, I kept thinking to myself that it just wasn't fair. These were the good guys, doing the right thing.

I learned quickly that if you are going to fight for the patients, or what is right or just, you will assuredly encounter people who are against you. And sometimes, these people have too much power and you are bound to fail at times. But you don't lose if you strike out, you lose if you quit trying or quit the game.

Martin Luther King Jr., wrote the famous "Letter from Birmingham Jail" after he was arrested for standing for inequality. Nelson Mandella was locked for 27-years by the South African apartheid government for not giving into a corrupt system that was committing egregious human rights abuses against black South Africans. Gandhi was arrested by the British government for conspiring to overthrow the government that had colonized his land and people for two hundred years.

As King, Mandella, and Gandhi went to prison they inspired many to join their fights along the way. In my own world, Jessie and Joanie, did the same for me. They inspired me and I knew at this moment that this would be a fight I would endure the rest of my life.

If you have not been fired in this field, you are not working hard enough.

CHAPTER VIII

The 危機 Theory
There are no Small Moments

Chapter 8
The 危機 Theory: There are no Small Moments

In traditional Chinese, the word for Crisis is comprised of two symbols. The first symbol, "危 (Wei)" pertains to facing an imminent danger or threat. The second symbol, "機 (Ji)" describes an opportunity presenting itself.

Edward Lorenz, pioneer of the Chaos theory, coined the term "Butterfly Effect," illustrating how a seemingly mundane event results in a significantly different outcome than would have occurred without the original divergence.

Or simply put, there are no moments in life that are too small and there is no crisis too great. Because life is full of chaos, presenting each moment as a crisis, leaving us with a choice between the Wei and Ji – ultimately determining the course of the future.

Amidst a treacherous winter snowstorm in sub-freezing temperatures, along the side of a small two-lane highway walks a six-year-old girl all alone. There are two vans approaching, one from each side of the highway. The first one stops and picks up the girl that clearly has her life in jeopardy. The man, not sure of what to do, turns her into the police station.

This random person affected so many lives by stopping his vehicle and instinctively taking action to do the right thing. This man saved my daughter's life. This was Kylee walking down the highway. She left a note for Adrianne saying that she was walking to my house across state lines to get food. This moment was the beginning of my butterfly effect.

They butterfly effect is quite prevalent if you look into history. On June 28, 1914, Archduke Franz Ferdinand of Austria and his wife were assassinated in Sarajevo. This is most prominently considered the moment that triggered a series of events that led to World War I. While the assassination plan had failed that day for 19-year-old Gavrilo Philip, he had left the scene and had a seat at the Deli. To his surprise, the Archduke's driver took a wrong turn and the vehicle ended up right in front of that exact deli. As he slammed on the brakes, the car stalled and Philip had a clean shot and assassinated the Archduke and his wife.

One wrong turn by a driver leads to events that sparked World War I, followed by the rise of Hitler and Nazi Germany. Essentially, this leads to World War II, the Cold War, and the ongoing state of war we are seeing today. Because of one wrong turn.

But this is just as effective in positive ways. On December 1, 1955, Rosa Parks refused to give up her seat on a crowded bus in Montgomery, Alabama, eventually leading to her arrest. In the streets of Montgomery, protests ensued with their spokesman Dr. Martin Luther King, Jr. leading the charge. And the rest of the civil rights act is history, because one woman refused to be a part of the system that was unjust.

A more scientific view looks at the water cycle on Earth. The sun heats the water in the ocean, causing some of it to evaporate and cooler temperatures allow it to condense into clouds. The wind pushes the clouds across the earth and cloud particles collide and fall to the earth as forms of precipitation. The precipitation either goes back into the ocean, lakes, or land. When it falls on the land it creates it becomes part of the "ground water" that animals and plants use or it may run over the soil and collect into the ocean again for the cycle to continue. In fact, there is always the exact same amount of water on earth since it was first formed two billion years ago.

Licensed to Steal

It started with another random phone call from Adrianne in which she was overly-hysterical, even for her standards. She had been quite distant for some time and she is on the phone bawling and I cannot quite make out what she is trying to say other than "Cops" and "Kylee."

My instinct told me that something serious was going on, so I walked out of class and headed to their home, across state lines. As soon as I arrive, she pulls me into her room and shows me track marks on her arms. She had been shooting meth, looks awful, and she shows me the note that Kylee had left her about walking to my home, across state lines.

This incident started what is called a CHIPS (Child in Need of Protective Services) case with Adrianne in which she would be monitored for a year by the court with potential of losing her parental rights to Kylee.

She failed her first drug test and no one told me. Then after failing the second drug test, Adrianne's family finally got in touch with me. The social worker on the case, did not even have me listed as Kylee's father.

I contacted her and told her, "I am the father of the child. I own a house and I will be taking her home with me – not Adrianne's family." So, I picked up Kylee and told Adrianne we were going for the weekend and that I would not be bringing Kylee back.

But remember, social workers have power over other people's lives. They get this power by taking a few classes and getting a degree. And now they have the right, as given by the state, to decide what is best for another human. They are far from prepared to handle real-life situations like this.

The "butterfly effect" of this scenario is that social workers tend to be one of the most depressed professions based on a Health Magazine article. This tends to lead to unusually high rates of alcoholism among social workers.

The educational system prepares kids how to take tests, remember things, and repeat what they were told. Students are told what to think, not how to think. And who are the people enrolled in these programs? It is people that come from privileged families and backgrounds that are yet to experience life.

Anyone who thinks freely surely doesn't fit the mold of a college curriculum. They don't look to answer the questions, the look to question the answers. And if you have been a victim of the system and have a criminal record, you are not going to be able to get any federal Pell grants and will not be able to afford the overpriced education.

As of 2015, the United States owes more than $1.2 trillion in student loan Debt! There are not enough jobs, or enough well-paying jobs, that people are going to pay these loans back. Eventually they will cut back on loans and the wealthy prevails again as the only ones with the opportunity for further education.

And it is those who get the benefit of going to college that enjoy upward social mobility, and essentially making the rules and decisions. But they have never been taught how to think freely and openly. They repeat what they are told to think.

This is what made Socrates such a unique person in history. He didn't do it for profit, wealth, or fame. He never accepted anything for his teachings. And he encouraged people to think about why they go about their day the way they do. How profound for 2,500 years ago! How profound for today!

I took Kylee back to my house, which turns out is against the law to take her across state lines – despite the fact that she is my biological daughter. I had never received any information in Adrianne's case. After I pick up Kylee and bring her to a safe place, Adrianne flips out, bashes me to the social workers to intentionally try to get Kylee put in foster care.

At what point do we stop and ask the child what she wants? Get her perspective? Although only in first grade, they seem to have more insight than an outsider with no experience in this kind of situation.

For three years I had no contact with Kylee and thought I had lost her forever. She had been neglected and abused and missed most of first grade. I finally get her full-time and she is in a good place with plenty of support with my siblings and parents.

Knock. Knock. Knock.

The social workers come in to my home and do inspections on my life. Checking into my background to see if I can care for my own daughter, yet you let her live with Adrianne for a year while she was shooting meth daily? Nor did they ever even notify me, I had to wait to find out about all of this from Adrianne's family.

I am not trying to put Adrianne in a negative light. She was in a lot of pain. In all actuality, I did try to get her into treatment as did everyone close to her. She was a lot like my grandmother who suffered from alcoholism and no one got to see the real side to her. Adrianne is kind, loving, and a wonderful human being that is in so much pain she completely lost herself.

Taking the Mask Off

We both had our own agendas and would talk bad about the other parent, which essentially just made the entire situation worse. Adrianne would come in-and-out of our lives which was confusing Kylee. I tried to share this openly with the social workers. I thought it was great to have them helping my case, so I shared everything with them and they appeared to be listening and they talked to me as if they really cared about what I had to say.

In reality, they had been manipulating me to build a case to take Kylee. I had completely and fully trusted in them. I said that I wanted Adrianne to be able to see Kylee because they cry for each other every night. They wanted to see each other and I thought that I was doing the right thing by not keeping them apart.

In the back of my mind, I also recognized that I had finally started to receive some sort of acceptance from her family and was even viewed as some sort of savior. Part of me started to imagine we would eventually get back together. Here, I had my own house, working a great job, and raising Kylee.

Adrianne would come back around and we tried to make it work again and again. One day, I came home from work and it looked to me like she was trying to make a drug deal. As I tried to swipe her phone, she dialed 911. Eventually I got hold of the phone and threw it across the room, ending the call and prompting the police to show up and barge into the house.

I had been trying to help Adrianne get her life together. I even gave her an old car to help her get around. While she was at my house and making this drug deal, I flushed the keys down the toilet because I knew if she left she was going to hurt herself and she was slowing killing herself with her habit – it was the only way I knew to stop the problem.

In short, I was arrested for domestic violence. I was told that the fact that she was afraid was enough for them to press charges. I was put in jail for about a week without any hope of getting out. I was certain I would be able to talk my way out of it, but it was just like back at Divine Redeemer.

The Gift of Powerlessness

This was just a loss of perceived control, because the truth is we never had control to begin with and it is moments of this that are reminders of our own powerlessness.

We face many rock bottoms in our journey, which turns out to be the greatest gift we can receive. If enlightenment is the cracking, or breaking away, of the ego – is there any better way than to hit a hard rock bottom? Each time it reminds of us our powerless of everything, our overall lack of control, and forces us into a surrender.

As I paced around the jail cell which seemed like an eternity, I couldn't sleep, eat, or function and was a wreck. I remember a guy in there with me was awaiting a murder trial and he told me, "Stop being crabby. You are already here. All that matters now is your attitude."

At the time, I wanted to knock him out, but he must have got to me subconsciously because I nodded my head and agreed. And he must have planted a seed in my head, because I go back to this moment at times in my life when feelings like this arise and he was always right. We never do have control over things, but it is how we look at things that make the difference.

In the first line of the serenity prayer we ask our higher power to grant us serenity, or peace, for the ability to accept the things in which we cannot change, or lack control. While simply stated, this is quite a difficult task and involves going against everything that we have been told since we were younger. We are trained to control, crave control, and told that surrender is a form of weakness.

However, this is another one of the great paradoxes of the universe. Surrender, as it turns out, is one of the most incredible strengths one can possess. Surrender is the bridge between acceptance and change.

Any time we face an obstacle, event, or moment in our lives, we are granted only four choices:

1. Change the situation;
2. If we can't change the situation, change the way we think about the situation;
3. Completely accept the situation without judgment
4. Do nothing and let everything build up

Back to this moment while sitting in jail, the ideal move would be to change the situation but I soon found out that this was beyond my control. In changing the way we think about a situation, begins with complete acceptance. This means looking at the present moment without any judgment or complaints.

It is what it is. I am in jail because I was charged with domestic violence. It is easy to complain, judge, justify, blame, or criticize the situation but nothing changes. As Eckhart Tolle states in *The Power of Now*,

> "Anytime we complain we are only rejecting the now."

This is acceptance. Acknowledging the situation, without judgment, for what it is in the present moment. Surrender is taking the next step. This has to do with stop fighting the forces that are beyond your control and use that energy and apply it to the things you can.

Which leads to the second line of the serenity prayer, "the courage to change the things that we can." It's important to highlight the word courage, because any type of change is difficult and takes some form of risk. Change, or growth, only occurs when we are willing to take a step outside of our comfort zone. And that is why we call it the "comfort zone," because we find great comfort there in knowing what to expect. But, the problem lies when we start to expect more from our comfort zone, without venturing outside this place where nothing ever changes.

All living things are either growing, dying, or dead. We are in need of growth, yet growth requires some element of risk. Of all problems that substance use causes, this is one of the most significant. Because when we use substances to take risks, we don't really grow. Furthermore, we learn to depend on this substance for future similar risk-taking activities which only further stunts our growth.

This takes immense courage to take a deep look at ourselves, our lives, our current situation and say that we need help and want to make a change. While in the jail cell, I cannot change the situation. I accepted it, I completely surrendered to it, and now the next step was to change the things that I can – my attitude or the way I think about the situation.

There is an old story about an upstart shoe company that is trying to expand their brand internationally. The Regional Manager sends his top two sales executives to Australia in an effort to sell to some remote villages to the aboriginal tribes. After a couple of weeks, the Regional Manager calls his top two salesmen for an update.

"This is the biggest waste of time," says the first salesmen, "I want you to put me on the next flight out of here. You don't understand, the Aborigines do not wear shoes, they have never heard of them, and have no interest!"

The Regional Manager obliged with the salesman's request and set up for the next flight home. But before doing so, he called the second salesperson to let him know that it was a wasted venture and they would be coming back home shortly.

"What are you talking about?" said the second salesmen, "I need you to send me as many shoes as you have in stock! You don't understand, the Aborigines do not wear shoes nor have they ever even heard of them! This is an untapped market!"

In the exact same situation, one man sees a crisis and the other an opportunity. This has to do with changing our perception of the situation.

So, here I was in jail and fearful of the unknown. I had just put up my house as collateral last week to get Adrianne out of jail, and now here I sit in a cell of my own. I had bailed her out a couple of times and she had become the target of an FBI Investigation, which landed her in a state prison. My intentions were good, but now I sat locked up as powerless as ever before.

The State's Game of Chess

On the day of the arrest, my best friend Joey saw the final scene played out on the street as I was getting forced into the back of a squad car in handcuffs. As always, he took care of things for me and contacted my family to make sure Kylee was OK. My mother picked Kylee up from school and was able to keep her at her house while I sat in jail.

Another random synchronicity of the universe that we like to play off as "coincidences," but there are no coincidences in life. Every event and moment happens for an exact reason for things to play out as planned. The chances of Joey driving by my house at the exact moment that I am being put in handcuffs is astronomical if you use pure logic, but once you are able to completely surrender to the universe you realize that these types of interconnected moments happen throughout the day.

Eventually, I plead guilty and my case would be dismissed under the stipulation that I did not have any similar offenses during the next year. Relieved, refreshed, and satisfied, I planned one of the very few vacations in my entire lifetime. I booked a flight to Arizona to spend a couple of days with my brother Larry that I hadn't seen in 18 months.

But, on the way to the airport, I get word that the social workers have went to the judge in secrecy, stating that Kylee was in danger while living with me because I allowed her to see Adrianne. There was never a court order stating she could not see Kylee and I was doing my best to try to keep the peace between everyone. She was trying to get better and I was doing what I thought was best to help her along the way. Kylee and Adrianne were crying to see each other and it tore me apart seeing them both in pain and the obvious solution was to bring them together, with no idea that it would lead to all of this.

I thought that I could save Adrianne. Not just her, I've always held this belief that I can save others. They developed a plan to remove her while I was in Arizona. Now I realize that if you are not healthy enough yourself, you cannot help anybody else.

Taking the Mask Off

As soon as I get the news, I turn around and head to the courthouse and skip my flight. I sat in the room crying, pleading, and begging them for Kylee. Of all people in my life, my sister Koryn was there with me. This is the true Koryn – the amazing, strong, compassionate woman that would do anything for what is right. I wish she saw how amazing she can be in her finest moments like this. I guess this is why I get so angered and bothered with her, because I see myself doing the same things. But as we sat there, it really wasn't that big of a surprise as she has always been there at moments like this for me and always says something truly enlightening when I need it the most.

She is a Buddha amidst a nation of greedy selfish leeches. It reminds me of the story of Lambert, the sheepish Lion. An old cartoon that tells the tale of a lion that was raised by sheep and doesn't realize that he is a lion. One day, the wolves are about to eat all the sheep and Lambert is just as scared as all of the other sheep – not realizing that he is indeed a lion. Eventually he sees that all the sheep are in danger and his true lion-instincts come out, chasing the wolves away. That was Koryn for me in this moment, just as she always has done.

In the courthouse, it became a battle between the social workers of two different counties.

There was a social worker from 2 different states involved, blaming each other, trying to decide the fate of my little girl.

We use the phrase, "stabbed me in the back," when someone betrays our trust by means of deception. I used to always think it was just a figure of speech because someone snuck up on you and proverbial "stabs you while you are not looking." But the analogy is so precise, because that is the exact feeling it leaves in your body. It feels like that person truly penetrated a blade through your skin and into your organs leaving you broken.

This was the same pain I felt when Kylee had told me that someone else was her Dad. It was perhaps even more disheartening because I truly was trying to do the right thing in this situation. The social workers took the words I was saying, twisted them, and told the judge that this was an emergency and that Kylee had to be removed from her home. They never told me about it, I had no idea of this emergency, they had planned to do it when I was out of town. It was a planned coup d'état of my daughter by the social workers.

Eventually, I did get a copy of the records on both sides and saw the documentation of their conversations. Here we are in the United States of America in the 21st century and we have two government agencies fighting over the rights of my child, all in the "Land of the Free?"

It is quite disturbing how these decisions get made that impact lives and families forever. Giving such power over to a twenty-something-year-old with minimal life experience should be the criminal offense. They are allowed to control the lives of others based on their own preconceived notions, beliefs, and ideals. This is the true "dangerous situation," allowing someone with such little understanding and knowledge this incredible amount of power.

It goes back to the educational system. Those who follow instructions well are the ones that are deciding the fate of my child. They listen in school and repeat what they are told and receive high marks. This leads to them going on to further their "education" by enrolling in colleges where they are further trained what to think, but not think freely. Then we grant them with a piece of paper, a license from the state, and give them the power to decide the fate of an innocent child.

And how do we get this message across? How do we tell people that everything they have been told is a lie and part of a corrupt system?

How can we ask someone to awaken, who doesn't yet know that they are sleeping?

Surviving off Hope

I went home devastated, angry, and depressed. The only thing that kept me going was that I did have a tiny ounce of hope. And hope is an underestimated powerful tool that can keep anyone going despite whatever obstacles they may endure; yet without hope, a man cannot survive in even the most miniscule challenges.

My source of hope was the original social worker, which told me that I could go back to court. That was the only thing that I was hanging onto at this point, one little tiny speck of hope. But that is all I needed to keep fighting.

Remember when I said I needed to surrender while in jail and conserve my energy for something that I could control? Here was the time. That little bit of energy that I saved up could now be expended at this last chance that I had to keep my baby girl.

Kylee had went to her Grandpa Tony's house, Adrianne's father. I refused to give in and I called all the lawyers, the guardian ad litem, psychologists, counselors, and social workers. I got everyone involved, moved all my chips to the center of the table, and went "all in."

In using the Texas Hold Em' analogy above, when someone is running low in their stack of chips they start to feel pressure. They know that their hands are numbered as they see their pile of chips slowly dwindle away and the rest of the members at their table are looking at any opportunity to wipe them out. Then, that player is looking for just one opportunity, one chance, and one piece of hope to make some sort of comeback. As soon as they get any type of hand that they believe gives them a chance to make that comeback, they slide all their chips to the center of the table and state, "All In!"

If they win the hand, they usually get a big enough stack of chips to keep playing and turn things around. But, obviously, a loss in this scenario and the game is over.

This is where I stood with this court case. I was so crushed at this point, that this was it. If it didn't work out I was going to go insane and snap. I spent ten days in a hotel in the same town that Kylee was, spending as much time with Kylee as possible. This meant leaving my job at Homer's House which eventually led to my termination, but I had much bigger priorities at this point in my life. It would only be two months later and Homer's House would be shut down for good.

My days at Homer's House were gone anyway, it was the farthest thing from my mind. In fact, everything was far from my mind – my mind had stopped. All the senseless thoughts, bothers, minor inconveniences, bitterness towards family were all gone. Just like the time I sat alone in my mother's house with the broken leg after losing Kylee the first time – it was all gone.

This is the awakening process. Just shutting down all the senseless things that we make up in our heads and the only thing that remains is our true selves, our reality, and our spirit. Although it is typically done in deep concentration or meditation, I had it forced upon me once again. My mind was gone and everything had disappeared which gave me a moment of clarity. It is the most surreal feeling you can experience as you are completely aware of what is true and what is important. The trick is practicing meditation and learning how to do this on your own which comes in time. I was fortunate enough to have this thrust upon me for the second time in my life.

Now, I intentionally use the term "fortunate," in this scenario explaining again the power of changing the way we think about things and total surrender. Surrender has to do with finding your flow in life, going with it, and understanding that the obstacles are there for a reason.

Which is why I refer to these two darkest moments in my life as fortunate blessings; because without darkness one would not know light.

Just like in meditation, when you come out of these phases of complete mindlessness, you return with a new outlook and refreshed sense of what is truth. This time, this forced surrender, would last for ten days while awaiting a court hearing.

The Story of Tony

It was time to go see Kylee who had been staying with Tony, her grandfather. This man used to hate me and the feeling was reciprocal. I was a punk kid that lied to him and got his daughter pregnant. His anger and hatred was likely justified and I would have felt the same about myself if I were him. When I was awarded custody of Kylee, he was sure that I would never let them see her again. However, that was far from the truth.

Through this tragedy, they saw the real me and I was able to see the real Tony. And while I was in his home town, he was happy to let me come over every day for supervised visits. If I had never shown him truth and love, it would have never been given back.

As we sat there talking, I realized that it would have been very easy for me to take Kylee and never let them see her again. Some people actually advised me to do so. "She did it to you, you should do it back to her." But as Gandhi said, "An eye for an eye, makes the whole world blind."

This is the power of love. While my ego was tempting me to do so, I knew that it was in Kylee's best interest to be around her family. This opened the door to creating a relationship with Tony. During those ten days, I had called everyone and agreed to anything they wished. At this point, the only thing that mattered to me was Kylee. That is it, which was the only truth that existed.

Finally, after a ten day wait, the social workers asked the judge to return Kylee to me and his response was quite unforgettable. He lit them up, screamed at them for saying that one day a child is in danger and the next that she is perfectly fine. He remarked about how they had abused their authority. I thought, "Finally, someone with some common sense!"

It was clear that I could have had a law suit on my hands for this mistreatment, but I lack any type of follow through skills and quite frankly, I was emotionally drained. As much as I despised social workers, I didn't have any fighting in me and I had won. Now, I see that it is a systematic problem that gives social workers with no training this type of power, then overworks them, and turns people into numbers. When they have 30 people on their case load, they stop treating each person as a human but as it states, "a case."

One month later while in court, the judge at the hearing looks to Tony and said, "Tony, you have been to every single hearing since this case started. What do you have to say?"

You could have heard a pin drop in that court room. Time froze. My heart was trembling, palms sweating, as my entire life was in the hands of my former enemy. Everyone stood in silence.

With a shaky voice and tears coming down his cheek, Tony said,

"She should be with Cortland."

I think everyone in the courtroom was in shock. This man hated me and in that moment he had the power to determine the fate of Kylee. It would make sense to say she should be with his daughter, Adrianne, or with himself. And for him to tell the courtroom that his daughter should not be entitled to his only granddaughter is one of the most remarkable acts of selfless love that I have ever experienced.

Though this experience, we had grown fond of each other and he started to see that I truly loved Adrianne and I did my best to help her. We took off our masks and got to know each other and the fear was gone. The need to protect ourselves was gone.

Then in this moment of truth, Tony took off his mask for the entire courtroom to see his true self. With tears rolling down his face, this man showed it all for the world to see.

Later on in life, someone told me a story that Tony had once saved this judge from drowning in a nearby lake when they were children. In that moment, like this one, Tony had showed his true character by reaching out and saving the judge. Perhaps that is why the judge relied on Tony's judgment so heavily in this case. Because he had already seen Tony without a mask; so when to say everyone in the courtroom was shocked, it is likely not true, the judge knew the truth would come from the man who removes his mask to serve a greater purpose.

Case closed. I was awarded sole custody of Kylee that day.

The Prison within the Prison

A few months later, the FBI had arrested Adrianne and she was facing a 17-year prison sentence. The day that I went to pick up Kylee for the final custody hearing, I was met by the FBI and asked about the information that I had regarding Adrianne. I really only wanted Kylee but somehow got tied into the middle of this ordeal. Adrianne would come around fighting with me, I tried to help her many times, and it continued to haunt me.

The FBI set me up in a hotel and I was to invite Adrianne over. They set up a video in an alarm clock on the table and they were watching everything in the other room. She started talking about all her dealings and selling and I sat and listened knowing that everything was being recorded and this would likely land her in prison.

She told me about everyone who had bought from her including local doctors, lawyers, social workers, etc. Nobody was immune. She could not understand why she was the target of this investigation when everyone was involved and just as crooked. .

I had tried multiple times to get her into treatment and she adamantly refused. She was going to die or get killed at this point, and I wish I had the skills to help her. She didn't need to be locked up in prison, she needed treatment for her mental health, emotional, trauma, and addiction. This is how we treat drug users. We lock them up like criminals; don't offer any help or rehabilitation. Just lock them up in cages, then act surprised when it doesn't work.

All the while, major corporations are getting rich off the prison system. First, with the overcrowding of prisons the privatization of prisons came to rise in the 1980s. In any for-profit business, you find ways to maximize profits in ways such as getting cheap labor and cutting corners whenever possible. Furthermore, these prisons lobby to congress to enforce strict laws for non-violent drug offenses to ensure the beds stay full. Meanwhile, congressmen (the law makers) have stocks in these prisons and are profiting off the laws they sign into action.

In the notorious Kids for Cash Scandal, Two judges, President Judge Mark Ciavarella and Senior Judge Michael Conahan, were convicted of accepting money from Robert Mericle, builder of two private, for-profit youth centers for the detention of juveniles, in return for contracting with the facilities and imposing harsh adjudications on juveniles brought before their courts to increase the number of residents in the centers.[46] They received millions of dollars in payments to hand out sentences of convicting juveniles in prison, destroying lives, while they profit. And these are federal judges in which they are paid for by our tax dollars. Next time someone complains about their tax dollars helping out a single mother, perhaps they should look at to their tax dollars that support this kind of corruption that puts kids behind bars.

An increased prison population helps out more than just the prison industry, many other corporations have invested in prison labor. At least 37 states have legalized contracting of prison labor including corporations such as IBM, Motorola, Microsoft, AT&T, Dell, Honeywell, Target, and many more mount their operations inside of prisons.

This is also known as slavery.

In fact, this idea of convict leasing arose after the Civil War. The South was built by stealing Native American land and utilizing free slave labor to build America into one of the wealthiest nations on

---

[46] Urbina, Ian (March 27, 2009). *"Despite Red Flags, Judges Ran Kickback Scheme for Years." New York Times.* Retrieved 2009-05-02.

Earth. But after slavery was abolished and African-Americans were emancipated, the corporations needed cheap labor.

Freed slaves started getting charged with petty crimes and sentenced to many years in prison. Once in prison, they were leased to work picking cotton and building railroads – just slavery with a different name.

After the Drug War launched in 1971, the prison population has skyrocketed by locking up African-Americans at an alarming rate to work for free for corporations. We really have not changed, we just find new and creative ways to hide the atrocious human rights crimes better.

The elite make the rules, which make more money, by punishing the poor in this new form of slavery. This is not ancient history; they are still doing this today. Many Fortune 500 companies today have contracts with prisons for prison labor, reducing overhead costs of employing people. Meanwhile, the United States has the highest incarcerated population of any nation in the history of civilization – all in a land that proclaims itself "The Land of the Free."

The United States is home to just five-percent of the World's population, yet has 25-percent of the world's prison population. As these prisons become overcrowded, they needed to outsource to the private sector. Private prisons were then built by corporations which created contracts with federal and state governments. This means that the more prisoners in the jail cells, the more money the prison makes. To ensure this, the corporations sign contracts with governments to guarantee occupancy rates sometimes as high as 90 to 95 percent for more than twenty years.

Now that the government is obliged to pay for 95-percent occupancy, they are going to get their money's worth and lock up as many people for as long as possible. This has led to mass incarcerations for minor non-violent drug offenses and the mentally ill. All the while, these corporations have gone public meaning that anyone can purchase stock. It is a mass marketing scheme to profit the rich at the expense of the poor.

The Power of One

All of these ongoing issues with Adrianne were adding up, my life continues to be effected, I've lost Kylee multiple times and I couldn't keep hurting myself by trying to help others. It came down to me choosing between Kylee and Adrianne and it was a no-brainer. I still had all my own issues, I had done my best, and now I got in the middle of this situation and I wasn't going to risk losing Kylee again. They say nothing ever goes away until it teaches us what we need to know. Well, maybe this was my time of finally choosing a different path in life and detaching from a toxic situation.

Adrianne was sentenced to 25-years in prison. The guilt is still with me today over this entire situation. Part of the reason I am so passionate about the treatment of patients is because of Adrianne. If you saw her, you may only see a drug addict that gave up her child or a criminal. That is how she is viewed in the prison by staff and guards and it affects how we treat people.

Adrianne was a loving, caring, wonderful person who the world chewed up and turned her into a monster. Then calling her names, judging her, and kicking her while she is down, only further tortures her soul.

This is what happens in the mental health industry. We see the behaviors of people, have preconceived ideas, and judge them accordingly. We decide who is good and evil and only intensify the problem with how we treat patients.

It has to stop and it can. It starts with one person showing support and caring that can change a million lives. The butterfly effect starts with each one of us and with each moment of each day, we spark events that change millions of other events unknowingly.

A smile at a gas station may change the person's mood behind the counter, who changes the attitude of the people she treats each day, maybe one happens to be the CEO of a company who decides to respond to a charity request because his mood is lifted, donating money to kids in need. The kids prosper with the much needed gift and assistance and are able to make a living they never had and in turn, give back to others and build sustainable communities. This is how it works, one smile, one moment, all day.

As for Adrianne, she made it out of prison and they have asked her to speak about her story of hope and recovery. I asked her how she made it through her sentence and she told me that everyone was mean to her, roughed her up, didn't listen, and treated the inmates like animals.

"But the dentist," she said, "kept me going. He was good to me and treated me well."

She also talked about positive reinforcement such as getting little certificates each time she completed things and how that still sticks with her in all she does today. But it was one man, the dentist, gave her the ounce of hope she needed to not give up, but rather surrender.

He treated her like a human, like an equal, with the dignity and respect that we all deserve. He will never know the difference that he made, nor did he do it to make a difference, but he did it anyways.

That is what faith and character is all about. It is doing the right thing, even if you are the only one. And not doing so because you are seeking something in return, but because it is the right thing to do.

CHAPTER IX

Vulnerability Removes the Mask
The Student is Ready

Chapter 9
Vulnerability Removes the Mask:
The Student is Ready

Vulnerability is often associated with weakness. There is certainly negative connotation with the word. The English Dictionary even defines the word as 1) capable of susceptible to being wounded or hurt, as by a weapon; 2) open to moral attack, criticism, temptation, etc.; 3) open to assault, difficult to defend.

However, vulnerability is simply removing our mask and revealing our true selves. There could be nothing more powerful in the world such as holding the power, courage, and strength to be in a state of vulnerability.

The mask takes shape from the day we are born and constantly bombarded with message that build this masks we wear. As Kanye West once said,

> *"Society has put up so many boundaries, so many limitations on what's right and wrong that it's almost impossible to get a pure thought out. It's like a little kid, a little boy, looking at colors, and no one told him what colors are good, before somebody tells you, you shouldn't like pink because that's for girls, or you'd instantly become a gay two-year-old. Why would anyone pick blue over pink? Pink is obviously a better color. Everyone's born confident, and everything's taken away from you"*

Another example is in the way we raise men in this society, is that we teach them that it is only acceptable to have one emotion, anger. When an infant or toddler boy cries, we comfort them. Then one day, they come home from school crying and the switch gets turned off. Suddenly, it is no longer ok for boys to cry.

Imagine the confusion this must create in a child's mind. This is invalidation in its most pure definition. A boy is upset and is literally told that it is not OK to feel this way and that we must act differently. We are taught to mask our feelings from a young age.

The day we tell our children that it is no longer OK to cry is the day we put on their mask for the first time.

Then, to ensure they never experience the power of vulnerability, we actually validate the mask. We pride ourselves on being tough and associate toughness with not showing our true selves. That is the opposite of toughness, which is simply hiding from reality. And we have built an entire society on this model.

Tony took off his mask in that courtroom, revealed his true self in a state of undeniable vulnerability with tears running down his cheek, and told the judge that Kylee should live with me – instead of his daughter. That is insurmountable strength!

People flock to those who are open and reveal their true selves, or are more vulnerable. Vulnerability has to do with loving your entire self, the good and the bad, and unabashedly revealing it for the world to see.

Think back to a time that you were first falling in love with someone and the incredible euphoria that came along with it. You loved every single thing about the other person, including all of their flaws. This happens as they remove their mask to you. Someone takes a risk by revealing their true self to another and making themselves vulnerable. In turn, the second person does the same and they remember the heavenly joy that comes with being ourselves.

This is the beauty of children as they are in the most vulnerable form by enjoying everything about themselves, life, and all those around them. Then one day, someone judges them, insults them, or makes them feel bad about what they are doing. This, too, is the beginning of forming a mask. We then learn that we cannot be vulnerable at all times or we get hurt. Masks have always been used for protection. In ancient times, for physical protection in battle. Today, they are used for emotional protection from a different kind of battle we face daily.

The Weight of The Mask

The irony of all of this is that following my arrest, I had been "disqualified" from any direct contact with anyone labeled "vulnerable." In essence, my actions that led to my arrest were a result of pure vulnerability – which is synonymous with love. I threw away car keys to prevent someone in danger from picking up drugs that would have likely killed her.

But looking back at the wording, along with realizing the true meaning of vulnerability, perhaps they are right. This was a turning point in which I was not qualified to work with people who were vulnerable, because I still had a heavy mask on my face that I wasn't ready to remove.

I had masked my emotions my entire life. As a youngster it was by projecting anger to cover up anything real, then it was drugs and alcohol, and then the co-dependency and trying to save Adrianne.

Throughout it all, I have added on more shame and self-hatred which only exasperated the drinking. It is almost as if with each drink of booze, my false self grows a little stronger and the mask grows thicker.

Eventually, I had to fill out a stack of papers and information to get my disqualification reversed. Externally things started to progress as I was able to work again and landed a job at a massive company with numerous group homes in the area. I was given a company cell phone and pager, got to make my own hours, and would work as a consultant for these homes.

At the same time, I finally had Kylee living with me full-time with Adrianne out of our lives. She is now in second grade and doing well in school. I had my own house, a family dog, and appeared to have everything together.

My external presentation would never suggest the immense inner pain, struggle, and turmoil that I was experiencing. And that is the indubitable influence of the mask. The mask says, "look at me, I am fine." Even though, inside I am dying and begging for help, I would never ask in a million years because to ask for help is considered a weakness. Although it is one of the greatest strengths one can possess, the ability to know that you cannot do it alone and reach out for help is a slaying of the ego and a connection to the true self.

In making my own hours, I was basically free all day long. I was paid to do whatever I chose. It was the perfect storm for an evolving addict, who was now using substances to block any feeling or emotion. My drinking was a nightly occurrence and with nothing to do all day, it soon became an all-day event. I rarely went to work and was getting paid to sit at home and get drunk.

My old friend, Jim (the one from the Introduction to this book), moved nearby and we spent a lot of time together. Jim came from the St. Paul crowd that I used to party with in my adolescent days. We had always been very similar and shared a unique connection. Thinking back to when we hung out together at the old House, he revealed his true self to me. Perhaps that is why we were always so close, we both put up these tough-guy facades to the world and knew that deep down we both had these huge hearts that wanted to express love.

Jim was a lost soul and his love typically came out misdirected as hate or arrogance. But when we hung out with each other, we were able to be vulnerable, and be our true selves. He started coming around since he lived nearby and we shared Oxycontin, Vicodin, and drank away all emotional pain that tried to creep into my consciousness.

I used to tell people that I was "living the dream," or that I had found my "dream job." This was based solely on the fact that I was getting paid to get drunk and high all day. This was my dream at the time. I could drown my emotions every day without having to worry about getting paid. And I do think there is some truth to this being a dream state of my life. Because in order to dream, one must be sleeping and one could never fully awaken without periods of sleep.

Behind the scenes, it was not quite as glamorous. I was trying to raise Kylee to the best of my ability, but my ability was severely reduced due to my ever-expanding addiction.

You see, humans have progressed and evolved based on their ability to set goals, achieve them which allows growth, set higher goals and continue to advance. This is done by altering our behaviors, such as working harder, trying new things, developing skills, and gaining insight. We evolve by changing our behavior to match our goals.

With addiction, this formula is inverted. We start to change our goals to match our behavior. I was a perfect example of how this works. My goal of opening a group home started to vanish as I became quite satisfied with my life situation. The goal started to change to making it to work on time, which eventually digressed to just show up enough to keep your job, and eventually to make it through the day. All of this happens so subtly that you do not even realize it is happening around you.

It is like if you put a frog in a hot frying pan, it senses the heat and immediately jumps out due to the imminent threat of danger. However, if you put a frog in a frying pan at room temperature and then heat it up, the frog stays in the pan as it cannot notice the gradual change in heat and will eventually die when all it had to do was jump out of the pan. That is how any addiction progresses and seems so simple to get out of, but we are unable to notice the changes in our environment that seem quite obvious to others.

Kylee would come home from school to a very inconsistent father. If I was drinking, I would play with her and spend time with her, but if I was not drinking I usually sent her off to play with her friends. When it came time to do homework, I was either too intoxicated or hungover from the night before to help her though.

I am so sorry Kylee. I tried my best, but I really fucked up.

I still carry around a lot of guilt about this and have not fully recovered. I intentionally use the word "guilt," because for most of my life I had substituted that with the word, "shame." There is a significant difference between guilt and shame, and I had been carrying around the latter the majority of my life.

Guilt refers to behavior, whereas shame refers to self. Guilt states that "I did something bad," whereas shame states, "I am bad." As you can see, shame can be far more detrimental to one's psychological functioning.

As Brene Brown puts it,

> *"Shame is highly, highly correlated with addiction, depression, violence, aggression, bullying, suicide,*

> *eating disorders….Here's what you even need to know more: Guilt is inversely correlated with those things. The ability to hold something we've done, or failed to do, up against who we want to be is incredibly adaptive. It's uncomfortable, but it's adaptive."*

It's no surprise that shame is highly correlated with addiction. It is another emotion to bury in the bottle of alcohol. I've already had it engrained in my head that I am a bad person, now the behaviors are starting to match which was a recipe for a shame-based depression and addiction.

Fortunately, Kylee does hold the superhero gene. It is the same one that my mother and brother possess. It is the gene that allows the person to return love for hate, naturally. The one that can see the beauty in the most diabolical environments, the good in the most putrid evil. The one that when you tell them there is a light at the end of the tunnel, they tell you that there is no tunnel.

She is an amazing person and she always will be. She is living proof that the Lord will never give you more than you cannot handle, because for all she has been through in her life to come out as such a kind, loving soul, is nothing short of a miracle.

There were mornings when she would wake up hungry and I would just give her a few dollars to go to the bakery for some donuts. This is when I started to organize my life around drinking. Alcohol had become a higher priority in my life, which is the typical pattern of addiction. The substance hijacks our brains and our neural reward pathways until it replaces our values and priorities.

While I did recognize this was happening, and each morning I swore I was done, but this is shows the incredible power of addiction. I saw the chaos surrounding me and I tried to stop drinking. I probably dumped all the alcohol out of my house so many times that my kitchen sink got alcohol poisoning. Twenty-four days was the longest I had ever made it without any alcohol, I could never fully abstain from using.

The mind starts to play tricks on you when you try to quit drinking. It tells you, "see I've been sober for 24 days, I don't have a problem. I can quit anytime." Or you begin to compare yourself to others and say, "at least I am not doing heroin." And of course, we justify it by saying, "at least I still have my job, my house, my daughter, so I don't have a problem. In fact, I deserve a beer for all this hard work."

And that is all it takes. We convince ourselves that there is plenty of reason why we should be drinking.

My entire life, I had always had something to mask my true self. We all do, we are raised this way. As a society, we find it so difficult to be alone in our own thoughts and with our self. We live in a distraction society. Most people cannot go a full hour without checking their phones, emails, social media, etc. All this behavior is preventing us from getting in touch with our true nature and purpose.

If we take time to be alone with our self, we could learn to love every aspect of our self and be comfortable to share this with the world. Then we would no longer need a psychological mask in public, display our self in full vulnerability, and allow the world to share our love.

Now, I have free time, money, and quick access to alcohol. My tolerance has increased not just with how much alcohol it takes to get a buzz, but more specifically, it takes more alcohol to drown more emotional pain. I need to drink more to drown more emotions. Not just childhood pain, but the shame I felt from dealing with Adrianne and how I had been raising my daughter.

Living Funerals

Amidst my daily routine of drinking myself into oblivion, I received a sobering phone call one afternoon from Jim.

"Big Al is dead," Jim said with tears in his voice," He's dead. He's gone. He was in a boat accident."

Big Al was a mutual friend of ours. He lived nearby and we used to play football with him on the weekends. He was a good man, kind to everyone, loved to laugh and genuinely enjoyed life. It just didn't seem fair. How could this happen?

Grief after losing a loved one is one of the most complex things to understand. We are dealt with a web of emotions and reactions. It creates changes physically, emotionally, spiritually, and socially in our lives. Everybody grieves differently and there is no timetable as to when someone can "recover" from the loss of a loved one.

It is a surreal feeling and the memories remain vivid forever. Emotionally charged events are always more remembered. It is not so much the significance of the event, but it is the intensity of the emotions.

At this time in my life, my emotions were regularly at the bottom of a bottle, and for them to be charged this high explains the intensity of the emotions I felt when hearing the news.

The funeral was the same type of feeling, but with all of us together in collective silence. No one said a word, everyone was still in shock and our worlds had just suddenly stopped. There was nothing to be said among all his closest friends, it was just a surreal moment in which all of our lives were forever changed.

A few months later, we all got together at the bar to celebrate his life. A typical western tradition of mourning, where we get together and celebrate life by sharing all the things we loved about the person after they have deceased.

As everyone took their turns shouting out their favorite Big Al Story, I had one of those significant moments where something just suddenly makes sense. Someone turned a light on inside my head and it all come together for some reason.

"Why don't we talk about people like this while they are still alive?" I asked the group. And everyone nodded their heads in agreement.

His death helped me awaken. I could see, hear, and sense how deeply people cared about this young man and the energy was so real that night. Everyone had removed their mask, allowed themselves to be vulnerable, and the love energy was rampant in that tiny bar that night.

It makes me think we should have things called "Living Funerals" in which we get together and share these stories while the person is alive. Take off our masks, tell each other how much we love them, and maybe it would build greater connection, peace, and harmony.

I wondered if anyone had ever said these things to Big Al while he was alive? This was a transforming moment in my life. I thought that from this point forward, I am telling people what I think is great about them while they are alive. I am going to present to everyone their living funeral celebration. Why wait until someone is no longer alive, to share how we feel about them? This is the danger of psychological masks, we are so afraid to tell people how we feel that the only time we can truly share our deepest love for them is when we know they will never hear it.

> *"True love is unconquerable and irresistible, and it will go on gathering power and spreading itself until it transforms everyone it touches."* – Meher Baba

I first learned about this from Jerry about being kind to others and not being angry all the time. Then I felt the truth through those heart-wrenching blows from losing Kylee. It was learning from Tony the loving energy that comes from forgiveness and surrender. Now, the death of Big Al and the truth about vulnerability was starting to make sense to me. I started to recognize how we truly feel about others and how we hide it.

It is as though every time something destructive was happening around me, it became a moment of transformation. This is why pain is not really pain, it is a lesson waiting to be learned.

This is always much easier to see in hindsight. While going through emotional pain, it is very difficult to consciously see the situation as it is and look for a lesson to be learned. While I was working at this large company, it was a pretty disheartening time for me and I was ready to give up.

Who are the Sick Ones?

Nobody cared about the patients, including my boss. What kind of boss would allow me to never show up and still continue to pay me without ever questioning anything? I once went to Arizona for two weeks, faxed in my timecard from Tucson, and was still paid for my 80-hours of "work."

I never went to any of the houses, I sat at home and drank, while watching NYPD Blue re-runs all day long and trying to take care of Kylee when I could fit it in with my drinking schedule.

Kylee was doing much better than before, but in comparison to her previous life, anything would have been an improvement. I started to make promises to her when I was drunk that I could not keep, I unintentionally invalidated her, because I needed to drink. Her needs always came second. I taught her about life, but it was consistently inconsistent. I did the best I could with what I knew at the time, I was passing on generational pain.

Everyone at this company was doing the same, passing on generational pain to the patients we were paid to provide care. One staff member, Bianca, used to antagonize clients to the point of chaos only so she could sweep in to rescue them and be the savior. Who are the mentally ill ones here?

It was disgusting, just one big scam. They purchased these big houses, took the money, and did the minimum to provide anything that resembled "care." Our trainings took a handful of minutes and were only done to meet state regulations to ensure the gravy train kept rolling to fill the owner's bank account. Medications were never monitored, leaving staff to just take them home to get high off patient's medications.

There was a mother-daughter group that ran some of the houses that became foster parents. Now, by becoming foster parents, I mean they would bring in more developmentally disabled people at their home after work. They ship them off during the day, put them to bed, and collect an extra thousand dollars every month from the county. They were awful to these patients, then went home and brought in more just to accumulate more income for services they were not providing. It was basically fraud and a complete scam of the system.

Who are the sick ones here?

Greed is always going to exist as long as we continue to glamorize it in our culture. This mother-daughter group were sick with a diagnosis of greed. It is no different than any other behavior addiction, they were attempting to fill their emptiness void with money and possessions believing it will bring happiness.

And it does, temporarily. Anything from the external can only bring pleasure, it cannot bring joy. Pleasure is temporary and will eventually fade, whereas joy is everlasting, pure, and comes from within.

I was no different in trying to fill my void with alcohol. By reaching, grasping, and clinging to anything external we start to hurt others in our efforts to end our own pain.

Hurt people are the ones that hurt people. Directly or indirectly, consciously or subconsciously, it is when we are hurt that we crave external pleasures which always result in hurting others.

At the time, I didn't understand any of this. I only saw things as they were, without understanding the hidden message, meaning, and life lessons. All my hopes of saving the world were dead. This is the world of psych. This is life as we know it. It is all just one phony place where we put on our masks and pretend to be something we are not. And I am just a small part of this dysfunctional existence.

The Story of Wanda

Just as I reached to throw in the towel for good on the sick industry that abuses the sick, I had some things happen to keep me breathing. This is a recurring theme in my life, people come along at times of need. If I was ready, they would appear.

"When the student is ready, the teacher appears."

Every now and then, the higher-ups at this company liked to play this game of rotating the houses in which we monitored. There was no reason for doing so, other than create an illusion of change. They put a new set of houses on my rotation, which meant I should probably check-in and introduce myself as the new consultant.

In one of the homes, is where I meet Wanda. She is smarter than any of the executives at this company and understands the bigger picture. She has denied numerous promotional offers which defied logic in such a low-paying industry.

She was the first person I ever encountered in a truly awakened state of being. It was never about money, fancy titles, or any self-promotion. She was content just running her house with her staff and the six residents. They gave her the toughest clients and she got them to do more than anybody else.

This was all done by creating a different type of culture. She cared for the patients and made sure her staff did the same. Those patients had great lives because of her, she is the one that made it all happen. You won't read about her in the paper, doesn't have a lot of money, or fancy cars, but she made the lives of those around her better – and that is the kind of "richness" our society ought to value.

My teacher had appeared. Sometime the best form of teaching is by just doing the right thing and knowing that others are observing and modeling that behavior. She never used violence, threats, or punishment. But rather inspired through kindness, love, and compassion to empower these patients to see the beauty they already possessed.

> *"Power is of two kinds. One is obtained by the fear of punishment and the other by acts of love. Power based on love is a thousand times more effective and permanent than the one derived from fear of punishment."* -- Ghandi

Like Wanda, Ghandi lacked rank, office, title, or wealth and his life exemplified what he preached: love, compassion, justice, equality and non-violence.

Although Wanda may not have been freeing the Indian people from British Colonialism, her story is similar as her methods helped free those under the oppressive regime of the mental health industry. It was Wanda who granted their freedom of the three unalienable human rights of life, liberty, and the pursuit of happiness.

She bore no mask, nor did she know of one. Some would say that she was making herself "vulnerable" and subject to being taken advantage of from others. Others would say she was making herself vulnerable, which opened the door to sharing love and granting freedom to those she served.

Section III
THE BOOK OF OBSTACLE

Chapter X:	The Phantom of Society	211
Chapter XI:	The Ego Has Landed	235
Chapter XII:	Down the Rabbit Hole	261
Chapter XIII:	Soul Contracts	283
Chapter XIV:	It's All Synchronicity	297
Chapter XV:	The Dark Night of the Soul	315

CHAPTER X

The Phantom of Society
A Villain's Perspective

Chapter 10
The Phantom of Society: A Villain's Perspective

Enlightenment is a process. It is quite rare for one to have the Hollywood-esque spiritual awakening overnight. Also, enlightenment is a state of being rather than reaching a particular destination. In reaching our natural state of being, it means discarding all the untruths we have been led to believe since the time of our birth.

Like peeling an onion, it refers to removing layers upon layers before reaching our core. Similarly, in peeling away each layer it can bring tears to our eyes as we work to find the truth about our core.

In listening to countless first-hand testimonies of Near Death Experiences (NDE), nearly 100-percent share a similar experience. They will explain this indescribable loving energy that surrounds them, they lose all sense of time, and there is no language or words to be spoken. They communicate telepathically and have a full understanding of everyone in an instant. About eighty-percent of those who experience a NDE share that their lives are forever altered, and claim a psychological change that highly resembles that of an enlightened soul.

For years, non-believers have downplayed this as hallucinations, but these experiences are beyond what science can prove. I've heard some cases of a child witnessing a phone call that his father made in another state. Or one of a man that had damage to the parts of his brain that are responsible for visualization, making it impossible for it to be a hallucination, yet he shared the same experiences.

The after-effects of the person typically include a newfound unconditional love for everyone with detachment from societal standards. They tend to be less religious, more spiritual, and more easily engaged in philosophical thinking. They carry a more child-like joy and an increased sense of wonder. They become more charitable, mindful, and hold a greater natural ability to flow in the present moment. All of life's little paradoxes and puzzles seem to make sense and the person has increased awareness, intuition, and psychic ability.

These heightened senses are the same as the enlightened person. I intentionally use the word "heighten," because these are all things that each one of us already possesses deep inside, but they only can grow once we break away the false self or ego.

Each time part of our old self dies, we get glimpses of this enlightened state as well. For me, it seemed to happen each time I hit rock bottom that part of my false self-died a little bit and I caught glimpses of this feeling. The problem was that I thought I had the answers and I started looking for shortcuts, not realizing that enlightenment is an enduring process.

It is the difficult parts in life that create food for our soul. This is the time that we are forced to break away our false self, which in turn, allows our true nature to take control.

Ego Trap: Confusing the Ego for Soul

I like to think of my time working at this company, as the deep REM cycle of my sleep prior to being awakened. As my pain and frustration grew to the point of breaking, I was given a chance to meet Wanda and she showed me that it doesn't have to be this way. She showed me how one person could make a difference. This is one of those little synchronicities of the universe that help us understand reality and open our minds to a sense of purpose.

There was this nursing line that we had to call to check messages and I started to hear a silent, confident, and lovely voice on the line. Her name was Jill. I had never seen her, but every time I heard her voice, I felt as though it was someone talking directly to me. As I look back at this moment, I realize it was actually my ego looking for the next thing to fill the inner void.

Wanda allowed me to re-open my mind and in doing so, it allowed me to listen to my spiritual instinct. I already knew, well before I ever met Jill, that she was going to be a part of my life. I knew this deep in my intuition, a part of us that we usually deny, but it grows stronger the more we learn to use and trust our sixth sense. We were not soul mates, but we had a soul contract. Our souls had been brought together to teach each other valuable lessons.

The popular belief is that we are human bodies that possess a soul, but the truth is that we are souls that have a temporary body. All animals rely primarily on instinct and telepathic communication.

Humans did too, until they started to evolve into "civilized" beings in which written and spoken language took away the need to further develop instinct. It is still there, but it takes time to build it up again. Just like any muscle that goes unused, it will never strengthen until we put it to the test. Intuition is one of the spiritual muscles that we kept stored away and deny its existence because it is something that science has not yet been able to explain.

Hindsight is always 20/20 vision; and looking back at this moment it is easy to see the train wreck that was about to ensue with this connection. However, we had a soul contract and this had to be carried out. It has all the making of the perfect storm; the raging alcoholic and the classic co-dependent fairy tale romance.

At the time, I had started hanging out with Bianca. Yep, the same Bianca that I trashed in the previous chapter. But, Bianca was a drunk, too. And us drunks always seem to find each other. As we are sitting around drowning our sorrows together, she tells me about a new worker, Jill. She tells me that everyone is going out and Jill will be meeting up with us and I happily go along.

Jill walks in and in. She has long, dark hair and is wearing a black and pink silk shirt covered with a green sweatshirt.

It felt right, which is a trap of the ego. How can it possibly be love when we are both out trying to make our best first impression? First impressions are typically our greatest mask we wear, we put on display a persona that we think the world wants to see. It is the furthest thing from our true selves. Then, it was our masks, who thought they were supposed to be together.

Love is the most powerful force in the universe. It is the only thing in the world that is true. This is why so much of our literature, movies, and music revolve around love. When we feel it, we know. Everything just clicks and makes sense.

Time stands still, we slip off our masks, and start living as opposed to merely existing. Books, movies, plays, and songs try to recreate this feeling and it has the ability to spark this same emotion in us in which we all so greatly crave, because after all this is our true self.

Here comes the ego trap.

Lust is not love. It feels like love, looks like love, acts like love, but it is far from pure. Lust obliterates common sense and intuition in the most sensible people. It becomes an altered state of consciousness in which MRI scans have proved that the same areas light up when a person is experiencing lust as when an addict gets a fix of cocaine.

Just as in the mind of an addict, the inner voice can be screaming "danger" but it is too late because the ego is in charge and convincing you this lust is actually love.

Co-Dependency

The definition of insanity is doing the same thing over and over and expecting a different result. Here, I was again in my search for wholeness craving something externally to fill that inner void.

I had originally felt as though I met another part of myself. I could be myself around her, my true self, and she was the first person who didn't want to see my mask, but the person behind it. Yet, unknowingly at the time, this was actually the beginning stages of her addiction – her co-dependency.

Co-dependency goes along the exact same stages of any addiction. The drug of choice is the relationship. The addiction comes out of good intentions, but can become compulsive and destructive. The co-dependent person gets involved in a relationship with an addict and it feels good to provide care for them and help them out.

Which seems harmless, right? On the surface, it is just as harmless as the addict who has a couple beers after work to help relax after a stressful day.

The problem is that they both feel good, which is highly reinforcing. It actually works on the same neurological pathways in the brain which focuses on pleasure and reward. Suddenly, fixing up the person makes the co-dependent feel alive. It brings them to life and they soon start to become compulsive in their own behaviors of fixing up and helping. The same way the addict starts drinking more often and compulsively to help themselves come alive.

The first time my brother met Jill, we were at a bar and I showed him my new shoes that Jill picked out for me. He gave me a look as to say "who the fuck are you?" I was wearing some $100 Kenneth Cole shoes. My entire life I had always worn tennis shoes until the soles literally were ripped away and then I would buy another hand-me-down pair. But Jill noticed this and was able to step in and clean me up a little bit, so I would be more acceptable to society.

Soon, the co-dependent starts having a sense of over-responsibility to manage for the family. Within months, she moves in with Kylee and me. I stroked her ego by calling her the "Lion Tamer" by her willingness to walk into the lion's dean and be a part of the chaos in our little home without blinking an eye. However, the additional chaos only enabled her addiction of co-dependency. More chaos, meant more fixing which meant a greater high.

Just like the addict, her tolerance was starting to increase and she needed a greater fix.

I think my family sensed it right away. They knew my previous relationships were with free spirits and wounded souls like Adrianne and Nicole. Then, when they met Jill something was off. She was trying to turn me into a civilized person who ate with a fork and knife, used proper dinner etiquette, and they knew she was putting a mask on me.

But, as our addiction for one another grew, it was easy to push this off. She was filling my inner void and providing for a motherly figure that Kylee never had. We felt we had this connection of oneness, but looking back it was all an illusion. It was like putting batteries in a flashlight by using something externally to connect and together have the ability to shine light through the darkness.

My life was filled with all the pleasures I could imagine. But, just as I had done before, I was mistaken pleasure for joy. Because joy comes from within and nothing external can ever bring us joy.

Self-Destruct Button

Nonetheless, the external pleasures brought happiness and a sense of peace. Temporary or not, there was happiness in my life – but that was the problem.

I have the tendency to hit a self-destruct button whenever things start going well. This has to do with my ongoing shame. When we believe we are bad people, we feel that we do not deserve happiness or good fortune. This leads to a subconscious effort to sabotage and destroy everything we had been seeking consciously.

Perhaps this is the reason that I have always carried such strong resentment towards people who possess traits of greed. They work on opposite ends of the spectrum. With greed, people try to fill their emptiness by accumulating as much as possible and wish to be the center of attention. In self-destructive individuals, we tend to give everything away and tend to want to stay out of the spotlight because we are highly aware of our deficiencies and fear being exposed. When fortunes do come our way, the tendency is to spend recklessly because the message of our subconscious mind still tells us we are not deserving.

A drunken fight that instigated a riot, along with spitting in a police officer's face, put me behind bars once again. The self-destruct button was pressed once again at the time when things finally appeared to be looking up.

This was my second assault charge within a year and I was looking at a minimum of six months in jail. Had I been black or poor, there is no doubt I would have spent that time in jail. But, my mother gave me $7,000, bailing me out of another ugly situation. As I sat watching my lawyer delay the case over-and-over, eventually the charges were dropped.

I actually felt like a cheat. I looked at all these black kids in line, most of them younger than me, that had far less crimes and were sentenced to far more time. The difference is they did not have money. People like my friend Jim would go to jail for up to four months at a time because he didn't have a security blanket to bail him out. It was quite embarrassing, I got out because I had money, because I was born into a better situation. Why should money be the deterring factor as to who serves time? I could only imagine what was going through the minds of the other inmates as they saw that I was pardoned because I had money.

The next six months of my life might as well been a sentence for the pain, humiliation, and despair I was about to endure.

There were also new rules created by human services, which led to be being disqualified again and could not have direct contact because of the two charges. I would not be allowed to work anywhere that does background checks, so I take a job at a dermatology clinic in the wealthiest suburban area of the Twin Cities.

To this day, the doctors at this clinic were some of the worst individuals I have met in my life. They abused their power and authority and turned it into a sick game. Reprimanded, ridiculed, and belittled if papers were in the wrong spot, if there wasn't enough paper, or if their clothes were not put together for them. The patients were just as bad coming in with a sense of entitlement just because they had money.

Here was an epiphany. Just months before, I was the one with the money that was being released from jail and now I am on the other end of the spectrum watching the wealthy indulge in unnecessary operations to chase external pleasures to fill their internal pain. Self-destructive people allow themselves to be used because it fulfills the self-image of deserving the abuse. With greed, people look at each situation and ask "What is in it for me?" They are more self-driven, which leads them to exploit others without thinking about it because they are attempting to accumulate more for themselves.

I could not be more of an outsider in this place, I would have fit in much better in a jail cell. I try to remember this experience and keep it fresh in my head to ensure that if I ever become a person in power that I never treat another human in this manner. I was literally becoming physically sick due to my discontent at this place and felt I was losing my mind.

In Randy Pausch's *"Last Lecture,"* he makes the reference to brick walls coming up when we are working towards goals and dreams. He states that brick walls are not there to keep us out, they are there to remind us how bad we want something – and to keep others out. While working at this dermatology clinic, this was a brick wall that made me miss psychiatry. It made me realize how bad I wanted to make a difference and I was motivated to change.

The final straw was seeing Dr. Madook's picture on the cover of some magazine and it made me nauseous reading about these high praises for this man who treated his co-workers as less-than-human. It was all about the money, it was the greed, chasing after possessions and exploiting anyone that may get in his way.

Everything in life is a lie. It is all backwards. I had been right ever since I was a child. I always knew there was something more to life than what it appears. My time spent at this clinic was an exaggerated view of the phoniness of the world, but a microcosm nonetheless.

The Co-Dependent Fairy Tale

While I was down, it felt great to look up and have Jill at my side. It also felt great for her to have someone who was down to be able to pick up. These self-destruct moments of the addict can create the greatest high for the co-dependent.

Again, with good intentions the co-dependent gets a high off caring for the person who is struggling. They start to enable the addict to continue to use and make poor decisions despite ongoing consequences because they feel it is helping them by providing care – but internally it actually feels really good. The co-dependent and addict need one another.

After the self-destruct button is hit, then the co-dependent rushes in with her cape to do all the work and everyone rallies around and says "that poor co-dependent." Plus, the co-dependent person typically has the extreme need for approval and acceptance and become quite hurt when their workload is not appreciated. But when it is noticed, it feels good and suddenly they have purpose.

One-hundred percent of the time, this is the same story. Then the deeper the addict goes into the addiction to the drug, the deeper the need to change/fix and the greater appreciation and admiration that is being received from others

Then the addict gets better, starts to help out in areas and make up for time lost. This creates turmoil, because now what is codependents role? What is her purpose? How does she come alive? She has no need to be controlling and dominating, because the addict is picking up his share and suddenly, she is back to where she was before looking for approval and it is gone. So she slowly starts to agree that it wasn't that big of a problem to encourage the addict to use again - because those were the good times.

Just like an addict will use to relieve anxiety or depression; a codependent fixes people as a means to fill the need for approval. Then the addict gets sober, they need to learn with anxiety in a healthy way; a codependent needs to find a healthy way for purpose and approval.

One of three things can happen after the addict recovers:

A) The codependent works on their issues and also gets healthier in relationships - such as less-controlling, better boundaries, develop trust, healthy ways of managing self-esteem, no longer responsible for what happens to others;

B) The codependent doesn't change, problems continue in the relationship, there is turmoil, and the addict relapses. But then, everything goes back to "normal." The codependent gets there drug of "fixing and caring" for the destructive person and the addict gets there drug back. It is an unhealthy cycle;

C) They get divorced and then codependent finds another addict; and addict finds another codependent. This cycle continues until they change.

This does not make one party wrong and the other right. It is a combination of both parties trying to find a way to find wholeness. The co-dependent does so in compulsive/destructive ways to find approval.

Jill's parents were extremely controlling with alcoholism running rampant through the family bloodline. They wanted, or demanded, her to always be clean, perfect, and perform otherwise she would not be accepted. Her feelings did not matter, nor were they relevant. She did well in school, work, and life because that is what was preached in her household. The message was that she did not matter, but the image that you portray is of utmost importance.

This is likely all her parents knew and just handed down the same teachings generation-by-generation. As children we do not have anything to make a comparison with, so the home environment we grow up with is the only one we know. In dysfunctional homes, it becomes a cycle of abuse until someone can finally step outside the chaos and do things differently.

I saw a cartoon that accurately depicts this cycle by showing the husband yelling at his wife, and in turn she is yelling at the child, and in turn he is taking a hammer to his teddy bear. This is just within the one family, then it tricks down to the next generation as well. Hurt people are the ones that hurt people.

This is where Jill and I are the same. We both knew that something wasn't right and wanted to step outside of everything we had been taught and choose for our self. I did so by screaming, yelling, gambling, drugs, and alcohol. Jill did this by leaving her home in small-town in the Midwest to live in California. She went against the grain of her family experience and expectations. She moved back after witnessing an accident that took one of her friends and she had saved the other by performing CPR. She was always looking for more. This we had in common.

We were walking into a perfect storm. Jill, the co-dependent; I was the raging alcoholic; and a 10-year-old girl that was about to be a teenager. To top it off, Adrianne was going to be released from prison early. She had originally been sentenced to 25 years, but serving good time, and turning in the kingpin she was scheduled to be released when Kylee was around 14 or 15.

Fights started emerging quickly between Jill and Kylee, always leaving me in the middle as the judge. Kylee wanted Jill to leave which arose from a fear of abandonment from women. She was not used to all the rules that Jill brought into the home.

As Jill took over all the homemaker duties, this allowed my drinking to progress. As chaotic as it was, we all served a certain function and we knew what to expect. Jill had seen me without my mask and I had seen her without hers. Jill wore a couple masks and they are so engrained that it takes a lot for the true self to come through. Her first mask is the one that she wears for society, the one that is so engrained in her head from her upbringing that your image you portray is more important than who is underneath. The confusion this must have caused created a secondary mask – one of anger, rage, and control.

Jill's false self was a perfectionist due to what she had been trained to believe her entire life. She walked into a perfect situation, a home filled with chaos, no rules, disorder, and dysfunction. This worked perfectly to fill my self-fulfilling prophecy of not being good enough and I was allowed to start acting the part.

Kylee saw far too much of this. We truly did love her and when things were good they were great, but everything was progressively getting worse. As I wrote these words, I heard Kylee say, "I think things are important like you guys did; like big houses, grades, not about scratching pans."

I wish I could have been better for her, now she thinks that money is what is important. She is an amazing person with a beautiful soul and just tries so hard to please people. That is where I know that she will find the path again someday, it is in her blood. With greed, people seek things to fill a void and will never be satisfied. But Kylee, only wants to make others happy.

Having to let go of Kylee and hope to be around when she is ready has been the hardest thing my entire life. Everyone used to always tell me what a great relationship I had with her while she was growing up, but no one says that anymore. It started to vanish the more I refused to let go.

There is a story of the Boy and the Butterfly. One day a boy came across a caterpillar in a cocoon. He noticed a small hole in one end of the cocoon and he saw the butterfly struggling to get out. The boy became concerned and wondered if the butterfly would ever make it out. So, the boy decided to help. He snipped the edge to make the hole bigger so the butterfly could quickly emerge. But as the butterfly came out, to his surprise, it had a swollen body and shriveled wings. He waited for the wings to expand and the butterfly to gain strength and fly. But it never happened. The butterfly spent its entire life crawling around with a swollen body and shriveled wings.

The butterfly was supposed to struggle to get out of the cocoon because that pushes the fluid out of its body and through its wings. Without the struggle, it can never fly. Struggling is a part of any growth.

Like the story of the Boy and the Butterfly, I was watching her too closely and wanted to hurry up the process and her path to enlightenment. It doesn't work that way, we need to learn from our own experiences. Pain and destruction may ensue, but if I am kind, accepting, and loving then she will return to me when the pain sets in – and that is when we awaken.

But if I do not have a relationship with Kylee when she goes through her trials, tribulations, and pain – then she will not let me in when her transformation takes place.

> *"I cannot tell if what the world considers 'happiness' is happiness or not. All I know is that when I consider the way they go about attaining it, I see them carried away headlong, grim and obsessed, in the general onrush of the Human Herd, unable to stop themselves or to change their direction. All the while they claim to be just on the point of attaining happiness." – Chuang Tzu*

The Phantom of Society

In June of 2014, I created a website, which all stems from the notion of removing our psychological masks. This book is my time to lead by example and remove my mask.

This information has never been shared before publicly or privately; hence, I have been wearing a mask for protection. I preach about inner peace, tranquility, and serenity is the direct result of "taking the mask off," so that is what I am going to do in the remainder of this chapter.

Eventually, I cheated on my wife Jill.

There you go, I said it. That is all the information you need to make a decision about my character and place me in the category of "good" or "bad." It really is that black and white. I am the bad guy and she is the victim. This is how our society works; we create a villain, and then demonize him/her, which allows for justifying complete blame.

This starts from the time we are children: Batman is the "good guy" and the Joker is the "bad guy." We categorize everything and everyone into two black-and-white categories of "good" vs. "bad." While this is entertaining in movies, television shows, and stories, it is highly detrimental when we place all of life into absolute categories.

In elementary school when they try to teach us about American history and we seem to skip over essential parts of modern history such as the Korean War and Vietnam War. When asked about it, we like to describe it as the communists are "bad" and we are "good." We had to invade others homeland to stop evil from spreading in the Pacific. If you tell any story from the perspective of the villain, you will almost certainly understand the reason behind the actions.

So, let me go along with this mask that society has placed on me as the villain in this scenario. This alleviates blame off of everyone else which makes the mask so appealing for everyone else.

As I remove this mask, let me start by apologizing to everyone that I have let down by my horrendous actions:

First off, I need to apologize to my now ex-wife for the pain that I have caused. On the day that I confessed the truth, she was so devastated that it put her body into shock. The mental anguish created physical Debilitation to the point she was hospitalized and had intent to end her own life. She did not deserve that kind of pain, nobody does. She grew up always doing the right thing, went to school, got good grades, on the honor roll, graduated from college, and then helped me raise my daughter. We started our own family and everything in her life was going as planned, as it should when you always do the right thing. She had always been in control of her emotions, but hearing these words literally took the life out of her as she could not breathe, talk, or walk because the emotional pain was overwhelming.

This turned her mad, angry, and untrusting of the world. I am responsible for this and I am sorry. I will never forgive myself and I am sorry for the tremendous pain that I have caused.

Then to my children, who now will have to live separate lives. Their entire world is now shook up as they will have to adjust to living in different homes, with different rules, and making difficult decisions.

Children do not deserve this type of cruelty. They will have to hear about how their father destroyed the once-happy family from their mother and vice versa from their father, creating dissention and confusion. I did this and I am responsible for this pain. To even think about how lives have been changed hurts me so deep that it brings about physical pain in which I can never fully recover.

To her family that took me in, accepted me, befriended me, and tried their best to include me – I am sorry for letting you down. They saw me as different and I did not fit into their culture, yet they accepted me as one of their own as a part of the family. Then, I broke their daughter's heart and left her devastated. They needed to stop their lives to pick her back up, get her on her feet, and begin her new life. As I watched this play out like a scene from a movie that is too difficult to watch that you need to look away, but I couldn't look away. Because I created it and I had to watch it play out with remorse, shame, and regret.

Then there is my family. After years of failures, letting them down, and hurting them, I finally had stability in my life. I had struggled my entire life to rebuild this trust with my own family, only for them to watch it all implode once again. They had to watch this horror scene unfold and couldn't believe that they had been so foolish to trust me with their hearts, knowing that this is how it would always end.

They were forced to pick sides between me and my ex-wife, and they were able to empathize with her as they have been on the receiving end from my hurtful actions in the past.

I am also sorry that it took me so long to speak and I am sorry that I had been wearing this mask for so long. Life really is more beautiful when we take off our mask, we get to see the world as it is. When we expose our flaws, our shortcomings, and our weaknesses, only then can we grow and evolve.

Now that you have seen behind my mask, let me see behind yours.

To my ex-wife, I am sorry that the pressure of being "normal" became too intense for you to bear and you rushed into a marriage with someone you truly did not share a spiritual connection. Because of this, there is resentment because the man you married does not fit the mold of "manly." I am sorry that I am not into hunting, fishing, fixing cars, yard work, and repairing things around the home. I apologize that because of this, resentment grew to the point that communication was cut off with your husband for not being someone he never was. You did exactly as you were told and were sold the concept of the "American Dream" and would do anything to achieve it. I am sorry that you r desire for "normalcy" grasped you like a drug-addiction to the point you sacrificed lifelong morals and values in an effort to inflate your image. You moved in too soon with a man you barely knew with his teenage daughter without developing any type of true relationship for society's acceptance, and I am sorry the world pushed this on you.

I also feel the need to apologize that society lied to you about how life was supposed to be and that you believed in this illusion of the American Dream. Sometimes you do everything you are supposed to do and things still go astray. We all have a script of how we feel life is supposed to go and sometimes those scripts do not match up. I am sorry that this was your first encounter with this reality and I'm sorry that I didn't fit your knight in shiny armor. Later, you were told you could not have your own children which altered your life plan to the point of having a mental break down along with verbally attacking the person closest to you – your husband. I am sorry you felt these verbal assaults on others were your way of coping with life's adversity that we all face. And I am sorry that once your world started to fall apart, that you chose me as the scapegoat for all life's problems. And I am sorry I accepted this role.

I am also sorry that you believed if you changed enough externally, it would fix things internally. Big house, fancy cars, and material possessions will always fade away and will only create temporary happiness; whereas, true joy can only come from within. You were led to believe that having a baby or two was the missing link to your lack of joy. I'm sorry that after paying for in vitro and having two children still did not change anything. And I am sorry I could no longer wear my mask at your family functions and pretend everything was OK.

I am sorry that our kids saw us fighting, screaming. I am sorry that the kids started going into the corner and screaming and fighting as well. I am sorry the kids looked scared all the time.

So yes, I am sorry that I cheated on you. I am the villain.

I am sorry my actions shook up everything in your world, your fairy tale world in which the beauty trains the beast to be civilized and they live happily ever after. I'm sorry for destroying your mask and deciding I was no longer going to participate in this phony play you were showcasing to the world.

I let you see behind my mask and I wanted to see behind yours. I was the Phantom and you were Christine. I showed you the deformities behind my mask and my need to be loved, my need to be real, and my need to be myself. I need my kids to see real love and genuineness, rather than build them a mask of their own.

But, this is not just the Phantom of the Opera; this is the Phantom of Society – it seems real, but it really doesn't exist.

To my children, you will not have a life like that of your friends. You will get to see a mother and father that are happy; you will get to see love. You will not have to see me repressed, unloved, or unhappy. You will not have to see a marriage which is silent, bitterness, or anger. You will not see a fake life and then try to imitate it when you are adults. You will never hear a bad word about your mother from me and you will never see us fight ever again.

As my role as the villain, living with a mask under the stage, I would like to apologize for my actions. I knew something was wrong and I could not do it anymore, I need to be loved. But I am the villain, and I am sorry for playing this role.

And to my ex-wife's family, I am incredibly sorry that you taught her that her self-worth is based on being married and having children. That your traditional beliefs were so engrained in her head that she never got to express herself and develop a true identity. She has the intelligence and work-ethic to be many things, but she only found her worth in being a housewife. She wanted to be a doctor and had the ability, but was pressured into social work. I am very sorry that she had to see this fake life while growing up and then mimicked all she knew to be true. She was domesticated to the values of getting together and hugging one another, then leaving events and not speaking for one year. You created a robot to take center stage and

I apologize for spoiling it to her that it is just an act and everything you taught her was a lie.

Now, everyone in your small community knows. You have a divorced child, and in your inverted values, feel that you have failed as parents. I am sorry for the anger you have towards me and that you had to see you daughter suffering. And I am sorry for exposing her to the truth and destroying your play.

She is now going to nursing school and following her dreams – not the ones you built for her. But, I am the villain, sorry for allowing her to be herself.

And to my family, I am sorry that the dysfunction led to us developing unhealthy roles and that I was chosen as the scapegoat. This allowed for you to focus on someone, rather than looking in the mirror, which prevented you from ever experiencing growth for yourselves. It gave you relief when I made mistakes, as it allows for these roles to fulfill. I am sorry that by acting out in dysfunction that it eased your stress and enabled you to point fingers and blame. I am also sorry that because of all the finger-pointing, it forced me to seek help and treatment and better myself while you continue to stay stuck without ever being able to look in the mirror after all these years. I am sorry that because of taking the role of scapegoat, it has prevented you from addressing your own issues.

While you are living the "American Dream," you are depressed on the inside. As Kanye West once said in his lyrics,

> *"We're told we're living the American Dream; but the people highest up have the lowest self-esteems; the prettiest people do the ugliest things."*

I apologize that I am no longer living that dream, but that is what happens when you wake up. You stop dreaming. In which, I am happy to understand it was all an illusion. But, I am sorry for being the villain in your play.

I am sorry that we live in a society that as soon as we are born, we are told about the "American Dream." That we grow up, go to school, learn what the teachers ask us to remember, get a job, pay bills, get married, and have children. I am sorry that those that tell us this are making money off of the tuition, weddings, mortgages, vacations, and even the toys for the kids. The American Dream is a marketing scheme and it always has been.

I am sorry that we are taught we can only love one person, even when it goes against everything that is in our hearts. Then we are told if we break that vow, we are set to spend eternity in a fire pit. We get pressured into getting married at a young age and having children, then told we are evil if we realize that the marriage was not meant to be. So, in my first thirty years, I am supposed to find my soul mate that just happens to live in the same geographic area that I was born? I am sorry men have desires and when consistently denied, that they begin to act out only to be labeled as the bad guys for doing what is natural - to seek love and affection.

I am sorry that people still think in black and white, that if someone is a cheater, that they are a bad person. I am sorry people cannot look beyond that, and see the whole picture. It is acting out of dysfunction. Life is not about who is right and wrong. It is about love. When love is missing, things go terribly wrong.

I am sorry that love is not ever really missing, but people are afraid to show it, from shame, pain, and hurt. It all forces us to put masks on and when that happens, love gets withheld. I am sorry that people do not see that love is all that matters, it is all we have. We are here for only a short time, and most of us are living a fake life.

I am sorry people think there is only one way to raise happy, healthy kids, and that is by living this lie.

The current divorce rate is 50-percent, and those still married, but unhappy, is about 35-percent. If you have that deep emotional connection, marriage can work and can be good. But we are all so busy just trying to be "normal" that we end up depressed. Then we wonder what happened.

I am sorry that I ever believed in the "American Dream." I am sorry for you if you still do not realize that it is a lie. I am sorry to everyone that cannot see the truth.

I am the villain, the bad guy, and I am sorry.

CHAPTER XI

The Ego Has Landed
Pride Toxicity

Chapter 11
The Ego Has Landed: Pride Toxicity

In Western society there has been an ever-growing new religious practice of self-worship. Capitalism has taught us how to put ourselves first, compete with one another, to win at all costs, and not to stop or slow down to help out our fellow human. It has taught us that we are solely responsible for our accolades because of our hard work; and that others simply have the tools in place but they just need to put them into action.

It is quite ironic. The word pride has turned into a virtuous characteristic, yet all ancient philosophies and religions point out the destructive nature of pride – or self-love. Nothing feeds the ego greater than pride.

Pride is another major ego trap that sets us backwards on our spiritual journey and it is a difficult one to recognize because our society values this trap so greatly. Pride becomes so toxic because the ego thrives on pride, it over indulges on pride, over-inflates itself, and nothing helps the ego grow greater than pride. Pride creates:

1) Separation from Others
2) Spiritual Blindness
3) Self-Absorption

This chapter will address each of these toxic forms of pride on a societal scale as well as the destructive nature for each individual.

Separation from Others

One of the wisest words ever spoken came when Mahatma Gandhi stated:

> *"The true measure of any society can be found how it treats its most vulnerable members."*

So what does that say about modern society? About the American capitalism system which is designed to help the rich get richer, while the poor get poorer.

While in the West, we refer to poorer countries as "developing," we are simply referring to developing into more like ourselves. They are developing materialistically. However, in the East, they refer to the United States as a spiritually developing country as we are slowly starting to understand the corruption of the elite and see behind the façade and see that we are all interconnected.

Chapter Eight explains how the elite make the rules in the Private Prison industry, but they do this in all lines of business. They spend millions of dollars each year to lobby to congress to pass laws which favor them making more money. The law makers (congress) then invest money in these industries knowing that they make the laws that make them more rich. For example, members of Congress invest in Arms Manufacturers that make weapons and then they are the ones that decide if our country is to go to war – which will benefit their fortunes at the cost of life to young men in the service.

In Chapter Two (State of the Psychiatry Industry Address), I remarked on how the psychiatry industry has a repeated history of torturing patients and using faulty methods for thousands of years. They have not been fully accepted as medicine until the past fifty years with the birth of pharmaceuticals – hence, the ability to make money and profit the rich at the expense of the poor.

Today, psychiatrists simply drug the mentally ill in a multi-billion dollar pharmaceutical industry. What makes us think that we have it right this time? Are we really working to help those in need or is this a way to secretly profit?

The Great Recession of 2009 led to a $4.35 billion reduction in spending for mentally ill, leading to an increase in incarcerations. The mentally ill have simply been moved from hospitals to prisons. It is more profitable to keep the mentally ill in jails and prisons than if we were to provide treatment.

At the same time, while banks were giving out loans freely and acting irresponsibly, they asked for the tax-payers to bail them out. Also we increased military spending and our budget for defense now exceeds $850 billion per year. That is more than the next 26 countries combined! If we have money to bomb other countries, then we should have the money to help them.

But again, war is far too profitable for it to subside.

John Kerry, the secretary of state, has made more than $26 million off his investments in the Arms Manufacturers since the start of the War in Iraq in 2003. The man who decides to go to war is directly invested in the companies who make weapons, of course he is going to choose war every time. Therefore, the defense budget will never shrink.

This is the danger of pride on a societal level; it creates wars, nationalism, and artificial borders. We grew up being brainwashed into believing America is the greatest nation on earth. It was hard not to believe with parents, teachers, and all adults spreading the propaganda.

As we grow older and travel the world, we see that other countries do not envy us, they do not dislike us for our freedoms, they do not really have an opinion of us, and they certainly do not need us. In evaluating the statistics, it is quite obvious of the lies we have been told to create separation from others.

As Aaron Sorkin eloquently stated in 2008:

> *"We're 7th in literacy, 27th in math, 22nd in science, 49th in life expectancy, 178th in infant mortality, third in median household income, number four in labor force and number four in exports. We lead the world in only three categories. Number of incarcerated citizens per capita, number of adults who believe angels are real and defense spending..."*

Also 13th in starting a business, 47th in press freedom, our GDP ranks 12th, 39th in income equality, 10th in economic freedom, and 11th happiest. Sorkin fails to mention that the United States also leads the world in cosmetic surgeries. So there you have it: We have fake beauty, a lot of weapons, and lock up more of our own citizens than any other society in the history of mankind.

I would refer to that kind of society as ***primitive*** (in regards to spirituality) ***savages*** (in regards to locking up their own citizens, while spreading terrorism to other countries to exploit them of their natural resources). Yet, we use the same term of primitive savages to exploit our enemies and justify our invading of foreign lands.

Personal pride works the same way in creating separation by ranking people by social class, how they dress, those who are mentally ill, race, career, intelligence, age, etc.

Spiritual Blindness

Spiritual blindness has to do with our over-inflated ego growing so large that we feel we are solely responsible for the positive aspects in our life. We have a need to always be right, find ourselves easily offended by others opinions, which can be projected as playing the victim due to only recognizing the flaws of others as we believe we can do no wrong.

This is a common trap on the spiritual journey as we start making positive changes in our life and then we start to compare our spirituality to others. A common saying in support group meetings is,

> *"Religion is for people who are afraid to go to hell;*
> *spirituality is for people who have been there."*

While this gets people riled up and a feeling of connection, the irony is the spiritual blindness that is building in the room. The reason most people get turned off from religion is because of rejection and judgments; yet, here we get a group of self-proclaimed spiritual beings doing the same thing but believing it is ok because they are spiritual.

In regards to mental health and psychiatry, this is where my story continues. I felt that I finally got my big break and landed a job at the largest hospital in the state, the county hospital. The largest such facility in the area and serves those with the most severe mental illness.

Again, I was giving myself the credit for everything as we have been trained to do so. This exaggerated love for self – pride – was an ego trap and I was hooked.

Licensed to Kill

There is a lot of spiritual blindness in the psychiatry industry. It is a field that externally looks like a helping field as we are allegedly "providing care" for those who are the most in need. But as pride has entered this field, the egos have grown and it has become far more destructive than healing.

Since the creation of the Devil's Dictionary (DSM), the rise in diagnoses for mental illness continues to skyrocket. With every newly created disorder, there is most certainly a psychotropic medication as the cure.

As the formula was previously pointed out in Chapter Two, this is not a field of healing people anymore; it is a marketing scheme to benefit the rich. More diagnoses equals more prescriptions equals more money for drug companies and psychiatrists. The law makers can purchase stocks in the drugs which will allow for the laws to continue benefiting the cycle of madness.

> *"Death by medicine is a twenty-first century epidemic, and America's war on drugs is clearly directed at the wrong enemy."* –Dr. Joseph Mercola

According to the Journal of the American Medical Association, 290 people in the United States are killed every day by prescription medication.[47] Approximately 106,000 deaths per year are the result of the prescription drug use – some legal, illegal, overdose, or taken as prescribed.

Even when these drugs do not directly kill the patient, they are slowing down or altering the person's natural state of consciousness.

---

[47] Starfield, B. (2000). The *Journal of the American Medical Association* (JAMA) Vol 284, No 4. Johns Hopkins School of Hygiene and Public Health.

It is like applying and a bandage without ever addressing the underlying concern. The body becomes accustomed to the new state of consciousness and requires more medication (tolerance) and if the person is to stop taking the drugs they have serious side effects (withdrawal).

The DSM itself states that the only two symptoms someone needs to be physically addicted to a substance is tolerance and withdrawal. Hence, we are purposely getting people addicted to drugs and eventually killing them all to profit those on top.

As we fight this War on Drugs, we are targeting the drugs in which the corporations do not have their hands in the pie quite yet. They are targeting the "illegal drugs" specifically marijuana.

Yet, the biggest killers each year in the United States are tobacco, alcohol, and prescription medication. The three categories which are legal, but we are not going to go after those companies because they bring in far too much revenue. That is spiritual blindness at its finest.

Heart disease, cancer and respiratory disease are the three leading causes of death in the United States. It is estimated that smoking cigarettes accounts for more than 350,000 deaths annually in the three aforementioned causes.

The fourth leading cause is accidents or unintentional injuries. Leading this category, is the subcategory of drug overdoses – with more than half of those as prescription drug overdoses. More people die each year due to a prescription drug overdose than from car accidents.

In making this argument, people will often refer to the prohibition of alcohol and how it was such a complete failure. However, that is not necessarily true. That is more propaganda from the booze industry telling you that we need alcohol or we will go insane.

In actuality, alcohol was creating problems in America for many years and they were pushing for prohibition for nearly eighty years. Once it went into action in 1920, there was a great reduction in public drunkenness, crime, and cirrhosis of the liver. This is because the majority of the people just stopped drinking. However, the alcoholics continued to find a way to get alcohol – just as drug addicts today will always find a way to get their supply.

Crime did not increase until after 1930. In 1929, the stock market crashed which eventually led to the Great Depression. One out of every four Americans were without work. Crime started to increase at this time, because people were in need of putting food on their table – it had nothing to do with alcohol.

In 1933, part of Roosevelt's campaign was to lift the prohibition of alcohol which would open 1300 breweries and increase jobs and tax revenue. It had nothing to do with people needing alcohol, it had to do with the economy needing people working and the government profiting off more people drinking. It took more than six decades for alcoholism to reach the pre-prohibition rates.

Adios to Affluenza

A couple years ago there were two notorious court cases that were circulating around the internet regarding young adults and drug-related offenses.

The first child was arrested for possession of Xanax, a benzodiazepine, in the state of Florida. In the state of Texas, a different child was arrested for driving under the influence of alcohol (with a BAC three times the legal limit), after stealing two cases of beer, along with valium (a benzodiazepine) and THC in his system at the time. He was driving 70 miles-per-hour in a 40 mph zone. Once his friends told him to slow down, he sped up intentionally. He then crashed the truck, killing four people and severely injuring two more.

Both are first-time offenders. Who spent more time in jail?

In the first case, the young adult is dressed in an orange inmate jump suit. The judge issues her bail bond of $5,000 before wishing her a sarcastic farewell with a childish-like wave saying, "bye-bye." She replied back the same phrase, only in Spanish, "Adios." This resulted in her bond being doubled to $10,000, in which the judge then mocked the child by wishing her well with the exact same phrase, "Adios." In nervous frustration, she then flips the bird to the judge and fires back more expletives and lands a 30-day sentence in jail.

In the other case, it is the story of the wealthy and white. In fact, this young adult is so wealthy that his legal defense team argued that he has never been able to learn consequences for his behavior since his money always gets him out of trouble – coining a new disorder, "Affluenza." Although this is not a legal or medical term, it worked, and the child was put on probation and sent to a rehab facility that features horseback riding and massage therapy.

While there may be something to the argument that this child was raised in such a way that he didn't know any better, why can't we argue that the first child was raised in such a way that she didn't know you can't tell the judge "Adios?"

It seems like a rather harsh penalty. Especially since the wealthy white child would get out jail free based on the notion that he was raised in such a lifestyle that he does not have the ability to determine right from wrong. Yet, he was not only was taking a similar substance, he was also driving a vehicle and twice the posted speed limit, he had three times the legal limit of alcohol in his system (for an adult, he is only 16), stole the beer from a Walmart, also had THC in his system, and killed four people. But he didn't know he couldn't do that?

But don't take my word for it, here is an explanation from Judge Andrew Napolitno regarding the sentencing of the minority child's case:

> "I think [Judge Rodriguez-Chomat] grossly over-reacted, I think the judge brought on her contumacious behavior, and he violated the procedures," Napolitano continues, "She is innocent until proven guilty, she is charged with an illegal possession of a prescription drug, she has no priors."

Typically in a case like this, the person will be released on Recognizance (ROR) – basically meaning that she would not have to post bail with a promise they will attend all future court hearings. Rodriguez-Chomat posts bail at $5,000 based on his indifference towards her and then doubles it to $10,000 because she said, "Adios." She reacted to his over-reaction and he gives her 30-days in jail? Where is the justice here?

> "If someone misbehaves in your courtroom, you have to display some sort of tolerance," Napolitano continued, "If you are angry at a person, you cannot sentence a person in anger because that is not the right or fair mental framework. Here is the rule on contempt, if you tell somebody not to do something and they do it – you can sentence them for contempt. But if they do it spontaneous on their own and you are offended by it, you send them to another judge for sentencing."

And this is just the quantifiable punishment that she would go on to face. She became a media sensation on YouTube. With titles such as *"Flipping the Bird to Judge,"* being viewed more than 15 million times; *"Judge DESTROYS Ditzy Rich Girl,"* with more than 7 million views; *"Judge Doesn't Take Crap From Disrespectful Girl,"* has more than 700,000 views; *"Woman Curses at Judge, Flips Bird,"* with more than 450,000 views; *"Judge Flips out After Getting Flipped Off,"* has more than one million; and *"Dumb Girl Gives Middle Finger to Judge,"* with 117,000 views.

Besides being viewed upwards of 25 million times by the general population, the titles are incredibly misleading of the entire incident. She took a couple of Xanax and was arrested, after receiving her sentence she simply states, "Adios." The judge then abused his power. He initiated the entire incident as stated by Napolitano.

Judge Rodriguez-Chomat has a violent, disrespectful history of his own, as well as receiving the second lowest approval rating among local attorneys. As a representative, Rodriguez-Chomat was advocating against school vouchers while sending his own kids to private schools. After being called a hypocrite by fellow lawmaker Carlos Valdes, Rodriguez-Chomat grabbed Valdes by the tie and started a brawl with him in public. Imagine what kind of sentence he would have handed out to himself for that incident? But who judges the judge?

Notice how this part never makes headlines? Our society doesn't want to hear that, our society wants to hear about a disrespectful girl – as the YouTube titles indicate. But four days after this case, she made a second appearance and apologized to the judge for her actions, admitted to being under the influence, and had her sentence dropped. This video never seemed to get shared on any of my news feeds.

Just three weeks from her original arrest, she has passed all eight of her random drug screens, was attending rehab classes, working towards her GED, and doing clerical work. She is improving her life, but we still only remember her in her darkest moment and crucify her for something that was erroneously titled and unjustifiably marketed on social media. It is truly unfortunate that this young child had to deal with the wrath of public condemnation during her worst moment, because a power-hungry judge couldn't control his anger. Yet, we never share when she comes out of the darkness and makes positive changes in her life.

Ironically, the video entitled, *"Judge DESTROYS Ditzy Rich Girl,"* has more than seven million views as if we want to cheer and applaud some judge for taking care of a spoiled rich girl. But that is not the case, she was under the influence (which explains the so-called "ditzyness") and if she was rich…well then she would have never seen the inside of a jail house because she would have likely been suffering from Affluenza.

The Good Side of Psychiatry

Of course labeling all of psychiatry as bad is another ego trap. It would be labeling all people of one category as "bad"; which again creates separation and a fight of "us vs. them." I did get to witness all of the amazingly powerful side of psychiatry while I was at the county hospital as well.

Again, these were the "sickest of the sick" patients that came into this facility. The "sicker" the patient means the "harder" the work. This deters the phonies away, as they can make their money anywhere, but those who are there for the clients find this place as beautiful as the patients they serve.

The facility is loaded with intelligent, passionate, and enthusiastic people. I have been humbled by my past experience and I am a believer in psychiatry again. I am making more money than I have ever made in my life, better benefits, hours, and around pure genius. I am 100-percent on-board with being a perfect employee to ensure I never end up in another dermatology clinic.

So much of your experience depends on your surroundings. Here I was at the very bottom of the totem pole, whereas before, I was on top as an LPN at former jobs. I was truly humbled and at the same time excited to be a part of a place in which I was bound to learn and grow.

The most amazing part was to see how genuine kindness of the psychiatrists. They did not fit the mold of the horror stories we hear about psychiatry. They cared for the well-being of the patients and showed curiosity in the lives of others. It was quite intimidating to be on this low end of the spectrum. There was no chance I could be the loud mouth here, even if I wanted to, and I was happy to stay quiet, listen, and learn.

Doctor Wagner believed in minimal medication – a theory unheard of in a field in which 90-percent of the visits ends with a prescription to a psychotropic drug. He was a big follower of Sigmund Freud and believed more in psychoanalysis. I could sit and talk to him for hours, and he likely would have obliged.

He treated me as an equal and was happy to share as he sensed my equal enthusiasm for the field.

Then there was Doctor Solly who once lived in his car and took his first college class at a community college at age 32. Dr. Solly did not believe in committing patients. He told me, "If they are living under a bridge and not hurting anyone, why do we feel the need to control people?" I instantly loved the man. He took time out of his day to talk to me, teach me, and listen to what I had to say. He showed me that these giants in this industry truly believed in me.

And of course, the great Doctor Peters, the former pig-farmer turned psychiatrist.

Peters was a true revolutionary. He would strip patients of their medications and find out what was not working. He was not afraid to speak up when executives told him his clients were staying too long in inpatient. He fought for what was right and just and always took time to speak to me. He was the first one to treat me as an equal. He gained absolutely nothing by being my friend, talking to me, and treating me well.

I was in unfamiliar territory of being at the bottom and was ready to bolt due to the discomfort. But, Dr Peters included me, listened to what I had to say, and encouraged me. He helped build my confidence and altered my life on a different course for the better.

Malcom Forbes must have been talking about Dr. Peters when he was quoted saying,

> *"You can easily judge the character of a man by how he treats those who can do nothing for him."*

This is the quintessential virtue of empowerment. While the term "empowerment" is thrown around in the mental-health industry, it is a term that is not often defined or understood. It is an elegant-sounding term that looks good on a treatment plan, but is it ever carried out?

Empowerment comes from altruism – the practice of acting out concern for the well-being of others, without regard to your own self-interest. It comes without judgment or criticism, and a deeper understanding of our fellow man. Empowerment has to do with being happy for others and praising their accomplishments. This doesn't require any effort, knowledge or skill. It can be as simple as smiling at a passerby, treating the gas station clerk with respect, or simply being able to identify with someone in a struggle.

The beauty of empowerment is that empowering others also empowers us. It is a contagious phenomenon which is the basis of the 12-step program. The 12th step tells us to be of service and help the next person who walks through the door. This is what has kept Alcoholics Anonymous strong for so many years, altruism and service.

All these doctors at the county hospital seemed to thrive off each other's altruism. They took less money to work with sicker patients. In our competitive, me-based society, it is quite unheard of to see the greatest providers take a reduction in pay for more difficult work. However, as I look closer, it really is not that big of a surprise. You see, these doctors were real healers and providers that want to be there for the patients. It actually makes perfect sense that they would all wind up at a place in which they could provide the greatest good.

There was Doctor Coller, another great man and incredible genius; Doctor Winter had a huge heart; and Doctor Jackson always took time for everyone. Another one of my idols was Doctor Halt, an old, retired medical doctor that came in to see patients twice per week and you would never have guessed he was a doctor by his presentation. I learned so much from them by just observing how they went about their day, but they also took time to talk to me. I gained so much insight and knowledge about diseases, medications, side effects, commitments, and the legal system. It was a mind-blowing experience every day.

The Bad Side of Psychiatry

But it was not all sunshine and roses.

There were plenty of storm clouds, poisonous thorns, and toxicity. Just like any place it is bound to have its share of negativity, poor patient-care, and those in it for the money and benefits. I sat right next to two of those – Carol and Penny.

Sadly, this is more of the norm in psychiatry. They would come to work and make fun of the patients, ridicule them, and refuse to listen to what they had to say. This persistent ego-driven, need for control has reared its ugly head everywhere I have been.

Carol constantly complained about her patients, her life, and her general unhappiness. Yet, she liked living a fancy, luxurious life. It was quite clear that what she presented on the outside was a mere mask to disguise to cover up the pain she was hiding internally. She took out her frustrations on the patients and Penny seemed to get easily influenced in this dysfunction.

Which many of us have done at times, it is easy to fall victim to this mode of thinking. Misery enjoys company. My head was clear and I was able to see it this time and recognize it for what it was. At times, Penny removed her mask and showed that she had a caring heart of her own. She was in a lot of pain herself, which is why it is crucial that you must be healthy yourself before trying to help others. Otherwise, you spread toxicity rather than love.

One of Carol's patients committed suicide just a week after a visit with her. I could not even fathom the pain that would bring of hearing that kind of news. In school they tell us we need to learn to detach and leave the work at the door, but that removes the human element of a field that claims to be "human services." I could not tell you how Carol felt, if she felt anything at all. It would be safe to say that she followed the status-quo of "detaching." I felt bad for the patients that ended up with her, because if they did not like her and spoke up, they were labeled as "difficult" patients and she would be sure to pass on this information to future providers.

In situations like this, the patients have no chance because our own issues get projected on them and we are unable to see what is really going on beyond the surface.

I saw a woman there who had been stable on Prolixin for 20 years. She was unfortunate to end up in the hands of an ego-based physician, Doctor A, on the inpatient unit. Dr. A decides to change this woman's medication under the medical rationalization of,

"Because I am the doctor and I know what is best."

The patient quickly went downhill and instead of putting her back on Prolixin, Dr. A committed her to the inpatient unit. This person's life, that was stable for the past two decades, was now committed based on something beyond her control. Her voice was never heard. It was a picture-perfect example of abuse of power and control.

I watched things like this happen on a regular basis and it occurred to me that I could see how people can grow negative and burnt out in this field. We had a handful of patients come in just to fill out disability forms, most of them who did not need it, and it all just depended on which doctor they saw that day. However, some truly did need it and it is such a subjective field it makes sense how some people view psychiatry as fraudulent.

The Sick Ones

I also had my first glimpse of the sickening pharmaceutical industry in this position. The "sales reps" came in non-stop pushing their drugs to the doctors. It was all a repugnant game they were playing. The more signatures meant more money. The more prominent the doctor that signed off, the more money they received. I intentionally put quotations around "sales reps" because they were not truly selling anything it was closer to bribery or prostitution.

The drug companies send in young, gorgeous woman that look like models to flirt with the doctors until they agree to prescribe their drugs. Or they offer luxurious gifts such as entertainment suites at sporting events, dinner's at the most pricey restaurants, and other lavish items to entice the doctors into prescribing their drugs.

Which leads back to the opening comments of this book, are we really doing the right thing this time with the over-medication? The United States holds only five percent of the world's population, but we consume over 80-percent of the world's pharmaceutical drugs. Are we that sick? Or is it the drug companies that are the sick ones?

All of this keeps the lower rings of society down. The rules have been created this way to favor those in power. And all of this has to do with the love, infatuation, and addiction to money and wealth. We are knowingly killing people for the benefit of a few. This is the real mental illness; that we allow this to continue.

This was just a microcosm of the entire system. The worst case I witnessed firsthand was Doctor E. His wife was a sales rep for Abilify. Most doctors will tell you it is like Vitamin A; it is not effective for much. It probably gets about seven percent of the market. But for Dr. E's patients, about 70-percent of his patients were on Abilify. So his wife makes commission, he makes money for prescribing the drug, and they invest in the drug which allows them to live their affluent lifestyle and retire early.

Conflict of interest does not seem to apply in this industry, because the entire thing is a conflict of interest.

While E's wife had an "in" with this doctor, many other reps had tools of their own to push their drugs. They created a database to see which doctors prescribed which drugs most often; they got to know doctor's prescribing tendencies. The sales reps know more about doctor's prescribing practices than the doctors know themselves – because they don't chart their own prescriptions.

She gets commission when he prescribes her drug, they make money off their investments, and their portfolio grows. He gives presentations and speeches which are funded by the pharmaceutical companies and the rich get richer. All the while, they are keeping the sick people sick. This is how we live.

She would come in and talk about happy hour, their nanny, and their lifestyle which made me nauseous. I had to put on a fake smile to ensure I didn't upset this "wonderful" doctor that I could hear in his office telling people they had to take Abilify, even if they were doing well without it. The patients suffered so the doctor and his wife could go on luxurious vacations.

Some laws have been passed to cut-down on some of this, but they haven't exterminated this practice completely. That is because the pharmaceutical companies lobby on both sides of the hall in congress to ensure that whoever is elected they will support the industry. In 2014, pharmaceutical industry spent $229 million in lobbying to Democrats and Republicans ensuring the gravy train will keep rolling despite who is in charge.

Self-Absorption

While it is easy to point the finger, I was no different than Dr. E. I was just on a smaller scale. In my first year at the county hospital, the maximum raise that was allowed was three-percent – I received a six percent raise. In my second year, the same thing happened. I had been doing all the grunt work, sucking up, and doing whatever was needed to show my gratitude to be back in psychiatry. I never said no to anything, but eventually started to burn out.

> "Achievement is the beginning of failure;
> Fame is the beginning of Disgrace."
> - Chuang Tzu

At the same time, Jill was getting promoted and getting raises as well, so we decided to buy a big house in the country. So here I am living the same way, trying to accumulate as much material wealth as possible. Chasing after a green piece of paper, which we decided to give value and spend our lives doing whatever to obtain more.

We were very *proud* of ourselves. Showing off and living for other people. It was complete phoniness, our false selves were busting out of control. Naturally, my alcoholic drinking was at its peak as was Jill's codependency. We were living behind our masks, and worse yet, we were comfortable to stay behind them forever.

As expected, our false selves thrive on destruction. We were constantly arguing with each other over petty things, it was more of our emotional pain projected at each other. Jill couldn't get pregnant which was only adding to the hurt and suffering. I started missing work after being their "golden boy" for the first couple of years, suddenly I was unreliable and inconsistent.

The fighting progressed, which was also destroying Kylee as she had to endure all of this while she had her own struggles of being an adolescent along with the situation with her mother. Kylee ran away a few times and we had to call the police. Once they found her, they took her to a hospital in and placed her on a 72-hour-hold after she told the cop she was going to kill herself.

Wow. What just happened?

My little girl that I fought my entire life for and have worked so hard to improve her life was sent to the hospital for suicidal ideation? How did all this happen?

We also taught Kylee a lot of good. When things were going good, they were going extremely well.

However, those times were getting fewer and further between the chaos. We would have nightly talks about work, school, and life. Kylee was on the A Honor Roll and captain of the cheerleading team and excelling at life.

All of us were, on the outside. We had this huge house with four bedrooms, three bathrooms, multi-level house that shouted "look at me!" We looked great to the outside world, but inside things were on the verge of erupting.

This is the work that pride plays on the ego in the spiritual warfare. Our self-love, or pride, had inflated our ego to the point that nothing else mattered. We now had to protect the ego – the false self we were living.

This image I have painted for you is the premise of the idea of enlightenment. Our society of consumerism and materialism teaches us that the only way we will be happy is by owning more, having, more, and looking a certain way. We are brainwashed into believing the notion that happiness comes from the outside.

While it is true that it will bring temporary satisfaction, anything that is external will eventually fade away. This is why you see so many celebrities in rehab, or former athletes committing suicide. They identify only with their external existence.

We have created this notion that we are all separate and the path to happiness is by competing against each other, owning more than the next person, and the one who accumulates the most is the winner.

We live in a linear-based existence in which we believe life is a race to the end, we push others out of our way, put our selfish needs in front of our dying brothers in this faulty belief system.

I see kids walking around with clothing titled, "YOLO," which I found out stands for "You Only Live Once." This is a product of what we teach!

Which is why enlightenment is a process of breaking away from all these untruths. It is engrained in our heads that we are all separate from each other and that we only live once. The truth is that we are all one organism, experiencing this life as individuals subjectively.

Here we were in our home, all of us looked to be excelling. The money is flowing in, Kylee is going to State for poetry and on the honor roll. It was a huge success, what a turnaround from where things were only a few years ago.

But, why does it hurt so much? Why are we all in so much pain? I though this is what we strive for in life and this is what makes people happy. We were living the American Dream, with emphasis on the "dream."

Here I was, living the life of all the adults that I knew were insane and phony. I was Dr. E for God's sake! Why am I surprised? I climbed to the top of this mountain only to realize that it was all an illusion. This was just a creation of the mind in this dream state in which we live in and call reality.

Life is a dream and that is all. We are not a human body that experiences life with a soul. We are a soul, that is experiencing life with a human body. This existence is a dream state and the purpose is to awaken from this dream and see life in all its beauty as it is supposed to be.

We have so many people running around chasing after the next best thing and trying to live up to other people's expectations. Go to school, get a job, get married, have kids, enroll your kids in sports and compete some more. We are all depressed, maybe the numbers on the diagnosis for depression is accurate in this country. Judging by the way we are living, we are mentally ill.

Without any healthy release, the pain, chaos and turmoil kept pouring in. Jill eventually got pregnant, but had a miscarriage which only led to more emotional pain which was misdirected at each other. Then came the word that Adrianne would be released from prison early for flipping on the top guy in the drug ring and she had a charge thrown out for good behavior. Another wrinkle to our already dysfunctional existence.

Kylee had always dreamed of this fantasy life with her mother. She believed that as soon as Adrianne was released that everything would be magical and the pain would subside. But when Adrianne got out, she still had to take care of herself, which Kylee took as further rejection and more suffering.

My expectations were that I could keep all of this bottled up and pretend to be "normal," hoping it would all eventually disappear. However, I am the one that has always reacted to this stuff; the lies and dysfunction on the inside always comes out with me.

This false existence that I was living was driving me insane. I had become everything that I was against my entire life. I always knew that there was more to life, always had an inkling that the way we are told to do things is not true. Yet, here I was the most fake of all the people I knew. It was boiling up inside and it was only a matter of time before some type of explosion. Outside my home, people were applauding my accomplishments, but inside I had one hand on the bottle and another on the self-destruct button ready to blow it all to hell.

CHAPTER XII

Down the Rabbit Hole
Path to Freedom

Chapter 12
Down the Rabbit Hole: Path to Freedom

"Have I gone mad?" asked the Mad-Hatter. *"I'm afraid so, you're entirely bonkers",* Alice replied, *"but I'll tell you a secret... all the best people are."*

The exchange above is from Lewis Carroll's notorious fictional story, *Alice in Wonderland*, which in my professional opinion stands with more validity than today's psychiatric and mental health paradigms. In fact, Alice shares the same view as some of the greatest thinkers of all-time, such as Socrates who once declared:

> *"Our greatest blessings come to us by way of madness, provided the madness is given us by divine gift."*
> Plato too referred to insanity as *"a divine gift and the source of the chief blessings granted to men."*

On the first page of the classic story, we find Alice is disinterested in the dull, boring, everyday existence in which she resides. She peers into her sister's book to see it has no illustrations or even conversations, which to Alice has no use or interest. She ponders the idea of making a daisy-chain, but lacks the energy or motivation to take the time to pick the daisies. She is disinterested in 'normal' life. Then, suddenly, a talking white-rabbit runs past her; he appears to be late. Of course, Alice is curious about this bizarre occurrence and follows him down the rabbit hole — and most of us will be familiar with the rest of the story.

Along with Alice, many classic stories have this same message of the truth-seekers journey. Dorothy from *Wizard of Oz* is annoyed and bothered by the dull farm-life in rural Kansas before a twister sends her on an inward journey of truth. Belle, from *Beauty and the Beast*, is ridiculed for not going along with the daily routines of her small town in France. Ariel, from *The Little Mermaid*, has a desire to explore life above the sea and has a belief that there is an entire existence that others do not dare to explore.

We are naturally intrigued by these films because it touches part of our inner core that feels the same way. We have a longing to discover the truth and to be free, every single one of us has this desire. Yet, when we try to carry this out in the real world, it is then frowned upon leaving great confusion.

Between the ages of two and four, 95-percent of children are considered highly creative, imaginative, and curious about the world around them. By age seven, this number is down to less than five-percent. During these crucial years, the mask is created as children are discouraged to be creative, taught how to act, behave, speak, and the socialization process begins. We are taught to color inside the lines or you are "doing it wrong," discouraged from stopping to smell the flowers and play in nature. If a child knocks over a cereal box in the grocery store they are told they are "bad." But, then, they encouraged to sit in front of a television set which further creates a mask. With the ever-increasing violent programming on television and video games, the average American child will have witnessed 8,000 murders by the time they finish elementary school.

Will this lead to them being more violent? It is hard to say, but it is clear that each of these messages – subliminal or deliberate – is stored in the subconscious mind. Instead of being guided with love and connecting with the universe, we are being trained to fear the world and separate from others.

As everyone wears this mask from age seven on up, the mask builds and builds and builds and it controls our lives. It leads to society of people that are depressed and anxious. Just walk through the store or the mall and see how many people will go out of their way to avoid eye contact. Yet, when jogging in the park or when around children, everyone is more engaging with one another, energetic, laughing, and smiling. Children and nature help remove these masks.

Then as we grow old, we realize that we were wearing this mask our entire lives. As we sit on our death beds, we never ask to see our bank accounts, our trophies, our awards from work, or our bonus checks. We seek to be with loved ones as long as we can. Our masks are removed.

That is the secret to life, to remember who you were before the world told you who to be; to remove your mask and remember your inner child before we were socialized. Each moment is an opportunity to either to develop the true self or develop the mask.

This is true freedom.

I have met people who have been incarcerated who have more "freedom" than those who make more than six figures per year. Freedom has nothing to do with legal rights, it has to do with ability to be your true self. It is something we all desire and something we can all do.

There is an old story of a prisoner who is locked in his cell. One day, the King comes by and tells him he will grant him his freedom. The prisoner is ecstatic and thanks the King profusely. The King leaves for the day and the prisoner anxiously awaits for the King to return. Day after day, the prisoner starts to grow more anxious waiting for the King to return. He knows the end is near, but has no idea when the King will return to fulfill his promise. As weeks and months go by, the prisoner starts growing irritated, worried, and fearful that the King will not follow through or has forgotten about him.

One day, out of a furious rage, the prisoner cannot take it anymore and starts to shake the jail cell door furiously. At that moment, he notices the gate door slides open. It had been unlocked the entire time and his freedom had already been granted.

Freedom and spiritual awakening can be used synonymously, because true freedom is what spiritual awakening is all about.

There are a few key signs that dictate that you are nearing a spiritual awakening. They do not all come at once, they do not come in any particular order, but they all do occur. It is important to note that spiritual awakening is a process and enlightenment is simply being, as a way of life.

1. Questioning the Answers
2. You No Longer Fit Your Life
3. Unexpectedly Meeting a Soul Mate
4. You've encountered death
5. You want to go "home"

While there are indeed more signs, these are the most prevalent and striking signs. At this point in the story, I have had brief glimpses of each of these, but they need to be profound to the point that you can tell something is changing.

Questioning the Answers

I have always had this "quality," which ironically is viewed as an annoyance or nuisance. Anytime we go against the grain, there is going to be opposition and resistance. In fact, just questioning the grain creates turbulence. The mantra of the crowd is to "not rock the boat."

The problem is that change does not happen by doing what we have always done. If Rosa Parks followed the grain and moved to the back of the bus, there would not have been protests in Montgomery and that much-needed spark to create change.

If the Wright Brothers just accepted that it was impossible to fly as fact, we may still not have the airline industry we have today. They were viewed as rebels, outcasts, lunatics, and crazy in their times for challenging that status-quo.

This is a positive sign that enlightenment is on the horizon. You will feel lonely, distant, and confused. Wondering why do I think so differently than everyone? Am I crazy for feeling this way?

I've had these thoughts all my life, I speak up, and I get shut down. After repeating this so many times it becomes disheartening. It gets easier to believe into what the crowd tells you to believe. Erich Fromm writes about this in his book, *Escape from Freedom*, in which he discusses man's persistent struggle for freedom and then the paradoxical escape from freedom once it is gained.

With freedom comes great uncertainty, discomfort, and incredible unexpected responsibility. This, as Fromm suggests, it what drives people away from freedom as it is easier to blend in with the crowd than to stand alone. The illusion is that it is safer to go along with the crowd, than to embrace freedom. It is easier to answer the questions, than it is to question the answers. And if the answers to the questions are along the lines of "that's just the way it has always been," only further shows the need to question everything.

One of the most powerful images in modern history is of "Tank Man" in Tiananmen Square in 1989. While China is under martial law and the tanks are rolling down the streets, one individual student carrying a bag of groceries decides to literally take a stand. He stops in front of the tank and refuses to move. The tank tries to move around him, and the man stands in front of the tank again. This is on live television, crowds watching, expecting the man to get run over and truly uncertain of his fate and destiny. The man even opens up the tank and yells at the driver.

After the student starts to walk away, the tank fires up and starts to head down the street again and "Tank Man" runs in front of the tank again and halts the line of tanks, all by himself. Even more courageous, this happened the day after the Tiananmen Square massacre in which similar tanks were running over protesters and killing anywhere from 300 to 2,600 civilians (no official numbers have been recorded or released to the public).

In the heart of one of the more un-free places on earth at the time, one college student was the most free man on the planet. Away from the crowd, in the face of uncertainty and risk, one man symbolized freedom of mind.

You No Longer Fit Your Life

In the documentary film, *I AM,* by Tim Shadyac he describes his journey from being a wealthy film director soaking up the lifestyle of the elite to understanding the true meaning of life. He opens the film by telling the viewer it is a story about mental illness and shows images from movies such as "One Flew Over the Cuckoo's Nest," as that is the typical image that comes to people's mind when they think of mental illness.

After sharing his story, he ends the film saying,

> "I told you it was about mental illness."

Shadyac explains how else can you describe one flying on a private jet, living in multi-million dollar homes when down the street there are people searching through garbage cans for food or people in other countries without clean drinking water or places to live. The real mental illness is living beyond our means and believing that we are separate, rather than connected.

Western culture has taught us since the time of our birth that we are all separate and that we must compete against each other. The only way to success is to accumulate as many things as possible.

In Gail Godwin's book, *Heart: A Personal Journey through Its Myths and Meanings*, she shares a narration between Carl Jung and a Native American chief in New Mexico in 1932:

> "Chief Mountain Lake: 'See how cruel the whites look, their lips are thin, their noses sharp, their faces furrowed and distorted by folds. Their eyes have a staring expression; they are always seeking something. What are they seeking? The whites always want something. They are always uneasy and restless. We do not know what they want. We do not understand them. We think that they are all mad.'
>
> "When Jung asks why he thinks they are all mad, Mountain Lake replies, 'They say they think with their heads.'
>
> "'Why of course,' says Jung, 'What do you think with?'
>
> "'We think here,' says Chief Mountain Lake, indicating his heart."

This is a profound dialogue which depicts the many differences between the old world and the new. And by old, I am referring to eastern philosophies and that of many Native American tribes. Only now are Westerners starting to adapt these "old" philosophies, ironically labeling it as "new-age."

We are always wanting more and therefore, will never be satisfied. As soon as we achieve material wealth, we want the next big thing. We convince ourselves that, "once I have this, then I will be happy," "If I have a new job I'll be happy," or "once I find love, I'll be happy." While these things do bring temporary pleasure, it is short lived and we soon are seeking something else just as Chief Mountain Lake has observed.

The other message of this dialogue is the power to think from the heart, our true self. Now this may sound like some utopian, hippy mumbo jumbo talk, but there is scientific evidence to back up this notion. Since in the West, we are always in need of proof, scientists continue to work hard to prove the theories that the East have been practicing for thousands of years.

The human heart is the first organ to develop after conception. It typically begins to develop around 20 days, as compared to 90 days for the brain. As we know, the heart pumps blood to all organs of the body, but it has a greater function – an intelligence of its own.

According to neurologists, 60 to 65 percent of heart cells are neuron cells, not muscle cells. The heart is proven to work similarly like the brain by sending out electromagnetic waves that carry essential information.

Even more fascinating is the connection between the heart and brain. We are told in school that the brain sends out signals to the body, and that part of the body carries out that function. Which one could only assume this includes the heart. But the heart actually sends far more signals to the brain, than the brain does to the heart! These heart signals influence emotional processing and higher cognitive function.

Doctor Masaru Emoto took it a step further in his rice experiment, in which he places rice in two jars – one that says "thank you" and the other says "you fool." For thirty days, school children would walk by and say these words out loud. After one-month, the jar that said "thank you" was hardly changed, whereas the jar that said "you fool" had become moldy and rotten. Again, this experiment scientifically backs the ancient philosophies and theories of the power of thinking from the heart.

Thinking from the heart is pure, untouched, and loving energy. Whereas, thinking from the brain has been influenced by the outside world and is a reflection of our false self.

This is the second sign that a spiritual awakening is near. I had moved into a large, expensive house, in a private gated community. We had two luxurious cars, golf club memberships, and hiring people to do our lawn work. What had I become? This was everything I have always been against!

I grew to become a part of this culture of separateness and competition. As we were earning more money, we accumulated more external luxuries to cover-up the internal pain. Deep down, I knew this was not me. I was no longer fitting my own life.

This, too, can lead to depression, isolation, and loneliness. It becomes quite confusing, which is why many people tend to go back with the crowd – because it is comfortable. Even if we know it is not right, it is comfortable, and it is easier to go back to the old way of living.

Here I am with everything I ever wanted and more on the outside, but on the inside I was empty as ever.

I did not fit this way of life, and in hindsight, that should have been a clue that I was doing something right. If enlightenment has to do with breaking away from everything you know, it makes perfect sense that you would not fit in.

As Kurt Cobain once said,"

> *"They laugh at me because I'm different, I laugh at them because they are all the same."*

You Unexpectedly Meet Your Soul Mate

The word "soul mate" has been misused by Hollywood and romance novelists. We have this idea in our head that a soul mate is some sort of perfect fit and people live happily ever after. But instead, it works the same way as enlightenment – your soul mate points out what is lacking or missing in your life, helps you break away from these chains, and propels you to find your true self. This means disagreements, arguments, and challenging everything that you think to be true.

Elizabeth Gilbert describes a soul mate as a mirror, which I agree is the most appropriate term. You see your reflection in somebody else and share a deep connection and understanding. Also, like in a mirror, you see things about yourself that you may not like and may want to change that you did not notice before.

This is the third sign that a spiritual awakening is on the horizon. I add in the word "unexpectedly," because it really is something quite different than you had imagined.

First, we need to understand the term. The word mate derives from 14th century Middle Low German term which translates as "comrade or companion." Two-hundred years later the term first was used to describe "marriage." The Merriam-Webster dictionary still today first defines mate as *an associate or companion; friend or buddy; an assistant to a more skilled worker.*

Perhaps this is why meeting our soul mate happens quite unexpectedly.

I met my sister's boyfriend, Shandon, and he became my best friend instantly. I admired much about him, and we talked about deep emotional subjects. No one in our family could quite comprehend how or why this guy liked me. I was bad-mouthed, gossiped about, and told that I was a bad guy, but it didn't matter to Shandon. He didn't see it. He only saw the true me because we instantly spoke from the heart and never wore our masks in front of each other. While my family was describing my mask, Shandon never saw the mask, only the true Cortland.

There is much literature and research regarding the family systems theories and the roles attached in dysfunctional families. Along with these roles, families tend to not talk about problems, don't express feelings openly and honestly, and communicate indirectly. My role was the scapegoat which is to help the family by taking the focus off the family's problems by pulling negative attention towards myself.

This is not asking for a pity party or sympathy, this is just the nature of the family systems roles in dysfunctional families. The scapegoat often looks angry, defiant, rebellious, and rude on the outside. But on the inside they are hurt, afraid to trust, misunderstood, feel rejected by the family, and hopeless. The scapegoat is typically the second-born and tends to do poorly in academics, involved in criminal activity, alcohol, and drugs. The path for the scapegoat to escape his/her role is permission to be successful, supportive confirmation, along with structure and consistency.

And while it is a dysfunctional family, it is still functioning and it is all that they know. When someone goes outside of their role, it changes everything and creates animosity. We grow accustomed to our roles and any change disrupts the entire dynamics of the family.

For me to have a lot of money, big house, and fancy cars did not fit my family role. I was supposed to be the one in jail or homeless – which I have been both. When I was in jail or homeless, the family was more accepting of me because I fit my role. But now that things had changed, they were not as accepting. This is not saying that my family is bad people; they are actually following 100-percent of what research has shown for the past 50 years.

It works for all the roles. Larry was the mascot – using humor to ease the tensions of the family. When he tried to be serious about things, people told him to not be so uptight. Koryn was the hero, and when she was studying abroad in Africa and volunteering with political campaigns it stirred things up because her role was to overachieve to show the world that the family is normal. Reggie was the lost child which means they isolate to avoid the family chaos, and when he was coming around all the time things felt awkward for everyone because he was breaking the family dynamics. And Sharon was the placater, or people pleaser. This is the giving, caring, loving member of the family that has the highest tolerance for dysfunction. When Sharon speaks out of the dysfunction and stops being supportive, it throws things off.

This was my time in which I was going out of my role and it caused resentment in the family. People saw us going out, partying, having fun and thought that I was poisoning Shandon. But nobody was there. We talked about politics, religions, philosophy, and the meaning of life. It was a true, deep spiritual connection.

We had completely different beliefs when we first met – I was a bleeding-heart liberal and he was a crack-pot conservative. By the end, we are both libertarians. At first, he was an atheist and I was a God person. Eventually he transitioned into a devout Christian and I developed a spiritual sense that recognized much broader beliefs. We affected each other's hearts, by opening up our own and being honest with each other. He could be tough on me, and vice versa, because we built a bond of sacred trust.

"Man, I have never met anyone like you," Shandon said to me one day, "You are just so open about all your flaws."

He got to me. He just gave genuine compliments. I made myself vulnerable and took off my mask, and he wasn't afraid to do the same. This is how relationships are formed and connections made. We saw each other as we truly were.

They say when the student is ready, the teacher appears. It was true as we taught from each other and learned from each other. As I began reading about Buddhism, he seemed to already have a sense of these things. He knew what was real, he loved nature, being outside, and enjoying the simple things in life.

"Can you see this?" He asked me while we were waiting to tee off at a golf outing, "How lucky are we to be living in this moment in time and to just be outside golfing?"

Shandon is a deep person, full of love. He got my dad to laugh and swear – things I rarely saw in my entire life. I got to see my Dad without his mask, all because of Shandon. He brought pure, genuine, unconditional love to a family that had been starving for the last two or three decades. He brought the family closer together with his ability to relate to everyone and enjoy life.

With such a pure heart, I wondered how could he be an atheist and he told me the story. He said when he was younger he saw a dead bird and he thought he had killed it, after that he just shut down. He is just a pure soul. This is why when I hurt him, along with everything he had previously heard from the family, he couldn't handle it – because he saw the mask the family warned him about.

We had shared each other's company for years without our masks, and then I showed him my ugly mask. I do not blame him for his blind rage and hate that ensued. It was my own dysfunction, my self-destruct button, and family role that came into play.

You Encounter Death

I spoke previously about the power of Near Death Experiences and how those who encounter death have an increased spiritual connection. They got a sneak-peak preview as what lies ahead, the afterlife, the truth.

But, encountering death as a sign of a spiritual awakening does not have to be your own death. I've spoke candidly about my connection and relationship with Jim. We were the same person, with completely different upbringings – that was the only difference. I just shared in great detail my emotional bond with Shandon, but most of those deep talks involved alcohol. We needed a substance to help remove our masks. With Jim, we never needed substances to show our true selves.

While we were living in the city, Jim had lived with us for some time. He was constantly struggling with keeping jobs and having a place to stay. I would have been the same if it weren't for the security blanket of my family. Jim didn't have that security blanket, so I took on that role for him. Every time he was in trouble, he called me. No matter how long it had been since we last talked, he knew that if he called me that I would be there.

Jim had a big heart, too. He wanted to help others who were suffering and in pain. So he started inviting sketchy people into our house, making everyone uncomfortable. I couldn't have these people in the house around Kylee while I was at work, but I didn't have the courage to tell him. We needed to ask him to leave, but I couldn't do it. So, in typical co-dependent fashion, I had Jill do the dirty work for me and she asked him to move out.

A few months later, Jim was in trouble again – but he didn't call this time. It turns out, the pain had become too much for him and he hung himself and died.

I still carry a lot of guilt regarding this to this day. I would blame Jill for kicking him out, but it was just a ploy to try to project my guilt and pain onto somebody else. All I could ask myself is "Why didn't he call this time?"

Suicide is complex and also carries a lot of stigma. People just say the word, hear the word, or read it and they get an uncomfortable feeling. There is no worse feeling in the world than to hear of a loved one taking their own life. We are quick to ask what we could have done differently, take on the blame, and have millions of unanswered questions.

One of the problems in our society is the immense difference between the words "suicidal" and "suicide." If someone tells you they are suicidal, people want nothing to do with it. There is no chance you are going to tell someone you are suicidal if the reaction is worse than telling them you have some sort of fatalistic contagious disease. They shun you, tell you to "never talk like that." The message here is, do not tell me how you feel because it makes me uncomfortable and it is wrong to feel that way. That is suicidal. Whereas suicide, brings about the most horrendous pain and sorrow one can imagine.

This is the danger of stigma and the deaths it creates. People often say suicide is selfish, but they do not understand the pain of the victim. Nobody wants to die, nobody has ever wanted to die, they only want the pain to go away. Suicide is the result of the emotional, psychological, or sometimes physical pain is so prevalent that the best option to stop the pain is to end life altogether.

There is nothing selfish about that, it is the type of pain that you would not wish on anybody. But if we change the connotation associated with suicidal, perhaps we can change the times we have to hear the word "suicide."

Jim's death shook me up, opened my eyes and gave me a moment of clarity. But that's all it was, a moment. How many of these moments will it take? How many times do I need a tragedy to help me awaken?

Encountering death is part of the process. It shows us the value of life, the importance of the little things we witness each day. Albert Einstein said,

> *"There are two ways to live life. As if nothing is a miracle, or as if everything is a miracle."*

Moments like this teach us to choose the latter.

You Want to Go *"Home"*

In encountering death, we see that we are all going to die. But the secret is to have your false self die, before your physical body dies. Because if we can do that, we see that there really is no death. In this discovery, we break away from all the lies that our false self has been telling us and we finally start to see that we are all connected. We begin to understand that we are all eternal beings, experiencing life in the form of a human body.

Our true nature, god-like essence is best described as pure and radiant love. We know this feeling when we experience it, we feel it through all our senses and awareness. This is what I mean by "home." We want to return to our true self.

In our physical "home," things were imploding quickly. Even with all the material possessions, I was empty and I knew that I didn't want any of it, so I searched elsewhere. I was never at the house, went out golfing and drinking at all hours of the day. I felt as if our perfect little home had been set ablaze and I needed the quickest way out.

I had tasted the truth, and I knew what I had in that home was fake. I wanted to return to me true "home." I picked up lessons from losing Kylee about love, from Jerry about being genuine and kind, from Shandon about enjoying the simple things – and everything in that home was fake.

Jill and I had on our masks, our false selves were hurting each other. My drinking escalates, which leads to her greater need to control. Eventually we both snap, and it turns into an ugly fight. Our stress and frustration had been on overdrive for too long and we both exploded. And after the damage had settled, we were able to cool down. We had not communicated with each other for so long, at least during this altercation we shared our true emotions which ended up resolving part of the struggle. This is a common cycle in dysfunctional communication. Everything is internalized until a huge blow up in which all is revealed, and everything is temporarily solved.

After the fight, we decide to try the fertility doctor one final time in an attempt to have a child together. The fact that Jill was unable to get pregnant was an indicator for me that we were chasing this fake life. We have the big house and now needed a family to fit the societal norms to show the world we are OK.

At the same time, I was growing addicted to the money and possessions and decided to go back to RN School. This would occupy my time and my mind – the baby, school, work – I will be too busy to have to deal with any inner turmoil. This is highly encouraged in our society, to stay busy is to be successful. This is no different than filling our void with alcohol or drugs. We are suppressing what needs attention.

The more we try to run away from pain, the more it builds. Furthermore, we never learn the healthy ways of handling pain. Our pain continues to grow and we continue to run, it only continues to pile up and the only thing we know to do is run away. As the saying goes, "pain is inevitable, suffering is optional." Suffering is only the result of untreated pain.

As the Buddhists teach, all pain comes from desire or attachment. It is no wonder that the nation that prides itself on consumerism is suffering so greatly from depression. We have filled our homes – both our internal and external – with material excess. It is time to clear the clutter and rearrange our lives to bring about a more peaceful existence.

Feng Shui is the simple interaction between humans and their environments. This has been practiced by the Chinese for centuries in rearranging our environments to bring about different energies that increase our quality of life. It has grown into the West as a form of interior design, working the same way – cleaning out the clutter and bringing in objects that bring about a change in energy flow.

This works in our external homes in which we live in, but also in our internal "home" in which we want to return. We can rearrange the thoughts, beliefs, and attachments in our heads that are creating clutter in our minds and use the ancient Feng Shui techniques to increase positive energy in our lives.

And this is where I stood. I knew that I wanted to go "home," but I didn't have the slightest clue as to how to get there.

It reminds me of The Wizard of Oz in Dorothy's journey. It is symbolic story of great spiritual reference. Dorothy wishes to go "somewhere over the rainbow," knowing that there is a better existence that what she is currently living. She lands in Oz and is told the only way to get home is to see the Wizard and he will grant any wish you desire. She is told in order to see the wizard, all you need to do is follow the path (yellow brick road).

This is all symbolic of the belief that the one true way to eternal bliss (you may call it heaven, enlightenment, nirvana, etc.) is to follow the path that we have put in place. At the end you will have to ask the wizard (symbolic of organized religion) to grant your wish to go to the one place you know as "home." Along the way, you meet a Tin Man, Lion, and Scarecrow. These are also symbolic aspects of the self – tin man is seeking a heart (compassion); lion is seeking courage; and the scarecrow is seeking a brain (wisdom).

Along the way, the scarecrow shows multiple acts of intelligence coming up with ideas to help the crew, the lion is brave in defeating the witch, and the tin man is always crying out of love and compassion. At the end, they meet the wizard to discover that he is just an old man hiding behind a curtain – just like organized religion abusing their power behind a charade.

The Wizard then gives them each a gift which represents their wishes. The Scarecrow receives a diploma, the Tin Man a heart-shaped watch, and the lion receives a medal of courage. He shares that they had these features within them all along.

At the very end, the Wizard attempts to bring Dorothy home in a hot-air balloon as one final attempt to convince her that he is the only one who can bring her home, but Toto releases the balloon as he symbolizes intuition. As Dorothy begins to cry, thinking she will never be able to return home, Glinda comes along.

> *"Oh, will you help me? Can you help me?"* pleads Dorothy

> *"You don't need help any longer,"* Glinda replies, *"You've always had the power to go back to Kansas."*

> *"I have?"* asks a confused Dorothy.

> *"Then why didn't you tell her before?"* asks the Scarecrow.

> *"Because she wouldn't have believed me,"* replies Glinda, *"She had to learn for herself."*

CHAPTER XIII

Soul Contracts
Fate and Destiny

Chapter 13
Soul Contracts: Fate and Destiny

There are no coincidences in life. Coincidence refers to a couple of things lining up as a part of a meaningless chance. As you become more in touch with the oneness of all that is, it is quite apparent that all these synchronicities are not by chance.

Quite often you hear the terms "fate" and "destiny" used interchangeably. Both terms refer to one's future in life, but are quite different. This is best described as thinking of fate as the hand you have been dealt (no control), and your destiny is how you play the cards (a result of your choices).

In each lifetime, our soul sets out to accomplish a certain set of learning tasks and creates "soul contracts" with others to ensure this task is met. This refers to our fate, such as daily people, places, and things we encounter daily. We do not control where we were born, our families, race, or social background. This is all predetermined. Prior to entering the world of human form, we have already arranged soul contracts with everybody we have ever encountered. Each person has a specific meaning and purpose in which we are supposed to learn a specific lesson. Upon fulfilling the stipulations of these soul contracts, we manifest our destiny.

At this point in my story, we had been trying to get pregnant to no avail. Eventually, we went into the doctor to discuss options regarding in vitro fertilization. Feeling helpless, we decided to give it a try – something we had previously stated we would "never" do. This is part of the fate aspect of life, and learning to trust the process. All the failed attempts at pregnancy had to do with the time not being right.

Our desperate attempt to bring a child into this world, only further demonized me from Jill's family. They had never approved of me, and this only added fuel to their disgust. Jill's sister had named her the guardian of her children in case of an unforeseen death. But as soon as I was brought into the picture, she rescinded those rights from Jill as I was deemed incapable of raising a child according to her family's standards.

They are the stereotypical rural small town family – heavy drinkers, outdoors type, religious, and conservative political views. They fit the script perfectly by drinking all day, hitting and ignoring the children, and then going to church on Sundays. Then on Monday, they are back to judging anyone who does not live exactly as they do.

There is an old Leadbelly song, *Ain't It A Shame,* that describes this chaotic way of living. The singer mentions different acts which people should not do on a Sunday (the holy day), and then finishes by informing the listener that they can do these the other six days of the week. Each verse, the act gets a little more vulgar to the point of domestic abuse:

> *"Ain't it a shame to go fishing on a*
> *Sunday, ain't it a shame....*
> *Ain't it a shame to have a drink on a*
> *Sunday, ain't it a shame....*
> *Ain't it a shame to beat your wife on*
> *a Sunday, ain't it shame....*
> *When you got Monday, Tuesday, Wednesday.*
> *Oh, Thursday, Friday, Saturday, ain't it a shame."*

I do not blame them, do not think they are bad people, or think any less of them. They are just highly misguided. As Jesus states on the cross of those who have crucified them,

"Father, forgive them. For they know not what they do."

This is the socialization of a culture in rural America. From generation-to-generation, it is passed down that this is the way the world operates. The cycle never changes until someone can break out of that pattern and see the dysfunction of it all. Jill was able to see through this façade, which propelled her to move to California to see the way the rest of the world operates – rather than the little that was known within the tiny confines of this small-town. Yet, the engrained messages never left her soul.

While I do not condemn them, or fault them for their way of living, it is also important to bring awareness to any type of socialization that further creates this illusion of separateness. Organized religion serves as many wonderful purposes in the world, but it has been the cause of nearly every world conflict since recorded history. In theory, religion was meant to bring people together to see the oneness, yet it has only brought about the opposite by furthering the cause of separateness.

In vitro fertilization is considered unnatural form of conception (occurring outside the Woman's body), which is what upsets certain religious communities. Jill's brother-in-law associates this with working with the devil. So here we have a couple trying to procreate and bring loving children into the world, and instead it creates separation all because of the manner in which it was done.

Despite the increased tensions, Jill was able to rise above the disapproval of her family once again. We followed through and they extracted eight eggs. Which eventually dwindled down to four, and on the day of insemination only one embryo remained. Jill started bawling as the likelihood of having a child together appeared to be out of our "fate."

"You know what, this is actually good," the doctor told us, "you know you will be getting the strongest one."

This seemed to be just a way to comfort us, but it was the last ounce of hope we could grasp. But without hope, there would be nothing left. A man begins to die the day that he stops longing for Tomorrow.

With everything going on, one instant sticks out in my memory like it was yesterday. It was a moment of truth, an unmasking of our egos in the face of some of our greatest turbulence. Upon coming out of surgery, Jill was looking for me with her arms out, wanting a hug. That's it, just looking for a hug but I had not seen that side of her for too long. We were in too much pain and attached to the masks we had been wearing, we forgot what it felt like to be vulnerable and show our true selves.

You need to experience darkness, in order to appreciate the light. This is what made this moment so powerful and fresh in my mind. I had been living in darkness, we had been living in darkness for far too long – and this was the brightest, most refreshing light I've seen in years. This was the truth. The same truth that we only know as toddlers before the world tells us who we are supposed to be. Then we do not see this truth again until we can break out of the mask the world has created for us, and awaken to our true reality. In this moment I saw the love that she was always trying to hide.

On December 19, 2009, Bayonna was born.

Was it fate? Was it destiny? Whatever it was, it was without a doubt part of a greater plan beyond any of our control. In birth and death, we are able to experience God by appreciating the beauty of all life. Because in these moments, we wear no masks, we allow our true selves to shine. At our core, each and every living thing on this planet is God. Enlightenment is the ability to become aware of this. God is only pure, radiant, unconditional love energy.

Everything was better, all the misery had subsided. Destiny was on our side and things were finally coming together. Finally, we could be at ease with no more dysfunction. Or so it seemed.

This dangerous mindset of believing that we will find inner peace once things come together will leave use constantly chasing external people, places, and things. It will never be enough and we will never know peace. This is another one of life's paradoxes, as later we discover that life actually works by us first finding inner peace, and then we watch as all the things start to come together.

As this is happening, I am approaching the end of school and prepared to take the nursing boards. Ever since leaving Divine Redeemer, it has been my dream to work with disadvantaged youth in the mental health field. I came across a position that appeared to be my "dream job" working with kids in a prison. Everything seemed perfect, this was my destiny. I had played my cards right and I was certain this was all part of some greater plan.

And it was, but it was a part of my ego's plan. But my soul had a different plan. My soul had some other prearranged contracts that it needed to fulfill to ensure that I was meeting all the tasks I had set out to learn in this lifetime. This is how fate works.

I failed my boards by a fractional margin, and was quite confused. It did not make sense that I wouldn't pass, since I thought I knew my destiny and had played my cards right. Well, with fate, sometimes no matter how well you play your hands, someone else can have you beat with the flip of the final card.

In August of 2010, I take the boards again and pass with ease and take a job as an RN Supervisor at a psychiatric rehab facility. I'll be making more money that I could have ever imagined for myself, far more than if I got the job working with kids. Perhaps this was the real destiny, I had finally made it. We had the house, the new baby, and income beyond anything we had experienced. I thought the pain would have no chance against all these external forces.

The day of my interview, I am highly confident and sure that I am going to make an immediate impact at this place. It is an old, rundown, apartment complex that appeared to be awaiting someone to teach them about psychiatry.

Enter Riley Schonner

This woman would change my life forever and guide me on the road to enlightenment, and make the person that I am today. Without any doubt, this is fate. My soul had a contract with this woman, a prearranged agreement that we would meet in this lifetime to teach me the lessons that I longed to learn.

Once again, my plan for myself was not the best. I thought I knew what was best, but that is how the ego takes control of our lives. It was another lesson to accept what is, surrender to the process, and drop the illusion of control.

Riley wanted to hear my thoughts, which came unexpectedly. I had been quiet on my beliefs for so long and she encouraged me to speak up. It's as if she saw everyone in the world wearing a mask and it was her objective in life to remove them all. She encouraged participation and involvement, and before long I started speaking up at meetings.

In a way, it was the same thing as when I was a patient at Divine Redeemer. While at Divine Redeemer as an adolescent, I had been beat down and given up on life. There was nothing anyone could say or do to get me involved. Then it started with the nurse Tim, who just wanted to talk to me and treat me like a person. Eventually, I started to listen in group and see everyone else being vulnerable. I participated and realized the power of vulnerability.

This was a lesson I learned at 18-years-old, but was falling back into the same patterns. This is a stipulation in soul contracts. There are built-in backup plans, just in case we are not learning the lesson or we fall astray. I had learned this lesson many years ago, but I was slipping again. I was in emotional pain with the marriage, alcoholism, and never addressing my pain. I continued to run from my pain, and was starting to shut down.

On the outside, everything looked perfect. The pain was covered up by external luxuries, but inside I was dying. I was drinking nearly every day of the week, and barely managing to get by.

Then, like Tim did so many years ago, Riley wanted to know me as a person, hear what I had to say, and showed sincere gratitude. I had so many thoughts, ideas, and beliefs that had been bottled up for so long it was like an emotional eruption that was about to take place.

Just as Riley was with her staff, her staff was with the clients. We worked with them as people, as individuals. She believed in meeting the client where they were at, treating everyone the same and all as equals. We would get to know the clients, what works for them, and be there for them.

With the staff, she held 30-minute supervision sessions with each one of us weekly in which we would address concerns, issues, and suggestions. There were many staff with four-year degrees in psychology in their first position in psychiatry, and pursuing further education. I had the experience, they had the formal education, and it was put upon me to give advice, teach, and guide them on their career path.

Riley had no ego, she only knew her true self and shared it with everyone. She would go over each diagnosis, the reasons why, and she would educate the entire staff. She took time to personally guide each and every person – staff, client, or family member. I was really settling into this place and learning every day and granted the confidence to supervise other and make important decisions.

Addictive Thinking

Behind closed doors, it was not quite as glamorous. Although we had far more money than we would ever need, somehow bills were piling up. I was spending money recklessly, golfing, and drinking with Shandon each night. I purchased a Mercedes Benz and then a BMW. It was a, "look at me, I'm good! I am not a bum," type of purchase.

Of course, this was only covering up the deep truth; any enlightened soul would see right through to my deep insecurities. Purchasing luxury items is highly effective in temporarily bringing happiness and jolting the self-esteem, but it is just like a drug. It gives you that quick fix to forget about what is going on inside, but when that initial "high" fades away, it creates a rebound effect. Like the drug, after the glamour of the luxurious item fades we end up in more pain than before because we never addressed the real problem, and we are already striving for more. We see the short-term effect one car brought us, so if we buy a second car it should bring even more happiness.

Our tolerance increases and we experience these "withdrawals" from luxurious purchases. It only leaves us chasing more externally, while avoiding the suffering going on internally.

Looking around me at the person I had become made the suffering even more severe. As I was chasing external riches, I realized that I have turned into the person I swore I'd never become. I think I knew this at a subconscious level, but I was not able to pull this to the surface at the time. All I knew was that it hurt, and the only way I knew to drown the pain was with alcohol.

Jill was tired of the drinking and I had tried to quit multiple times. I had all the excuses in the book as to why I kept going back to the booze. I would justify my drinking by stating that I worked hard all day and deserved something to relax. I would place the blame on Jill, stating that I only drank because she was too controlling. I tried to rationalize my use of alcohol by telling myself that it was medicine and the only thing that would calm me down, I would be out of control without alcohol.

And when you create this type of addictive thinking, your mind starts to get hijacked by your addiction. You will do anything to defend your drug of choice, it is never the drug's fault for any of the consequences in life. I would be hammered while trying to watch Bayonna and would convince myself that I had only one or two drinks, because that was the outward lie I had told so many times. I started calling in sick to work, and placed the blame at the way things were changing at work. It had nothing to do with the alcohol!

Looking back, it is just an all too familiar story of anyone who has suffered from addiction. Use the drug to mask the emotions, start to see consequences, develop addictive thinking, consequences become more severe, isolate and blame, until either an intervention occurs or you shut down to the point of death. It is the same story for everyone, only the details change.

With each sip of alcohol I took, it was as though it was kryptonite for my ego. I was drowning my true self, while inflating my ego to the point that I thought I was above everyone else. I admired my luxurious life and thought I had it all figured out.

I started to see things from a different perspective, which only makes sense that your vision becomes cloudy when your eyes are covered by a mask. I started criticizing everyone's decisions, coming down on people for minor mistakes, and even stopped teaching the staff that was eager to learn. It was just another means of avoiding emotions and intimacy. It was a cycle that was spiraling out of control.

It was around this time, that fate had struck again with some shocking news. Jill was pregnant. She is not supposed to be able to get pregnant, but it happened.

Unsure what we are going to do, Jill plans to run a day care at the home. Now, this interferes with my plan. And by "my plan," of course I am referring to the ego. This was never my dream. My dream was to save money, open group homes, and save the world. That was my "destiny."

Yet, I had the cards (fate) in place, but I wasn't playing the cards (destiny) the right way. I could have been saving money all along, but was out buying cars, expensive golf outings, drinking, and spending more than I was taking in – following word-for-word the description of the self-destructive personality.

This gave me a new outlet, a new area to place the blame for my unhappiness. It was Jill's fault that I was not reaching my destiny, my dream. She would blame the dysfunction on my drinking, and

I blamed the drinking on her dysfunction. A battle neither of us would win, which is probably what we secretly craved. We thrived on the dysfunction, as it was the only form of function we knew. It was a game we played, in which we masked things for so long until there was a huge meltdown and we would make up.

The next phase of addiction and addictive thinking involves being secretive about how much or how often you are using. This will prevent others from blaming the drug on any problems if they are not aware of how much the drug is being used. Every addict has their hiding places, along with the progression of the severity and desperation of finding better spots to ensure the stash is safe. I reached the point where I was hiding one-shot bottles inside of Bayonna's dirty diapers and would pull them out when Jill wasn't around.

Fading Dreams

I should have never been allowed to keep my job at the psychiatric rehab facility. Riley had seen something in me, which I likely did not see in myself. She got me to reveal my true self, and she knew how to get behind people's masks. She saw my passion, saw that I was learning, and knew that there was something deeper inside that I hadn't yet found. Her father was an alcoholic, she likely knew what was going on all along and was waiting for fate to play its course with me.

With a negative mindset, we start to see the world as a negative place. While my pain was increasing at home, I started to change the way I saw the world. I started noticing the staff that did not want to be there. They cried that it was all a fraud, that they do nothing but write notes.

They were right. It was a fraud, they wrote fake notes, fake plans, and no one really cared. We really do not do anything at all. I started noticing everything that was wrong with this place that I had once loved only months ago.

We were getting paid $8,500 per patient, per month, while we only granted $87 per month to the patient. Where is all the money going? All these fake plans, goals, and notes were just a façade for the county to ensure we received funding.

People had serious lifelong ailments, and we claimed that we would be able to rehabilitate them in 90-days? It was basically just a holding place after being released from the hospital. The groups lasted about ten minutes, if we did them at all. We tried to cancel them if we could, to avoid the embarrassment.

Everything I had worked for my entire life since being hospitalized, all my passion was fading. The internal fire had been extinguished. The entire industry is corrupt. What am I even doing here?

We commit people just so we can have control over them. We don't rehabilitate anyone, nor do we even try. Here I was getting all passionate about this and it likely made me the laughing stock of the community. I can only imagine that everyone was pointing and laughing behind closed doors at this guy who thinks that we actually are helping people. The joke had been on me all along. I started to become paranoid that I was part of some mass conspiracy.

This confusion and paranoia only added to my depression, which had to be conquered with more booze. If I tried to stop drinking, these thoughts were too overwhelming and I couldn't handle life.

However, I was not done learning from Riley Schonner. She had started me on a path, she had been an angel in my life. Our souls had a contract to meet, that was fate. What I did with that encounter determines my destiny.

For the first time in my life, my outsides were matching my insides. I was finally dying on the outside, too.

CHAPTER XIV

It's All Synchronicity
The Good and the Bad

Chapter 14
It's All Synchronicity: The Good and the Bad

I am often asked, "How do I know if what I am experiencing is a coincidence or a synchronicity?" I simply answer by referring back to the opening line of last chapter, "There are no coincidences."

Synchronicities are two or more events that have no causal relations, meaning no cause-and-effect connection. Yet, there is a significant meaning attached. The more "random" the number of incidences or connections, the less likely this can actually be a "random coincidence."

For example, French writer Emile Deschamps was first introduced to plum pudding in 1805 by a stranger named Monsieur de Fontgibu. It was ten years later, when Deschamps noticed plum pudding on a menu in a Paris restaurant and wanted to order some. The waiter told him he had just sold the last order, in which to Deschamps surprise was ordered by Fontgibu. Many years later, in 1832, Deschamps ordered plum pudding once again while at a dinner and joked "the only thing missing to make this setting complete is Monsieur de Fontgibu." In that same instant, the now senile Fontigbu entered the room.

Carl Jung first coined the term synchronicity and states,

> *"When coincidences pile up in this way, one cannot help but be impressed by them – for the greater number of terms in such a series, or the more unusual its character, the more improbably it becomes."*

Jung believed that experiencing these synchronicities serves as a role similar to dreams with the purpose of shifting one's egocentric conscious thinking to greater wholeness. These synchronicities occur more frequently at the time of transformation, and once we become more aware, we start to see them on a daily basis. At this point, it is quite apparent that there are no coincidences.

In Lewis Carroll's, "Through the Looking Glass," he depicts this is dialogue between the White Queen and Alice:

> "That's the effect of living backwards," the Queen said kindly, "it always makes one a little giddy at first."
> "Living backwards!" Alice repeated in great astonishment, "I never heard of such a thing!"
> "But there's one great advantage in it, that one's memory works both ways," said the Queen.
> "I'm sure MINE only works one way," Alice remarked, "I can't remember things before they happen."
> "It's a poor sort of memory that only works backwards," the Queen remarked.

The last line, *"It's a poor sort of memory that only works backwards,"* was one of Jung's favorite quotes in describing synchronicity. Basically stating that synchronicities are the universe sending us messages that we already knew, and we are just remembering something before it happened. The more we are in tune with these message, the quicker we can find our purpose in life.

In the last chapter, I spoke about fate and destiny and how they work together. Our ego has a plan that we think what is best for us, but our soul knows what is best for the universe. Once we start listening to these synchronicities and following what our heart knows is best, we start to see many more doors start to open for us. This can be defined as "flow." You know when you see someone working in their flow, because they are good at it, work from the heart, and look forward to getting up each day and continuing what they were meant to do. Door after door opens for this person and almost appears to be "lucky," but really they are just answering the call of the universe by being aware and listening to the messages that we all receive.

Another example is one of the greatest writers of all-time, John Steinbeck. He knew that he was destined to be a writer and did vast amounts of research as to what type of novel people would be interested. He wrote four novels about 17th century France, as he research had indicated what people wanted to read, yet nothing sold. As he looked out in front of him, he saw a lot of poverty in California and started to write about what he saw (a sign? a message?) and what his heart was telling him. This led to writing about things such as the Oklahoma dust bowl in Grapes of Wrath, which is one of the greatest classic novels of all-time. Furthermore, it changed the way people viewed the Great Depression and those suffering. His heart's intelligence was telling him that he had a greater purpose for the universe and it wasn't until the stopped listening to his brain, and started listening to his heart in which he found his flow.

For me, I was going through a transformational time of my own. Many times, these transformations begin by going through what is commonly referred to as the "dark night of the soul." There are countless number of spiritual gurus that share moments on the verge of suicide before turning their life over, or celebrities that went through countless hours of working meaningless jobs before getting their big break. It comes to a point in which the seeker knows that there is much more out there than what they are experiencing, but they do not quite understand what it is. It is the time when their memory is starting to work circular, rather than linear.

My end was coming soon. I was getting sucked into another black hole, and getting prepared to hit the self-destruct button again. Perhaps this time it would be fatal. I had no idea what was happening to me, but I sensed an eruption about to take place. The same way animals instinctually can tell when a natural disaster is about to occur.

In the 2004 Tsunami, of all the incredible stories of survival, the one that is often overlooked is all the wild animals that had "sensed" the disaster and moved to higher grounds before the floods took place. Many scientists like to play off this animal instinct that resides in all of us. The difference is that human brains became more developed and we were able to articulate and communicate, which took away our natural ability to feel and understand telepathically. Animals still have this ability, but as we evolve as a species it has been taken away from us. But we still have it in us, and like any skill just needs to be practiced, which is how psychics are able to accurately understand others and see events before they happen.

My grandmother had incredible intuition and it runs in our family. My intuition is far more accurate than it is incorrect, and by the way things were going, it was a combination of common sense, intuition, and similar patterns in which I sensed an inner tsunami on the horizon.

A Tale of Two Physicians

I had gone to the same local clinic a couple times seeking help, which is a highly difficult thing for a man to do in Western culture. This alone is a message from the universe propelling me to write this book. This stigma alone kills people daily, because we are afraid to ask for help. It is viewed as a weakness if you ask for help, yet it takes incredible strength to be brutally honest with yourself and tell the world that you are in pain.

But when you get pushed into a corner, you only have so many options. If I didn't have my children, I likely would have thrown in the towel and given up. But I knew I had to at least try something before everything fell apart.

My first encounter was with Dr. Donnder, and he told me I had chronic fatigue syndrome.

"There is nothing you can do about it," he told me as he shrugged his shoulders, "they have some support groups out there that you could try."

Not too long later, I went to see him again. Although, he did not recognize me and did not realize that he had previously had me as a patient and diagnosed me with chronic fatigue syndrome. This time, he told me that I might have tuberculosis.

Was he just guessing at things here? He did not know my name or anything about me. It was apparent that he did not care. Everyone was right, all of this is just a big money-making scam. Nobody cares about the patients, it is a matter of getting them in-and-out of the office as quickly as possible just as any business works. He does not see a person, he sees dollar signs when people come into the office.

"No, doctor," I pleaded, "I think I am depressed. I can't get up in the morning, I no longer enjoy the things that I used to love. I don't know what is happening to me."

I got no response. He looked at me as though he was saying, "What do you want me to do?"

This is what helps the stigma grow. I am terrified to open up and share what is going on because I have been brainwashed into believing that there is something wrong with me for asking for help. Then, I go to a professional and use all of my strength to share what is going on, and this is the respond I get? Why would anyone ever return?

The reason I returned is because I am about to have a son and I want to be healthy so I can support my kids. It was May of 2011 and I am desperate at this point, so I made another appointment. I was trembling with fear and shame as I waited for my name to be called in that waiting room, knowing I was going to have to open up once again to another doctor who does not care about me.

In walks Dr. Michael Braker.

When you reach out and have pure intentions, often you are sent an angel. This man, in the next few moments, changed everything for me. His actions altered the course of my world and everyone around me. Another synchronicity in the middle of the dark night of my soul.

"Hi, Cortland," he says with a genuine smile on his face, "I'm Doctor Braker."

Empathy refers to feeling the emotions of others. We all have this ability, some have it greater than others. It has to do with recognizing what other people are feeling, and you take on that same emotion. It is another animal instinct that has been lost along the way of the left-brain dominance of the western culture.

Dr. Braker must have sensed my anxiety, fear, depression, and shame as he walked in the room. With is simple introduction all the tension in my muscles suddenly faded. How did he do this? One simple introduction and I felt better already, as though it was this man's genuine kindness and compassion that just lifted a weight off my shoulders. I knew I didn't have to fear him and that he wanted to help me.

He spoke to me for about one hour, and talks to me like I'm a human being and not just another number on his daily list of things to get done. He was clearly going to be behind schedule because of this, but it did not seem to bother him. I likely had more anxiety about his schedule and the next patient than he did, he was in the moment and knew that I needed the time.

At the end of our conversation, he prescribes me with Celexa and stated that he wanted to see me again in two weeks to monitor the side effects. He wasn't just one of the pill pushers that I previously shared my disgust about. He believed this medication would help, but more importantly he wanted to know how it worked on me rather than just sending me on my way.

Two weeks go by, and I find myself waiting a room again for Dr. Braker. He knocks on the door, peeks his head in real quick just to check in on me.

"Hey Cortland!" he says with a grin, "I'll be in shortly, just running a little late."

A small, seemingly meaningless gesture makes such a difference. He knew my name? I couldn't believe it. And he took time to acknowledge that he was running late, understood that his client's are people too, and still has a smile on his face.

For all I know, he could have been helping someone like myself the first time I came in. Maybe he needed an hour with someone else that day. Just by popping his head in and letting me know he would be late, showed that he valued my time and helped me relax.

He never judged me and was always 100-percent present. He was never looking at his watch or trying to get out the door. In the past, I have always had doctors that come in, not know my name, never listen, know nothing about me, and try to get the appointment done as quickly as possible. That is why I never asked for help, it seemed as though I was an inconvenience to doctors, as though they had people with "real" problems and I was just a grown man complaining about life.

A month went by, and I was feeling great. Hardly drinking anymore and starting to actually enjoy life. I was climbing out of this black hole that was about to devour me and everything I cared about.

All because of the provider that took time to hear what I had to say and feel what I was feeling. Everything in our society has become about making money, and the most money as possible. This means seeing six patients each hour, in-and-out, send out the bills. In the fast food industry, the quicker they make the food, the more they can get to the next customer and the income increases. Health care is quickly taking on this model. We are not too far away from having drive-thru clinics!

Especially when we are dealing with mental health, such as depression, it seems counter-productive to just write a prescription and send the client on their way after a 10-minute talk. The person is hurting, in pain, struggling to find the courage to share what is going on. They need someone, a person, not a pill.

There have been studies conducted on doctor's who have been sued for malpractice are always the ones that lack empathy for their clients. Even if a doctor gives a wrong diagnosis or causes harm to a patient unintentionally, but shows empathy, it is highly unlikely that they will get sued for malpractice because they person felt cared about. On the other hand, a doctor who comes off as cold, does not show compassion is far more likely to be sued for something minor because the person senses the lack of compassion.

In a sense, a doctor should be liable for damages if they are not empathetic or compassionate. Isn't that the entire purpose of health care? It's not just about the physical health, but our emotional health has been scientifically proven to correlate with physical health. People are far more likely to heal from physical ailments when they are in a better frame of mind. It is the doctor's duty to "care" for the person they are seeing. If they lack this component, perhaps they are in the wrong line of work.

I had the exact same problem that I had a few months ago, symptoms of depression. One doctor (Braker) showed compassion and I noticed immediate results. Whereas, the other doctor (Donnder) acted as though I was an annoyance to him, and my symptoms got worse. It was a tale of two doctors - It was the best of times, it was the worst of times.

Synchronicity in Every Step

Every interaction matters, it was another soul contract that each one played its purpose. The first one drove me deeper into despair, and the second showed me the light. By simply knowing my name and being interested in me, it changed my life. He made me feel comfortable and I was able to open up more. This is the same old story that continues throughout this book, love, compassion, caring for one another. This is not groundbreaking information, it has been taught by all the ancient philosophers, religions, and healers throughout time. Dr. Braker did more for me in that one hour, than all previous physicians have done for me in my entire life combined.

People told me that I was euphoric. They were right, I felt euphoria in everything. I had never been this happy, and I expected this to fix everything. This would eliminate my need to drink, my anxiety would be gone, I would be OK around Jill's family, right? Wrong.

I thought I had a cure without having to do any real soul work. Nothing works this way, and all short cuts end up making things twice as difficult in the long run. We still have to work on ourselves, the medication is a boost to get us in the right mindset to start doing the work. Anyone who has been truly depressed, understands the viciousness of the cycle. You are feeling down, and know that you need to get up and do something, but you lack the energy or motivation to do so. Then, because you are unable to do so, you feel guilty that you are unable to get up and do something and feel worse about it.

It gets to the point that you get hungry and know all I would have to do is make a sandwich. But, then I think, "yeah but then I have to get out the bread, put the peanut butter away and the knife will be dirty. That is just too much effort."

As ridiculous as that sounds, even worse the depressed person is fully aware that this is ridiculous which only furthers there depression. They know that it is not logical, but they cannot snap out of it. The medication works as a tool to make it so the person can function through the day and start working on their self to get out of this state of mind. It is not a, "take this pill and everything is fixed." That is a huge misconception that has been created by the mass media and marketing campaigns. Nothing is that simple, but we are in a pill-taking society in which we expect anything can be solved by taking a drug.

When we are first born, there are some changes that take place. The first life lesson we receive is a literal pat on the back which teaches the infant to breathe in air. We have all the tools in place, we just need to adjust to our new surroundings. Next, we need to learn to eat without the umbilical cord. It doesn't take long and we learn to adjust. Once out of the womb, we need to start doing it on our own and make adjustments rather quickly. This is how all growth takes place, we need to have action, have some failures and learn from them, and continue to take action, and see the progress along the way. All growth occurs in this same pattern.

But I felt better than I had ever felt in my life and my fear was always that this feeling would go away. It was the same thing with drugs and alcohol, I was afraid that feeling would go away which led me to indulging. Furthermore, I had developed a physical dependency to alcohol and still needed my drug and continued to drink. It was everyone's greatest fear that I would be drunk when Jill went into labor and I would miss the birth of my son.

First, it was always being drunk while watching Bayonna and I made excuses, lied, and hid the truth. Then it was at all of Kylee's school events that I would either miss because I was drunk, or only attend if I had a few drinks. I would always say that I was going to quit, but I never made it more than 24 days. And at this point, I truly meant it. I had every intention of quitting each time that I said I was done, but I couldn't follow through. I have had enough, but something kept pulling me back in.

Then on June 30, 2011, Rocky was born.

I was not drunk and I saw my son born. I could not believe it. My entire life, I had dreamt about having a son and now I did. I held him in my arms and again felt the unconditional love that exists in every living creature. It is the love of God. It is the only truth in this world.

The problem with drugs and alcohol is they do a great job fooling you into believing that you are experiencing this feeling. Drugs give you an artificial spiritual connection, a taste of reality, with an ultimate price you pay in the end. Once I had this euphoric feeling while holding Rocky, my brain was triggered to have a drink of alcohol.

Dopamine is the pleasure chemical in our brains. We all have dopamine and it gets moved around when we are experiencing things that bring us joy and pleasure. With drugs and alcohol, these systems are manipulated and an unnatural amount of dopamine is flushed into our neurological pathways creating an intense sensation of happiness. But, the brain also has a built-in mechanism known as homeostasis which always brings the brain back to a balance.

When using drugs, you only get to rent that dopamine rush. Everything that you experience, you have to pay back at some point. After the initial rush, the brain creates balance which creates the "hangover" or "crash" effect because you need to pay back what you have been recklessly using. This leads the user to need more of the substance to feel the same effect – also known as tolerance. As this continues over time, the user eventually needs to use the drug just to feel normal because their brain's balance is so depleted of natural dopamine.

After years of abusing alcohol and relying on drugs to manage my mood and emotions, I had no other way of feeling happy besides when intoxicated. This meant both physically and mentally, I could not be happy unless I was under the influence. As I held Rocky, my brain was triggered with true, pure joy and love. My dopamine system was activated naturally, but I was unfamiliar with this feeling. The only thing that I could familiarize this feeling with was being drunk. While in this moment, all I could think about was going home and having a drink.

Can you imagine that? Here I am going through this beautiful moment, all my dreams being realized, and all I can think about is, "Man, let's get this over with so I can get a drink."

This was the beginning of the end for my false self, and I finally consciously was aware of it.

Now, I am writing all of this well after the fact. In the moment, I did not know why I was wanting a drink. All I knew was that I needed alcohol, and I knew that it was wrong to want a drink in this moment. But, I couldn't control how I felt, nor did I know why I felt this way. It was an incredibly awful feeling with no comprehension as to what was going on inside of me.

Prior to this moment, I had been arrested for a DWI not too long ago and went back to jail for the third time. I have been drunk and missed holidays with the family, or too hung over to participate. Every time there was a big moment coming, when I knew that I couldn't drink – that was the exact moment in which I grabbed the bottle. It made no sense to anyone, myself included.

I ruined Jill's high school reunion which was important to her because of my inability to control myself. I missed Kylee's parent's day at basketball cheerleading, meaning she had no one to escort her during the pregame ceremonies – the only kid on the court without a parent by her side.

"It's OK, Dad," she would tell me. But it was not OK, whether she truly believed it or not, I know now that it was not OK. I was drunk on her birthdays. We took her to the amusement park, and then I got hammered in the beer gardens and drove her home. I drove drunk with her in the car far too many times than I wish to mention.

Joey's cancer benefit, we got trashed the night before and showed up late. Reggie's wedding we were almost too hung over to make it to the ceremony. Then, of course, I was coaching a little league baseball team and we advanced to the state tournament. For months, we had been preaching to them the importance and significance of this tournament and how all their hard work would pay off this weekend – and I got drunk the night before and was too hungover to coach in the biggest game of their lives.

I was turning into my grandmother. Why can I not stop? I really no longer want to do this. All the times I told everyone I was going to quit, I never really had a desire to stop. I just wanted to stop getting in trouble, but now I had no desire to do so and it kept happening.

I would be determined to quit, put all my mental energy into doing so and then after one week, I was right back at it. I absolutely hated myself for this, but without the alcohol I was going crazy. And when I did drink, I had enormous guilt for not being strong enough to abstain. I felt like a complete loser and it was pure torture going through this week-after-week.

The absolute worst part of it all was the moment I was holding Rocky and thinking about alcohol. I tasted both heaven and hell in the same moment. I felt the greatest love this world knows, followed by the enormous pain of wondering why I was thinking about getting drunk.

On the morning after he was born, I was planning on going to the hospital to visit Jill, Rocky, Bayonna, and Kylee – our entire big family together for the first time. My dad, Larry, and I decided to golf at 7:00 a.m. before heading to the hospital.

Dark Night of the Soul

After nine holes, Larry and I decided to stop in the club house. Well, it was more like I decided and Larry just went along for the ride. It's his gift, he provides unconditional support. He is an amazing man who had no idea what was about to come. Neither did I.

"Let's just have two beers and then finish the last nine before going to the hospital," I suggest instead of just grabbing a candy bar as we had told our Dad.

This was the intention, have a few early morning beers to make golf a little more fun and then be on our way. We knew Dad was waiting outside so we had to go quick and thought it would be funny. But Cortland after two beers, is a much different person than Cortland with zero beers. You see, Cortland with zero beers truly only wanted to have "a couple beers, finish the last nine holes and go to the hospital."

But Cortland with two beers then thinks, "Well if this feels this good, what if we had a shot." And then another, and another.

Jill calls and I am drunk, and she knows it. She has become such a pro at this by now, she can tell you what I've been drinking and how much I've had just by my voice and face – and typically she is accurate.

In my head, I know that this is that breaking point that I had feared for so long. I thought maybe I had overcome it with the medication and with Rocky being born, but I couldn't avoid this dark moment.

Back to the tsunami analogy, the tsunami starts with an earthquake underneath the ocean which is only felt by those that are closest to the storm. Then the sea level actually drastically drops and creates this surreal scene which has everyone a bit puzzled – it is the calm before the storm. Then suddenly the sea level starts rising at an unnaturally rapid pace which has people starting to sense that something bad is about to happen. As they start walking into shelter, they see an enormous wave roaring toward land which creates devastating destruction.

Then, another calm. The sea level drops and everyone can relax. Only for a moment though, because the next wave comes and it is far bigger than the previous one which brings the ocean onto the land and everything is destroyed.

My tsunami had begun, and I knew it.

Not knowing how to handle the situation, I turned on my automatic switch which has dealt with uncomfortable emotions my entire life – booze. I kept drinking and my Dad eventually came in and left knowing that we had to go the hospital. Even Larry stopped drinking at that point and that is the last thing I remember.

I woke up around eight or nine at night in the backseat of a car in my garage, no idea of how I got there or how long I had been there. I called Larry to take me to the bar and he said "no." He said he would only come over to the house to spend time with me if we did not drink. This was my number one drinking buddy that I could count on for anything. We always drank just as much as each other and did just as stupid stuff together, and he told me he would only visit me if we didn't drink? What the hell happened?

If Dr. Braker did not arrive in my life when he did, I would be dead without any doubt. I would not have made it past this point, this is where the story would have ended. There are no small moments in life, every moment, every interaction is an opportunity for something great. All it took was for him to treat me like a human, and it started me on a path to recovery.

This was a turning point for me and I was getting started on this path, right before this big fall. Right before the Tsunami, Dr. Braker told me to stay off the beach that day. That's all it took. The tsunami still happened and I lost everything I owned, but I was still alive.

I went to him when I was at my perceived lowest, and he put a spark in me that gave me hope. While I sat there alone in my home after this Debacle, I still carried with me that little bit of hope that he had provided.

As stated in the Shawshank Redemption,

> "Fear can make you a prisoner, but hope can set you free."

This was the dark night of my soul. I was broken in mind, body, and spirit. There was a collapse in all meaning in my life. Nothing made sense anymore. And yet, there was a mysterious sense of hope. It's almost as though we need to go through this dark night of the soul, a total destruction of our reality in order for us to create a new one. A new reality, one that is built on interconnectedness and does not require sophisticated meanings or scientific explanations.

At the time, the pain and suffering of the dark night seems never-ending. Stuck in an eternal black hole in which everything has crumbled.

The real battle is recognizing the dark night for what it is, realizing that without the darkness we could never see the stars, and knowing the crumbling away we are experiencing is the crumbling away of the false self. The death we are experiencing, is the death of the ego.

CHAPTER XV

The Dark Night of the Soul
Hitting Rock Bottom

Chapter 15
The Dark Night of the Soul:
Hitting Rock Bottom

The Buddha taught us that in all of life there is pain. And, yet, also taught us that pain is inevitable but suffering is optional. While in theory, it sounds quite practical. But how do we prevent pain from ascending into suffering?

Hope. That's it, just hope.

Suffering is simply the absence of hope. Though the resurgence of hope can transform the suffering back into manageable pain, and with pain can come growth. Hope is typically the last thing taken from a man before he completely crumbles into a state of despair, loss of control, and destruction. And often, we find hope in the most unlikely of places. Sometimes it takes someone to believe in us, when we are not able to believe in ourselves that provides the hope, the lifeblood, which is needed in these dark nights.

In a lecture, I once picked up a bottle of water and asked the audience how much the bottle of water weighed. They all gave their different guesses and techniques at trying to give the most accurate answer. The truth is it does not matter how much it weighs. What matters is how long you hold onto the bottle of water. If I hold onto it during the entire lecture, it starts to feel heavier and heavier and harder to hold. I start to feel "pain" up and down my arm and eventually it starts to interfere with my ability to give my lecture (suffering). If I were to continue to hold onto the bottle, I would start to get angry, irritated with people, unable to concentrate, or focus on what is being said. My primary goal is to get rid of this bottle of water and everything else is secondary.

That is how suffering works. It is the inability to let go of the pain and allow it to run our lives. Pain is going to happen in life, but we choose whether or not we are going to suffer. In this analogy, all I have to do is put the bottle down and suddenly my mood shifts and I can resume life; the same goes for pain and suffering.

Wish and Hope

Now, I need to differentiate between wish and hope. We use these words interchangeably, but they could not be further from synonyms. Wishes are just things that we would like to come true, such as winning the lottery. But, hope is far greater than that. Hope refers to accurately seeing positivity in the future. It reminds us that tomorrow might be a better day. It is the power that allows us to envision cancerous cells dying, relationships rebuilding, and financial burdens being lifted.

Sitting alone in despair at my house, Jill's mother stops over to pick up the car seats and I can feel myself crawling out of my skin. Just when I wanted the pain to go away for good, I was faced with another moment of immense suffering.

She had every reason in the world to demonize me, judge me, and hate me. But, she never did. She seemed to always realize that things were not entirely my fault, and never viewed me as the evil villain destroying her daughter. Like my own mother, she somehow has the ability to look beyond the mask and see people's true character.

"Never give up on an addict," she would tell Jill.

I had lost all reasons to live, the suffering was inescapable, and like everyone who becomes suicidal the best alternative to escape the pain was to end this existence. This is why the scariest state of mind someone can tell you that they are in, is one of hopelessness. Without hope, there is no future. And when one gets into this state of hopelessness, it is a black hole in which nothing anybody can say can bring you out of it.

Because that is trying to solve problems with the left-brain, but logic is not capable of solving depression. Every single thing you could possibly say, the person has thought of millions of times in their own head. Logically, depression does not make sense even to the depressed person.

The left-brain tells us, "I wish I didn't feel this way," "things are not so bad," "other people have it worse," "look at the bright side," "just look at things positively."

Whereas, the right-brain uses images and emotions and no words are necessary. Jill's mother, without saying a word was able to send me the messages of hope, when I lacked in belief in myself. That subliminal/telepathic message is the only difference between me pulling the trigger and ending it all that day.

My brother Larry has suffered from depression most of his life. He has lost many friends and people stopped talking to him because of his inability to "snap out of it." While I was going through these dark days and wanted to end it all, my brother Larry sent this to me:

> "You have always been there for me during my darkest days. Being friends with a depressed person is the most difficult, yet kindest, thing you can do for another person. You cared for me when I didn't care for myself."

August Landmesser

In 1931, there was a worldwide financial collapse and a global depression. This was especially true in the war-ravaged Germany after losing the First World War and paying repercussions to France and Britain. This led to the rise of the Nazi Party, in which a man named August Landmesser would join in an effort to land a job. Four years later, he met the woman of his dreams and they were engaged to be married only before the Nuremburg Laws prevented this from taking place.

While the masses were joining the Nazi Party in Germany and watching the country rebuild, Landmesser was able to see the truth. There was an entire nation rallying around this party that was bringing a nation out of poverty and back into power, but Landmesser was not impressed. In 1936, a crowd of people were gathering to watch the launching of a navy vessel in Hamburg in which they all stood to proudly salute Der Fuhrer, Adolf Hitler. But, not Landmesser. While there were a handful of people not saluting, none were as obvious and Landmesser with his arms crossed and unimpressed with the brainwashing of the masses in front of him.

This image surfaced in 1991 and has become quite notorious on the internet as it shows thousands of men saluting Der Fuhrer, with a circle around Landmesser as he chooses to think for himself.

In my own little world, this was Deana on that day. Everyone close to me had joined the masses to kick me while I was down, and with very good reason. Yet, she decided to stand alone, against the crowd, and see behind my mask. The easy thing to do would have been to join the party, create the master race without an inferior like me as part of their family, but she chose the road less traveled. She chose to be like August Landmesser that day, not caring what the result would be, but knowing she was standing up for what she knew to be true.

And while this moment of courage by Deana provided enough hope for me to carry on, the pain was still unbearable. I knew that the marriage was over as I had begged, cried, and pleaded with Jill to no avail. She finally had enough, and I saw that this time it was really the end.

At the same time, things at work were falling apart as well. Riley was helping as much as she could as she knew that I was struggling. But she also had patients and other employees to worry about, and I was losing all respect that I had recently built up over the years. I was rarely at work, and when I did make it there physically, I was still absent mentally and emotionally.

Everything was crumbling once again, the self-destruct button had been activated just as I have done so many times before. It didn't make sense. How was this possible after I had worked so hard to turn my life around?

The problem was that this castle I had appeared to have built, was under a poor foundation. The outside was decorated with gold and chrome, though nothing to protect from the wind, rain, and storms of life.

> *"And so castles made of sand, fall in the sea, eventually."* – Jimi Hendrix

Addiction is one of the most complicated diseases in the world. It is the only such disease that convinces you 100-percent that you do not have it. Imagine having a broken arm, feeling the physical pain, recognizing the symptoms and yet refusing to get help. Others would see that you are struggling and in pain, but you deny that it exists and start blaming it on everything else.

This is how the substance eventually hijacks the brain. The addiction convinces the person that everything that is happening around him/her has nothing to do with the drug, and they will defend the drug at all costs. This is why, so often, it takes people to hit a "rock bottom" before going to treatment – or to be forced into treatment by the law. It is the only way to get someone in the door to look at how their mind has been abducted by a chemical that used to bring them pleasure.

I swore that missing Rocky's first three days and my failed marriage were my rock bottom. How could it possibly get worse?

Well, the problem is that there are "high bottoms" and "low bottoms." What I mean by that is we can have these experiences that open our eyes and create problems to the point we can no longer deny our addiction. Though, in these instances, we still have our material possessions, employment, some friends and family. This is the stereotypical case of the "functional alcoholic."

The low bottoms occur when we start to lose these things. The person who hits the low bottom is quite obvious to everyone. But, I was only hitting my high bottom at this point, because to some outsiders, it still did not appear that I had a real drug problem. I just had to learn how to control it.

Furthermore, when you have low self-esteem and battling depression on top of addiction, there is no limit as to how far deeper your rock bottom can go. You may be sitting at the lowest low you could have ever imagined, but we become stuck without believing in ourselves, without hope. And all we can do is keep shoveling deeper and deeper and the rock-bottom's progressively get worse.

Firecracker Open

Every year, Jill's family hosts a golf tournament deemed "The Firecracker Open." It is a family reunion which has been taking place in their family for the past fifty years. It is a big event to their entire extended family, which brings in over 100 people from all over the Midwest each year.

Rocky is now one week old, and I am vowed that missing that week was my rock bottom and there is absolutely no chance that I would drink today, especially being around Jill's family.

I make sure that I get a chance to golf with Jill's father and brother in the morning as an opportunity to rebuild some of the trust that I had lost. Trust is like a game of Jenga, it takes a long time to build up with precision, carefulness, and delicacy. But one mistake and it comes crashing down, destroying everything that was once in place. Then, to build it back up again, you must start from scratch and the more times it crumbles, the less confidence you have in making it last.

When it comes to addiction, trust is even more difficult to produce because of the inconsistency in behaviors. I would be great most of the time, nearly 100-percent of the time, but you never knew when I was going to have one of my implosions. That was the tricky part, how can you trust a ticking time bomb? You know it is only a matter of time before it happens again. And, if it happened once, you can play it off. But when it becomes a consistent pattern of inconsistency, people are hesitant to get close again.

However, I am quite excited for this opportunity and a chance to try to rebuild things and prove that those behaviors were in my past. I have never fit in with her family, her father has always judged me and viewed me as some terrible person. He doesn't understand me, nor does he want to understand me. He is a drunk himself, which might be the source of his pain. He is doing the same thing as me, searching for joy by external resources. We are both hungry ghosts, searching for love in the wrong places. Hate is only misguided love, so his hate for me was really never about me. Though, that is difficult to understand while you are going through it.

Plus, neither of us believe we are alcoholics. Our world is just a reflection of ourselves. If I were to look in a mirror and get mad, the reflection cannot help but to also show anger. If I am to laugh and smile, the reflection does the same. This is how the entire world works, if I am a miserable addict, I am going to see the same in this man. At this point, I still do not think I am an alcoholic. I look at all the things that I have accomplished. I have money, cars, nice job, and a big house. That is not an alcoholic. A drunk is a guy that lives under the bridge, at least that is what we have been made to believe. I am just a guy that likes to have a good time, I work hard, and I deserve to have a good time occasionally.

As we are getting closer to teeing off, I start to have all these thoughts in my head and the excitement quickly turns into anxiety and near panic. I had been recently prescribed Klonopin for such reasons, and quickly popped a couple to try to ease my nerves.

I feel relaxed talking to them, but he still will not engage. He just sits there and thinks and analyzes everything, whereas I needed to talk about everything. He has nothing to say, which has my anxiety out of control. This is the problem with using substances to curb emotions such as anxiety or stress. You can't take a drug without it having a rebound effect, you have to pay it back at some point. My anxiety was temporarily lifted, but as the medication wears off, along with the struggles going on externally the symptoms came back harder than if I would have taken no pills at all. Furthermore, relying on a substance takes away from learning how to deal with situations such as this in a normal way. I am cheating myself out of an opportunity to grow as a human.

Anxiety speeds up the body such as increased heart rate, high blood pressure, tense muscles, racing thoughts, and on edge. This is our body's natural survival system to "fight or flight." Of course, it was designed back when humans were first like any other animal and survival was more based off physical fight-or-flight. As we evolved, it is more of a mental fight-or-flight. While this system amps up, drugs such as alcohol or benzodiazepines work as central nervous system depressants – which means they slow the body down.

They naturally will take away all these unwanted feelings of anxiety. The problem is that the brain is always creating balance and once the drug is slowing down the body, the brain puts its foot on the gas pedal trying to amp the body back up. Once the drug wears off, the anxiety is greater than it was before. Our body then remembers that alcohol and benzodiazepines work so well to reduce this anxiety, which is where the habit, or dependence, is created.

As I am playing out this entire doomsday scenario in my mind, assuming that he is thinking the worst, it is really just his personality. Neither way is right or wrong, but I start to take his non-engagement personally and created something that was never really there. I am starting to physically feel pain because of this, emotionally hurting, feeling insecure and I am need of something to make this go away. I needed to take a couple more pills just to finish the round. This one round of golf symbolizes how quickly addiction can happen, once we start to rely on the drug to take away an unwanted feeling, the cycle quickly progresses out of control.

We finished the round. I made it. Exhausted mentally from the torture I put myself through. As I go in the clubhouse, my brother

Larry, friends Shandon and Jim, and my Dad are checking in and ready to play a round.

The Love Tackle

After everything that just happened in the last week, I couldn't believe it, but I actually wanted to have a drink. As they all sat at the counter having non-alcoholic beverages, I cracked a joke asking for a beer. It was dead quiet. Nobody even found it funny, maybe because they all knew that it wasn't a joke. It had gotten to the point that I couldn't even joke about drinking a beer with the group of people that were closest to me.

I was able to manage to sneak in a couple of shots before we got started and we all headed out and had an enjoyable six holes. The sixth hole ends right at the clubhouse, with a long walk before getting to the seventh hole. It is not uncommon for people to stop in the clubhouse and grab a drink at this point, and actually incredibly common for any of us. But, not this time. There was no alcohol involved in our group, besides what I had snuck in before we started.

As we finish the sixth hole, the only thing on my mind is how I am going to get into the clubhouse to get another drink or two. I tell everyone that I am going to stop in the clubhouse to use the bathroom. Everyone already knows what is going on at this point. There is that same silence when I cracked the joke about the beer just a few hours ago. In fact, they tell me not to go in and just go in the woods – which is typical on that course out in the country. But, I insist that I need to use the bathroom in the clubhouse – because I needed another shot.

Here I was, sneaking shots from the people that I used to spend the most time drinking with. The people that were the most supportive of me and I am lying and hiding things from them, because I know that they are starting to disapprove of my habits.

Eventually I come back out to the seventh hole, and everyone has already hit their tee shot. I am stumbling around and my Dad grabs his clubs and leaves the course in disgust. He knows that I am hammered. They call me out on it and I deny everything and start to get defensive towards the group. Everyone is disgusted with me, nobody more than myself. I can't believe that I was in this state again. I swore I would not drink today.

Everyone is done golfing. We paid for 18 holes, and golfed six, because nobody wants to finish the round. So we head back to the reception at Jill's parents' house with nobody having a scorecard to turn in for the tournament. Everybody in her extended family sees me stumbling over the place, unable to talk, or function and it is not even 6:00 p.m. Even Jill's brother is mad at me and he has always been the one to stick up for me. But not anymore.

Larry and Shandon are sitting next to me, looking uncomfortable the entire time and refusing to drink. Here I am again, one week after missing Rocky's birth and I am doing it all over again.

Then suddenly, it all goes black.

Next thing I remember is I am lying on my mother's front lawn with no recollection of how or why I am there. Shandon and Larry show up and I am certain that they came to be my drinking buddies again, they won't judge me like everyone else.

"Let's go to the hospital," Shandon says in a serious voice.

"Ok," I laughed, "is this just your way of getting me out of here so we can go to the bar?"

"No, I'm not taking you to the bar," he remains serious, "Would you be willing to go to the hospital? I'll give you a ride. You were taking Klonopin, Ativan, and a bunch of shots. I'm afraid you are going to overdose and we need to get you checked out."

I start laughing again, not sure what to think of everything.

Maybe this is what I wanted. This was my way of asking for help. As strange as it seems, this was the only way that I was ever going to ask for help, I had to be forced in to treatment. To ask for help was always viewed as a sign of weakness from my perspective. I believed that addiction was something you could control, I just needed to stop drinking. I couldn't believe that things have gotten to this point in my life, but I must have known that I needed help.

"Ok," I said, "let's go. I'll go in."

I think this surprised everyone that I agreed. Maybe it is because of my level of intoxication that I agreed, because it was able to subside some of that fear. On the car ride there, I tried joking with Shandon but he continued to be serious the entire time. Things were starting to set in and I couldn't believe that my life has gotten to the point that I am admitting myself to the hospital for an overdose.

As we pulled into the parking lot, I think everything got too real. We all started to have a sense of fear.

"Ok," I trembled, "you made your point. Let's just turn around now."

I was serious. I no longer wanted to do this. I had no idea what the intention was, but I made it up in my mind that I was not going to follow through with this intervention. This was far too real, I could see the hospital and we were pulling up to the ER doors.

"No, we are really doing this," Shandon said as he looked at me with tears in his eyes. He knew he was putting his best friend in a tough situation.

"You are really doing this to me?" I asked, "I'm going to lose my job. Thanks a lot, Larry."

My last effort to place the blame on somebody, as Larry immediately started crying which brought back flashbacks to when I was younger and was getting hauled away in police cars. Everything I had worked for was getting washed into the sea. Then as Shandon was talking to the receptionist, I made my move.

"Well, this isn't the first time I've done this…" I said to Larry as I slammed the door on him and took off running. Downtown, in a blackout state, barefoot, and I start running with no idea as to what is going on.

Then, I am tackled from behind. Somehow Shandon caught me. How did this 220 pound guy chase me down after I got a head start?

Love, that's how.

If you are pure in your intentions and God enters you, you cannot be stopped. Who knows what would have happened if he did not catch me in that moment. Then he was able to talk to me and convince me to go into the ER somehow. I am a bull-headed drunk, and somehow he convinces me to go into the hospital.

Here is a case in which Shandon gave me tough love, which was necessary to save my life. If we did not have great rapport to begin with, it would have never worked. I would have started fighting him, or I would have never agreed to go in the car to begin with. This is how the entire industry works, this is how the world works. You must build relationships first. People do not care how much you know, until they know how much you care.

They bring me in to detox, but I have been working in this field for far too long and I know what to say to ensure they will not keep me. I am told that I need treatment and I agree with them. Although, this is quite common for people in the Emergency Room to state that they need treatment. At that time, it is obvious, but as they sober up their mind goes back to playing tricks on them.

Others Hope in Me

I was set up to go to outpatient treatment. It was a dinky little place behind a Super 8 Motel in an obscure little building in a small town. Not quite what I had imagined when I thought of treatment. I went in for my intake and was scheduled to begin the next week.

However, I had not had a drink in fourteen days at this point. I have been scared straight, there is no need to go to treatment – another common belief as the fear of the unknown convinces in any way to not try something that is new.

I wake up the morning of my first day of treatment and I convince myself that I am fine. I don't really need to go to treatment, I stopped drinking, and things are getting better. I don't even have any desire to drink anymore after the night of the Firecracker Open. Jill agrees with me, that things really are not that bad and there is no need to go to treatment. I am not a true alcoholic or how could we be living like this?

As the time approached, she says, "Just go one time and see what you think. What do you have to lose?"

Group started at 6:00 p.m., but for some reason I had written down 6:30 p.m. So, I arrive at 6:15, and was fifteen minute late. I walked in, they guided me to the group room where I would begin my treatment. No idea as to what to expect was on the other side of that door, my entire body was shaking as I was terrified of the idea of treatment. Really, I was just terrified of the idea of doing anything uncomfortable without the aid of alcohol.

I opened the door and there they all sat, all eyes peaked up at me. There was Jerry, Sharon, Mindy, and Albert all sitting in a circle. Michelle ran the group and she peered at me with welcoming eyes that I will never forget. The fear instantly dropped. Everything did. Somehow, I knew I belonged just by the looks of the eyes of those in the room. I was seeing myself in all of them and all my worries simply vanished in an instant.

Without the help of Shandon, Larry, my mother, and even Jill's mother seeing the good in me, I am certain this entire thing would have collapsed. How could anyone see the good in me after the past two weeks that I put them through? None of these are coincidences, these angels were put in my paths to help guide me home. They helped guide me to this group room that was a necessary block on my path to enlightenment.

After the 1996 bombing of the Oklahoma City Federal Building, Garth Brooks wrote a song entitled, "The Change." This song was dedicated the emergency personnel and rescue workers that spent countless hours searching through the Debris and rubble looking for trapped victims.

With the acts of terror and natural disasters that have followed in the past two decades since then, we see these images quite often and the same song comes to mind. In the opening lines, Brooks talks about a rescue worker saving someone and a voice asks "what good is it, while thousands more are dead?"

And the chorus goes:

> *"I hear them saying, you'll never change things;*
> *And no matter what you do it's still the same things;*
> *But it's not the world, that I am changing;*
> *I do this so, the world will know, that it will not change me."*

These angels of mine stood alone and against the masses, with nothing to gain and everything to lose. They challenged everyone and stood up for what they believed and knew to be true. Life is simpler when you go with the crowd, there is far less risk involved. But true joy comes from with following your heart, despite every reason to go against what it is telling you to be true.

While this was going on, I didn't realize that I was working the steps of a 12-step program. Somewhere deep down, I was starting to see that I was powerless over alcohol and my life had become unmanageable – defining the first step. The second step is about hope. Hoping that a power greater than ourselves can restore us to sanity.

The deeper the despair, the more powerful is the hope. While I lied alone in my house that day, which may as well been considered my death bed, it was the smallest ray of hope that was guided upon me by Deana that gave me the courage to carry on. It gave me the emotional image of a better tomorrow and a belief that this too shall pass.

It was her belief in me, when I didn't believe in myself that taught me to "never give up on an addict."

Section IV
THE BOOK OF WISDOM

Chapter XVI:	Recovery	335
Chapter XVII:	Freedom to Be Me	355
Chapter XVIII:	Relapse	369
Chapter XIX:	Forced Surrender	387
Chapter XX:	The Lunatic is on the Grass	405
Chapter XXI:	Disillusionment	425

CHAPTER XVI

Recovery

Abstinence is not the end; it is the beginning

Chapter 16
Recovery: Abstinence is not the end; it is the beginning.

On April 20, 1999, Dillian Klebold and Eric Harris walked into their high school with automatic weapons and opened fire at the staff and students at Columbine High School in Littleton, Colorado, leaving 19 dead. I still remember the images on the television screen as the nation stood in shock as the horror unfolded right before our eyes.

A few years later, Michael Moore made a documentary in regards to gun control with his film "Bowling for Columbine." Of the most interesting points that Moore came up with in this film is his short two-minute interview with Marilyn Manson. At the time, Klebold and Harris were big fans of Manson's music and the mass media needed a scapegoat. Manson was criticized and blamed for the attack, and out of respect he canceled the final five shows of his tour that year. As the two spoke about the music industry, along with the corruption of government, the interview concluded with the following exchange:

> **Moore:** *"What would you say to these two if you had an opportunity to talk to them?"*
> **Manson:** *"Nothing. I wouldn't say one word to them. I would listen to what they had to say, because clearly nobody else took the time to do so."*

Now, my purpose is not to pardon these two and the atrocities they committed on that day. But, rather examine how our society understands mental illness and the role that we all play. Manson's final line of the interview sums up the entire problem – nobody is taking the time to listen.

We all come into this world with a clean slate before we are domesticated by parents, grandparents, teachers, churches, television, friends, and the billions of other messages we receive. This is all part of the socialization process of the American psyche. We train everyone to be the same, and to be "normal" as part of the process. While in school, you are told what to think, not how to think. Then you must fall into a certain category or else you fall behind in the race to the finish line. Once you get behind, you lose purpose and meaning in life.

It is a survival of the fittest mentality. But that is not how humans evolved. We evolved by expressing love towards our fellow man, showing compassion, and caring for others. The competitiveness of our society may appear to be evolving our species, but in reality we are digressing as we continue to create a greater illusion of separateness.

In August of 2013, America was on the verge of yet another school shooting. There have been countless numbers of mass shootings since Columbine as the media has nearly sensationalized such events, which has led to copycat acts over the past 15 years.

At Ronald McNair Discovery Learning Academy, just outside of Atlanta, Michael Brandon Hill entered the school with a rifle and nearly 500 rounds of ammunition. He was mentally unstable and had lost the will to live, and intended on taking others out with him.

Less than a year after the dreadful Sandy Hook shooting had left 26 dead, America was on the verge of another deadly elementary school disaster. But it was a woman with the last name "Tuff" that exemplified mental toughness that comes from the heart is mightier than any toughness that comes from muscle or violence. Antoinette

Tuff, the school bookkeeper, noticed Hill and took time to talk to him and shared her personal struggles.

Tuff shared her difficulties of raising a disabled child, having her husband leave her, and failing in business. She convinced Hill to put down his weapons, and later states that he did not want to be doing this.

"I thought the same thing, you know, I tried to commit suicide last year after my husband left me," Tuff had told Hill during the altercation. "But look at me now. I'm still working and everything is OK."

Eventually, Hill agreed to put the gun down and discontinue his plan that would have surely resulted in multiple losses of life.

"It's going to be all right, sweetie," she tells Hill at one point. "I just want you to know I love you, though, OK? And I'm proud of you. That's a good thing that you're just giving up and don't worry about it. We all go through something in life."

Sometimes "giving up," is the strongest thing you can do. This is the power of surrender. As dramatic as this story is, the climax of it is that Tuff was not even scheduled to work that fateful day. It was only because of a shift change that had Tuff working in the front office that day and was the first to encounter Hill in the school.

Still believe in coincidences?

Learning to Connect

A synchronicity of my own took place the day I walked into the group room at outpatient treatment. I walked in and everyone was smiling and happy. I didn't get it. Why are they so happy and nice? I always thought treatment was a form of punishment for people who couldn't handle their liquor and got in trouble with the law. I was here as a final attempt to save my marriage, and happy is definitely not the emotion I would use to describe how I was feeling to be at treatment.

Then there was Michelle, the counselor. She welcomes me to the group and asks me to have a seat in the circle. This is nothing as to what I had expected. Neither was Michelle. She is a motherly type, very welcoming. It was like coming home to see Ma. She had hot chocolate out for us and with a huge grin she says, "Well c'mon in. We've been waiting for you."

How true were those words? We are the ones we have been waiting for all along. We all have the power within, and in this little tiny office building was a place in which these counselors allow us to recognize the power we possess. Michelle is very welcoming with a genuine expression on her face of love and compassion. Yet, at the same time, I can see fierceness in her eyes. They call her "The Mama Bear" as she is going to take care of her cubs, but you best not cross her. And you see this in her the first moment you make eye contact.

"Hello, welcome," she says with a smile, "We are just finishing up check-ins. Let's have everyone tell their story and what brings them here."

In no other walks of life, would you encounter a group of people with such differences sitting around talking for two or three hours. We had a young man working construction, a nurse, a punk-rocker guy, professionals, students, and everything in-between. Some were mandated to be there to fulfill court obligations, while others (like myself) just saw their life starting to crumble around them.

One guy shares his story and his history of violence with his girlfriend and some of his pending legal charges. He is following court recommendations and trying to stay out of future trouble.

I remember thinking, "man you are lucky to be in trouble with the law so early in life."

Most people wouldn't view this as "luck" per se, but because of the stigma attached to addiction most people do not seek help until they get to a point in which they are forced. Either forced by the law, relationships, financial, or health, are the typical reasons people enter treatment.

But treatment is not about just learning to stop drinking or using drugs, it is about learning how to live life. If you never learn these things as a child, you will not just figure it out magically, and sometimes we need some "unfortunate luck" to bring us to the right spot where we can learn, develop, and grow.

Here, this man just told his story with all his mistakes and everyone just accepted him as he was. Nobody viewed him as a bad person, nor judged him. They knew him without his mask on and they knew that he had a good heart. In fact, they were all encouraging him.

This has been the power of Alcoholics Anonymous for nearly 80 years. It is just a group of people with a common struggle, getting together in a circle, sharing their stories, providing feedback and support. We open up, make ourselves vulnerable, and nobody is judging us. We see each other without a mask and we feel good about ourselves. It is a powerful, spiritual moment, every time people step into the room.

Addiction treatment programs initially took up this model as a means of saving money. They looked at it and saw that you could charge somebody $100 per hour to talk to a counselor, but then the counselor is going to be too busy to see everyone. They took on the A.A. model, and figured now you can charge six or seven people all $100 per hour – bringing in $600 or $700 per hour for the treatment center.

However, they quickly realized the power of group therapy. The connections are so much stronger as the participants are going through the same thing as each other. Soon, all therapy started including some form of group therapy as they saw the magnificent impact of people getting together and sharing with one another.

Connectedness, which is all that is going on. We are learning how to be together as one, just as we are intended to be. We spend our entire lives trying to form this sense of identity, or ego, and become miserable. Then, we are "forced" to meet with a group of people once a week and talk about the most real things in our lives – and we heal. When you look at it from this perspective, it is common sense as to why this method is so effective. It is natural.

We don't sit around and talk about sports and weather, we get together and dive right in without our masks.

The Dangers of Separation

But as we grow more and more separate from one another, we become attached to our masks that create a fake identity. In our fast food society, we feel we do not have time to spend hours in therapy. We do not have time for other people, we do not have time for ourselves.

The ironic thing about time, is that we all have the same amount of time each day. Whenever you tell yourself the lie, "I do not have time," it is better to reframe that statement as "This is not a priority in my life." Then, we are taking accountability and realizing that some things are not as important.

As psychiatry has found its own way of increasing revenue, it has actually created more separateness. The marriage that psychiatry has with the pharmaceutical companies has killed all forms of psychotherapy with the emphasis now placed on prescribing medications. People want the quick fix, they would rather take a pill than talk to someone – and a group of people is out of the question.

Then as the atrocities described at the beginning of this chapter take place, the message from the media is that they were mentally ill and needed to seek treatment. While that statement is partially true, when are we going to evaluate the type of treatment they need? In the story of Michael Brandon Hill, they told us that he was "not taking his medications." Perhaps, we shouldn't be prescribing a medication that if we stop taking it we are capable of shooting up a school. When will that be addressed?

Never. It will never be addressed in the mass media, because they are highly funded by pharmaceutical companies. Since the 1997 act allowed pharmaceuticals to market on television directly to consumers, it has become one of the greatest advertisers on television, newspapers, magazines, and radio. It would be a massive conflict of interest if the news stations condemned the drugs. Instead they say that these killers only did so because "They are crazy and not on their medication." You will never hear them say, "They were on a medication that if they stop taking, they will go crazy. And that is what happened today."

The same was true for Adam Lanza, the shooter at Sandy Hook. Medical experts from Yale University conducted a 126-page report that indicates that "his mental illness was not the factor, but the fact that it went untreated." It also mentions many times that Lanza refused to take his medications. Columbine killer Eric Harris was on Luvox, an SSRI medication. Patron Purdy went on a shooting rampage in 1989 and was on the antidepressant Amitriptyline and the anti-psychotic drug Thorazine. And the list goes on and on with more than 90-percent of school shootings linked to psychotropic drugs.

James Holmes, the shooter in the Aurora movie theatre, had four prescriptions including sertraline (generic Zoloft) and Clonazepam (benzodiazepine that has "hypnotic properties"). Of course, benzos mixed with alcohol only exaggerate the effects and they discovered 48 containers of booze in Holmes apartment indicating that he was likely combining his drugs with alcohol. Holmes, actually did seek help about 38 days prior to going on his shooting rampage and told his psychiatrist, Dr. Lynne Fenton, that he was having homicidal thoughts and fantasies of killing groups of people.

Again, this is not pardoning the killer, but looking at a highly disturbed individual who was seeking help and the "treatment" he received was dangerous drugs. But this was not new to Fenton, according to a 2004 DEA investigation she had been prescribing without documentation: Claritin and Ambien for her husband, Xanax for herself, and Vicodin and a sedative for a co-worker with a headache. It is a society in which we seek a powerful narcotic for any of life's complications.

Fenton, however, did contact authorities and told police about the threats, but nothing was done. Maybe all they needed was someone like Antoinette Tuff to talk to him. Clearly that is what he needed, as he started to send death threats to Fenton after she stopped seeing him. Many cries for help were made, albeit not healthy cries for help, and our answer was to provide him with drugs.

Now, I realize that these medications truly help many people each day. The problem lies in the fact that we go to a doctor or psychiatrist telling them about our problems and the immediate answer is a drug. We need human connection and interaction, we need to be able to feel compassion and love. You will not get that in a drug. This is how we become addicted to drugs so easily, because it gives us that temporary feeling, but when we pay it back with the rebound effect, we are worse than before – which leads to use seeking more drugs.

Beneath The Surface

There is usually some big event like this that leads us to seeking help. Nobody is going to seek help on their own, because they just feel they drink too much. There is going to be a breakdown along the way in some area of life – legal, financial, family, health, or spiritual. But this event that takes place is just scratching the surface. The event itself, is not what makes you an addict. The event is what opens your eyes to what is going on beneath the surface.

It's like seeing a duck swimming against the stream of a river. This always fascinates me as all we can see is the duck gracefully floating on the water, yet can go against the current of the river. What we do not see, is all the effort, energy, and strength that is going on beneath the surface. The part that our eyes cannot see is the fast action of the ducks legs kicking the water to allow it's body to go in the other direction. Once the duck gets closer to us, we can see through the water and watch their magnificent feet in action. But first, we need to get close enough to see this take place.

This is how counseling works. We all have our stories on the surface level, but we need to build trust with one another, and create a sense of closeness before we can see the strenuous activity that lies beneath. And that is the part that moves us all.

They all tell their stories and I am fascinated by it all. Perhaps I would have even judged these people if I worked with them, saw them on the street, or in a bar. Now, here we were all together, as one. I was already part of something greater than myself – I was part of a true community.

"It's time to tell your story," Michelle says calmly with the entire group gently focused on me. They all had this look of genuine care, compassion, and curiosity. What a beautiful thing it is to have someone else curious about your life and to be curious of theirs. It is the foundation of all relationships.

"I've been sober for 17 days," I said proudly, "I missed my son's first couple days because I was out drinking. I have always been drinking and I cannot stop. I am a jerk, manipulate people, lie to them, and a bad person. I am at a complete loss and I have nowhere to turn. So I am here."

Wow that felt good! I was able to be completely real with this group of strangers. I was instantly comfortable with them. Likely because they were so vulnerable with me and shared their dark secrets, I felt it was OK to do the same – and it felt good!

We were all in the same boat – hopeless, in serious pain, and at the end of a long line of troubled lives. Yet, if we are all in the same boat, then nobody would try to sink this ship. That is the bond that brought us together. A group of outcasts, brought together by our addiction.

At break, the group goes outside to smoke but I am still trying to keep my distance. I still fear getting too close to anyone as I just had a devastating end to my relationship with Shandon. Michelle talks to me about the process of group, the assignments, what to expect, and the length of the program. She tells me that we present all our assignments in group, which seems a bit scary, but I have been taking Celexa which was providing some sort of relief.

Again, medications can be helpful for many people. It was allowing me to get out of that black hole that I was in. It is not a fix-all problem, but giving me the boost required to get out of the dumps and be able to function in the world.

Returning from break, the punk-rocker presents his step one. He puts it all out on the line, shares his stories, his life, the guilt, and just lays it all out for us. Not what I was expecting from this guy. He is just being completely real which creates an automatic connection to the group.

It hurts, but it is also quite refreshing to finally see and hear real truth. Nothing is sugar-coated, side-stepped, and short-sighted here. This man just took off his mask and showed us his deepest scars. Yet, we all saw the beauty, not the scars. This was also reassuring, seeing that I am not alone and there are others like me. It was like we are part of some secret society or freak-culture all getting together to learn how to live as humans with Michelle there to guide us how to be decent humans.

I felt happy being in this group. Amazing how just a couple of hours ago, I was asking "Why the hell are these people so happy and nice?" Now, I was feeling pretty good about things.

Being part of a group felt good. I felt like we are all the bad guys from our tribe, of course, I thought I wasn't as bad as the rest of the group – but I was our family's version. Everyone has been right all along, I am the bad guy but it is refreshing to know that there are others out there who share this sort of shame. Seeing everyone rally together provided stronger hope that I could turn things around and maybe I can become normal one day.

He finishes his step one and we sit around, provide feedback, and discuss things. This takes us until the end of group and I was quite intrigued. It was enough to make me want to return on Wednesday for the educational lecture. The lecture goes for two and a half hours, but it keeps me interested the entire time with some important information.

"That wasn't even PVD," my group told me, "wait until you hear him talk."

Why Don't We Teach People To Remove Their Masks?

This group has me connected already after two days and I am soon sharing more of my life and feeling accepted. Here we have a group of people with very little in common becoming a tight-knit group that are struggling through the darkest nights of our souls. How is this possible? And why do we not practice this in all walks of life and education?

Imagine in school if just one class period per day was devoted to treatment-style education. Everyone gathers in a circle and presents assignments in which they share the deepest parts of their true-self, imagine the connectedness we would all feel.

We go through our entire adult lives without ever using the Pythagorean Theorem, or Achilles and the Trojan War, nor the Tea Tax Act of 1789. We memorize dates, numbers, and stories, while we go through school with angst, aggression, and insecurities. We single people out because they are different from us, and know nothing about the battles they are fighting at home.

What if in 1995, Columbine High School had a program in place in which one hour per day was dedicated to group therapy instead of Ancient Greek Literature? Maybe Klebold and Harris could have shared some of these dark thoughts and feelings they carried inside, that they felt excluded, rejected, and hurt.

Like in our group, they would have been offered support and compassion by opening up and becoming vulnerable others would have done the same. It would have changed the dynamics in the classroom, lunchroom and hallways. And by the time they were seniors in 1999, maybe life would have had a different ending for all those involved.

I was now at 24 days sober – the longest I had maintained sobriety since the first sip of alcohol was 26 days. I was feeling pretty good, but it was also strange. It was uncharted territory for me. I was feeling emotions that had been bottled up my entire life through shame, anger, drugs, co-dependency, and booze.

My true self wants to come out and is on the verge.

The problem is that I wasn't sure who this true self really was or is. I had no idea. Nor did I know how to express these thoughts or feelings, this was all new to me. When I spoke, it came out as self-directed anger. I went on a rant for about thirty minutes about all my downfalls, shortcomings, and misery I have caused to those around me. I hate all the things that I have done to myself and I hate the person that I am.

"You know it is a disease," Michelle says to me calmly.

"Bullshit!" I scream, "That's not true. That is such a cop-out! It is like ADD and all the other made-up nonsense."

"There is scientific evidence," she responds with a warm smile and friendly demeanor. She is completely unfazed by my outburst.

Of course, facts have never interested me and I refuse to budge with all the information she throws at me. Which is why I cannot even recall the conversation, I simply blocked out her explanations as I did not want to hear it. I am one of the loud-mouth, opinionated people that makes sure everyone knows that I am right. This is the mask I created and I put it back on.

Michelle just stares at me with her gently fierce expression and says, "It's time for the video."

The group just quietly shakes their head in agreement. She sends us to break early and tells us that she will have a video when group resumes. This is her way of being fierce and gentle at the same time.

She puts on this corny video of an old guy from the 1980's, which looks like some sort of PBS special. He introduces himself as Dr. David Ohm's with these cheap graphics on the screen that look like it was made in someone's garage. I have already decided that this guy is a loser, and is only seeking a way to make money. I remember thinking, "Really? This is the almighty video that everyone thought I should see?"

Yep, it was.

Somehow, this old guy on the screen captured my attention. It must have been one of those soul-contracts that we make with people that we never actually "meet." We can have soul contracts with anyone, whether we meet them in-person or not, as long as they had a purpose to help us meet our life objectives. He had grabbed a hold of my true self's attention, because something was making me listen.

I am an Alcoholic

Then, for the first time in my life, he had me finally admit that I am an alcoholic. Not out loud, but to myself. It was a huge blow to my false self, my ego. It was a wake-up call that challenged everything I thought I knew.

Mike Tyson famously stated, "Everyone has a plan until they get punched in the face." This was in reference to boxing, and is often used in all sports analogies in reference to how we abort our plans once we are tossed a huge obstacle. I had a plan for myself, we all do, we call this the ego's life plan. This was the punch to the face that Tyson explains that had me aborting the ego's plan for myself.

"You see an alcoholic doesn't get drunk every time he drinks," Ohm's says in the video, "It's just that he cannot predict once he takes that first drink, whether he will have two drinks or will end up drunk."

I nearly fell off my chair as he said these words. I literally felt the ground moving, and I think it was my true self seeing an opening and trying to get out. It was the loving self who had been held back and pushed down for 34 years and shouting out loud, "I told you that you are not a bad guy!"

Synchronicities are when all the world just makes sense, when you remember something that you have never been taught before. I was hooked and listened to the entire video with an open mind. All my preconceived judgments about the corny video had evaporated. My false self-had started to die.

Everything was changing in this instant. My true self, my soul, finally saw an opening and an opportunity to shine.

The statistics and evidence Ohms gives in the video were overwhelming. He told stories of twins separated at birth with one ending up in a positive environment and the other in an alcoholic home, yet the rates of alcoholism were the same. He talks about the brain waves, blood marker, how we break down dopamine, and countless studies explaining how it fits the disease model. I was having a battle inside myself.

This is what the Christians refer to as spiritual warfare. It is an internal battle that goes on within ourselves between our soul and ego (or God and Satan). It refers to resisting, overcoming, and defeating the enemies (ego) lies. The ego sends three battle fronts: temptations, deceptions, and accusations.

These are the battles that we are fighting daily, and up until now, the ego was winning the war.

Although this is a current struggle with all people, no matter what the religious belief, we all have this battle. This moment, I was feeling the battle going on and was conscious of every little game the ego has been playing on me over the years. My ego had me believing that I was a jerk, a manipulator, a bad father, and a bad person. I must have had a soul contract with Dr. David Ohms as an agreement that he would provide support for my soul in this spiritual warfare as the evidence was too overwhelming for my false self to fight anymore.

It was the first time my true self had emerged in a long time and it was a bizarre feeling that words could not describe. I wasn't sure what to think and was in a confused state of mind. All the deceptions and accusations about me were all part of a spiritual battle inside my head, and I had been wrong my entire life.

The video ends and Michelle asks, "What do you think?"

Well, what I wanted to say was, "What do I think!? You just made me see a truth that no one has told me and hid this from me my entire life." I wanted to kiss her, hug her, and kill everyone who participated in feeding the ego lies and supporting the battlefront of my false self. I was stunned, confused, and mad at myself for falling victim to this lifetime of deceit.

"What do I think?" I say in a much calmer voice than the internal dialogue, "Umm, that is just a lot to take in."

Group continued for another hour or so without me speaking another word. My world had been changed, I was reborn. I refer to my birthdate as July 9, 2011, as that was both the death of my false self and the resurrection of my true self all at once.

All my past lessons were instantly transformed from failures into life lessons. This was the true turning point in the awakening process as for the first time, my true self had the upper hand in this internal struggle.

The next day, I woke up a new man. I started researching more about the disease model of addiction and found unlimited evidence. I ran around sharing this with everyone like when Charlie discovered he had found the last golden ticket in Charlie and the Chocolate Factory. I start telling everyone that I have a disease, I am not a bad guy, I am a decent person and I just need to remove this barrier.

"No, that is not true." This was a typical response from my family and those closest to me, "I suppose everything is a disease now."

Perhaps this was foolish of me. For some odd reason, I anticipated that everyone would welcome me back with open arms and admit that they were wrong. I have no idea why I thought this would happen, it was likely wishful thinking. Or naive thinking, after all my true self was still an infant; and just as all infants do, we view the world as magical place where everything consists only of love.

This is quite common when the addict starts to make life changes and lifts the addiction and "bad traits." Even though they have caused pain and hardships to the family, it becomes the family norm. This is all done subconsciously, nobody realizes it is going on, but the family has become accustomed to the addict being the person that messes up, screws people over, and causes problems. When the addict gets healthy, it throws off the entire balance and people do not know how to take it until they get healthy themselves.

Although, there were a few with open minds, the ones who still loved me listened to what I had to say and were curious to know more. There it is again, curiosity. It falls hand-in-hand with unconditional love. See, people like Larry, and Joey all came to me and were curious about this disease model. They never gave up on me, which is unconditional love. It means, without condition. They were not waiting for me to change my ways to love me, not waiting for things to be perfect, they loved me no matter what I had done. And with that, comes curiosity about my life, they wanted to know more.

I had only been to four sessions of outpatient treatment, and already started to feel the difference in my life. Now, I finally got a chance to meet this "PVD" guy that everyone told me about. I was excited, but also a little skeptical as I never like when people get over-hyped – they never live up to the expectation. Nonetheless, I was excited just to come back to this little office building in the middle of nowhere. It was even more exciting to have

We checked in and sat in the lecture room as all the people from group and their family members joined us shortly thereafter. The end for my false self was near as I was about to meet PVD for the first time, the false self-had no chance.

The man that eventually stuck the dagger in my false self was about to make his way into my life for the first time. I must have had a significant soul contract with this man prior to entering in my physical body, because every lie, deception, and accusation about myself was about to be destroyed in an instant. Our contract states that he will reveal to me the truth that I had always known.

This would be the atomic bomb of spiritual warfare and I have no choice but to fully surrender.

CHAPTER XVII

Freedom to Be Me
Jailbreak from Addiction

Chapter 17
Freedom to be Me: Jailbreak from Addiction

In Pink Floyd's rock-opera album, *The Wall*, the main character is a man named Pink who builds a metaphorical wall around himself to seclude himself from the outside world. The album begins with Pink's childhood of his father dying in battle in World War II, followed by abusive teacher's in an outdated education system, an overbearing mother, and his estranged wife. All these areas of his life continue to help him "build his wall."

Towards the end of the first half of the album, Pink starts to getting more aggressive and shouts out loud that he "doesn't need anything at all" to the world as his inner pain continues to build. The second disc opens with his final cries for help for anyone "out there beyond the wall" only to realize it is too late and the wall he built is too powerful for anyone to reach him.

At this point, Pink becomes hopeless and dives deeper into his state of despair to the point he overdoses on some type of drug while waiting in his hotel room prior to a concert. The medics find him passed out and revive him, only so he can get back on his feet and perform another show to the crowd.

Prior to going to treatment, this is the point I had reached in my personal story. I had fallen deep into despair, before a near overdose on prescription medication and alcohol hospitalized me for one night. Just like Pink, I was able to get revived and went back to work, put on my mask as if nothing had ever happened. The show must go on!

Taking the Mask Off

The album ends with Pink questioning if he has been guilty of all the pain and suffering in his life. He goes to trial and claims to be completely crazy. His schoolmaster and wife testify of his shortcomings, while his mother rushes in and tries to protect him one final time. In the end, the judge takes all of this evidence into consideration before giving his ruling with the line:

> *"Since, my friend, you have revealed your deepest fears;*
> *I sentence you to be exposed before your peers."*

After this sentence in handed out, the judge demands for his wall to be torn down and Pink would no longer be allowed to isolate from the world. He would have to face his fears, his innermost demons, and reconnect with the world.

This is what enlightenment is all about. It is about breaking down the walls around us and living freely. Sometimes we need a judge to deny our insanity defense, and make us relearn how to live life the healthy and natural way.

I use the story of *The Wall* as it coincides with this point in my journey. I had given up, was no longer fighting, and had accepted the fact that I was crazy. There was simply something wrong with me as no sane person would continue to create this amount of pain in the lives of others.

In walks PVD. He was my judge that was about to force me to tear down my wall – or in my case, take off my mask.

His lectures have been built up by everyone in group and the other counselors. Anytime things are overhyped, I instantly am turned off by it and looking for any reason to go against what everyone says. I had the mindset that it would be overhyped and that I already was prepared to give my insanity defense.

Cortland Pfeffer; Irwin Ozborne

The Legend of PVD

He walks in and it was nothing like what I had expected. His presence is immediately felt as soon as he enters the room. He has an energy that grabs the attention of everybody in the room like nothing I've ever felt. He is a big guy, over six feet tall, and has the classic old-school mustache like the Monopoly Man. His voice is demanding, powerful, confident, and compels you to hear what he has to say.

There are two types of people in this world – thermostats and thermometers. Ninety-five percent of people are thermometers, the walk into a room and they measure the temperature of the room and they adjust to their surroundings. The other five percent, such as PVD, are the thermostats. These are the people that walk into a room, and they change the temperature of the room and all the others around them adjust to the new setting.

I have been around the mental health field for more than 20 years in all different types of settings. This man is simply the best and there is no comparison. He is the Babe Ruth of mental health.

I was unaware of it at the time, but there was all this hype and talk about his greatness in which I wasn't fully ready to buy into. Then he walks into the room and it is quite obvious there is something to the hype. It is like when LebRon James was dubbed the "next best thing" when he was a sophomore in high school. Then he walks onto an NBA court as an 18-year-old kid, completely unfazed by the big stage, before stealing the show and backing up the anticipation.

He opens up by explaining substance dependence in a short five minute description that tells my life story. It was one of the most unbelievable things I had ever heard. I was completely floored. And by, "I", I mean my ego. My false self was about to get crumbled to the point in which my true self was finally about to have the upper hand for the first time in my life.

As the lecture progressed, he spoke about shame, healing, and family involvement. It was though he was speaking a truth in which I had always known at my core, but never heard it described in such a clear, concise, indisputable manner. This man was unlocking my door to freedom. He was unlocking my self-imprisoned cell that had been barricaded many years ago.

The stories he used to describe things were insightful, meaningful, and he added a sense of humor. This was a man who was truly in his flow. He was put on this earth to teach people about addiction and to see him in work was like watching Elvis Presley or Michael Jackson perform in concert, Tim Hanks or Marlon Brando acting, Michaelangelo or Picaso paint, or listening to Socrates or Jesus preach.

I mean it. I really felt as though I was watching Jesus work as I saw him bring in the lowest members of society and heal them right before eyes. It was a daily miracle that he performed. You can read ten thousand books on enlightenment and each one may make you feel closer, but the problem is that enlightenment is far too powerful to be described in words. It is something that has to be experienced. Each Wednesday night, I was witnessing enlightenment in action in which there are no words that could describe.

I remember thinking, "I am watching God in action." At first it seemed a little exaggerated, only discover how truthful it had been. I learned that we are all God (or Jesus, Buddha, Allah, Source, Great Spirit, Creator, One, etc.) The name you choose to use does not matter. However, PVD had already learned this – but more remarkably he was putting it into action.

Anyone can read a book about these things and feel good in that moment. That is the easy part. It feels great and feel like we can make a difference, but then you put the book down and life comes back around and challenges you to not apply what you have learned. This is another form of spiritual warfare that is a constant battle throughout life. Somehow, PVD not only knew all of this, but he was living it.

Of all things, this man was free. He was free from any type of suffering or pain. He gets into character when telling his stories without any form of embarrassment. He wants his audience to challenge him so he can discuss things in greater detail – and he has a remarkable descriptive answer for every question.

He explains that when you use a substance to deal with a difficult emotion that you are cheating yourself out of a learning experience. The problem, as PVD states, is that it works so effectively that it becomes highly reinforcing. As this pattern continues, we never learn how to do things the natural way.

Boom! A light goes off in my head.

This is real. Everything he is talking about is the absolute truth. Everyone, including myself, has the completely wrong perception about me. I feel alive for the first time in years, I feel like I have been re-born.

Reborn because I feel like an infant again, everything is so new and exciting to me. He has removed my mask and I can see things from a different light. I can look at my face in the mirror and see that I am not the mask that I have been wearing all these years. The grass is greener, the sky is bluer, the light in people's eyes is brighter, and the world is a beautiful place.

I continue to go to the groups with Michelle and start opening up. Each week, PVD does another lecture and these moments are a regular occurrence. It is like I am in heaven. All the guilt and pain is washing away and my ego is diminishing.

This is the Tet Offensive of spiritual warfare, my ego has no choice but to surrender. It is all happening so quickly and so soon that I am overwhelmed with all this knowledge and changes going on internally. It as though I have been given a secret on how to live life.

At the same time, I have a strong working relationship with Dr. Braker, as he actually listens to what I have to say and believes in me. I am building so many powerful allies in my support system that my ego is trapped by the power of my soul, the love of my true self.

I am healed! I am like the Phoenix that has been burnt to the ground and is rising from the ashes into a much more pure, radiant, and energetic form. This was a true resurrection that only a few months ago would have seemed impossible.

Enlightenment refers to light being shed on something, or light entering your awareness. As Rumi states, "the wound is wear the light enters you." Through all my pain and suffering in life, it has opened wounds in which the light was entering and my soul was able to feel the light. It was the first rays of light my soul had felt in years and it was eager to burst out of my physical body.

Immediately, I want to share this secret with everybody. I want to be Dr. Braker. I want to be PVD. I am ready to heal the world. I have become high on recovery and became completely obsessed with it to the point I was receiving warnings from Jill and PVD. But, I can't control myself. It is like locking an animal up in a cage its entire life and then one day telling the animal it is free. Of course it is going to run wild and explore all there is to see in the beautiful universe. It no longer wants to be contained to the small quarters of a kennel or cage. The animal knows that there is a greater truth and can never return to its former life.

One day, I get to see PVD in action in a group. At break he calls somebody into his office and gets him to confess to the group about a relapse. How did he get him to do that? What did he do?

"Guys, the only way this works is by being real," PVD tells his followers, "If you don't want to be here, then don't."

Wow! That was refreshing and different. I have never seen a clinical director of a program come out like that. He was not concerned about bringing people into the program and making money, he only cares about helping people succeed and live the life they deserve. He saw the beauty in everyone, and if they were not ready to break free, he sent them home.

He had clearly broken away from the ways of the world and society. He knew what was right in his heart, and he followed it. This is how the enlightened person behaves, they have destroyed the lies, walls, and masks that have been placed around them and they are true. They become a vessel for God and you can see it in them with all their actions.

PVD would share to us about his days of using, I have never heard a counselor do this before. In the mental health field, they typically do not want the patients to know anything about you. I have always found this to be backwards logic. By hearing PVD share his story, it gained everyone's respect and attention. We were allowed to ask questions and he gave truthful answers. If we pushed the questions too far, he would let us know and he would give us specific reasoning.

Just as the Viet Kong sacked Saigon after the Tet Offensive and the American troops withdrew, there was a sense of freedom in Vietnam for the first time in a couple of centuries. Generations of people had no idea what it meant to be "free" and they had to learn how adjust as a society. This is the same confusion that was going on internally for me at this time. My true self had destroyed my ego and now I had to figure out how to live as a free person.

Learning to Live

This was the hard part. All the habits of my false self had to be removed. These were old habits, beliefs, and thoughts that had been engrained in my head since I was born. These were the after-effects of the war. Similar to the long-term effects of the bombing of dams, dykes, unexploded bombs, napalm, and agent orange used on the Vietnamese people. Although they won the war, these were the long term effects they were willing to risk in an effort to be free. But that is how important freedom is to those who have been suppressed for so long. This is how much I was willing to sacrifice for my freedom from myself.

PVD kept working with me, talking about isolation, shame, trust, and the process of healing. If I could ever give anyone what he gave me, I would be able to die content knowing that I had done something special for the universe.

He was the first person to put me in the forefront and made me start to question all the lies I had been telling myself. He would not accept my insanity plea, and instead, he forced me to face my deepest fears and remove my mask.

If you ever can convince someone to do so, to remove their mask and have them embrace their inner beauty, you will be forever immortalized. You will live on for generations of the families you save. Just as the people of Vietnam took only one day to change the name of Saigon to Ho Chi Minh City to honor the man who dedicated his entire life to freeing them from generations of empirical rule. Although Ho Chi Minh never lived to see the promised land, like Moses, he knew it existed and was on the horizon – and that legacy was good enough for them and the people they served.

After seven weeks of intensive outpatient treatment, I decided to skip the five months of aftercare as I felt I was ready.

"Thank you PVD," I told him as I declined his recommendations of aftercare, "But I need to go out and heal people now. It is time for me to be you."

Ahh, the ego wasn't dead. The worst part about it was that my true self did not even realize this was the ego fighting back. I thought it had been destroyed.

I returned to work and was ready to save the world. I found every opportunity to spread my newfound knowledge. I tried to save everyone, I loved healing and I wanted to rush into this as soon as possible. But, of course, I was not ready. I was not fully healed myself, I rushed to the end of the book and did not sit around and enjoy the journey.

I was just reborn and trying to be the new savior. It took Jesus 30 years before he started his ministry and teachings, and here I was a few weeks into my rebirth and thought I could jump right into that role.

If people were not ready, not on board, or didn't get it, I simply judged and criticized them – the opposite of what a healer is to do.

My intentions were great, but I had no idea what I was doing. I was like an infant granted a superpower, running around thwarting lightning bolts at everyone and causing as much damage as healing.

There were moments when I got it right, and everyone saw the potential. Riley was there to guide me and teach me how to use the superpower. She already possessed this super power and knew how it worked. She let me experiment and when I went too far, she reeled me back in. And when she saw it was working, she let me loose. I was like her hunting dog on a leash, I wanted to go after anything and everything that had a scent. But she was a trained hunter and knew when the time was right and she was training me so I could do this on my own without a leash.

My new support system of PVD, Riley, and Dr. Braker were always there for me. They saw me make mistakes, they saw me go against their advice, and they always welcomed me back. They are all angels that were working together with their own unique abilities to help bring my true self to the surface.

When you keep hanging around with snakes, you get bit. If you surround yourself with angels, you become enlightened.

In the final track of *The Wall*, Pink's wall is finally torn down and he is reborn to a world in which he is now unfamiliar. To his surprise, he sees that he had people on his side the entire time that were waiting for the day the wall was brought down. While he tried to plea insanity, and then felt that it was a punishment to tear down the wall, he realized it was the most necessary pain he would ever endure.

The final song is titled, "Outside the Wall," and the album ends with the following words:

> "All alone, or in twos;
> The ones who really love you;
> Walk up and down, outside the wall;

This piece embodies the sense of community that brings this world together. If one is unable to tear down their wall, or remove their mask, those trying to get in will eventually give up and you will live a lonely life. Fear, pain, oppression, and isolation create these walls/mask that endanger society and humanity. It is the duty of every conscious person and community to never rest in attempting to bring these walls down that separate us and remove the masks that keep us hidden.

Although Roger Waters has never given an official explanation of this hymn, looking deeply it is clear that this song has a double-meaning in that their true-life band "Pink Floyd" is banging their heart against the walls of society, making their stand for change, and waiting for humanity to break down these barriers. As evidenced in the final lines of the song:

> And when they've given you their all;
> Some stagger and fall, after all it's not easy;
> Banging your heart, against some mad buggers wall."

In the video, children are picking up the bricks from the torn down wall and likely starting to build their own walls which indicates the cycle is going to continue of new generations putting up their own psychological barriers

Once the music fades, you hear a voice ask, "Isn't this where..." and then it cuts off. This is an intentional message attempting to put an end to the cycle of generational pain, oppression, and barriers.

Taking the Mask Off

If you turn up the volume on the first track of the album, you will hear the words muttered in a question form "…We came in?" This is to portray the non-stop cycle of psychological barriers that we continue to build by raising children to build walls and wear masks. Then a new story forms with new pain, trauma, and suffering. As we go through this cycle, we learn that we need to break out of our personal wall, we get put on trial, and realize that the only way to freedom is to "tear down the wall."

As this is done, we are reborn and we see the world as an infant once again. Everything is new, everything is fresh, and everything is unconditional radiant love. Though, at the same time, there is a sense of familiarity.

Then we ask ourselves, "Isn't this where we came in?" As soon as we ask that question, the cycle starts again as the ego never truly dies. The ego starts creating new pain, we build new walls, only to ask for them to be broken apart again.

The album ends with Pink breaking the cycle as he stops in mid-sentence by asking, "Isn't this where…."

CHAPTER XVIII

Relapse
A Deeper Rock Bottom

Chapter 18
Relapse: A Deeper Rock Bottom

…We came in?

Yep, my cycle was about to repeat again.

And I wasn't the only one on the verge of a recycle. There was a patient, Abigail, being admitted to the psychiatric rehab facility I worker at for a second time. Before she arrived, the staff that remembered her from a previous stay were shouting out advanced warnings.

"Oh no," they pleaded, "This is terrible. She is a sociopath! A monster!"

Word got out that Riley was going to visit Abigail at the hospital and was thinking about letting her back, which had the staff shook up. Their world was about to change, not realizing that they had the ability to change the world of another in a positive direction.

Once again, the staff is creating labels and judgments that will likely to lead to destruction of someone in need. She made their job difficult and inconvenient because she required additional support. They became comfortable with doing little work, and if she were to return they were going to be challenged.

They had been through it once, had her removed, and now they had their comfort zone being threatened and they went into defensive mode. They were prepared to lash an assault of labels and judgments to remove her before she can be admitted. While none of this is done consciously, this is a result of being attached to the material world, believing in the illusion, and creating the walls of separation.

> *"Nothing ever goes away until it teaches us what we need to know,"*

Pema Chodron writes the quote above in *When Things Fall Apart: Heart Advice for Difficult Times*, he continues:

> *"Nothing really attacks us but our own confusion."*

While it was clear for me to see that this was the message that the staff needed to learn. I was also being hit by a recurring lesson of my own that I was not fully aware. While, I was prepared to take on the world, I was quick to judge others and take their own inventory.

Throughout this text, I continue to refer to the notion that we are all one. We all come from the same Source and are experiencing this world subjectively through different experiences. The quickest way to forget this notion is to start comparing to others, judging, or creating some level of hierarchy as to where each person is on their path.

If we are all one, then that means every person. It is a simple concept to say and think about, but putting it to action is the difficult task. The person behind the counter at the gas station is you from a different life (perspective). The annoying guy talking too loud on his phone, is also you. The ignorant, racist guy on the bus that irritates you to the point you nearly lose your temper and start a fight – is also you.

Each of these people you encounter is also God. So when you get taken advantage of someone in a business deal and are reflecting at the end of the day, you may ask, "God, if that was you, why did you treat me this way?" With this perspective, you can identify the lesson that was meant to be leaned with each scenario. Or for deeper perspective, you may ask, "Why did I treat myself this way?"

"We are taking Abigail on as a patient," Riley told the staff in a quick ten-second meeting after returning from the hospital.

It was that simple, she understood it already. She wasn't taking on "Riley," she was taking on each one of us, the creator, the source, and herself.

The staff lost it. They all went crazy hearing of this news and all I am thinking is that this poor patient has no chance, especially if this is what the entire staff has this preconceived belief about her before even being introduced. This is not new, I have seen this everywhere.

"Imagine if this was your daughter! Or someone close to you?" I pleaded, "We can not only take on the easy cases."

As I look back, I was getting pretty close to figuring it out. I had the right idea, but coming off the wrong way. Because this person is your daughter, it is your sister, your girlfriend, wife, brother, uncle, friend, and yourself. Viewing the world from this lens automatically opens up our ability to be empathetic and instantly re-connects us as one. The message was right, but the delivery was creating more separateness.

The staff was made up of mostly 20-something-year-olds that grew comfortable sitting in their offices, doing short groups, writing fake notes to appease the county, and did not want to be inconvenienced. When a tough case comes along, they do not want to do the work because it shatters their level of comfort and ease.

Attachment Theory

I read Abigail's chart prior to her admission and saw that she was a 19-year-old girl that was adopted from an orphanage in the Philippines at age three. The fact she is in an orphanage her first three years indicates severe trauma as those are the most important years of our lives in regards to creating connection to the world, trust, and security.

Attachment is a deep and enduring emotional bond that connects one person to another across space and time. Many studies have shown the importance of early childhood relationship with their caregivers in terms of social, emotional, and cognitive development.

John Bowlby started recognizing this while working as Psychiatrist at Child Guidance Clinic in London in the 1930's, in which he treated emotionally disturbed children. This led to his research and identifying his attachment theory in 1958, stating that infants have a universal need to seek close proximity with their caregiver when under stress or threatened. He also noted that children felt extreme distress when separated from their mothers, even if they were fed by another caregiver.

Bowlby suggests forms one primary attachment and that will act as a prototype for all future social relationships. He also states that there is a critical period in the first five years of life to develop a secure attachment. If an attachment has not developed during this period then the child will suffer from irreversible developmental consequences, such as reduced intelligence and increased aggression.

We are social creatures by nature and come into this world looking to form attachments with others, because this is how we will survive. The detriment of attachment is not food, but care and responsiveness. Which further shows that love, above all else, is the most basic human need.

Harry Harlow did a number of similar studies on attachment in the 1950s and 1960s by studying the mechanisms by which newborn rhesus monkeys bonded with their mothers. The study was conducted to discover the basis of the bond that newborns have with their mothers. The behavioral theory suggests the bond exists from one that would provide food. Whereas, the evolutionary theory states that infants need to touch and cling to something for emotional support.

In one study, the monkeys were reared in isolation in which many died and others were frightened and acted abnormally. Once they grew older, they could not interact with other monkeys. The second study separated monkeys from their mother and gave them options of two surrogate mothers – one made from wire and the other with a soft cloth, both which provided milk. All the monkeys spent more time with the mother made of cloth, even if she had no milk. They would only go to the wire mother when they were hungry and then spent the remainder of the day with the soft cloth mother.

Furthermore, when a scary object was placed in the cage, they rushed to the cloth mother for support. The monkeys were also more willing to explore, or take risks, when the cloth mother was present. This allowed Harlow to conclude that for a monkey to develop normally they must have some interaction with an object they can cling to during those critical first few months.

Similarly, Konrad Lorenz did a study on geese during their critical period of 12-17 hours after hatching. He took a large number of eggs that were about to hatch and put half under a mother goose, while he kept the other half close to himself as they hatched. When they hatched, he imitated a mother goose quacking sound and discovered the young birds regarded him as his mother. This shows that imprinting can occur without any form of feeding needing to take place. If no attachment is made with the birds within 32 hours, it is highly unlikely any attachment will ever develop.

In 1964, Rudolph Schaffer and Peggy Emerson went a step further to identify the stages of attachment as follows:

- A) First three months: Indiscriminate attachments – respond equally to any caregiver.
- B) After four months: Learn to distinguish people – prefer primary caregiver, but accept from anyone.
- C) After seven months: Special preference for single attachment figure – shows fear of strangers, unhappiness when taken away from special figure (separation anxiety), seeks security and protection.
- D) After nine months: Multiple attachments – starts to become more independent and forms several close attachments.

In noting the multiple attachments that form depend on who responds accurately to the baby's signals, not who spends the most time with them. They are more likely to form bonds with those who play and communicate with them rather than who feeds and changes them.

Back to human development and our client Abigail. We know that her first three years were in an orphanage without that much-needed bonding and attachment. She was adopted at age three which left a little bit of time to develop some form of bonding, but much of the early years has already created irreversible trauma.

A few years later, her foster parents divorced and she never saw her father, leading to more separation anxiety. And this is just the crack of the iceberg of her story, there is no way of knowing the pain that this girl has went through and was enduring her entire life.

On the day of her admit, in walks a short, five-foot tall Filipino girl with a bright smile and high energy. I couldn't believe it, this was the "evil patient" in which we were trying to get rid of because there was no hope for her?

I worked often with her, spoke with her daily, did any intervention I could. It was my goal to save her. I pushed for change and confronted staff frequently. She would sneak out the house at night, drink alcohol, smoke pot, steal from others, and having sex with anyone willing in the nearby proximity.

Eventually, we needed to have a sit-down talk with her. Abigail was brought into a conference room to be addressed by Riley, Rochelle, and myself. This was my opportunity to become PVD.

I started talking and explaining everything to her that I had learned from the master himself only a few months ago. Then something magical happened. After a long, emotional conversation, the question was put directly on her, "Will you go to treatment?"

She sat back, leaned her head against the wall, closed her eyes, huge tears ran down her cheeks, and she nodded her head "yes."

I pumped my fist in excitement as though symbolically saying, "I did it! I did it!"

Letting Go of Outcomes

"You have a gift," Riley told me with her eyes tearing up. I was ecstatic; the entire room was filled with pure joy, unconditional loving energy between the four of us.

But it was short lived. A few days later, Abigail had stolen more and Riley had no choice but to discharge her from our program. I was devastated, crushed, and defeated. This all happened while I was gone and I didn't have a chance to defend her. The staff explained how she was evil, manipulative, and a sociopath.

"How can everyone just give up on her?" I yelled at the next staff meeting. I got in everyone's face and was disgusted with them for pushing to get her kicked out.

"Maybe you were fighting for the old Cortland," Riley said to me politely, "The 18-year-old Cortland that everyone gave up on."

Damn. She was right. Riley taught about transference and counter transference all the time. She was like PVD in a way. She is a genius in the field and always knew what was right for each person, including her staff.

She just understood things. She was correct again about Abigail, this was not a failure because we planted the seeds. Sometimes that is the best thing you can do for a patient. It hurts when the staff fights so hard, give everything they got for the person, only to see the treatment fail. It hurts, you feel bad, worthless, and burnt out.

This is not only about the psychiatry field, but whenever you try to help any person in general. When it doesn't work, you don't see the results you were hoping, it can be frustrating. It all stems from the unhealthy attachment to your personal hope, feelings, or beliefs on the outcome.

That is the ego at work. We cannot control the outcome. When the true self is at work, you are able to spread love, surrender, and let go of any outcomes or results. You never know the impact that you have on a person's life. All you can do is what your heart is telling you is best in that moment and trust the process that things will work out in time.

When I was younger, I was at a gas station and a woman asked me for some money because she had some car troubles. Unsure of what to do, I told her I'll see how much I have after I fill my gas tank. In reality, I was questioning whether or not I was doing the right thing. Something seemed off, but I decided to give her $20.

While it seemed like a good gesture, my ego was still in control at this time. I watched her talk to someone in another car and they took off, I decided to follow them. We went to a rough part of town and into a run-down neighborhood. I parked behind a car to ensure she did not see me, only to watch her give a handshake to some guy in which I saw the money exchange hands and then she quickly shoved something in her pocket – yep, a drug deal.

I was so upset with myself, I felt so scammed, lied to, and taken advantage of by this person. How dare she!

It was only later on the drive home when my immediate ego response had subsided that I realized I had no control over what she was going to do. Based on the information I had, all I did was give her money. I gave money to one of God's children that was hurting at the time, what she did with the money was beyond my control. I attached myself to the outcome and became hurt by it, but that wasn't my journey. If it wasn't me, it would have been the next guy. She would have found a way to get her fix.

Then I thought, what if I had said no to her because of my preconceived beliefs about her. But, then, the story turned out to be legit and person-after-person continued to say "no" to her until she had to commit a crime to get money to repair her car? Or what if I said "no" to her and she was going to buy drugs, and person-after-person followed suit until she had to rob someone to get some cash? We never know the results and we are not responsible. We are only responsible for our actions.

I realize now that her addiction had hijacked her brain, though she will not forget the time she took money from a stranger. Maybe not today, nor tomorrow, but someday down the road when she is ready to make a change, she will remember the kindness of that stranger's heart. This may propel her to start giving back to others, the way a kind soul did to her. We may never know where that story leads, but I do know it is not up to me.

In regards to Abigail, my first red flag should have been my fist pump. Right there, I had made it about me. As it turns out, she was never using marijuana. I had become so obsessed with chemical dependency and my personal journey, that Abigail had read about it and she told me what I wanted to hear. I was trying to advance to become some great healer so fast that it had blinded me to only seeing what I wanted.

Trigger – Urge – Slip - Relapse

This had triggered me, and at this point I didn't understand triggers. I was done being all about recovery and started counting my sober days out loud to everyone. My marriage was still filled with pain and

I didn't understand why Jill couldn't just let it all go. The problem was that all the damage I had done to her was real. Even though it was my false self, my addicted brain, it doesn't take away what had been done.

She had lost herself and I was ready to move on without dealing with anything. And at 84 days sober, I used again, this time it was pills. After this slip up, I mustered the courage to go to my first AA meeting in hopes to find another PVD - a permanent savior. However, it just didn't happen. I was disappointed but was able to stay sober through sheer will power alone.

Though sober, I was still bottling things up, explosive at home, and fighting at work. I felt a relapse coming, I felt defeated and hopeless. I still cannot do it even after everything I went through. The shame was piling up high enough to build a wall around me, driving me into further isolation, torture, and pain. As PVD would explain, I was trying to "White Knuckle" my recovery. I thought I was mentally tough enough to do so. But the problem is recovery is not about intelligence or mental toughness. The smarter you are, the more at risk you become because you think you can outsmart the disease.

My ego had not died. It was alive and well and I felt a giant attack was on the verge. While I felt like chief Crazy Horse after surprising the world with the victory over my ego, as Crazy Horse did to the United States Army at the Battle of Little Big Horn. Though, it was only a matter of time before the powerful United States Army, or in my case my ego, would avenge the embarrassing defeat.

My problem was that I thought I had won the war once I stopped drinking. I thought the spiritual warfare was over. But as it turns out, that was just the beginning. Abstinence is not the solution. Abstinence does not equal recovery, it only opens the door to recovery. PVD told his groups time and time again that, "Recovery is not about getting sober, it is about growth as a human being."

As I refused to listen to the advanced warnings, eventually it became too much to overcome and I had a night of using medications. And then another and another.

Then it was Shandon, my best buddy that first took me into detox, called me up and said "let's grab a beer."

And just like old times, we went out and he got hammered and I was taking medications. We used to get so drunk together that we have enough drunken war-stories that we could fill up an entire book. We had many good times together, good long talks, before the alcohol takes a toll and we start acting foolish in which we only remember half the evening. We offered the truest versions of ourselves, without our masks on, and then wake up and not talk about any of it. Instead, we picked on each other like brothers, made fun of each other, and then went out drinking and the cycle continued. Tonight we went back at it again, it was like getting the band back together.

"Man, I missed drinking with you," Shandon exclaimed to me, "such great times."

Great times until my sister Sharon, his wife, called him and said, "Like father, like son."

Shandon was heartbroken by this, and so was I. I knew that I was going to be the one to take the blame. So, we were already feeling bad and the only way to escape that pain is by drowning it in the booze and the pills. The full-blown relapse had begun.

Nightly using to the point of blacking out and passing out in a random area of the house or garage had become the norm. It got to the point that Jill could take no more and needed me out of the house. We had two young kids, Kylee, nonstop fighting, and me not even coming home sometimes.

As soon as Jill left the house, I started using and trying to hide it – though she always knew. She couldn't even trust me to leave me alone for 30 minutes. I was in a teenage mindset in which any chance I had, I was going to do whatever I could to get my needs met. At this point, my number one need had become using whatever pills I could find, from my parents, or brothers, or friends, it did not matter. I had convinced myself that I was not drinking, so I was ok. My priorities had shifted, the only thing that mattered was getting my fix and then the rest could fall into place. Or like the mice in the Peter Olds and James Milner 1954 experiment.

In this experiment, Olds and Milner were to identify the pleasure centers of the brain in mice. They fed these pleasure centers with electrical shocks and then cocaine and the found that this altered the mice survival priorities. Some mice chose not to eat, sleep, drink water, or have reproduce as they would rather starve to death waiting for their next fix. I was like these mice, my survival means had changed.

But, I still have a prefrontal cortex, even if it was not receiving all the messages. This means that I could still feel bad about these actions, carry guilt, and feel alone. This led to more and more use. One night, Kylee had felt so bad that she drove me to a friend's house and had to try to find her way home (this was pre-GPS days). The next day, she had to pick me up from work in the midst of a snowstorm. She couldn't find me and nearly ran out of gas on her adventure through some of the worst areas of the city. But, I determined that I'll never hit a bottom. How in the hell can I not quit using?

Then I was hit with another shockwave. While texting Shandon, I tell him "I am feeling great right now,

(I had gotten pills from my friend who had cancer.) I feel good."

I'll never forget this response as it is glued in my memory, "I just feel sorry for your kids."

The Mask Returns

All of a sudden, he was against me too. Now, I am some terrible person and evil monster to the man who invited me out for a few drinks just a couple weeks ago? What happened?

One day he told me that I have a dark side. Of course I have a dark side, which is what has been showing to the world through the mask I have been wearing. But, throughout our relationship, Shandon never saw the mask. He saw right through it, he saw to my true self.

I felt as though for the first time he saw my mask and it immediately fooled him. Instantly, he believed that this mask was my true self. He had always been different and with his first glimpse of the mask, he was blinded. How ugly can one mask be?

I was hurt and felt like this was my bottom. My one true friend that didn't ever see my mask, now thought the mask was real. It was as though he was enlightened and someone took it away from him somehow. Which is not uncommon, since we all come into this world enlightened and it is taken from us – in fact, some of us never get it back. Some of us only get it back when on our deathbeds. Though it was strange to seen a grown man have this gift and suddenly lose it overnight.

Eventually, Jill and I decided a divorce was in the best interest of everybody involved. Shandon agreed to let me live with him as long as I stayed sober. My family had abandoned me, I felt like a bum, and I could not believe that my world was crumbling around me so fast. I lost the will to live at this point, I had nothing left.

On January 8, 2012, I am staying at their house and Jill came over for a family get-together. I was watching the kids and started taking some pills to avoid the immense emotional pain in which I am suffering.

Shandon is a paramedic and has a good understanding of how narcotics work, along with my past history, and takes one look at me and knows that I am high. I deny everything. He gives me a sobriety test and I pass everything according to his standards.

The next thing I remember is Shandon standing over me with a bag of pills. I must have passed out and they found everything. He tells me that they are calling my work and the police if I do not go with the paramedics to the hospital.

I have been in this role before with Shandon, just a few months ago. I still trust him, believe he is still on my side, so I agree to go. Just like before, he comes into the hospital with me at the Hospital and I get admitted.

But there were no psychiatric beds available at and the next closest location is across state lines. I was given a high dose of something and instantly pass out before being put in an ambulance for a three-hour drive.

Before anyone had ever met me, Shandon had already told the social workers and doctors that I am a "con-artist, a manipulator, and a drug addict." He had ripped me apart, but I do not blame him. He was in crisis mode, again. Once we reach this crisis state, we really cannot judge anyone. The number one concern is to avert the crisis. It took them a long time to make the decision on admission.

To this day, I have no idea when he decided all this about me, but I still feel physical pain throughout my entire body thinking about it. Like a knife through my heart. I was heartbroken, devastated, guilty, and felt like a complete failure.

My first phone call is to Riley. I tell her I will be back to work as soon as possible, I am being admitted under false pretenses. Everything in my life is snowballing faster than an avalanche of consequences. To me, my life is over. I have officially given up and I will commit suicide as soon as I get out of wherever I am going next.

CHAPTER XIX

Forced Surrender
The Gift of Letting Go

Chapter 19
Forced Surrender: The Gift of Letting Go

The concept of surrender is a difficult one to grasp in Western culture. This derives from the socialization process in which we teach to "fight until the death," "never give up," or "only the strong survive." When we hear the word surrender, we immediately picture a weakened military hoisting the white flag over their camp and resisting to a greater power.

Most simply defined, surrender refers to releasing control of something in favor of another. This does not have to be in militaristic terms. It can be as simple as falling asleep each night. We surrender the will to stay awake and keep thoughts with us, and we can only fall into a peaceful sleep once we surrender to the night.

Make no mistake about it, surrender is a battle term. In the terms of awakening and spirituality, surrender once again refers to the internal battle between the soul and ego. Surrender has to do with our ego giving up giving up all rights and authorities to the conqueror – our soul. This type of surrender, connects us with our intuition, our deepest self, and allows our soul to guide us rather than the ego.

It takes a great deal of risk and faith to complete the act of total surrender, to dive feet first into the unknown. But it is the essence of this book – removing our psychological masks is an act of surrendering the ego in favor of the soul.

There are a number of different types of surrender, but they all go through the same process. As Dr. Judith Orloff states in her book, *The Ecstasy of Surrender*, these steps are: 1) Resistance; 2) Acceptance; and 3) Letting Go.

As with any new skill, this requires practice. Luckily for us, we have a built in soul GPS system that makes sure that we are always on the right track. Once we start living for the ego, we eventually commit spiritual suicide and become forced into surrender. This is our built in emergency system, to ensure if we ever get too far off track of our soul's plan, a crisis is created that forces us to surrender to the soul.

Once back on track, there will be continued obstacles – which are meant to be there. It would be like signing up to run a hurdle race and then get upset that there are hurdles on the track. They are meant to be there, to help us grow and develop. The problem lies when we get so discouraged by the hurdles that we stop running the race altogether, which is where the soul intervention must take place to remind us of our purpose. Once following our purpose, we know it, because we feel it. We are in our flow and we look forward to getting up in the morning, we lose our sense of time when we are following our purpose, and our masks get naturally removed.

There are three main types of surrender:

1) Forced Surrender
2) Conscious Surrender
3) Total Surrender

Forced Surrender

It is just as it sounds; it is forced upon us as part of a divine intervention to get us back on track. I have had a few of these in my life, and this chapter focuses on my final forced surrender which allowed me to understand that I signed up for this hurdle race and that the obstacles are there to help us grow, not deter us from finishing the race.

I woke up in a hospital bed in the next state, not too sure of what was going on, where I was, or what they had given me the night before. It was a similar feeling to the opening chapter in which I intentionally took pills in an effort to end my own life, in which everything was just a blur.

I try to sleep it off, but it doesn't seem to subside the overall confusion. I feel like I am drunk, high, been in a fight, and suffering a concussion, in which everything I attempt to do is an incredible cognitive challenge. I am not sure if there could be a worse possible state-of-mind that I could be in before meeting a doctor that will determine my fate, which is exactly the decision the nurses made.

The doctor informs me that I had told the staff that I had stolen the meds from my work, in which I completely deny. He later decides that he is going to put me on Remeron because it works well with Celexa, which only adds to my doped up state-of-mind as I am still withdrawing from benzos.

"You told the staff that you had stole medications from your work," he says to me.

"I never took anything from my work," I reply, "I was doped up on a number of meds and I was likely being dramatic. That never happened."

"Well the plan from here is to commit you to inpatient chemical dependency treatment…"

My heart stopped. Actually, everything stopped. I was in a timeless, lifeless, mindless state-of-mind. But not a drug-induced haze, this was my forced surrender.

Shandon had given a report to the staff back in Fridley and that was all the information they needed to commit me. It is amazing how the process works in favor of committing someone. This is how the entire DSM operates. They create disorders with criteria that are so vague you can diagnose anybody, with any disease. Once you are in their power, your words have less and less significance. They seek a diagnosis, they seek something wrong with you to the extent that you A) meet a diagnosis; and B) that level of care will be covered by insurance. The entire system is a money-making scam, and now I was back on the other side of things, once again.

"My life is over," is what I thought to myself. I was hurting so badly at this time, like I have so many times before. It is never-ending. The big house, the cars, my job, my RN license, marriage, and kids, would all be taken from me. I had nothing to live for anymore.

It is amazing what addiction can do to our minds, and how it can take absolutely everything away from us, yet in convinces us that the drug is not the problem. To the outsider, it is quite obvious in this story that the drugs and alcohol have created these problems - but not the addict. Then, the addict suffers consequences, and instead of seeing the big picture, the thought process changes to, "I need to get better at this so I no longer get in trouble."

At first we go to jail and tell ourselves, "that was enough for me, I'm never going to jail again." But after a while, any external motivation diminishes. I ended up in jail three times and it became less scary each time. My final attachment was my "success." I could always cling to the fact that I am not an addict because I have a good job, big house, and nice cars. Addicts live under bridges, but I had success.

As with every addiction, eventually it gets to that too. This was just part of my process – the hijacking of my brain. The final thing I had left was about to be taken from me. I truly had nothing left.

That is exactly when it hit me.

"I have nothing left. Nothing,"

I told myself out loud. As I pondered on that thought of having "nothing," I realized at the same time that meant I was completely free.

"If everything is gone and I have nothing," I smiled to myself, "that means I have complete freedom."

The thought of losing everything brought me joy, and a sense of relief.

I had went through Dr. Orloff's three stages overnight. On the ambulance ride to the next state, I was resisting everything. The next day, I was forced to accept the nature of the situation. Then, after hearing that I would be committed, I surrendered everything.

This was the silencing of the mind and the clarity that I have felt before in my most defeated moments. It had returned, another divine intervention, in which I realized this always brought great freedom. I could just enjoy moment-by-moment as everything in my life was about to disappear. I could no longer attach to anything external, because it was being stripped away before my eyes. My anxiety, tension, and anger was all gone.

In Christianity this is often referred to as "the way of the Cross," which means finding Jesus in our most troubling times. However, the irony is that the Source, God, Jesus, Buddha, Allah, or whatever you choose to label your higher power cannot be found because it never was lost. It was always within, not without. The way of the cross refers to our times are so troubled that we finally stop resisting and in doing so the suffering seizes automatically.

Pain is inevitable, but suffering is optional. Suffering only occurs when we hold onto the pain and when we resist life. Whenever we resist what is, whenever we complain about our situation, we are rejecting the present which leads to suffering. All we have to do is stop resisting and we can see the joy of surrender.

I recall a phone conversation that evening from my brother Larry.

"But what are you going to do," Larry said to me via a telephone conversation from my hospital room, "I mean, with your job, your license, the house, the car?"

I could sense the panic in his voice. All my family had this same sense of panic –Jill, my sister, my mother, they all felt this doomsday scenario in mind. It felt great that they cared so deeply for my well-being, but what they did not understand that I never wanted any of the phony stuff to begin with.

This is the divine intervention. My soul saw that I was getting too far track off of my true self. It let my ego have some fun, but it got to the point it had to intervene and force me into surrender. I would have never done so on my own. My soul had to come and grab me and put my back on course.

"It doesn't matter," I told Larry in a calm voice, "I can do anything. Maybe I'll go back to school and be a teacher. I'll come back from it, I always do. I am free to do anything now."

That calmed his voice, and it was genuine. It wasn't just him fearing that I was going to commit suicide, it was a teaching moment for him to hear in the darkest night of my ego, my soul prevailed. I know it was a teaching moment, because he asked me to add this conversation to this chapter.

In his words he said:

> *"I was on the phone in your backyard talking to you for two hours. My mind was racing, emotions out of control, and had no idea what was going to come next. I couldn't even call you and talk to you. I had to wait for you to call. I knew how hard you had worked for everything, overcame so much, to achieve so much, and it would all be gone. My biggest fear was your response to losing everything. I feared the worse, for I feared for what I would do if I were in your situation. Then as we spoke, you spoke with such calming clarity that it sent me a message saying, 'It is all going to be alright.' That changed everything for me. I had already quit drinking and my anxiety about everything was through the roof. Now I had a reason to be anxious and with just a few words, just by you saying, 'I can do anything now. I am free to do anything now,' changed my perspective on life. It was the beginning of my awakening. That was my PVD telling me something that my soul had known all along. It would be another 18 months before I could put this theory into practice, but once I did, life started to change for me for the better. First comes the knowledge, then the practice, then the results are just automatic."*

I wasn't trying to be inspirational. Nor was I trying to send an assuring message to my family that I was not suicidal to ease their worries. I was just being real, maybe for the first time in my life. This is because my ego had totally surrendered to my soul.

Conscious Surrender

This occurs once we know we are on the right path and have experienced the dark night of the ego. We have all witnessed people experiencing their flow in life, those who you can see in their heart they are doing what their soul desires. It is inspirational, but nothing like the feeling of being in the flow yourself. To know, you are on the right path, in your personal flow, allows us to consciously surrender in times of need.

The doctor had not listened to a word I had said, and once again, my fate was in the hands of the social workers. She had spoke to Shandon who had demanded that they lock me up and throw away the key, figuratively. He had told them that I am conning and manipulative, and that they cannot listen to a word I say – not that they needed that advice, it seems to be a part of the culture to not listen to the words of the patient.

When Larry took his first job as an LADC at an adolescent treatment center, his supervisor told him that "I don't believe a single word the kids tell me, they are all liars."

"But why are you going to commit me?" I asked the social worker out of general curiosity. I had surrendered to whatever decision they hand down on me. In the past, this question would have been for an opportunity to jump at them, blame the system, but I was able to consciously accept and surrender to the situation. This is the forming of becoming a way of life. It was becoming the new automatic response, which takes time, effort and practice, but soon you no longer think about it – you just let go.

"Well, the nurse is reporting that you just sit in your room, do not participate in activities, do not eat, and are not going to groups," she told me in a condescending way.

While her report was accurate, not one of them had even stopped to say "hello," introduce themselves, ask how I am doing, or even knocked on my door to see if I was alive. I was coming down from a bender, on new medications, and four hours from home. Also, I've always been a picky eater – literally eat about six different things – and I am incredibly depressed.

Looking at my circumstances, it actually would make more sense that I stayed in my room. If I were to get excited, jump up, run into groups, and share my life – that would be more abnormal behavior, wouldn't it? Who are the insane ones here?

It reminds me of another story Larry told me when he first got into the field. The first client he worked with was a 5-foot-tall, 100 pound, 17-year-old female. They labeled her as anorexic because she was small, yet she always asked for seconds at lunch and dinner and ate more than the boys. She would then sleep through the day because the classes they offered were of "third grade level" and it would not help her graduate. She already had a plan in place to return home, get her GED, graduate on time, and enroll in college. But when she overslept, they denied her food! How can you label someone anorexic, then deny them a meal? Furthermore, on her chart it just says "Client did not eat lunch." Only validating the anorexia diagnosis.

Larry confronted the clinical director about this and was told, "You weren't here when she came in. She was just pushing her food around her plate and wouldn't eat."

"Maybe that is because her mother just lied to her and dropped her off here when she though they were going shopping," he responded, "most people do not eat, and sleep all day, when they are depressed. That is normal."

Two weeks later, he was fired for the first time in his life from any position. Because he had been there before, the symptoms were normal to life's circumstances. He spoke to her and found that she despised that diagnosis because she had been bullied all her life for being small and called "anorexic," yet she comes from a home in which her mother is 95pounds and her father is 140 pounds. Plus her parents were addicts, abusive towards her, always moving around, and she suffered daily abuse. But the only thing she hated was being called anorexic, because it was the only thing that she said was untrue.

I was in this same position. Nobody asked what was going on or why I was behaving this way. Hell, no one even stopped by to say hello. Instead, they just labeled me as non-compliant. How can I be non-compliant, if I have never been asked to comply?

It was quite a different experience than when I was 18 at Divine Redeemer. Yet, at the same time, it was similar to the fact that my life had been put in someone else's hands again. This time there was no fighting it, as fighting would have surely led to a commitment and it was not in my control – it never has been.

This is conscious surrender, knowing the situation, knowing I have no control, and able to let things go. This also goes through the same stages of surrender – I resisted their decision and the corruption of the hospital, but had no choice but to accept it for what it was – corruption. The last step, is to let go and let it flow.

Now, I need to make it clear that surrender is not just sitting around doing nothing. It is not refusing to get out of bed and waiting for God to make things better, there still needs to be action. Surrender is the ego giving over control to the soul.

"I'm really having a difficult time with everything going on," I told the nurse, "I was told that I am doing nothing, but no one told me about the groups. Nobody even stopped to say 'hi' to me, and I've been zonked out on medications since I've been here."

"You have a packet there," she responded.

"I do not remember getting that," I laughed, "remember I was in a drug-induced haze when admitted."

Inside I was furious, but it reminded me a lot of my work and the assumptions we make in order to commit people. Then, if we do not like them, we commit them. I was Abigail, and getting to experience the other side for the first time in 18 years.

This is the power of oneness, and realizing that in the universe we are all one. I am Abigail, and she is me. We are just experiencing the world from a different perspective. When I was on the other side, I saw the world through her lens and now I was physically experiencing it. This allowed me to surrender to the moment and know it was all part of a greater purpose.

Daily surrender

This is the final part of the process, and as the name indicates, it is an ongoing "battle" to surrender to the soul moment-by-moment. There is no point in resisting anything anymore, so I show up for meals at the hospital, eat the terrible food, pretend to be engaged, and go to group. While in group, I steal the show and just talk the entire time to pass the time.

In one group, they were talking about such things as recovery churches, which I found quite intriguing, and motivated me to do some research. In my free time, I found the little red book of AA, which blows me away and gives me new sense of connection.

So, like any addict, I stole the book for future reference.

While this new state of inner-freedom was taking control of my life and guiding me, I knew it was only right to get in touch with Shandon. He was doing what he thought was right at the time and he was hurting badly.

"You haven't hit bottom yet, you need to be committed," he tells me, "No one in your family will even talk to me. You need to take the blame with your family and let them know this is your fault."

It was quite odd how he had transformed from enlightened to unenlightened. I guess it is just as easy to fall asleep as it is to awaken. He must have been going through some very difficult times mentally and emotionally, he felt as though I had been lying to him for five years and that he had finally seen the true side of me. But that logic was inverted – he had seen the real me for five years, and just met my false self finally. Though, when someone is in pain, you cannot logically explain this to them.

My family brings in outsiders, we always have. Thinking back to when we were all kids, every single one of us had a best friend that was some type of "sociopath" or "loser." We seem attracted to bringing in the misfits and making them feel loved. All of us have this quality, we must see the good in everyone and learned it from our mother.

We are a strange group, but a loyal group. When Shandon came into the family, naturally we wanted him to feel love and be part of our crazy clan. Everyone built him up, told him how great he was, fed his self-esteem and made him feel welcome. But, when this entire thing blew up and the family told Shandon that he was wrong – he didn't know how to handle it.

This is not entirely his fault. My family wears a collective mask. While they adored Shandon on the outside, they never accounted for him doing any wrong. They inflated his ego with unconditional, and unrealistic praise. Then when crisis struck, the mask came off, and Shandon had not seen this side of the family – the part that might not just go along with everything you say. This is the Irish part of the family that would rather keep the peace than engage in a conflict. We avoid conflict and then when things get out of control, people clash. Shandon just happened to get hit by all sorts of things he had never seen.

He knew me, the real me. He had a fresh set of eyes when we met and held no preconceived notions or beliefs. People told him to be careful, but he didn't see this side of me before. He thought he was being the hero for saving me, for doing the actions that everyone else knew was right – and then he got judged the bad guy.

"Welcome to my world," is what I wanted to say to him. He was in crisis mode and while everyone else was standing around, he acted out and was now being judged. I knew how that felt, and I knew in a way, that he was the one who saved me for taking a risk, taking a chance, and diving into the unknown.

"I'm sorry Shandon. I love you," I told him, "I'll call everyone."

My sister Sharon had stopped talking to him and no one wants anything to do with him. They are upset at the way he handled things. At one point, he lashed out at my mother and telling her she is a terrible mom. The family is fighting and every repressed feeling over the years was coming out. It was an opportunity for a global unmasking, a family forced surrender, but of course, action is required.

When we surrender to the moment, things cannot fail. They may appear to be going wrong, based on what our ego wants. But they always go right, according to what the soul needs.

They call Larry, my mother, and Jill as collaterals. Larry tells them no commit is needed and that I am just going through tough times. My mother also backs me up. Then Jill, who I had put through the ringer with our two kids, would be the final piece to the puzzle.

"Just tell them the truth," I told her, "tell them how you see it."

She tells them, "Shandon is his drinking buddy. He is the one who took wanted to take him out drinking before his major relapse. They drink just as much as each other and always get into the same situations. Then, it suddenly changed."

They ask her about my behaviors at the hospital – not eating, isolating, and not showering.

"This is going to sound bad," she laughs, "but those are all quite normal behaviors for him. I can't get him to eat, leave the house, or shower either."

She resisted nothing. She told the truth, surrendered to the moment and let fate play out before us.

I was released, however, I was assigned a social worker to check in with me for the next sixteen days after discharge. Also, I was required to return to treatment and I chose to go back to the same outpatient program I had left since I was comfortable with everyone.

Once those 16 days were up, I withdrew from treatment against staff advice because the social worker was off my case. I add this story into the daily surrender portion, because it is clear that I had not achieved this at this point. It is a process, a daily process, a moment-by-moment process. My ego was still fighting.

This upset Shandon and I had officially lost him at this point. This was very painful, and still is to this day. I understand that he is extremely sensitive and we had created a unique bond. This is the other side of making ourselves vulnerable – the part in which we fear. When we make ourselves vulnerable, take off our masks, we take a risk. We open ourselves up for pain, but also open ourselves up for connection. Though we had connected at such a deep level, it was now gone and we were hurting.

He was devastated that he had taken off his mask to me and was humiliated. The things he was told about me, seemed true to him now. This hurt me as well, as I had lost a soul companion. It took years for me to stop hurting all over – part of my conscious surrender, and at times moment-by-moment surrender.

Initially when I felt this hurt from our lost relationship, it was my ego taking back the driver's seat. I knew I was getting discharged, so Larry drove four hours in the middle of a snowstorm to pick me up. I was embarrassed, ashamed, scared, lonely, and sad. I had no idea how to respond when I saw him. I have been so awful to him, more than anyone else, and he was the person coming to pick me up.

I couldn't handle this feeling, and since I couldn't drink, I needed a way to protect my ego. I needed to put my mask on – and good ole, reliable anger returned. As he was excited to see me, I barely make eye-contact or talk to him. I lay down in the back seat of the car and cry like a two-year-old for Burger King. As he searches the snow-covered town for a Burger King, he buy's me some food and I pass out in the back seat as he drives four more hours back home.

Not another word was spoken from me during that trip, creating more pain and distance, and allowing the cycle to continue. Although I was more aware, I was still unable to put my knowledge to practice. The ego does not take surrender seriously, it knows that it is a moment-by-moment struggle.

In recovery, this is known as the Pink Cloud. We first stop using the drugs, start feeling good about ourselves, with all this knowledge and ideas, and everything is good. The problem, or as it is perceived, is that life continues. All that a forced surrender does is allow us to get back on track. We still have to complete the race in which we signed up for; a race that we knew was going to have hurdles.

I was granted the opportunity to get back on the track. My first hurdle came with seeing the unconditional loving and accepting face of Larry, and I fell over and decided to just lay on the track.

CHAPTER XX

The Lunatic is on the Grass
Spiritual Gifts of Madness

Chapter 20
The Lunatic is on the Grass:
Spiritual Gifts of Madness

Family members and neighbors used to refer to me as "Psycho Cortland." This was always my weak point, when someone would call me "Psycho," I would lose it as if it were the worst insult you could ever throw at me. Perhaps it hurt so badly, because deep down I knew they were right – but what I did not know is what it meant to truly be a "psycho."

A psycho is derogatory term for someone who is psychotic. Someone who is psychotic is a person suffering from psychosis. Psychosis is characterized by a disconnection from reality.

That is it, that is all there is to it. A psycho is someone who is experiencing a disconnection from reality. However, nothing upset me more as a child and young adult as when I was referred to as a psycho because of the connotation with the word.

This is likely due to the historical nature of the word. In ancient times the common term was "mad" or "madness" which referred to those is a state of psychosis which would resemble periods of mania or hallucinations. People with bipolar disorder and schizophrenia are the most discriminated against people in the history of the world.

As I shared stories of the ancient days and how people with mental illness were mistreated, a large majority of those mistreatments were towards schizophrenics. At first the term was "mad," then we called them "crazy," then "insane," which became "lunacy" or "lunatics," and then of course "psychosis" or "psychotic."

Just as human have always done, when we do not understand something, we label it as different and persecute those people. But, this is the one group of people that are still left in the darkness. We still do not understand it. Even though we label it as a medical disease, they still end up locked up behind bars and it is the last group of people in society in which it is still socially acceptable to discriminate against.

Mental Illness: Disorder or Something More Profound?

So are those with a mental illness sick? Or do they actually possess something more profound? West African Shaman Malidoma Patrice Some explains that mental illness "signals the birth of a healer" and "good news for the other world." Dr. Some was shocked by the manner in which the Western world treats people with mental illness.

"I was so shocked. That was the first time I was brought face to face with what is done here to people exhibiting the same symptoms I've seen in my village," stated Dr. Somé in a Waking Times article in regards that all the attention was placed on the idea that the condition is something that needs to stop. This was in complete opposition to the way his culture views such a situation. As he looked around the stark ward at the patients, some in straitjackets, some zoned out on medications, others screaming, he observed to himself,

> "So this is how the healers who are attempting to be born are treated in this culture. What a loss! What a loss that a person who is finally being aligned with a power from the other world is just being wasted."

In the same Waking Times article, Dr. Some tests his theory by taking an 18-year-old boy with schizophrenia back to Africa and use the Shamanic approach. Rather than cursing him as mentally ill, they trained him as a healer. Within eight months he was considered "normal" and he returned to the United States four years later. He went on to a graduate program in Psychology at Harvard University. No one thought he would be able to function in an undergraduate program and with the treatment from a shamanic approach, he advanced well beyond what any "normal" student could do for themselves.

Furthermore, people with mental illness and addiction almost 100-percent of the time are going to have suffered some form of abuse or trauma in their lives. As a child, you do not understand the way things are around you and many times do not have resources or ability to make changes in your environment. This leads to mental illnesses and addiction as a means to cope. As these abused children grow up, they start acting out with undesirable behaviors and are shunned from society. Many of them end up being incarcerated.

Hence, our current system is further punishing the people who have been abused, neglected, and mistreated most of their lives.

The most common "disorders" that are the most highly discriminated against are the psychotic disorders – mainly schizophrenia and bipolar disorder.

Let's look at the spiritual gifts of all of these disorders.

Schizophrenia

In the very ancient times, in the shamanistic cultures they viewed schizophrenics as having a connection to the spirit world. They would train them as to how to use this power, this gift, to connect with their higher self and earn them the title of "healer." Eventually as civilizations started to form, governments were created, along with rules, laws, and norms were passed down to keep peace and order. This meant, to conform to those in power. Schizophrenia then became viewed as different, bizarre, chaotic, and mad. People with this "disorder" were then persecuted, drowned, buried alive, burnt at the stake, locked in institutions, cut off parts of their brain, or highly medicated to control these abnormalities.

So what is schizophrenia? Medically speaking, it is a diagnosis that is characterized by abnormalities in the perception or expression of reality and the sense of the self.

These "abnormalities" are described as hallucinations and delusions. Hallucinations consist of hearing things that do not appear to be there, and seeing things that do not appear to be present. Delusions are beliefs that appear "strange" and that only the person diagnosed believes them and they refuse to think differently – hence, refuse to conform.

On a side note, the next version of the DSM is planning on including non-conformity of a mental disorder. They have went from trying to be secretive about these things, to just being quite upfront. If you do not act as we want you to do, then you are sick. And if you are sick, you need to take this drug.

But this drug is expensive, so you need this insurance coverage.

However, these descriptions are clinical terms used to help give a diagnosis, which allows for treatment in a society and culture that has agreed upon the best way of treatment of any mental illness is a drug. In the past it was hospitalization in which they never treated the person, but rather abused them and labeled them as insane.

What would happen if we were to actually look deeper into what these "symptoms" include in non-clinical terms, but rather, in terms of the client experiencing them?

The hallucinations are nothing more than an over-sharpening of the senses and experiencing unusual sensations. It can feel like an out-of-body experience and having difficulty deciphering the difference from reality and illusion. Everything tends to flow together as one. The wall never ends, but rather flows together with the flooring. Auditory hallucinations or the "hearing voices" which is so often mocked and ridiculed is a part of being in tune with higher frequencies.

It is scientifically proven that we do not see objects as they are, but rather a transformation and interpretation made by our eyes and mind. The brain filters out what it deems to be unnecessary information. This isn't new age, make-belief information, this is physics. Some physicists have estimated that the percentage of light we see on the spectrum is between 1.5 percent and 2.3 percent! That means that there is up to 98-percent of things that we are incapable of seeing.

We communicate daily via invisible radio waves through internet, cell phones, television, and radio. Radio refers to sending energy with waves. Energy is transmitted across the globe without any direct connection. The end result is an announcer speaks into a microphone and the signal travels at the speed of light via radio waves, is received by another signal, and if we tune our radio dial to the right frequency we can hear their voice without any direct connection.

With all this being said, is it possible that if someone has heightened senses to see part of the 98-percent of the world we do not see? Or to hear things at a different frequency in which we are not tuned in? I would say it is almost certain.

Psychosis, such as schizophrenia and mania, has to do with cracking the ego.

The experience is so intense that words cannot describe. The ego, also known as the false self, is everything that we thought we knew to be true about ourselves. The reality, as we know it, is breaking right before our eyes. The ego, or mask, is put in place to protect us from danger – but it also is incredibly limiting. During this experience, you break out of this mask you have been wearing your entire life. You feel an intense amount of energy that takes you to the depths of your soul. Your soul is set free for the first time since you were an infant, which is the reason for such rapid changes. As a part of this, all your senses are incredibly heightened and you start to question everything around you. You ask things such as "Is this real?" "Am I going crazy?" "Did I Die?"

If we are able to resist nothing and allow this experience to continue we will feel other symptoms such as feeling connection and a sense of oneness with the universe. You begin to feel that you are everyone and everything, and they are all you. An intense level of understanding takes over and everything makes sense, you finally see to just "get it." All the answers to life are in the grasp of your finger tips. Along with the heightened senses of vision and hearing, you also are in tune with those around you almost to the point of feeling their senses, emotions, and thoughts. The sense of time disappears, all that exists is the present moment. All worries seem to disappear as an intense sense of love for everything appears and everything becomes incredibly sacred. Along with this connection, you also may begin to feel that everything is a test from your creator and you no longer see people in their worldly form, but rather see their souls and see the message they are bringing to you.

As this state of consciousness comes down, it changes everything. Your priorities and values change quite dramatically. It is as though you have been given the answers to all of life's mysteries and to return to the worldly form can be depressing.

I would like you to now go back and read the last three paragraphs and take them out of context. Just read what this experience of psychosis feels like to the person. Now, instead of saying psychosis refers to cracking of the ego, change the word "psychosis" for "enlightenment."

"Enlightenment refers to cracking of the ego." Now read those same three paragraphs describing the sensory experience. It is the exact same thing.

The difference is with enlightenment, people try many ways to achieve this experience through deep meditations, vision quests, soul dances, and psychedelic drugs, etc. Yet, those who are labeled as mentally ill and who have been discriminated against more than any other group of people, tend to have this same experience happen to them naturally. In fact, if you were to experience bipolar mania and explain it to someone the most common response is "I think you need help."

And by "help," in our society means to medicate the person so they no longer have these mystical experiences. Now, I do acknowledge that sometimes these hallucinations and delusions can be quite harmful in the sense they are asking people to act violently and they are seeing demons. This is likely due to the either trauma or repressed feelings. It is still a good sign that the person is breaking away from their ego, but they need to be guided by someone with experience so they can get closer to the enlightenment side of the spectrum.

Bipolar

> *"Have I gone mad?"* asked the Mad-Hatter. **"I'm afraid so, you're entirely bonkers"**, Alice replied, **"but I'll tell you a secret… all the best people are."**

The exchange above is from Lewis Carroll's notorious fictional story, <u>Alice in Wonderland</u>, which in my professional opinion stands with more validity than today's psychiatric and mental health paradigms. In fact, Alice shares the same view as some of the greatest thinkers of all-time, such as Socrates who once declared: *"Our greatest blessings come to us by way of madness, provided the madness is given us by divine gift."* Plato too referred to insanity as *"a divine gift and the source of the chief blessings granted to men."*

So, to best understand bipolar disorder the modern day epidemic of medicated "madness", down the rabbit hole we go…

On the first page of the classic story, we find Alice is disinterested in the dull, boring, everyday existence in which she resides. She peers into her sister's book to see it has no illustrations or even conversations, which to Alice has no use or interest. She ponders the idea of making a daisy-chain, but lacks the energy or motivation to take the time to pick the daisies. She is disinterested in 'normal' life. Then, suddenly, a talking white-rabbit runs past her; he appears to be late. Of course, Alice is curious about this bizarre occurrence and follows him down the rabbit hole — and most of us will be familiar with the rest of the story.

By today's standards and diagnostic references, Alice's disinterest in 'normal' life would very likely be diagnosed as a mental disorder. With this diagnosis, she would then be medicated for life, after a brief stay at a psychiatric hospital to stabilize her on the medications that are claimed to be capable of *normalizing* her mental sickness.

But, is Alice really sick? Or is she a creative, intelligent, deep-thinking, imaginative, or even gifted child? I would wager everything I own on the latter!

Bipolar disorder is one of the oldest recognized 'mental disorders', yet it remains one of the most misunderstood. As a psychiatric Registered Nurse, it is my belief that people with bipolar disorder are not "sick" – the *real* sickness lies in the treatment and medications they receive.

Formerly known as manic-depressive disorder or manic-depression, bipolar disorder refers to the experience of opposing poles with regard to a person's mood. Essentially, bipolar disorder is distinguished by the experience of *polarity*.

At one pole is mania, which includes intense energy, racing thoughts, feelings of euphoria, inflated grandiosity or sense of self, impulsiveness and risk-taking behavior. The other pole includes depression, which presents the opposite symptoms, such as fatigue (to the point of inability to get out of bed), moving or talking so slowly that others notice, a feeling of emptiness, loss of interest in things that were once enjoyable, difficulty concentrating or making decisions, and thoughts of self-harm.

It is important to understand the distinction between *moods* and *emotions* here. Moods are essentially emotional feelings that last for a period of time – typically for more than two or three days, which can be difficult to shift. While everyone has their ups-and-downs, bipolar disorder is far more disabling, with symptoms far more severe than a typical mood swing from happiness to sadness. The extremes of bipolar disorder can take you from feeling that you are omnipotent to the point of wanting to end your own life.

> *"It is no measure of health to be well adjusted to*
> *a profoundly sick society"* -- Krishnamurti

Just as Alice does in the opening chapter of her story, many people with bipolar disorder realize that "normal life" is far too phony, boring and constrained. They realize that there is much more to this mundane existence than what is commonly suggested. So, with this insight, one can see how easily it would be to slip into a depressed mood with thoughts such as:

> *— Why would I want to go through with this life?*
> *— Nobody understands me!*
> *— I am all alone.*
> *— Why am I the only one who thinks this way?*
> *— Maybe they are right, maybe I **am** crazy.*
> *— What is the point of it all?*
> *— What reason do I have to keep going?*

This depression sucks the life out of you, to the point that you lack the energy to even get up and pour a glass of water. *If I got up, then I would have to find a glass, wait for the water to filter, and then put the glass away... it is not worth the effort.* Furthermore, the person experiencing these thoughts *realizes* that this thought process is illogical, and destructive, which only creates a tidal-wave effect, inducing further feelings of sadness and dejection.

At birth, we are free — we are born with a clean slate and we see the world is magical. But as we grow, things change. We are trained to behave a certain way; we are domesticated to a set of standards that our society has agreed are "normal". We learn to create a mask and put it on every day; to conform. We learn to use different masks for different groups of people, different occasions, and different times. We are taught that this is "normal life", and that wearing these masks is "normal" human behavior.

*And yet this mask, this image that we create and send out to the world, is our **false** self. It is a learned function of the ego. It is only behind the mask that we find our true self — our soul.*

Manic episodes — those times of euphoria, grandiosity and impulsiveness — are triggered by the collapsing of the ego or mask. It is as though the soul is allowed to be free for the first time. Just like a dog that is tied to a chain its entire life and then finally breaks free, it runs wild, explores, and does whatever it can, because it can *finally be the animal it was meant to be.*

A spiritual awakening is much the same process. Like those times of mania, it involves taking off the mask and living as our true self for the first time. If treated as a spiritual *dis-ease*, this is the unexpected gift that bipolar disorder can offer — a short-cut to enlightenment. The mania pole can reveal to us our strongest and deepest desires, and exactly how our personal energy truly wishes to be expressed, while the depression pole shows us – in no uncertain terms – the areas of our lives that are not being lived in total alignment with our most honest truth.

But, like the dog that just got off its leash and is running wild without care, there can be great danger if those manic episodes that are not controlled. Experiencing and freely expressing the impulses of your true self for the first time, you may begin to test reality in life-threatening ways, such as trying to fly out a window, walking into the middle of traffic, etc. In contrast, if the dog (the soul) has always been allowed to roam freely, it learns not to run in traffic or to chase people, and knows how to regulate its natural energy and exuberance for life.

The key is balance; learning *always* to roam free, not just in moments of mania.

The Story of Karl – "The Lunatic on the Grass"

Back to my story at the psychiatric rehab facility, I was ready to move on with my life. Psychiatry is a fraud and I wanted to get out of that place. But, as previously mentioned, I had one soul contract that needed to be fulfilled.

We had a schizophrenic patient named Karl. His plan was to marry Paris Hilton and join the European golf tour. He told us that he was a pro golfer and he was engaged to Paris Hilton, this was one of his many delusions. The staff laughed at him and made jokes. It was easy to go along with it because I had given up, I no longer wanted to fight, and his delusions were quite ridiculous. I joined in on the fun as I was burnt out.

It is hard to go through your entire life as a revolutionary. It is mentally, physically, and spiritually draining. I had become the burnout staff that I had despised my entire life.

I had thrown in the towel and really had no energy to fight the system. I laughed at his delusions and didn't take anything serious. At the same time, my new escape had become playing golf. It gave me a chance to get outside, learn something new, and watch myself grow. It excited me to escape from everything and enjoy a few hours of the day. One day, I had a golf match set up after work, so I brought it my clubs and started swinging them in the office.

"You got a decent looking swing, Cortland," he says to me, "can I show you something?"

"This ought to be entertaining," I thought to myself as I handed my new clubs to the delusional golfer. I thought I would have some fun at his expense. So he starts talking about a couple pointers that actually sounded legit, they made sense logically.

Then he gets into a stance and something changed in the energy around us as he took a couple practice swings in front of me.

Wow! They looked like a real golf swing. I couldn't believe it, this schizophrenic delusional old man just took some of the nicest, smoothest-looking swings I had ever seen.

"Do those swings again," I asked.

He gladly obliged and I was floored by his precision and gracefulness of each stroke. We started talking about golf and he knew everything and more. I asked him about playing shots out of bunkers, downhill lies, in a divot, out of mud, and all his answers actually made perfect sense. Then he would demonstrate and it was like going to a golf clinic from a pro. I was in complete shock.

"It's hard to explain it in this office," said Karl, "it would be nice if we could go to a driving range sometime."

I am still quite a bit skeptical of him, so I go to my office and do a quick google-search. Sure enough, there he is as a highly successful NCAA Division I golfer. I had to do something, so I asked Riley if I could take all the residents to the driving range and she agreed.

We all packed in the van and headed over a college golf course. The course is overcrowded with the demographics consisting primarily of wealthy, white, college kids with expensive clubs smacking the ball around and admiring their shots with each other. As we get out of our van, Karl is wearing tennis shoes that are twenty years old, ripped up jeans, and looks like he hasn't been outside for a decade.

As I look around, you can feel the eyes upon us with everyone staring, laughing, snickering, and making comments to themselves. It was quite apparent that we did not belong.

We didn't have any clubs, so we asked to rent some.

"Sorry, we don't rent clubs here," said the attendant, "All we have is this old nine-iron that was left here by a child, you are welcome to use it but it is quite small."

Karl is about 6'5 which makes the club even more impossible for him to hold. The club is about thirty years old and made for a pre-teen child. I start to feel apprehensive about everything and am having doubts. This isn't fair to embarrass him any further.

"Sorry Karl, this is all they have," I tell him.

"This is fine," he says as he grabs the club, "It is a little small but it is fine. I haven't swung a club for many years, I wonder if I still know how to do it."

My heart started racing as his comment made me think that maybe this entire thing was another delusion. Now, we have this old schizophrenic golfer about to hit some balls with all these rich white kids that have already been pointing and laughing at us since we got out of the van.

As we start to walk towards one of the tee boxes, my heart is pounding and my nerves are out of control. This man doesn't deserve to be treated this way. With each group we pass by, they stop hitting their ball just to look at him and wonder "what the hell is this freak doing here?"

The stigma of mental illness was right in front of us. All we were there to do was to hit a few golf balls and go back to our home, yet it had become a scene as soon as we got out of our van as if to say, "Looks like the circus is in town."

It felt as if we were in some movie scene and you knew something was about to happen. I felt as if the Pink Floyd song, "Brain Damage" were playing in the background.

> *The lunatic is on the grass;*
> *The lunatic is on the grass;*
> *Remember games, and daisy chains, and laughs;*
> *Got to keep the loonies on the path;*

The opening lines of the song, Roger Waters explains that this is in reference to the signs that say "Please Keep off the Grass," and that disobeying such signs indicates insanity. He later states that not letting people on such beautiful grass was the real insanity. We refer to anybody as a lunatic or insane that does not live by certain rules that in reality, make no sense. Keep the loonies on the path, don't question the norm, is the message the higher-ups have placed on society for generations. The real insanity is to go along with it without question.

On this date, the lunatic was on the grass. This area of beautiful grass on the golf course was designed and reserved for the privileged class and this lunatic needs to be kept on the path, which refers to his group home. Don't let him outside and into my backyard!

We finally found a tee box that was the closest we could find to away from everyone, yet it was impossible with such a big crowd. And as far as we were from the gallery, it seemed we were still smack in the center as the swings certainly slowed down in other areas as they wanted to watch the circus that was about to take place.

"Well here we are," I said with nervousness in my voice, "Let er' rip Karl."

I put the bucket of balls on the side and our group sat back and watched as Karl put the first ball on the grass. I took a step back and looked around and it was quite clear that we were the main attraction that day.

Karl took the club, held it in the air and inspected it for a quick second. He then walked up and approached the ball before putting his club on the ground. He took one final peak into the driving range area as to look where he would be hitting before he put his head down and was glued on the ball.

As he began his backswing, time stood still. There was nothing else around and the world was silent as he took a flawless backswing with his eyes glued on the ball as the short club reached its peak over his head.

He then turned and led the club head directly toward the ball as the entire driving range waited in anticipation. The club had come down fiercely and then…SMACK!

The ball goes soaring into the air, higher, further, and more beautiful than anything I have ever witnessed. You could not make it up, it was like from a movie scene. My heart stopped, my mind stopped, and I just stared at the beauty of this ball in midflight before finally landing nearly 200 yards away.

Karl grabs another ball and he does it again, and again, and again.

Soon everyone at the driving range had completely stopped swinging and started watching this schizophrenic hit the ball like a professional golfer. He starts giving me the same tips he was giving me at the office, but now he is demonstrating and then smoking the ball better than the club pros at the driving range.

Suddenly, some other kids start walking over and they hear our conversation and ask for advice. Karl starts giving tips to everyone. It was the most amazing sites of my life, and the most hope building thing I have ever experienced.

Just as I was ready to throw in the towel, the guy who told me he was going to marry Paris Hilton just changed my world and all of those around him. He eliminated stigma that day, for those people, by just hitting some golf balls. He was no longer a freak, but a friend.

I saw God once again. All of his mental illness disappeared as he hit the ball and started working with others. This came along when I needed it the most, however, it bothered me that he sat there for two months and I never bothered to say "hello" and never got to know him.

I was planning on just going about my business and let him rot there. It was the exact same manner in which I was treated in my recent hospital stay and I had been doing it to Karl. I was too burnt out and in too much pain to care for this person. I saw him as a freak, just like everybody else, but learned more from him than from any professor, mentor, and person with an advanced degree. He taught me of acceptance, facing fears, and returning love for hate.

As we started talking more, he once said to me, "Cortland, you are the first person in twenty years that has explained to me what schizophrenia was and how it works. And yes, I think I might have that."

I was the first to tell him, the first to show interest in his life, and he started to listen. I taught him about the symptoms and he taught me about golf. He was not all delusional, but more importantly, he was a regular human just like everyone else that had been treated like an animal the past twenty years. We have not got it any better than we did before, we treat him as insane, mad, crazy, or a lunatic. In reality, he is breaking away from the reality that we see and is on the verge of being enlightened and we have impeded on his process by telling him he is wrong.

Eventually, he left our home and I do not know how his story ended. I did discover that his doctor was Dr. Jackson from the county hospital, who has a reputation for committing everyone. I gave her a phone call and let her know that he was not all delusional. I have no idea how she took it because I let go of the results. I did my best, which is all I could do. In the past, I would have fought and fought and fought. But, all that does is drive all of us crazy when we attach ourselves to results in outcomes. We are only responsible for our choices and actions, I have no control over what happens from there.

The moment at the driving range is one of the most unforgettable experiences of my life. I can recall the entire event as if it happened today. We look at a person with schizophrenia, disheveled, and lost their mind. But we don't see them as a human, we don't see this beautiful golf swing that resurrected his life.

He started talking to people differently and hanging out at the nurses' station. He was a different man after he hit a few golf balls. It proved to me that God exists in everything and if you are open, you can see him in everyone.

This is my best example of a soul contract. We needed each other. I needed him to give me hope and show me that my life of a revolutionary is worth it in the long run; and he needed me to realize there is more to life than what he had been experiencing.

It hurts me to know this is just one story that happens to have a happier twist. I think about all the others in psychosis that we mistreat and abuse. I have family members and friends that experience periods of mania that we laugh at and tell them, "take your pills" or "Stop acting crazy." We invalidate their periods of heightened senses, which is no wonder when people come down from periods of mania they become depressed. They get glimpses of the truth, get laughed at, and then return to a reality in which they know is not true.

Which is why psychedelic drugs become so appealing, it becomes a means to self-induce "psychosis" which happens to be the exact same thing as enlightenment. Stan Grof describes these periods of psychosis as "spiritual emergencies" as the person is cracking the shell of the ego but needs to learn how to embrace it, resist nothing, and understand that they are only waking up.

The problem is when people who do not understand this are trying to tell people what they are experiencing is not real. It makes those afraid to try to explain their experience in fear of being locked up or labeled as "crazy."

The world we live in is all an illusion, it is all a dream. Once we experience psychosis or a spiritual moment, we begin to wake up. But how do you explain this to someone who is still sleeping? How can you wake someone up, who doesn't know they are sleeping?

CHAPTER XXI

Disillusionment

Everything We Have Been Told is a Lie

Chapter 21
Disillusionment: Everything We Have Been Told is a Lie

On a trip to the zoo, as we encountered the Wolverine display it was clear that something was off. This poor creature was in a dead-sprint back and forth against a ledge that was about eight feet long. While the children found amusement in the Wolverine's bizarre behavior, most of the adults were able to show compassion for the "sick animal."

"Oh he is still doing that," said one of the adults behind me.

"Still!?" I asked, "How long has he been doing this?"

"Well, he was doing it last week, too."

For over a week, this animal was sprinting back-and-forth on an eight foot ledge? Wolverines in the wild travel up to fifteen miles per day and this one is in captivity in a room the size of a living room and has literally lost its mind.

But, is the Wolverine actually sick? Or is it a product of the unnatural environment?

When you think about it, there is actually nothing unnatural about the Wolverine's behavior at all based on its circumstance. A few more displays down the walkway and there is a black bear pacing back and force on a rock for the past month or so that is in an enclosure that is 0.0018 percent of its natural habitat as behind the glass everyday it has children, men, and women pounding at the glass, staring, laughing, and making faces and mocking this animal's misery in captivity.

These examples are what have been commonly referred to as *zoochosis*. This is the term used to explain when a zoo animal goes into a state which resembles psychosis; but nobody views this animal as sick, but realize it is because we have captured them and put them in an unnatural state of being. It is the smartest of these animals that realize the disorder around them and they enter into this zoochosis. Because they understand that this is not real, this is not natural, and that they are being played for as a game.

If the wolverine was a human, it would be diagnosed with ADHD and put on medications. The common treatment for kids with ADHD is Ritalin or Adderall – highly powerful stimulant drugs that have similar chemical makeup of cocaine and methamphetamine, respectively.

Think about that; If a smart kid is having a difficult time in an unnatural environment of sitting in a classroom for eight hours learning about meaningless activities and he/she acts out, then we label them as sick and dope them up on meth to help them focus.

Who is the sick one here?

Out of curiosity, I returned to the zoo a few weeks later and the wolverine was not in his display anymore. I went back again about a month after that and he was still not present. Nobody seemed to have a direct answer as to what happened to the wolverine – just pretend as if nothing happened.

Another month passed and I returned to the zoo again and saw the wolverine back in his display. He was digging a hole, playing and doing "natural" wolverine type things. He seemed happy, content, and no longer bothered by his tiny living arrangement. People walked by the glass case and took pictures and were happy to see the playful wolverine enjoying life in captivity.

What they did not realize is that this wolverine had gone into psychosis and they removed him for two months while doping him up on Prozac. Now he was ready to return to public display – similar to how we treat the mentally ill and chemically dependent humans in our society.

The Door to Enlightenment

Disillusionment is defined as a feeling of disappointment resulting from the discovery that something is not as good as it was once believed. As difficult as it can be at times to experience disillusionment, it is also a powerful spiritual experience as this is what opens the door to enlightenment. This is the point you stop seeing the world with all the attachments you have been brainwashed and you see it for its truth as it really is.

The illusions are everywhere – teachers, parents, school, work, television, media, internet, church, government, politicians, history books, etc. – therefore, the truth is underneath everything we know to be true.

In 1995, Canadian pop-star Alanis Morisette broke onto the scene with her album "Jagged Little Pill". Morisette had been pushed in to the industry by playing piano at age six, writing her own songs at age nine, and by age 10 she was on a television show "You Can't Do That on Television." By age 14, she had signed with MCA Canada and released her first album at age 17.

Jagged Little Pill was an enormous success worldwide with the edgy, alternative-style sound that had not been heard before. She went on a world tour for eighteen months before taking another eighteen month break to find herself. Alanis told MTV:

> "Basically, I had never stopped in my whole life, hadn't taken a long breath, and I took a year and a half off and basically learned how to do that. When I did stop and I was silent and I breathed… I was just left with an immense amount of gratitude, and inspiration, and love, and bliss."

She came back with the song "Thank You" which describes her process of surrender, letting go, getting off medications, having accountability, and remembering her divine nature. However, the song did not have the commercial success as her first album but it was clear that her mission trip to India and Cuba had opened her heart and soul to her true nature.

Similar stories have been told earlier in this book about film producer Tim Shadyac, who after a serious bike accident he started to see the world for how it was and gave up his material possessions.

More recently, actor Jim Carrey has gone through a similar transformation after battling bouts with depression for most of his life. He stated that he discovered that heaven is not a faraway place, but found right here in the present moment. Carrey goes on to state that he understands that we are all one and that he wants to make as many people with him as possible.

Of course, these are stories of disillusionment from people who are already at the top – and this is actually far more rare to achieve. More commonly, it is the people who hit rock bottom or who have suffered some type of discrimination, trauma, or abuse that are the ones who will see through this façade we all experience.

If you are of a minority race, you already see the injustice of the world on a daily basis which puts you closer to disillusionment. It just depends on how you choose to use it. If you start to identify with the fact that you are a minority and discriminated against and then turn it into spiteful anger, you go in the opposite direction. But, if you use this for disillusionment it can be a boost in the right direction to enlightenment.

It can take place in small increments such as seeing the wolverine at the zoo or golfing with a schizophrenic to destroy the illusions around us; or it can come in one major incident such as a near death experience or hitting the proverbial "rock bottom."

In Christianity this is often referred to as "the way of the cross," explaining how often the worst times of our lives is what helps the person find Christ. However, you cannot find Christ (or the divine, God, Source, or whatever you choose to call it) because it was never lost. It can only be found within.

But it is not the worst moments that bring us closer to finding this moment, it is the fact that we are more willing to completely to surrender. Once we hit rock bottom, we silence the mind and go into a forced surrender state and in this state is when the soul can shine through for the first time. This is why so many people in prison find God for the first time as they are into a forced surrender situation. But it is not the only way, we can surrender to each moment through meditation in which we can achieve this same notion.

A Sioux creation story says that long ago the Creator gathered all of Creation and said, "I want to hide something from the humans until they are ready for it. It is the realization that they create their own reality."

The eagle said, "Give it to me, I will take it to the moon."

The Creator said, "No. One day they will go there and find it."

The salmon said, "I will bury it on the bottom of the ocean."

"No. They will go there too."

The buffalo said, "I will bury it on the Great Plains."

The Creator said, "They will cut into the skin of the Earth and find it even there."

Grandmother Mole, who lives in the breast of Mother Earth, and who has no physical eyes but sees with spiritual eyes, said, "Put it inside of them. They will never look there."

And the Creator said, "It is done."

The Lies Our Teachers Tell Us

Disillusionment goes beyond just finding the divine and surrendering to the moment. It is involved in every aspect of our life.

Between the ages of two and four, 95-percent of children are considered highly creative, imaginative, and curious about the world around them. By age seven, this number is down to less than five-percent. During these crucial years, the mask is created as children are discouraged to be creative, taught how to act, behave, speak, and the socialization process begins. We are taught to color inside the lines or you are "doing it wrong," discouraged from stopping to smell the flowers and play in nature. If a child knocks over a cereal box in the grocery store they are told they are "bad." But, then, they encouraged to sit in front of a television set which further creates a mask. With the ever-increasing violent programming on television and video games, the average American child will have witnessed 8,000 murders by the time they finish elementary school.

Will this lead to them being more violent? It is hard to say, but it is clear that each of these messages – subliminal or deliberate – is stored in the subconscious mind. Instead of being guided with love and connecting with the universe, we are being trained to fear the world and separate from others.

As everyone wears this mask from age seven on up, the mask builds and builds and builds and it controls our lives. It leads to society of people that are depressed and anxious. Just walk through the store or the mall and see how many people will go out of their way to avoid eye contact. Yet, when jogging in the park or when around children, everyone is more engaging with one another, energetic, laughing, and smiling. Children and nature help remove these masks.

Then as we grow old, we realize that we were wearing this mask our entire lives. As we sit on our death beds, we never ask to see our bank accounts, our trophies, our awards from work, or our bonus checks. We seek to be with loved ones as long as we can. Our masks are removed.

That is the secret to life, to remember who you were before the world told you who to be; to remove your mask and remember your inner child before we were socialized. Each moment is an opportunity to either to develop the true self or develop the mask. What will you choose today?

It begins with our parents teaching us the values that were passed down to them from many generations. They teach us what they have always believed to be important which came from their parents, church, and schools. This socialization process puts labels and attachments on everything we see, read, and hear.

> *"The day we are born we are given a name, a race,*
> *a religion, nationality, and ethnicity. We then*
> *spend the rest of our life defending these labels."*

From the first days of school, we are told that Christopher Columbus discovered America – when in fact, he was lost and thought he was in India. We were told that people believed the world was flat and that he proved it was round and everyone believed they would fall of the face of the Earth. However, people knew the world was round for thousands of years before Columbus was born.

But is much easier to share this story to children as opposed to discussing how Columbus was a mass-murderer, a precursor for genocide of the American Indian, introduced the sex trade, and enslaved, raped, tortured the Natives that had welcomed him into their home.

Yet, we celebrate Columbus as a hero.

As the story continues, we are brainwashed into believing that Americans are always the good guys and that we are the greatest country on earth. The church promotes the same belief that their religion is the only true religion. And the entire culture gets you to believe that being white is the most powerful race.

It is all propaganda that was passed on down to us. When we are children, we believe what is told to us and we get bombarded with these messages that create further separation.

The history books spend a great deal of time on the Revolutionary War and the Civil War as to how wonderful we are as a society. Then in World War I and World War II how we jumped in to save the world. But they fail to mention what has really been going on since the Cold War – since we have been invading countries to steal their natural resources. Or how our country became powerful by stealing land of Native Americans by breaking every treaty we have ever signed and profited by using slave labor of Africans we stole from their homeland.

And we refuse to address any of those things. There is this unwritten rule in our society in which we do not talk about race, religion, or politics. Yet, those are the three things that are causing so many problems in the world. Those are the three things that create the most separation and if we do not talk about it, there is no chance it will get better.

We have enough money to end world hunger and to create world peace. But that will never happen with a capitalistic society in which war is a lucrative business. Peace can never exist because war is profitable. Imagine if spending millions of dollars on one missile that can damage a village and kill children, that money was spent to build homes, schools, infrastructure, and provide ample supplies of food, clean water and electricity? But the rich white man would not profit off helping.

The irony of all of this is that the more you look into these things, the more you get labeled a conspiracy theorist, paranoid, etc. Of course, that comes from people who have not broken through the illusions yet.

They do not want to believe that their government would lie to them, because they have been brainwashed since the beginning to believe that they are part of the greatest country on earth.

However, you can look up the CIA operation MK Ultra in which the government took citizens and gave them different psychotropic drugs in an effort to better understand mind control. Psychiatrists performed studies in which they put subliminal messages unbeknownst to patients in an effort to control their minds in part of the Cold War era.

This is one of many atrocities carried out by the CIA which are all public information and would not take more than a few Google searches to see that the American government is not above hurting its own citizens to benefit the elite.

The entire idea of national pride creates separation itself. Many of the astronauts who have traveled into space and looked below at the Earth see it in its natural beauty without borders and this led to a spiritual awakening as they became disillusioned to the lies of the news and media.

Recently deceased astronaut of Apollo 14, Edgar D. Mitchell stated of this experience:

> *"You develop an instant global consciousness, a people orientation, an intense dissatisfaction with the state of the world, and a compulsion to do something about it. From out there on the moon, international politics look so petty. You want to grab a politician by the scruff of the neck and drag him a quarter of a million miles out and say, 'Look at that, you son of a bitch."*

Spiritual Gifts of Mental Illness

In the previous chapter, when discussing the story of Karl, I explained the association between psychosis or mania with the same feeling of a spiritual awakening. Again, as we speak about those who have been most discriminated against, they are the ones with the gifts and closer to a spiritual experience that will take them beyond this dimension.

And it works this way for all mental "illnesses."

This chapter opened with the story of the Wolverine, who would almost certainly be diagnosed with ADHD if he were a human. People who have this "disorder" are typically the most gifted, creative, and intelligent people. But since they do not fit into a box for an educational curriculum, we drug them up with potent drugs that are considered a felony to possess.

These children are gifted because they realize that the information being fed to them in the classroom is not nurturing their soul. However, once they find something that clicks with their inner being, they are dedicated and more focused than anyone in the classroom – one-hundred percent of the time.

They do not have a disability, they have a different way of learning. Then we look for the quick fix to make it easier on the teachers and parents and we drug them up with powerful substances so they fit into the mold – so they are "normal." Yet, we are shutting off their innate creativity and inner genius.

Those who suffer with depression and anxiety provide spiritual gifts as this is also breaking down of the ego, it is part of the disillusionment process. This person experiences such difficult moods because it is hard to fit into this world that does not make sense to them. They are on the verge of a breakthrough and aware that everything around them is a lie. It is difficult to be an incredibly real person surrounded by an entirely phony world.

Obsessive-compulsive disorder is just a way for people with anxiety attempting to deal with the anxiety. But their compulsive and obsessive habits, all in an effort to avoid the discomfort, become a new disorder. Which one can only ask how difficult must the underlying condition be?

Even the most "difficult" of personality disorders can be a gift. We put together an article on the spiritual gifts of borderline personality disorder (BPD) which received serious backlash – not from the sufferers of the disorder, but more from the people living with those who have BPD. They were appalled that we suggested that people with BPD are loving, kind, caring people that have endured abuse – they wanted the world to know that they are "evil" people of the worst kind.

The Diagnostic and Statistical Manual for Mental Disorders (DSM) defines BPD as a pervasive pattern of instability of interpersonal relationships, self-image, and affects. It also includes problems regulating emotions and thoughts and can include impulsive on and reckless behavior.

Clinicians will refer to this illness as being "addicted to drama." We are told that those with this "illness" depend completely on the external environment for clues as to what emotion to feel. Symptoms may include behavior that is manipulative, gamey, attention-seeking, dramatic, self-damaging, and emotionally unstable.

The term "borderline" was first used in 1938 by psychiatrists to describe people who they thought to be on the "border" of diagnoses of neurosis and psychosis. This term is outdated as "neurosis" is no longer recognized in any diagnostic material and BPD is no longer believed to be a psychotic disorder.

In Western medicine and society all mental illnesses focus on what is broken in the person and what needs to be fixed. In the East and ancient cultures, shamans view mental illness as the birth of a healer and good news from the outer world.

From a shamanistic perspective, they "symptoms" of BPD include feeling intensely connected to everything; therefore, become highly affected by everyone and everything. They are not bad, they have a spiritual gift. They can sense the emotions of others instinctively and feel things that we cannot. They know how to make people feel as if they are reading your soul.

Dr. Marsha Linehan, the founder of Dialectical Behavioral Therapy (DBT) and leading expert in the understanding and treating of BPD, explains patients with BPD are like third degree burn victims. Just by walking by them, you may hurt them.

Linehan had her own personal struggle with BPD and was and hospitalized for 26 months in 1963. In her discharge summary it states, "Miss Linehan was, for a considerable part of this time, one of the most disturbed patients in the hospital."

It is reported that she had attempted suicide multiple times because she could not close the gap between the person she was and the person she wanted to be. The gap was insurmountable which left her desperate, hopeless, and homesick for a life she would never see.

Living with BPD is like the earth beneath your feet is constantly shifting and changing which keeps you off balance, scared, and defensive. It is a roller coaster of moods, thoughts, emotions, relationships, self-image, goals, and even your likes and dislikes at such frequent intervals it is overwhelming and confusing.

Is this a disorder? Or, like the shamans believe, is this a healer in training that already sees the truth and is strongly dissatisfied in the current reality? Whereas, the rest of us put on a mask everyday as we get dressed to go to a job we don't like, to make money to buy stuff we don't really want to impress people we don't really like.

Yet, those who have this innate sense of connection, we label them as overly emotional and difficult. We are labeling the future healers and spiritually gifted as insane and medicating them to be "normal" or more like us.

However, no drug has currently been approved for treatment of BPD, which is the sole reason that the number of those diagnosed has remained relatively low. The best form of treatment is individual therapy, which is the last thing the psychiatry industry wants. It is easier to label them as bipolar and give them a "mood stabilizer" or "anti-psychotic" medicine to chemically restrain them. Due to being doped up, tired, and sleeping all day the symptoms disappear and it is a quick success and an easy paycheck for the psychiatry industry.

As soon as a medication becomes approved for BPD, I guarantee the number of diagnosis will skyrocket immediately. You'll see.

While the experts are in the infant stages of determining the roots of BPD, it is actually a simple formula. This formula includes biological temperament, social invalidation, suppressed feelings, psychological trauma, stigma and judgments, and a yearning to escape the suffering of the phony existence in which reside.

The only time they do receive validation is when they act out in certain behaviors such as self-harm. It is the first time someone listens to them.

Inside the clinics the staff does not want to work with borderlines. Before they even walk in the door if they have that diagnosis, the staff is instantly on edge and wary of the person which negatively affects the treatment in which they receive.

When I was first told about BPD, it frightened me. I was trained in that it is all just "attention-seeking and manipulative behavior." I believed the way I was trained and that it was all fake and I didn't want to "deal with it" either.

I was taught that these people were "bad" and that we were "good" for the services we provided by ignoring and avoiding them. Yet, now I see that these are the people that have endured some of the greatest pain. And with this pain, often comes the greatest moments of clarity. As Rumi states:

"The wound is where the light enters."

But, instead of trying to help them through their pain to experience that light, we are adding to their suffering. With this pain and suffering, these people know the truth. They are the ones who understand life and the connections at a deeper level. Instead of validating them for who they are, we place a stronger mask on them to ensure they are never allowed to use the gift we don't understand.

Spiritual Gift of Addiction

There are stages of recovery from chemical addiction such as admitting, accepting, embracing, and transcending.

Admitting is the easy part, it has to do with being aware of the consequences of our substance use along with the loss of control. Or as the First Step states, "We have admitted we are POWERLESS over our addiction and that our lives have become UNMANAGEABLE."

Accepting has to do with surrendering and realizing that we will never be able to use mood-altering substances again. This has to do with making changes in our life. It is easy to admit, but to fully accept that this is a condition that will be with us forever is a difficult pill to swallow – especially because we are giving up our drug of choice which has been our most powerful means of coping with difficult emotions.

It is important to note that chemical dependency is not of a moral condition. It has do to with becoming dependent on using a chemical to alter mood and emotions. Which is why often someone with mental illness will develop chemical dependency; because they already have difficulty with their mood/emotions and the drug provide a temporary relief.

The spiritual gift aspect happens when we can embrace and then transcend the addiction.

This is also referred to as taking the mask off. We used drugs and alcohol to find our true self, to allow our soul to shine through, and recovery is about still having that longing to do so and finding a natural way to make it happen.

The person who develops a chemical dependency has a strong innate desire to take their mask off; they too, understand the phoniness of the world and have a strong craving to break through this illusion. Once they get into their active addiction, they create a new mask, and the stigma and judgments pushes them further and further down into a hole.

Yet, when they hit that rock bottom and lose everything around them – that is when they break free.

This is why you will hear so many people proclaim, "I am a grateful recovering alcoholic/addict." It is because they are grateful for their addiction because it is what made them the person that they have become.

Transcend means to rise above, go beyond, overpass, or exceed. The most hardcore addicts can many times transcend into the most spiritual beings we encounter once they put the same effort into their recovery that they put into their addiction. They have been through hell and back and have an entirely different view of the world. They make the world a brighter place for all those that they touch all because of their addictive ways in the past and their ability to break through the illusion on their path to enlightenment.

Every enlightened person has went through this period of disillusionment. Any enlightened person you meet has some story of going some turmoil whether losing a child, imprisoned, drug addict, losing everything, or through trauma and abuse. This is because the illusion has been so engrained in our minds that it is so difficult to break – but it can be broken by anyone at any time.

HMO Hitmen

My story of disillusionment carried into the very field that I work – health care, addiction, and mental health.

One would certainly expect in a field called "health care" that the field cares for the general health of the population. But, that too is corrupt. I met a former drug and addiction counselor that told me the story of his client "Susie" which led him out of the field in which he entered to help addicts recover, not bury them underground.

Susie was a 24-year-old girl who died from a heroin overdose after being denied residential treatment following a relapse. The average salary of a CEO of a health insurance company makes $13,000,000 per year with their average employee making $35,000. They are trained to "Just Say No" to claims, which enriches the man on top.

With all that money, imagine all the services and care people could receive, instead of increasing the wealth of one person? We could create an entire industry and call it "health care."

Corporations are making huge profits by getting people addicted to drugs (pharmaceutical industry), by creating diseases to justify drugging them (psychiatry industry), and then denying them the help they need for this addiction we created (health insurance industry).

In sharing Susie's story, it is clear that the sick ones are not those addicted to heroin, but those in offices deciding the fate of those in need.

Susie had completed residential treatment months earlier and had a chance to clear her mind and work on skills to avoid further harm. While working on building support, Susie had a relapse by injecting heroin over the weekend.

Heroin relapse is often fatal because after abstaining from using for a period of time, your tolerance significantly drops and your body can no longer handle the effects. Furthermore, heroin is at an all-time high as far as lethality. Back in the 1970s it was about 10-15 percent purity and now the numbers are closer to 70 percent pure heroin. Dealers have typically mixed alternative products in heroin to maintain greater quantities of their product, but with supplies and competition escalating, dealers need to provide higher quality for repeat business.

Susie survived the relapse but was in need of further treatment.

But her fate is handed off to a "clinical specialist" at the insurance company that lacks education, experience, or licensure. Instead, it is just a young kid in their mid 20's that has been trained to "JUST SAY NO!"

Literally, they are told to deny claims. In the medical industry, a claim is referred to as a "medical loss." Think about it; if you deny care, it saves the company money. If you save the company money, they have more profits.

How did such a corrupt system begin? President Nixon passed the HMO (Health Maintenance Organization) Act of 1973, which eventually gained many federal subsidies and virtually eliminated affordable individual health care plans.

In a meeting at the White House between President Nixon and John Erlichman (speaking for Edgar Kaiser) in promoting HMOs, Ehrlichman quotes Kaiser stating,

> "*All the incentives are toward less medical care, because—the less care they give them, the more money they make.*"
> - Mr. Ehrlichman quoting Edgar Kaiser to President Nixon on February 17, 1971

Why Is Disillusionment Needed?

The illusions are everywhere – politics, religion, education, economics, racial tension, how we treat each other, etc. They are so engrained into our minds that it is hard to comprehend this at first. In fact, some people are so deep under the spell that they will get angry and defend this illusion if you try to point it out to them.

This creates cognitive dissonance as everything we have believed to be true is starting to no longer hold any ground in our new belief system. Disillusionment is necessary because it is the key that opens the door to enlightenment.

In politics, we have a political system in which we get to vote between two different parties that are supported by the same major corporations. Then, no matter who wins, the corporate interests are served. Capitalism has to do with invading third world countries, putting natives to work in slave labor camps to mine for raw materials. These materials are then shipped (using oil from the Middle Eastern countries we have occupied for decades) to other developing nations to use these materials to produce goods in sweatshops. These sweatshops have such poor working conditions that they have placed "suicide nets" outside the windows to prevent employees from killing themselves while at work. Then the materials are shipped to the United States and sold for a profit to make us feel good about ourselves and someone at the very top gets a nicer paycheck.

Consumerism and materialism is the opposite of enlightenment. It is searching for pleasures and happiness from something outside of ourselves. The media – also owned by just six corporations – then implants these messages into our minds that we need to buy more stuff.

> "When you're watching television, you're watching the news, and you're being pumped full of fear. There's floods. There's AIDS. There's murder. Cut to commercial. Buy the Acura. Buy Colgate. If you have bad breath, they're not going to talk to you. If you have pimples that girl isn't going to fuck you. It's just a campaign of fear and consumption. That's what I think it's based on. This whole idea of 'keep everyone afraid and they'll consume.' – Marilyn Manson

Religion divides us up and we have a world at war constantly since the beginning of time fighting over who created the world and killing each other over the dispute as to what happens when we die.

However, all religions at their core teach the same concepts of unconditional love, acceptance, and oneness. Yet, man gets involved and it turns into greed and power and has corrupted the entire system.

Now this is not meant to be a gloomy chapter on the evils of the world. And it is easy to get taken down that path once you start to see the illusions that surround us. In fact, it can be quite depressing to realize that everything we have been told is a lie.

However, this is a necessary part of the awakening process. It is like going through a very bad nightmare or dream and then you wake up and can relax knowing that it was all just a dream. Disillusionment is necessary because it is part of breaking away of everything we have ever known to be true. It can make us depressed, anxious, sad, angry, or fearful. But the purpose is to get beyond those initial emotions and see the world for how it truly is – beyond the illusion.

We get a chance to return to see the world through the eyes of a child. Each day, we can wake up when the sun comes up and look at the world in all the awe and wonder. The pure ecstasy of each and every moment returns to us as it once did before our masks were created.

Just like having a lucid dream – one in which we know we are dreaming and we can control the outcome – disillusionment does the same thing. We see through the façade and we can appreciate the beauty in all living things. We lose all the fear and anxieties that have been engrained into our minds and we live freely just as we were meant to be.

Anyone of use can do this at any time. We all hold the key to our own freedom.

> *"Perhaps the biggest tragedy in our lives is that freedom is possible, yet we can pass our years trapped in the same old patterns." – Tara Bach*

When my brother quit drinking he was extremely depressed and was struggling with this concept. He would always tell me that he just wanted to be his true self.

"You have the power to do so," I would always laugh, "Just start right now."

The struggle always came with him looking for the right time, place, job, or situation. He always had a plan to start living once he reached some sort of destination in life. That is the idea that the Western World has taught all of us. Keep striving for something more and happiness will follow.

But the logic of that process is inverted. The truth is that once we find fulfillment, then all these dreams that we ever imagined start to fall into place quite rapidly.

And quite simply, we can find fulfillment at any moment against any circumstance. All we have to do is return to the present moment, recognize the illusions of life, and remove our mask. The rest will follow.

While disillusionment is necessary to take the next step; therefore, then the illusion is also necessary for enlightenment. Without the illusion, there is no enlightenment. And that is the fun part of the game is recognizing it is a game.

Section V
THE BOOK OF LOVE

Chapter XXII:	A Perfect Third Step	451
Chapter XXIII:	Ego Traps	465
Chapter XXIV:	Shadow Work	487
Chapter XXV:	The Revolution Has Begun	505
Chapter XXVI:	Taking the Mask Off	521

CHAPTER XXII

A Perfect Third Step
Resist Nothing

Chapter 22
A Perfect Third Step: Resist Nothing

While Karl is an example of a man with a unique spiritual emergency, I truly believe that everyone dealing with addiction is also going through some type of spiritual emergency. The craving behind the drug, alcohol, or compulsive behavior, is a craving for wholeness and connection. Addiction is a horrendous disease that will take everything from you, rip you apart, tear you inside out, and leave you morally, spiritually, and financially bankrupt.

This state of nothingness, this state of being completely broken is often referred to as "rock bottom." The beauty of the people involved in recovery, they have such incredible ways of spinning things into a positive light. One of the saying you will hear in community support meetings is, "my rock bottom was the foundation in which I built my recovery."

In terms of enlightenment, rock bottom is also in which the person's ego has been torn apart and broken to the point that it dies a miserable death. But it is a death of the ego, nonetheless. I am not glamorizing the process of addiction, as it destroys many people who never have the guidance that I was granted and tools I discovered to allow myself to die before I die – which is the secret of living.

The 12-step program is a spiritual based program that can benefit any person. It is a systematic process that deliberately breaks away the ego and helps people build their spiritual muscles. By spiritual muscles I am referring to things such as hope, faith, patience, humor, and connection - The good things in life that make life worth living.

Patience is a tough one. Everyone in western society struggles with patience, especially in our fast-paced, instant gratification culture. It becomes incredibly frustrating in our culture when we have a question about something and we cannot get the answer right away. We feel that we are entitled to a full explanation, with every single detail, of every event that takes place – no matter how big or small, relevant or not, it is our right to know when we want to know.

After my relationship with Karl had grown, I felt once again that I was ready and had the answers. I was back on track and ready to take on the world without my mask. I read through the Big Book of Alcoholics Anonymous in one sitting. I sped through the steps of AA so fast because I was ready to be healed.

But in "working the steps" there are no shortcuts. You cannot take the elevator to recovery. You work the steps, one day at a time, and it is a process. Life is a journey, not a destination. You are never recovered, you are in recovery.

The 12-steps are typically broken down into phases. In most settings (treatment centers, sponsors, support groups, etc.) it is quite common that the first three steps are put in the same category as the beginners steps.

They go as follows:

1) We have admitted that we are powerless over our addiction and that our lives have become unmanageable.
2) We came to believe a power greater than ourselves could restore us to sanity
3) We made a decision to turn our will and our lives over to the care of God as we understood God.

Additionally, each of the twelve steps has a spiritual principle attached. Step One is about honesty; Step Two is hope; and Step Three is faith. The first step is all about defining the problem, and the next 11 steps have to do with the solution. If we cannot be honest, we have no chance to change – and this works for all walks of life. It starts with honesty, it starts with exposing our lies to the light.

Step One – Honesty:

The paradox about step one, is that we practice it every day and in every moment. Step One seems so far away, and people who have had relapses convince themselves "I've already done step one, I get it now." However, relapse is also a process. We start losing our principles, our "stinkin' thinkin'" returns and soon we are able to convince ourselves that drinking, using, or old behaviors become rational or even ideal.

In the definition that I listed above is taken from Narcotic Anonymous, rather than Alcoholics Anonymous. The only difference is one word – addiction. They substituted the word addiction for alcohol because the person is not powerless over alcohol, they are powerless over what the substance does to them – hence, their addiction.

Once the lies are exposed to the light, they die, and the truth shines. You can get high on honesty, as I did. It felt so great, that I couldn't wait to jump into the next steps. Step four has to do with taking a fearless inventory of ourselves, and step five is revealing this list to one other person. On the surface, telling a complete stranger the deepest aspects of our life sounds like it is another step of honesty but it is actually about integrity. Step four is about the courage to dive into the shadows of our soul, all those aspects that keep arising at the most inopportune times. All the aspects of ourselves we have repressed, left in the dark, are coming to the surface. That takes courage. Step five is about owning up to our wrongdoings.

I prepared and did my Step Five with the pastor at the Recovery Church and it was simply amazing. I felt free, my shadows had been exposed to light. I owned up to my past. After sitting with the pastor for four hours and going over the darkest aspects of my soul, he finally spoke with a short response.

"It is all bullshit Cortland," he said to me, "you never had any control. It is all an illusion."

My secrets were dead. My ego was dead. The only thing that could live on was my soul.

Step Two – Hope:

A lot of people lose interest in the power of the twelve steps once they get to Step Two as it asks us to believe in a power greater than ourselves. This is when people confuse religion for spirituality for the first time. Once hitting rock bottom, remember we are spiritually bankrupt and now you are asking us to believe in a God? It seems insurmountable at this time.

But you can see why these are referred to as the "beginner's steps." We need to be honest with ourselves, then we need to have some element of hope that this will actually work. Then step three is about believing in the process.

The scariest person to work with is the person who has lost all hope. Viktor Frankl also speaks greatly of the aspect of hope in his experience in the Auschwitz Concentration Camp in World War II. Hope kept more people alive than anything external. The hope they would see freedom, see their loved ones again, and return to their old life.

Throughout this book, I have continuously went through phases of feeling hopeless before some sort of divine intervention had prompted me up with the smallest notion of hope that maybe things can improve. That is the power of hope, it can be the smallest amount and against all odds – but it can move mountains.

I want to clarify that there is a clear distinction between hopes and wishes. They are often used interchangeable, which can be detrimental. A wish is a desire for something that is currently not true. I wish I was taller, I wish I had a nicer house, I wish I was married, etc. Whereas hope has to do with a future event that has a possibility of coming true, such as I hope this is my last relapse, or I hope I pass this exam.

Simply put, wishes are for genies and hopes are for dreamers. Wishes are when we are in dire need and looking for an unrealistic outcome, but hopes include some form of confidence that the desired outcome has a possibility of being true.

Ever since being admitted to Divine Redeemer, and maybe beforehand when working with the neighborhood kids as a young adult, I had always wanted to work with kids. At first it was a wish, then it became a hope, and the path was surely unfolding before me to the point it was a certain reality.

Hope is the greatest of motivators because you can feel the outcome in your mind and emotions. I had an offer to work at the Prison for kids. It was my "dream job."

Everything makes sense, everything that I had to go through, all the paths I've been down have led me to this position. All my struggles, were only obstacles to show that I was ready to go down this path so I could work with kids. I felt on top of the world, realizing my dreams were coming true. It was my destiny and I was so thankful for everything that I had been through to make this a reality.

This leads directly into the third spiritual principle – faith.

Step Three – Faith:

Although the spiritual principle of the fourth step is courage, there is no doubt that step three takes a great deal of courage as well. Step three has to do with turning our will over to the care of our higher power.

As men, we are raised to do things ourselves, not ask for help, and take a great deal of pride in how we work through things on our own. This is what makes a man, a man. Now, as the pastor told me, "you never had control." That is a tough pill to swallow.

My father once told me,

> *"If you can go through an entire day without worrying, then you had a good third step for the day."*

It is quite a bold task. To not worry about anything throughout an entire day seems impossible. That is exactly what faith is about, completely turning our will over to our higher power.

I get a call from the kid's prison and find out that they have to rescind their offer as I had withheld information on the application.

What!? I couldn't believe it. This was destiny!

Then, I was reminded of the third step. It is not up to me, I never had any control, go through the day without worrying, understand that I have turned my will over and things will work out as planned. This is a concept much easier said than done. It is easy to preach this when things are going well, but when things don't' go as YOU planned, it becomes quite daunting. However, it is incredibly empowering to be able to live through a third step moment – the greater the challenge, the greater you are building the spiritual muscles of faith and patience.

I let it go. It wasn't meant to be, there was another plan in place. I had another interview at a drug rehab facility. Not expecting anything of it since it is an entirely different field and they were receiving all sorts of funding, I figured they would have much more qualified applicants, and my heart was still clinging to the prison.

Eventually I get the call and they offered me the job at the drug rehab facility. I was hired as a supervisor and would be making more than $90,000 per year as their first full-time RN.

This was quite the turn of events! I wasn't even surprised as I had detached myself from the prison job, allowed for God's plan to take over, and not concerned myself with the outcomes. We have no control over outcomes and the more we attach ourselves to outcomes, the more it will drive us up the wall.

Now, I can quit the psychiatric rehab facility and have my fresh start. I am involved in the Recovery Church, have my home group for AA, reading books on spirituality, and doing my daily meditations. Everything is turning in a positive direction. There was never a magical moment here, it was all part of the process. I took three steps ahead, one back, two ahead, one back, and so on. As long as we keep going forward, the process continues.

The next obstacle, I received a letter from the board of nursing notifying me that I am being investigated. I respond back and let them know that narcotics have never been missing from work and that I had told the ER doctor anything to put me away. I had given up on life and was attention-seeking at the time. There was a big conference about this case and after I started my job at the Drug Rehab Center, I received another letter stating that they do not believe my argument and that my license is suspended; but they will stay the suspension if I go to a program for three years for health professionals. However, it will go public that I had stolen medications.

Here is where it gets complicated. I am willing to turn my will and life over to the care of God as I understand, but does that mean just lying down and letting things happen? As in doing nothing? Everyone tells me to sign the papers, but it is not true. Is this turning over to the will of God or is this just being passive?

Faith may move mountains, but that doesn't mean you can't bring a bulldozer with you.

They told me "do not drag everyone through this." I think more and more about the situation and maybe I shouldn't drag everyone along for this ride. I need to just deal with the consequences. People lose jobs, houses, all the time. We will have to figure something out, but this is part of life. We will come back from it.

Just as I surrendered and turned my will over, my sister Sharon unexpectedly showed up with the proverbial bulldozer. She sends me a text out of nowhere that says, "You should contact Raymond Star, he specializes in this stuff. He was in the paper the other day, he fights medical boards."

It reminds me of an old parable about a man who was in a boat out at sea and fell overboard. He was stranded by himself with no one within miles and surely would never make it back to shore. After a few hours, a boat spots him and approaches the man.

"Wow, I am glad I found you!" says the boater, "you would have surely died out here on your own. Get on in!"

"No," says the man, "I am fine. I am waiting for God to save me."

The boater is unable to convince the man and finally goes on his way. A few hours later, the man in the water is barely staying afloat when a second boater comes along and spots the man.

"Hey man, today is your lucky day! Glad I found you, let's go back to shore," says the second boater.

"No thanks," says the man who has all but had his life sucked out of him, "I am waiting for God to save me."

Again, after being unable to get the man onboard, the second boater also takes off and heads for shore.

A few more hours pass and the man is on his final breaths trying to make his way back to land. Out in the distance a third boat spots the man and quickly makes their way over to rescue him.

They throw out a tube and yell for the man to get on board.

Again the man says, "I appreciate the help, but I am waiting for God to save me."

Eventually the third boat also goes away in frustration of the man's unwillingness to get onboard for safety and his irrational thinking.

It doesn't take much longer and the man drowns to his death. Upon reaching the gates of heaven, he is introduced to his creator.

"God, I don't get it," the man says to God, "you always said you would save me if I kept faith. How could you let me drown?"

God shakes his head and responds, "I sent you three boats out in the middle of nowhere, what else do you want me to do?"

My sister Sharon's text was my lifeboat. I only needed one.

This big-time attorney wanted a $12,000 flat fee before we even got started. Another synchronicity, I just happened to have exactly $12,000 in my account at the time. Talk about breaking down the ego and emptying everything, I went all-in once again. I emptied everything I owned into this man, into this lifeboat that was going to rescue me.

He hired a private investigator to get information from my work and those who know me. They get reports that no narcotics have ever been missing, all my reviews have been phenomenal, and he gets no information from any collateral contacts.

Riley writes him a letter letting him know that drugs had never been missing and that I had been a standout employee. The board had no case anymore and they dropped all charges. Once again, I took a gamble, and slid all my chips across the table calling "All In" and this time watched the nursing board fold before my eyes.

They give me a non-disciplinary referral to the health professional program. I felt I survived once again. I should be dead or in jail, why do I keep surviving?

This is part of trusting the process. God is sending us lifeboats all the time, but it is up to us to get on board. Then, of course, my addictive patterns are still in place. My soul is still having an internal struggle with my ego which is everlasting.

This small victory, and my ego has my mind tricked once again. My ego tells me that I am the one who did this, that I am the one who created this. I am the all-powerful one with all the answers. The issue is no longer the drinking. The issue has to do with letting go of the pain, releasing the past, finding new ways to cope, and to grow.

Step three is the heart-and-soul of the twelve steps. It goes from having hope, to putting things into action. That is the hard part. But the magic starts to happen as soon as we can put together this perfect third step. When we can learn to accept the things we cannot change, and find the courage to change the things that we can.

Change only happens once we are willing to do things differently. This concept is also difficult, because in order to do things differently it means to admit that your old way did not work. It means to admit that you were wrong in the past.

But the most difficult part about step three is that we do it every day, multiple times each day. Every time we are faced with a difficult situation, we can either change it, change the way we think about it, or let it eat us alive.

In the parable of the mule and the well, there is a farmer that has an old, useless mule on his farm just putzing around and stumbles one day and falls into a well. It turns out that this well is also run-down and has not been in use for years. As the farmer peers down the well, he looks at the hopeless mule suffering and in misery.

The farmer calls over his neighbors and they all try to come up with a solution to the unfortunate situation. They decide that the mule and well both have no use anymore, and they may as well put the mule out of his misery. They decide they are going to bury the mule alive and at the same time all the dirt will fill up the well which has been out of service for years.

As they pour down the first piles of sand, the mule gets scared and anxious. He starts to panic as he understands what is going on. They throw dirt on the mule and it lands on his back, he quickly shakes it off out of anger and then stomps on the dirt. Again, more dirt dumped on his back and he shakes it off, stomps on it and steps up.

This pattern continues. Shakes it off, stomps it down, steps up. Shake it off, stomp it down, step up. AS this pattern continues, eventually the dirt fills the entire well to the point the mule is able to walk out of the well.

You see, the very things that seem to be the obstacles that are going to bury us alive may actually be the obstacles that we need to save us. It is a matter of recognizing these obstacles as stepping stones, funneling our anger into a positive direction, realizing that everything has its purpose, and of course putting it into action.

CHAPTER XXIII

Ego Traps
Relapse of the Soul

Chapter 23
Ego Traps: The Relapse of the Soul

Ever since I was young, I have had this strange ability to sense the feelings and emotions of others. They tell me this is "empathy" and that it is a natural gift to feel others emotions, which makes others felt heard and understood, and allowing them to take off their mask and build close relationships.

While it is true, this is very beneficial in this industry, it goes even deeper. This is another healing superpower, that needs to be learned how use and kept under control. If not, it can be incredibly overwhelming leading to anxiety, depression, fatigue, and loneliness.

Imagine being in a crowded shopping mall or at a sporting event and able to feel the energy and emotions of everyone, yes everyone. It is incredibly overwhelming and not sure what is going on internally, which feels like social anxiety. But it is not a fear of public places, it is just an overwhelming feeling that takes over and tough to manage.

With this gift, it is natural to want to work in industries of healing. However, without proper guidance it is quite easy to confuse the emotions of others as your own. Such as, take on the other person's pain and think it is your own pain. Also working in places of low energy, such as the previous places of employment I have described can throw off your balance and soon you find yourself adjusting to the energy that surrounds you.

This may sound familiar. Everyone has this to some extent. There is a wide spectrum in which the most severe end are the psychics and fortune tellers that can read your energy and connect to the metaphysical world without effort, and the other end of the spectrum would be someone with Alexithymia – or the inability to read one's emotions. People with alexithymia include autism and asperser's. Asperser's is more of a direct opposite, as the person is very intelligent, ritual, and using strictly logic. Whereas the other end of the spectrum is known as "empaths" which use intuition, are highly creative, and actually feel what others feel.

Some other difficulties with being on the empathy spectrum include feeling responsible for how others feel, difficulty knowing what you want for yourself, you know a lot about other people without knowing them, some people get very uncomfortable around you, and you have difficulty setting boundaries. Setting boundaries is difficult because of the immense emotions you feel of others. No matter what you do, it is a lose-lose situation. Either you end up doing what others want and you don't feel good about it, or you stand up for yourself and then feel their emotions of anger, grief, and resentment.

While in the last chapter, I talked about a "Perfect Third Step" which involves letting go and having faith. As difficult as this is for me, with the added difficulty due to the symptoms listed above, it made me incredibly stronger and able to carry out greater healing practices in other areas of my life.

This is also set me up for a major setback known as an Ego Trap. There are a number of spiritual ego traps which arise out of our ego trying to find its way in the back door during our spiritual battle. The most common types are as follows:

1. The Trojan Horse
2. Knowing the Path versus Walking the Path
3. Wearing a Positivity Mask
4. Feeling Spiritually Superior

The Trojan Horse

During the Trojan War, the Greeks constructed a large wooden horse and left it outside the gates of Troy. The Greeks then sailed their battle ships away. The Trojans viewed this as a gift and opened up the gates and brought the horse inside as a victory trophy. The Greeks had secretly hid a select few men inside the horse and once inside the gates, they unlocked the gates and the Greek ships returned allowing the Greeks to siege Troy.

This also works in spiritual warfare and is one of the most common ego traps.

The Trojan Horse ego trap involves the ego disguising itself as the true self and becoming more spiritually advanced. After we completely surrender and start to see positive changes happening in our lives, we start to celebrate as if we are victorious and we made these changes by ourselves. The ego starts building strength, but it is disguised as the spirit.

It would be like someone practicing humility and then developing a sense of pride about how humble they have become. Or someone who provides service to others and receives praise to the point that they start to put themselves on a pedestal thinking that they are above others. This is referred to as the Trojan Horse because it is all the ego disguised as the true self.

Here I was at the Drug Rehab Center, my new beginning. It was as though I was the mule from the parable told in the last chapter and worked my way out of the well. I had a fresh start, felt great, and ready to take on the world with a new perspective and another opportunity.

I was sober and surrounded by addicts and nothing felt more like home to me. It was uplifting to be in the building and feel the emotions of others and know that each one of these people were like me, they were all healers that were trying to find their way. Each one of them just needed their own PVD to set them free.

They told stories about the medications they needed to take, past addictive behaviors, legal troubles, obstacles, and how they were making strides. They were all crazy, but they were all doing well. I felt as though I was in heaven, being a part of these little daily miracles.

The substance dependence field is so incredibly amazing as you get to witness these incredible changes in such a short period of time. Whereas, with mental health there are such deep imbedded troubles in the person's life that it may take years to start seeing positive changes; but with substance dependence, you remove the drug, provide encouragement and support, teach the person life skills, and you can see change in months, weeks, or even days.

My brother had a job as a CD Technician at a treatment center working on weekends while he was in school. He would tell me he saw "daily miracles" each time he went to work. He would see clients on their day they are admitted into detox, then their first few hours getting associated with the group. He then did not see them for a week, came back the next weekend and they are feeling good and buying into the program. The following weekend he would come in and they are starting to be the leaders of the group and you witness them passing on the same positive energy that was given to them on their first day. Then on the fourth weekend, they were ready to graduate and move on, in just one month a person goes from being a hopeless dope addict to a dopeless hope addict.

At my new job it was the same, but I got to see the tiny miracles each day. I was the first RN at this facility, so I was given the opportunity to create the job. I had the freedom to do groups, lectures, and select the topics. The atmosphere was pretty chaotic, and I absolutely loved every second of it.

I have always seemed to thrive on chaos; sometimes I create chaos to get the feeling of "home." When we are born, we do not know what love is or what it is supposed to be. All we know is what our home situation is, and that becomes our definition of love. We do not have the cognitive ability to determine if our situation is normal, abusive, or chaotic. This is why our future relationships and feelings of love always go back to our childhood home; this is where the definition of love was imbedded in our heads.

If you were to write a list of what your home was like as a child, specifically the emotions and feelings you felt daily, you would surely discover that you could alternate the word "home" for "love." Most, if not all, relationships would have similar traits that you listed as "home." My childhood was chaos, and I have been attracted to it ever since. I am not alone, my siblings Larry and Koryn also tend to attract chaos in their lives. Whereas, Reggie tends to isolate, but they were the oldest and youngest, respectively. Reggie spent most of the chaotic times isolating– which is how he handles it today. None of this is right or wrong, it is just the way it was and it created who we are today.

Despite some of the tragedies, disappointments, and daily annoyances, I am still in love with this job. Riley had created a monster be encouraging me to do some advocating for the patients and I was growing stronger. I was always giving advice and speaking out for patients. The more I did so, the more confident I became and wanted to do more and more. I was also on medication that was helping me, along with winning this court case against the board was making me feel invincible once again (Trojan Horse).

The ego gets you to believe that it is all you, it creates the illusion of separation and that you can do everything on your own. I start placing myself in the center of everything, try to show off my knowledge, and make everything about myself- everything that I have been against. I keep falling back into these patterns and as I put it on paper it is like watching a movie of my life and seeing the main character do the same things over and over. It gets frustrating to watch. But if it is frustrating to watch, imagine what it is like to be living as that character. Which plays into the second ego trap – Knowing the Path versus Walking the Path.

Knowing the Path versus Walking the Path

Again, knowledge minus action always equals zero. You can read this, write it, say it, teach it, but until there is action there will never be results. There are countless books on this material, even more articles online, or videos which explain the process of enlightenment but all this insight means nothing if it is not put into action.

Furthermore, you can read about enlightenment all day and sit in meditation for hours but eventually it needs to be put to practice. This is the difficult part. Because to be awake in a world that is sleeping constantly drags you back to the ego-driven mind.

Earlier in this book, I gave the example of the Wizard of Oz being symbolic of the path to enlightenment. It continues with ego traps. As Dorothy first lands in Oz she is greeted by the munchkins who are fun-loving characters who are symbolic of our inner child. They had been suppressed for many years by the Wicked Witch of the East (addiction, suppressed emotions, mental illness, etc.). They rejoice by singing the notorious song "Ding Dong the Witch is Dead." This represents the pink cloud phase of recovery in which we are celebrating the reunification with our inner child, true self, and seeing the world through a magical lens for the first time.

It doesn't take long until the Wicked Witch of the West (our Shadow) makes an appearance to let us know she is going to be following us along the way and will not make this journey easy. Dorothy is told a simple path to follow the Yellow Brick Road to reach enlightenment – the Wizard of Oz.

However, the truth is that the Wizard was not enlightenment but it was the journey in which she becomes enlightened. Because we are not humans seeking a spiritual experience; We are spiritual beings trying to learn from a human experience. There is no destination, it is about the journey.

The gang first sees the Emerald City and gets distracted by the Wicked Witch of the West's classic trap of deterring them off their path. She plants poppy flowers off the path which are beautiful and soothing to the eye but have intoxicating effects that can end the crew's journey. They know to stay on the Yellow Brick Road, but get excited by getting to the end and run through the poppy fields before Dorothy passes out. She needs to rely on the wisdom from the Scarecrow, the compassion from the Tin Man, and the courage from the Lion – the three aspects the characters felt they were lacking – in order to get back on the path.

For me, I had gained immense insight from counseling, treatment, daily readings, and all the soul contracts and life lessons from everyone I have already mentioned in this book. I certainly had my moments of walking the path but also got distracted by my own proverbial poppies along the way.

One of the greatest tools to stay on the path is to return to the present moment. To realize that everything is always perfect in the present moment and everything is always as it was meant to be. However, when we are amidst turmoil and chaos it becomes easy to get off this path.

It is like if you could not read and you looked at this page, you would just see a bunch of random symbols that did not make any sense. As you looked closer, you could recognize that there does appear to be some pattern to it but still have no idea what any of it means. Just like those who are still sleeping, look at life events as random events – but once you are awake you start to see these patterns are happening just as they were planned.

Being present, or practicing mindfulness is a difficult skill that takes years to master. One of the greatest baseball players in the history of the world, Alex Rodriguez, states that one of his goals is to be able to play an entire game in the moment. One of the greatest of all-time, and this is his goal!

In the present moment, everything is always perfect. If you ever are feeling sad, anxious, worrying, or complaining, you are not present. In the present moment you have no name, labels, past or future. You are able to just accept everything as it is, in perfect harmony. As you work on this daily, it becomes easier. You can do so by walking, focusing on one step at a time and you see it becomes easier and easier to let go.

It was not all rainbows and butterflies though, there were definitely some difficult times especially when attaching so greatly to others emotions. There were many sad stories as well as those of people improving. You never know the impact you have on others and you never know what will come once they walk out the doors. This refers back to not attaching to outcomes because we have no control. You will see some people doing so well, then later hear that they relapse immediately. Others appear to not be listening, but they get better and embrace recovery.

People return, but they cannot be judged. That is incredibly difficult for the person to return and likely already feel judged. I went back to treatment three times and if they would have rolled their eyes at me, or looked down on me, I would have never finished the program. People are always learning and if they are coming back, that means they are still progressing. We plant seeds, let go of results, and have faith that the plants will grow. It is all a process.

There was one woman I remember specifically. She was 32-years old and wanted greatly to get her kid back in her custody. She was a wonderful lady, very sweet, dedicated, and made vast improvements. She was doing wonderful but later relapsed and died. It literally broke my heart, it sucked the life right out of me to hear this news. Even typing it today gives me the emotional recall of the pain that was felt.

There was another woman come in who was on all sorts of controlled substances and prescription medications. They took her off everything and she suddenly got better. She looked like a new woman, finally reconnected with family, and was experiencing a new full life. At first, I did not want to admit her because I feared she would be "too much work." She truly amazed me. I remember sitting on the street with her as she waited for her taxi the day she was discharged. We had a long, deep talk that was uplifting and inspirational. Then, about one year later, she also relapsed and died. Stories like these completely drained me emotionally. This is the part where professors teach students "don't take your work home with you," but that is just not possible for me. How can you not take this home with you? You form an emotional bond with someone, then send them out the door only to hear that they are dead a few months later? If you do not take it home with you, then are you ever really bringing it with you to work?

There were others that seemed disinterested, did not care, would not listen, and had no desire to be there. This is not hopeless, because they cannot unlearn what is taught to them. At the very least, my goal is to make it so they never enjoy getting drunk or high ever again. Every time they use, they will think about the things they learned in treatment and it will no longer be fun because they know the long-term result.

People complain and say it costs money to provide treatment for those disinterested, or court-ordered. But if you look at statistics with people first diagnosed with diabetes and asthma, they end up in Emergency Rooms far more often with addicts that are non-compliant.

Wearing a Positivity Mask

Once we do have glimpse of spiritual enlightenment, we start to feel that we are failing if we do not always have that connection. We start to create a new mask, courtesy of the ego, which puts on an overly positive look on all things. We are trying to force positivity even when things are not going well.

However, this is beyond just an ego trap – this is American society. Read through your Facebook feed at any given moment and people put on a show as to how positive and wonderful their lives are to showcase to the world. While this is quite obvious over social media, it becomes a deadly ego trap when we try to apply this to our daily lives.

What happens is when we are hurt, sad, or anxious, we then suppress those feelings by putting on the positivity mask. But those feelings don't just disappear, they stay with us and build up stronger as our shadow.

There are rough spots and bad days, and there does not need to be a miraculous moment that changes everything – in fact, that is unrealistic. Life is always changing and moving, and it is the ability to stop trying to control the storm, instead accept the storm without judgment, it is not good nor bad.

As Vivian Green once said,

> *"Life is not about waiting for the storm to pass, but how to dance in the rain."*

It is like the tale of the Taoist Farmer which goes as follows:

Once upon a time, there was a farmer in the central region of China. He didn't have a lot of money and, instead of a tractor, he used an old horse to plow his field.

One afternoon, while working in the field, the horse dropped dead. Everyone in the village said, "Oh, what a horrible thing to happen." The farmer said simply, "We'll see." He was so at peace and so calm, that everyone in the village got together and, admiring his attitude, gave him a new horse as a gift.

Everyone's reaction now was, "What a lucky man." And the farmer said, "We'll see."

A couple days later, the new horse jumped a fence and ran away. Everyone in the village shook their heads and said, "What a poor fellow!"

The farmer smiled and said, "We'll see."

Eventually, the horse found his way home, and everyone again said, "What a fortunate man."

The farmer said, "We'll see."

Later in the year, the farmer's young boy went out riding on the horse and fell and broke his leg. Everyone in the village said, "What a shame for the poor boy."

The farmer said, "We'll see."

Two days later, the army came into the village to draft new recruits. When they saw that the farmer's son had a broken leg, they decided not to recruit him.

Everyone said, "What a fortunate young man."

The farmer smiled again - and said "We'll see."

There is no use in overreacting to the events and circumstances of our everyday lives. Many times what looks like a setback, may actually be a gift in disguise. And when our hearts are in the right place, all events and circumstances are gifts that we can learn valuable lessons from.

> *"Everything we call a trial, a sorrow, or a duty, believe me... the gift is there and the wonder of an overshadowing presence." – Fra Giovanni*

We never know what each moment shall bring, all we know is that it is an opportunity to learn and grow. Every moment, encounter, and situation is an opportunity to change ourselves and all of those around us. But having the mindset of all of this is one thing, living it is another. This takes practice.

On my second day at the drug rehab center, I was called into the office to meet the clinical director, Diedre. She spends the entire day telling me horror stories of this awful place that I walked into. However, I loved it, but was nowhere near being strong enough to speak up for myself – which refers back to the lose-lose situation I described. I continue to live for other people's approval.

This spiritual gift that I explained, it is like a human antenna, I feel what everyone feels which allows me to tell them what they want. It was great in the sense I could feel the patient's and connect with them, but it harms me when I get into situations like this and I just give her what she wanted to hear.

Instantly, I knew I was in for serious trouble. This woman is crazy, she seeks power and she is going to get it. Deep down I know I need to keep her in my corner if I want to survive at this place. In order to survive, I needed to create a fake-self, or a mask. This is what I have done my entire life. I have one-thousand masks that I wear. I would decide who I wanted to be, depending on my surroundings, and put on that mask to survive with that particular person.

Needless to say, I joined her side. She really had some good ideas, though they were always changing and it also relied on who she was around. She was sort of like me in that regard, very passionate, just highly misguided, and shooting around her own super powers without any direction or control.

She started removing people like flies. Chuck had been there 25 years and she got rid of him quickly. Mack, a counselor, was another one of her enemies was removed for standing up to here. I did not care for Mack either as he was too old-school and felt the need to belittle and punish the clients. He would yell, dominate, and demand. He was an angry man, but what I noticed is that his style actually worked with some people.

With this, I saw how diversity works. If we are willing to accept each other and different styles, we create a strong team. Though at the same time, it comes down to needing to heal the self before becoming the great healer of others. However, I also realized that there usually is not some magic, climatic moment in which this huge transformation occurs. Besides Bill W. or Buddha, in which they did experience enlightenment in a single sitting, it is more often than not a process. There will be small moments, and you certainly feel them as they happen. Other times, changes are taking place without ever knowing. Similar to how a child grows each day, we do not see the daily changes but they are so small that you do not even realize it until soon they go from an infant to a toddler. You watch a child trying to walk so many times and they keep falling down, but once they finally get it, it doesn't take long and they are running around the house. Such as with awakening, there will be small, gradual steps, but once you get it, it becomes quite simple and apparent.

As great as this new beginning was for me, it was also a trap of the ego. Things started to go well and my ego wanted all the credit for the newfound wisdom, energy, and euphoria I was experiencing daily. It actually fell into all categories of ego traps. I was being sucked in to believing I was the one responsible for all the changes and my ego was growing (Trojan Horse); I knew that this was happening, but continued to fall into the trap (Knowing the Path versus Walking the Path); and I put on a show to the outside world that everything was going well (Positivity Mask).

My marriage, however, was nonexistent. I have blown that completely, destroyed my family, and my connection to church was fading. To mask this pain, again I looked externally. This time it came in the form of bragging of my success. I would share with the world the amount of money that I was making as if that would take away all the hurt and sorrow.

Furthermore, I didn't need family or friends anymore. I was above them and they had too much to learn and too much growing to do. I couldn't hold conversations with them because they were not on my level of knowledge and life experience – leading to the next trap, feeling Spiritually Superior.

Feeling Spiritually Superior

The idea of being spiritually superior is an oxymoron in itself. Spirituality has to do with connection and the moment we start judging our path versus the path of others is when we have lost control to the ego. This ego trap works in the form of feeling good about growing spiritually and then starting to look down on others who are not as spiritual as yourself.

This could come in the form of if you meditate, if you read spiritual books, if you ride a bike instead of driving a car, become vegan, do yoga, spend time in nature, etc. As you are growing it feels good and you know the path and are walking the path. But the trap is when you start to criticize people who still watch TV, read the mainstream news, and spend money on materialistic items. If you are doing these things only to serve your own desires, you are the victim of an ego trap.

As I start learning new things, doing readings, and embracing my newfound spiritual lifestyle I want others to get on board. I am seeing changes in my life and I know the good that it can bring others and it became frustrating that they would not blindly follow me. Soon, I started looking to where they were on their path and trying to figure out what was needed next on their journey. While it comes from a caring and passionate place, it is putting me in a different category than them and is just the ego's way of getting back in the driver's seat.

I was providing powerful lectures which resulted in standing ovations, patients were writing letters asking for me to speak more often. This is exactly how the ego builds. I needed something external and I clung to it and it was building exponentially. It was ironic that I was telling people about how to find their true selves, while I was using it to build up a false self for myself

It was as though I was waving a flag to tell the world that I am insecure. Also, with this new attention I am quickly becoming a target of Deidre. I deserved it though. I was a loud-mouth, arrogant, healer. I am finally doing the healing that I felt I was meant to do, but that fulfillment alone was not enough for me. It was not enough to know that I am making a difference, I needed acceptance still. If I did not get it, I tried to create it by running my mouth and boasting about the wonders that I am creating.

One day one of the counselors shows me a book called "A Peaceful Warrior. "Perhaps he recognized me falling into these traps. It is a very deep spiritual book and I read it in one day. Then he gives me another by the same author, and then another. I start getting very deep into this spiritual stuff instantly and can not get enough. Another counselor then hands me a book by Don Miguel Ruiz called, "The Four Agreements."

This book was a life-changer to me. He describes truths that I have already known to be true, but words it in a way that I can comprehend. I have always been a feeler and I understood these concepts but never was able to put it into words – or even into coherent thoughts. This quickly becomes me new drug and I read all of Don Miguel Ruiz's books in one month. These books are teaching me things on such a different level that I am feeling an incredible connection to the universe.

I try to apply it to life and my marriage, but grew frustrated when it did not work and heal everything instantly. She is in a lot of pain, as am I. We rarely spend any time together and when we do it is not healthy. There is still constant fighting, which leads me to the golf course as an escape.

In the past, golfing was an excuse to drink. Now, it is a healthier escape as I am able to apply my spiritual lessons and learn about myself. I learn how to stay calm and balanced. One bad shot cannot ruin an entire round. There will be bad shots, bad breaks, but it is about how you overcome. You cannot take out your frustration by acting aggressive, or it costs you even further. It is an odd sport in which if you swing softer the ball goes further – because you need smooth, precise, relaxed, fundamentals. It also forces you to stay in the moment, one shot at a time, one shot can change your round – for better or worse. It is very spiritual to me to be out in nature and apply my spiritual lessons.

But it also isolates me from my family. The only time me and Jill are together is when the entire family is around. They benefit from everyone being together, all the children are together, and everyone is happy. Besides us, we are still in pain and I am still struggling with the emptiness. This is what they mean by you can be alone and not be lonely, just as you can be surrounded by people and be incredibly lonely. I was living the latter statement.

This is when I met Karyn, she is a former meth addict, stripper, with borderline personality disorder and in dire need of attention. It was a fatal combination of personalities. People with borderline strive off drama, they create drama because it makes them feel alive. It is like a drug addict. They need it to come out of the boring aspects of everyday life. One of the biggest means of creating this drama is through pushing boundaries. Now, here we have myself that is on one end of the empathy spectrum in which it is incredibly hard to set boundaries because I feel others emotions; on the other hand we have someone who pushes boundaries to create drama to come alive.

Although things started out innocent, it is a deadly combination for the perfect storm. The first few interactions were the calm before the storm. Everything is quiet, but you know exactly what is about to take place, the clouds start to darken and roll in fast and people go for cover to avoid any harm that is about to ensue.

It doesn't take long for the boundaries to vanish. It started as an escape while at work with a little harmless flirting. Soon it becomes daily talking and texting, and Jill is being completely ignored. I found something outside of myself to fill the void once again.

Just like that and the ego lands a knockout punch to the soul. That is how powerful and resilient the ego can be in spiritual warfare. In an instant the ego re-emerges.

I left Jill for Karyn. Jill begged me to stay with her. I had already made up my mind, I already had found my new outlet for my emotional escape. Jill's parents come over, just as they had many times before, but this time I actually left her for good.

After a few months, I see everyone is in pain and I decide to confess everything to Jill. I tell her it has nothing to do with her and it has to do with my emptiness and masking of emotions. I am unsuccessful in my explanations, she takes it personally, has a full-blown panic attack and ends up in the hospital. She is completely devastated once again. It's finally official, we are getting divorced.

Now my family hated Jill from the beginning. They knew she was not right for me, they knew it was all phony, but as soon as we started to have problems – they fell in love with her. It works quite well for the family systems dysfunction. I, the scapegoat, messed things up for someone else. Then Jill, the codependent, gets her validation through the victim role.

No one saw the way she treated me. They just see the end result and that I am the bad guy once again and now poor Jill is ruined. For the first time in our marriage, Jill is accepted because she is the new victim of my evil ways.

At mediation it became real. I couldn't believe we are really going to get divorced. Why? This is crazy! I am scared and confused and already feeling shameful before anything has happened. With Karyn I was having fun, but it wasn't real and I knew it wasn't real.

Back at work, things were also starting to fall apart. Deidre is not happy about me being with Karyn, either. While I enjoy working with people who are a little crazy, it also brings its own set of problems. Deidre tells me that I am OK one minute, then attacks me in front of everyone at the staff meeting an hour later.

I feel offended, but in hindsight I was sleeping during meetings, drifting off, dressing like a slob, and sending nasty emails to everyone. I am crumbling again and start deflecting the blame on her, when it is me who is falling apart inside. I am hitting my self-destruct button for the thousandth time.

Inside I am going crazy. Which is always only a matter of time before your inner world reflects to the outer world. Dysfunction internally will always project externally because the outer world is only a reflection of our true self and no mask, no matter how powerful, can prevent this from happening.

On top of this, I get notification that my drug program for professionals is starting. I will have random drug tests, they will write quarterly reports for two years, and I need to have a drug and alcohol assessment.

I return to treatment for the third time, but I am not worried, this is just a required assessment. I am doing fine, doing my best, there is no reason to recommend treatment. At the assessment, they ask for all my updates and I let them know that I have been sober, been doing great, and not having any problems.

"You never addressed relapse," PVD tells me, "You need to come back."

CHAPTER XXIV

Shadow Work
Addressing the Subconscious

Chapter 24
Shadow Work: Addressing the Subconscious

Relapse is not a one-time event, it is a process. There is emotional and mental build up to the physical event of drinking or using. And recovery is not just the absence of alcohol or drugs, it is about the rewiring of the brain to live a life full of freedom, inner peace, joy, and euphoria without the use of drugs or alcohol. Recovery has to do with removing our masks and becoming our true self – that is the only way it works.

But, in order to do so, we must dive deep into our subconscious mind, to the dark side of our personality – also known as the human shadow.

Carl Jung defines the human shadow as "that hidden, repressed, for the most part inferior and guilt-laden personality whose ultimate ramifications reach back into the realm of our ancestors and so comprise the whole historical aspect of the unconscious."

While it is needless to say I was furious about having to return to treatment – the fact I was furious shows that I had not addressed my shadow. It is common to think of a relapse as moment we drink or use, but that is just the end result. There is a buildup and return of addictive thinking patterns, the shadow starts to shine through, and before we know it drinking starts to make sense.

What is the Human Shadow?

From the time we are children, we are raised in a way that certain aspects are acceptable and others are not. Each time we are told that something is not acceptable, we suppress that part of ourselves. It becomes a part of our shadow. But this does not mean it disappears, it just stays in the darkness. The longer it stays in the dark, the harder it tries to be exposed to the light. It continues to come back around trying to get attention of our conscious mind. Along with the repression, we also create harsh attitudes towards these characteristics.

We start to see our shadow projected in other people, places, and things. We will see something in another we do not like and then it keeps coming up. For example, I may start to notice many people around me are full of greed. Then I will notice myself judging them. However, what I am disliking in others has nothing to do with them but rather an aspect of myself in which I am struggling with.

In primary treatment, we learn a lot about alcoholism, addiction, and the role that these substances play in our life. We develop tools to stay sober, but it is only surface-deep. Continuing Care is an opportunity for personal growth. There was a counselor there who had a men's group and started by having us talk about our feelings and diving deep into our shadow.

One guy would take a risk by sharing some deep aspect of himself and make himself vulnerable. This usually resulted with him putting his head down as it is something in our culture that men are not accustomed to doing. The reaction was always someone else taking a risk by sharing a part of himself. Once you have a group of guys taking risks and being vulnerable, something magical happened. It was like a spiritual connection every single week and real relationships were being formed.

It's like chopping away the layers of the onion. The onion is sweetest once you get to the core, just like humans – the truth is in our core. Removing the outer layers of the onion brings tears. In fact, it can be so painful, people publish articles as to how to get to the core of the onion without the tears including cutting under water, wearing goggles, or freezing the onion first. Similarly, we freeze our emotional feelings with things such as alcohol or drugs for an easier way to get to our core. Freezing vegetables, or feelings, similarly creates changes in texture and we lose the natural flavor.

In aftercare, you have a group of men talking about their core, their truest self, it involves peeling away layers which brings tears to men who haven't cried in years. At first, I was quite upset that I had to do this, but I was forced into it. Sometimes that is a sign that this is where you were meant to be. I met a man named Jack there. He was there voluntarily, he was in your face and I thought he was obnoxious. We did not always get along, but we both were fighting hard to stay sober. He changed me by challenging me all the time. It was another instance of a great lesson and teacher that I was resistant to. I still talk to Jack to this day, and he is the only one from our group. We are both sober. He was the last one that I thought I would still be talking to. As Abraham Lincoln said "I do not like that man, I must get to know him better."

As the weeks went on, I noticed my true self was starting to emerge again. Now, I'm about eighteen months old since my death and rebirth of July 9th. I have had a couple major mistakes, but it is still a learning process with so much new to learn. Like a toddler that touches a hot stove, it's a big mistake, but surely we learn not to do so again.

But as I learn more about "Cortland," I also learn that there is no "Cortland." True self is just another word for being open and letting thoughts go, not holding onto them, and not trying to generate them either. It is about being fully present with no past, future, judgments or labels. The love that fills you is enormous. This is unconditional love – love without condition.

This newfound joy brings about immense energy that I needed to learn how to spend. Once the soul comes alive like this, it is easy to follow its guides as everything becomes quite clear and apparent.

While this was an incredible experience, it wasn't just about forming relationships in that group. This small group was a microcosm of our outer world. It was teaching us how to embrace hidden parts of our shadow, make ourselves vulnerable, and connect with others in our daily lives. Plus, it would be one thing to do shadow work by yourself by working with a counselor or looking into a mirror, but this was far more meaningful as it taught us how to embrace ourselves fully on a weekly basis.

The previous chapter ended with many things appearing to fall apart in my life. But time and time again, it has proved that things need to fall apart so that they can fall into place.

Sometimes when we are forced into a situation, it is our spirit guiding us. We find ourselves wondering "how come I keep ending up in the same situation?" We ask/pray/beg for things to change, but this could be our souls way of telling us the situation will not change until we are prepared to move along and apply the lessons learned. This is one of those soul contract stipulations. I didn't seem to get the message the first time, and things always work out so you end up where you need to be.

Along with treatment, I am to get involved in therapy across the hallway with Dr. Nordway. I've been involved in therapy a million times before, without any significant changes. It does not work quite as magical as how they project in Hollywood.

Or does it?

I walk in and meet Dr. Nordway for the first time. He has the opposite features of PVD, but the same type of presence. He is a small, gentle man who commands your presence more by his innate wisdom. You can tell by the way he carries himself and looks at you that he has some answers ready for you to explore. He is welcoming, accepting, and approachable which allows me to be myself.

In our first sessions, he has my talking about myself and I enjoy it for once. This was a new experience in itself. He has me take the MMPI test to better understand my personality. The results come in:

Psychopathic deviant.

Great! Everyone was right all along. Cortland the psychopathic deviant, now it is official. But, Dr. Nordway did not see it this way.

"You make up your own rules," he said to me as a way of spinning the results, "this is not a bad thing. Plus there is a bell curve with these things and you do not fit in the bell curve."

While the counseling sessions were the same in the sense that I would share my life, feel sad, and move on. But, Dr. Nordway had a way of changing perception. He was able to twist my negative thinking and view everything about my life as a positive.

He taught me about cognitive behavioral therapy which is exactly what I had described above. It is about changing our perspective on situations. Basically, it is putting the serenity prayer into action. With each situation we ask ourselves:

1) Can I change the situation?
    a. If Yes, then grant me the courage to do so
    b. If No, then grant me the serenity to accept it completely as it is

2) Can I change the way I think about it?
    a. If Yes, grant me the courage to do so
    b. If No, let things get worse and disrupt other aspects of life.

"Where is the evidence that you are a bad guy," Dr. Nordway would challenge me, "If it only comes from your family, well are they healthy themselves?"

In using the formula above, the situation is that I feel bad about the things I have done in my life. Question number one asks if I can change the situation, which is no I cannot. In which, the formula suggests to go to number 1b; and grant me the serenity to accept this situation as it is without any judgment. That is quite a difficult task to ask of someone. Which is why we have question number two; can we change the way we think about it? There are only two choices and 2a sounds a whole lot better than 2b.

The reason we use the word courage is because change is hard for everyone. Especially when we are talking about changing a lifetime of distorted thinking patterns. This doesn't happen overnight, this happens by sitting in a counselor's office and working through these things one day at a time. That takes courage. It is not a weakness by any means to ask for help, it is a strength and takes bravery to admit that we have flaws and that we need help in correcting them.

While I was learning all of this, I was having struggles with my family still. I was trying to share all my new wisdom but kept getting rejected. One day when I was feeling really down, Larry sends me an email.

> "You are like Kanye West. You say what is on your mind, you do not hold back, you are highly emotional, and stand up for what you believe. Some people hate Kanye West and

others love him. For example, I happen to love him for his music and his character. I like how he is always himself and not afraid to speak his mind. Yet, others in my own family hate him. How can that be possible? It is the exact same man, doing the exact same acts, yet two people with very similar biological, social, and psychological wiring in their heads can have polar opposite views of the man? It is the same person, it just depends at how you look at him."

I'm Not a Bad Guy

After a storm had passed through my hometown, I took a walk through town to assess the damage. I saw the tree leaves, branches, and sometimes the entire trunks of trees knocked over. It was the tallest trees that were most prone to topple in these storms. They had grown so strong, but had lower center of gravity.

Some of the most impressive damage were the trees that had been completely uprooted. It was quite clear that in order for the trees to survive the storm, their true strength lies in their roots – which is quite true for humans as well.

"Cortland, look at this plant," Dr. Nordway said to me on one of my first days of therapy, "let's say it had a bad leaf. If you cut it off, that is great but another bad leaf will grow in its place. You need to fix the roots."

I feel like I have always known this, but this analogy really struck me deeply. It made me realize that addiction goes much, much deeper than what lies above the surface. In my soul, I have always known that the drinking was not the issues but rather a symptom of a much deeper core issue.

The first dead leaf was anger and I cut that off. Then it grew back as gambling, which I cut off. Adrianne then grew in its place and I became dependent on her. I cut off that leaf and drinking and drugs soon grew in its place and became judging of others. I tried to fix that by purchasing a big house and fancy cars, but the problem still hasn't been fixed. The next leaf was to stay busy with school, which is acceptable, which also makes it so dangerous. Then the drinking leaf grows stronger and I cut it off only to find that the addiction to recovery has grown in its place. Then it was church, cut off. Replaced by Karyn, and now that one is dead too. This pattern is never going to stop until I fix the roots.

The roots are where we come from, what develops in you as a child. It is your perception of the world, the life you created, and everything lies in the roots. The roots also provide the strength that keeps the tree up. Unhealthy roots will lead to an unhealthy tree.

The trunk of the tree is your core, the personality you have created. Everything builds off of the trunk. The main branches then grow to form our core belief system. Off of each of these core beliefs, smaller branches of personality traits develop. From there even smaller branches and eventually the leaves.

Leaves are always changing, fading away, falling off, and dying. These are our possessions, friends, money, and the things in life that will never last. Trees grow up, down, and out. The branches and bark get thicker when the cells beneath the bark are added that come from the nutrients sent up from the roots. Just like humans, as we feed our core beliefs and values, they grow stronger and more difficult to break. But it is the roots that hold up the tree, and it is the roots that provide all the nutrients that give the tree strength.

Just like humans, it is the roots, or the unseen that create what we see above the surface.

This analogy of trees is simple and makes sense, yet it is so hard for us to see that it works the same in humans. We judge people by what we see on the outside without knowing what lies beneath or understanding their past.

People with a damaged past are typically closer to a state of enlightenment as they are constantly seeking for some sort of truth. They have been locked inside a proverbial prison their entire existence and searching for freedom. We know we need to escape, but we do not have the tools or access to do so. The only way to acquire the necessary tools for freedom is to endure painful experiences and difficult times.

This sounds backwards, but it is one of life's paradoxes. In order to know happiness, you need to experience pain. In order to appreciate silence, you must face noise. And in order to be found, one first must be lost.

It is in these moments of pain, hopelessness, and despair that we are granted these tools. Every time I have been in one of these dreadful moments, I have also been given another tool to escape. Pain doesn't just show up in our lives for no reason, it is a sign that something in life needs to be changed and it offers us an opportunity to grow.

On the other end of the spectrum, when the upbringing is well it can create a different kind of prison. For example, if someone never experiences painful trials and tribulations they may become comfortable with their mask. They could potentially grow content with the lies and stories we create. While they may already be holding the master key, they do not realize that they are in prison.

In this sense, I would argue that ignorance is not always bliss. Ignorance can keep you imprisoned while hurting others who could benefit from the master key you possess. It becomes difficult to try to explain to someone that they are sleeping, they have no reason to awake from their dream. This creates further separation, then rules and laws are passed to keep the same people in power and the cycle continues. When, in fact, they are only building their own prison with bigger walls and stronger bricks.

Once people get to the point of getting treatment or any type of help, they are ready to awaken from the dream. There is always a choice. It may be jail, hospital, homeless, commitment, or treatment. But there is a choice involved. Some are not ready and they try to run, leave the state, or prefer jail. However, once you are in the chair listening, part of you is thinking about change. And when we think about change, it means we are thinking about breaking apart everything that we once believed to be true. That, in essence, is the process of awakening.

I have worked with, been in group with, and even been one of many people sitting in treatment that said it was the "greatest thing that ever happened to me." People who were facing severe prison time for dealing drugs, or multiple DUIs were adamant that as bad as the situation was externally, it was the point in their life that they decided to change. It was there alarm clock that told them it was time to wake up from this dream of life.

Like Albert, the man who had it all put together is someone that had his beginning from a tragic ending of another life. He just went with the flow of things. This is total acceptance. He never fought, took sides, or tried to change things beyond his control. He understood that life is not about doing, it is about being.

He did his job, spread love, and guided those who were open to it. This man's ego died a long, long time ago. While I strived to be like him, my ego still was alive and kicking, scratching, and clawing at any opportunity that presented itself.

Me and Deidre were fighting nearly every day. We were like two lunatics battling over who is more crazy. We both lose and so do the patients. Our anger put the entire facility into chaos, which was evidenced by two patients losing their life.

Then I made an ego-based mistake by feeling that I was more powerful that I truly was. It was a simple error, but Deidre seized it by jumping on the opportunity to get me fired. I was next on her list. She got me. She said I was prescribing medication and had me and another staff fired for making the same mistake.

I destroyed everything once again. I get fired and reported to the board of nursing again. When will it end? I give up.

This was another storm that knocked off some trees and branches. The branches were the parts of my personality that I became so attached to that I thought it was my true self. In reality, all attachments hide and cover our true self.

Our true self is like a magnet and each label we get as we go through life is like metal, it creates an attachment. This can include simple things like being a man, a brother, a father, or being a nurse. It continues to be other labels such as addict, jerk, and drunk. Since all these things are attached so greatly it is easy to think that this is who we are. The only way to get back to our true self is to detach everything. But, as you would expect, in detaching the metal from the magnet there is some serious resistance as this is the ego's way of protecting itself. Every time we try to detach, there is resistance. Which is why sometimes we need a massive storm to knock off some tree branches so others can grow.

I left Karyn as she was the most recent dead leaf that had to go. It had been torturing me and in order to bounce back, I needed to trim the dying leaves. For the first time in my life, I had something healthy to turn to. I had a support group of Dr. Nordway, my treatment group, AA, my readings, and even Jill was available. It was the first time I went to family instead of drinking, drugs, or unhealthy behaviors.

My support group gave me connection I needed, there was no inner void which I usually felt when things blew up. This time I am able to stay in balance despite the world around me seemingly falling apart. It was nearly one year to the day of my relapse that landed me in the hospital, now I am homeless and jobless but in a better state of mind.

I finally realize that none of this will last forever. For once, I do not react and try to fix everything, but just accept and embrace. Eventually the termination was reversed and I receive unemployment checks, but it really did not matter at this point. It was nice validation, but not necessary. Instead I was focusing on what I could have done differently rather than blaming the system.

We stopped paying the mortgage at this point. I had stopped caring about the money, house, and meaningless possessions. This may sound like throwing in the towel and giving up on life, but it was actually the opposite. This was about rebuilding after the storm had passed. I trimmed off the dead branches that weren't needed. The tree will regrow and new branches form in its place. The trunk is still strong, as are the roots.

For a tree to grow, it needs new cells to appear under the bark in the trunk and branches to widen and strengthen. For me, this meant feeling the feelings, staying present, not running, embracing my support group, daily readings and meditations.

Cortland Pfeffer; Irwin Ozborne

Creating New Files

The brain is like a computer. We have a subconscious mind and a conscious mind and we create files that are stores in our subconscious mind. Most of mine have been negative, but our brain doesn't know if these are true. Like a computer, it takes everything in as fact.

If we continue to tell ourselves we are a bad person throughout the time we are little, we have many files that are telling us what is true. Then each time something comes up in our conscious mind, we have these files stored in our subconscious to tell us it is true.

For example, if I have been told I am a bad person since my pre-teenager days and then again as I go through school and as an adult, I have a lot of files that have been created. Then as I go through my day, my self-talk is mostly negative as well. Then, something as simple as running late for work is happening in my conscious mind and my files stored in my subconscious immediately come up to remind me that there is "evidence" to support that I am a bad person and that is why I am late.

Shadow work has to do with re-wiring the brain and creating new positive files. We did this through reading books, meditation, cognitive behavioral therapy, affirmations, and mindfulness.

Dr. Nordway recommended a few books to me and it is something that I had never done before. I was never able to focus and my mind was always racing. This led to people considering me to be dumb and lazy. He prescribed some medications for me that he thought would help, without looking at me a drug-seeker. Soon, I was reading a different book every week. Most of them had to do with Buddhism, Tao, and Eastern philosophy.

These books seemed to connect with me at a deeper level. They were pulling out some sort of truth that I had always known but was unable to express. These books helped me break down the illusion and set me free.

Meditation was new to me at this point. It was something that I had always made fun of, likely because I didn't understand and only saw the mocking images on television because the western world mocks anything that it does not believe. It is implicit brainwashing of the media to conform.

The first few times I try, my mind goes crazy thinking about every thought that could ever be thought. With practice, reading books on how to do it, time, and patience, I start to figure it out. Patience is one of those spiritual muscles that needs to be practiced. Great peace comes in the ability to be patient and know that the universe that does not owe you instant gratification and answers. That is the trick that addiction plays on us, it makes us believe that we can reach enlightenment in one night.

Meditation allows me to stay present in the awakened, free, unblocked state of existence. It is the truth. This takes training of the mind to release everything, and only then are we free.

Cognitive Behavioral Therapy is a way to change our thought process. At its core it has to do with changing the way we think about situations. Throughout life, we always believe that our situation is the problem. But that is never the case, it is only how we think about the situation. Cognitive Behavioral Techniques is a process which teaches us how to change perspective.

Our thoughts create words, words create action, action creates habit, habit creates character, and character creates destiny. But everything begins with our thoughts. Thoughts have a life-form of their own, an energy of their own, which essentially create our destiny. The key to a lot of this is daily mindfulness, gratitude and affirmations.

Mindfulness allows us to stay present, in the midst of chaos, panic, or anxiety, a key is to just take a look at the surroundings and where are you at this moment. We can do this any time of the day – where am I, what is next to me, what is on the wall, who is in the room, what objects are here, etc. The ability to return the present moment, or practice mindfulness, creates a sense of inner peace and is especially useful during difficult times.

Studies have shown that keeping a gratitude journey – writing down three things you are grateful for each day – has the ability to significantly alter the way we view the world. Especially to put this together at the end of the day, when we are thinking about things we have to do, what we have done, or any additional nighttime stress. Instead, we switch the focus to just three things that we are grateful for and it can change perspective. Furthermore, as we do this for a period of time, we start to look for things and become more and more grateful throughout our days.

Affirmations are reciting positive thoughts to our subconscious mind. The law of attraction teaches us that we attract what we think about most. If we have recurring negative self-talk, these thoughts create energy that are sent out to the universe and we attract exactly that. Affirmations have to do with reversing this process and instead have positive self-talk and essentially attracting the positive into our life. Henry Ford said, "Whether you think you can or you think you can't, you're right."

All of these tools take time to rewire the brain. It cannot happen overnight. The ego trap is when we try too hard to do too much. Then we want to feel enlightened and put on a positivity mask rather than work on developing our soul. This is a classic game that the ego plays to get back in control.

All of this was teaching me to let emotions come and rise; feel them and then let them go. Do not run from them. It teaches us to let go of false agreements, do not attach or identify with anything, just love.

This was my true self and it was an amazing feeling. I wanted to rush and tell everyone, but instead only received rejection. They thought "here goes Cortland again saying he has it figured out." Normally, this would be a part I would send to my shadow and reject it, but the soul had grown too powerful to let it affect me. These tools made it easy to love and see the good in each person.

While this was going on, they had a training at my new job called Trauma Informed Care. This, too, is something that I have felt all along to make system-wide changes. The idea is to treat everyone as if they had been through some type of trauma – because most people have had experienced some form or another. This was created through studies in mental health, the idea is that it is very likely that everyone who walks through the facility has been in some type of traumatic experience. This is what I have waited for my entire career without being able to put it into words. This training revealed the truth. Everyone understands it, but the trouble comes into putting it into practice. People are still too influenced by the behaviors they see and are unable to look beyond the mask.

In order to make an entire society and industry change, a revolution is needed. An underground revolution that will change the way the world views mental health and addiction.

It is the only way.

CHAPTER XXV

The Revolution Has Begun
Demon's Last Stand

Chapter 25
The Revolution Has Begun: Demon's Last Stand

A revolution is defined as a sudden, extreme, or complete change in the way people live, work, etc. Unfortunately, the word is often associated with violence. However, violent revolutions are rarely successful. The reason is because the revolution is always going to come from the little guys, the ones who are being oppressed, and if they embark on a violent revolution they are going to get stomped.

The successful revolutions come by way of non-violent protests and civil disobedience. It comes by ways of people refusing to go along with the backwards ways of the world and refusing to fight violence with violence.

Most notable in carrying these out are Ghandi by freeing his people from British rule, Dr. Martin Luther King Jr. in the United States Civil Rights Movement, or Nelson Mandella in South Africa against the Apartheid Government. You could even go further to the teachings of Jesus and Socrates in regards to how we treat the poor.

There is a scene in the Ghandi movie in which the British troops are guarding the city gates. Ghandi orders his men, one by one to walk up to the gate and attempt to enter without using force. As they approach the gate, the British guards beat them down with their guns. Then the next group of Indian men walk and approach the gate and continue to refuse to resort to violence. One-by-one this continues as the British guards continue to beat them until they grow weak and tired and the Indian people eventually regain control of their city.

This scene sticks with me as it shows the commitment to the non-violent resistance to the oppressor and knowing that this way will always lead to victory. Once the world sees how the oppressor is treating those that are non-violent, it sparks a change.

If Martin Luther King Jr. would have resorted to violence in his protests, the media would have been all over it and change would have never happened. Instead, you would see African-Americans being non-violent and getting beaten and sprayed down with fire hoses showing that there was a need to make a change in public policy.

In the Vietnam War, videos were starting to surface about the atrocities being committed against the women, children, and civilians and it sparked outrage across America. Once the citizens of this country knew what we were doing they demanded change. The students protested across every college campus in American until eventually they withdrew the troops because the game was over for the elite who were profiting off the illegal war.

When a system has been in place for so long and it is creating a great deal of financial interest for those on top, the only way to make a lasting change is for a revolution. There needs to be an awareness of what is going on, followed by the public being notified of this, and then the change will instantly follow.

The mental health and addiction industry is no different. These people have been mistreated more than just about any other group of people since the beginning of time. There are different groups out there that are doing their best to spread the message and eliminate the stigma. This is great, but it is not enough.

Tupac Shakur made reference to this situation in describing his plight for African American rights, equality, and justice in his movie Resurrection.

> *"If I know that in this hotel room they have food every day, and I'm knocking on the door every day to eat, and they open the door, let me see the party, let me see them throwing salami all over, I mean, just throwing food around, but they're telling me there's no food.*
>
> *Every day, I'm standing outside trying to sing my way in:' We are hungry, please let us in. We are hungry, please let us in.' After about a week that song is gonna change to: 'We hungry, we need some food.' After two, three weeks, it's like: 'Give me the food Or I'm breaking down the door.' After a year you're just like: 'I'm picking the lock. Coming through the door blasting.'*
>
> *It's like, you hungry, you reached your level. We asked ten years ago. We was asking with the Panthers. We was asking with them, the Civil Rights Movement. We was asking. Those people that asked are dead and in jail. So now what do you think we're gonna do? Ask?"*

Can You Be Enlightened and a Revolutionary?

This concept may seem to contradict itself, but it is the only way. You need to have both. When you hear the word enlightened you likely think of Buddha or Jesus. When you think of a revolutionary you likely see the image of Che Guevara. It makes you wonder, how is this possible as these people are on such far ends of the spectrum.

However, that is not necessarily true.

We think of enlightened as a person who has it figured out, who can find peace in all moments, and has universal wisdom, love, and joy for the world. While this is true, what good does it do if we just have all of this information and keep it to ourselves? Instead of just sitting around in meditation or on park benches being one with nature, at some point we need to take this wisdom to promote change for humanity.

We need to ask ourselves, "Where do I personally find value, meaning and connection?" And once we have that answer, we follow our heart and we cannot go wrong.

Both Buddha and Jesus gave up material possessions and went on teaching the word of love and interconnection which founded two of the largest religions today. While religion has started to lose its way with man interpreting things as they seem fit for personal agendas, the point is that these religions were founded off the teachings of these enlightened individuals whose purpose was to go against the grain of their society to teach the truth.

Socrates did the same in ancient Greece with the same message. Ghandi, Mandella, Martin Luther King Jr., and even John Lennon all did the same thing.

The result is all of them end up being imprisoned and/or killed. Every single one of them. Because they are standing up to the oppressors and speaking the truth. They were all willing to risk their life or personal freedoms because they knew the truth and were willing to share it even if it cost them life on this earth.

These were all just ordinary people who understood the truth and were willing to risk it all. This is how the revolution has already begun. There are countless websites out there now that are preaching the truth with millions and millions of followers. People are getting fed up with the way of the Western World and we are on the verge of a breakthrough. It is a truth that everyone has known all along and it finally coming to the light. There are more followers now than ever before imagined.

The revolution begins with each person speaking up against the stigma and making a change. Each person that is involved in the industry and rather than being judgmental and going along with "that's just the way it is" can decipher what is right and wrong and willing to risk their job in order to help the patients that are suffering at the hands of those in charge.

The Other Side of the Jail Cell

While I have spent some time inside the jail cell, this time I landed a position working at a County Jail in a major metropolitan area. This position was created to bring about harmony and peace between departments as a recent major lawsuit had brought about serious discontent.

At the same time, I was finishing up continuing care of treatment which had helped me dive deep into my shadow, create new files, and rebuilding me as a human. Exactly as treatment is designed – to rehabilitate what was broken.

During my graduation ceremony, we go around the room and everyone gives me feedback. It was a strange moment in my life in which a group of men just went around and told me all these positive qualities about myself and what I had done for them. It was something I really had not received but it boosted my confidence.

The graduation ceremony concludes with the counselor giving some feedback. However, our counselor was not there today – instead, they had a fill-in counselor who happened to be the program director, PVD.

> "I think you need to stop enjoying being the new guy, the 'I'm learning guy,' the 'I'm growing guy,' the 'teach me, teach me guy.'" PVD said to me, "I think you need to become the guy who does the twelfth step. You get stuck in being here, in getting help. You need to step up. Become the leader, the giver, the teacher you already are."

It was amazing and also quite unexpected. I was expecting some type of praise for all the work I did, but instead, he challenged me to take things to the next level. He challenged me to grow. He challenged me to start the revolution.

This is one of the problems with the new ways we are teaching counselors and therapists. So much time is spent on practicing empathy – which believe me is utmost importance. The sad thing is that we need to teach empathy since it is an innate human characteristic. We are social beings and naturally have this ability. However, the stigma surrounding addiction and mental health is so strong that we need to teach counselors how to understand their clients.

Don't get me wrong, this is a great teach and necessary to build relationships. The problem is that there is not enough teaching in classrooms about how to grow. This is why so many people will talk about their counseling experience by saying, "Yeah it was great to have someone to talk to and share with but nothing really changed." That is because they person continues to just have a non-judgmental sounding board and build a relationship, but at some point they need someone to push them to change.

PVD has the natural empathy, but also has a direct approach. He wants people to get better and he will tell them what is necessary and then it is up to them to make that change.

I started to speak up for the patients and the jail and get to know each of them personally, along with the other staff including jailers and nurses. I was creating change and rising in popularity, which angered my boss. We were complete opposites and he believed in image and professionalism; whereas, I was more interested in saving lives.

We started to battle and I started to cross the line, which was ego-driven, which led to me either being fired or resign due to sending emails without approval. I felt crushed again as if I was losing it all – but I have had this feeling so many times before and this is always where the light enters. I knew I was meant to be there for a reason, but not the reason that my ego desired.

After my resignation, I received a very powerful reaction from the staff at the jail. It was overwhelming. Everyone in the building responded to me with care and compassion. I was receiving calls and texts from people to talk about how my presence will be sorely missed and about the great changes that were made during my short time.

The support was amazing and I felt like I truly did something right. But, I also felt guilty as could have handled it better and we could have grown together. It was just another life lesson, teaching me something, and leading me down the next road.

I remember hiring a young lady there because during the interview she told me, "We need to treat them the same as others. They are not bad people." I told her that is the reason she was hired, because of that comment. I told this to everyone.

The entire staff transformed. When I started they were yelling about the patients and complaining about how the prisoners take the taxpayers money to get free healthcare and at the same time treated them like animals. By the time I left, they were treating them with care and compassion.

We all learned that encouragement goes much further than correction. You find a positive attribute and you call it out in front of everyone. Correction should be done with love behind closed doors. In fact, the term "corrections" should be removed. If you just build a relationship and come from an awakened state of love, then things will change. If others do not accept it, that is OK, because you will still grow from giving love – I know I did.

State Hospital

As time passed, I had another job interview and it is at the State Hospital. It was the same place that I was committed to in March 1994 as an 18-year-old high school student. It was now November of 2013, almost 20 years later and here I was applying for a job.

It is the state hospital, so I doubted I had much of a chance to get any job there. This hospital houses the 110 "sickest" patients in the state, which meant it would also employ the most qualified staff.

In November of 2012, the Commissioner of Human Services had just allowed the state more staff due to the injuries that had occurred at the hospital. A recent lawsuit resulted in the state paying more than three million dollars for illegally using restraints on patients and using them as a behavior modification and not as a last resort.

It was known to be a "dangerous" place. So they needed to fill some new positions and my timing to be looking for work was perfect once again. I was hired the same day that I had the interview. Looking back, that should have been a red flag, but at the time I was ecstatic – I had arrived! My comeback was complete. I was going to work at the state hospital with the "sickest" patients. The place I had always dreamed of working. This too, was all an illusion.

No one has ever been let inside the State Hospital and no one has ever seen what takes place inside those walls. The administration claims that is due to HIPPA laws. On the news, employees complain about how scary it is and how they need more staff to feel secure.

All of this seemed scary, but I was excited to be there. It felt like home. The illusion started to crumble almost immediately.

I was in training with all the new staff and almost none of them had any experience in Mental Health or in Psychiatric care – another red flag. I was a bit surprised at some of the classes and some of the answers that were given. We would do mock talking with patient sessions and people did not know what to say to the actors.

Then came the mandatory day of class in which we were all required to attend. We were unsure about why or what it entailed and were only told it was "the most important day of training."

This critical training was the day they taught us how to "take the patients down." It seemed more like a football drill than mental health treatment. They told us how "dangerous" patients were and how they will hit and kick you. They talked about how unsafe it was and how we always needed to be on guard and prepared.

This is nothing like how I have experienced people with mental health. Statistics will also show that those with mental health have almost the same amount of violent crimes as the general population. We focused two days on how intimidating it was there and how we needed to be ready at all times. They were literally teaching us karate moves and self-defense techniques more than they were teaching us how to use force for two days; and we had only spent two hours on how to talk to them. Less than a day on the diagnosis and less than a day on the cause of these "illnesses" – all of which is trauma.

I glanced over the roster of the unit I would be working on - Unit E. The most senior nurse there had been there only three months. I asked the staffing lady about this, and she said, "You'll find out."

On my first day, a woman who had been working there for 20 years immediately shows me how to restrain someone. They were highly focused on using restraints. Next, a big burly man comes by us and says,

> *"I don't care what they told you upstairs,*
> *we do things our way on the floor."*

The new nurses and staff seemed to be afraid. Like any culture, if you are new, you usually go along. Or if you are in a place of dysfunction, you either become a part of it, or you fly under the radar.

What I saw in my time there was awful. It was a place that one group of people, the staff, had absolute power over another group of people - the patients. When there is absolute power, there is going to be corruption. These patients had no say in their treatment and were forced against their will to be there. While the staff could do as they pleased. I could not believe the things that I saw in that building. I thought we had come a long way since I worked as part of the "green team" that routinely abused patients. I was wrong. This was much worse. The difference is that I knew better this time, I was not going to go along with it.

I knew there had been a recent lawsuit and that there was a mandate to cut down on restraints and treat patients humanely. I realized that what they would do is restrain the patients and then fix the paperwork to make sure that it was justified, even though it would never truly uphold.

They would take a patient with BPD and give them antipsychotics for behavior control, and the patient would sleep all day and gain 50 pounds. They would conclude this treatment was beneficial by stating "no more behaviors" and laugh as they slept all day. The patients would be antagonized and if they argued, they would be restrained. I saw abuse of power as I have never seen before.

I didn't realize that when I was going to work with the sickest people in the state that it meant my co-workers, not the patients. Tell me who is the sick ones here? The person with a mental disorder or the person abusing their power?

They would tease the patients behind their backs, call them names, or make fun of their appearance. The medical director of the program (who is paid hundreds of thousands dollars per year) was teasing a young girl, born into poverty, about her hair. I saw patients get pushed and beaten and then the paper worked was completely falsified to say that they were "struggling."

"It's all in the paperwork." They would say and then laugh. Supervisors taught you how to fake paperwork. I could write an entire book on the numerous atrocities that I witnessed happen in that place.

It was like I was in a movie. I could not believe what I was seeing. Was it even real? No one said anything, so it made me believe that I was the crazy one for seeing what I saw. No one else seemed to see it or care to see it. I could not go along with this like I had in the past.

Knowing that there was a recent lawsuit, I reported things to my supervisor, which resulted in nothing happening. Then, I went to her supervisor with the same result. Eventually in about April, I was about to quit when I saw my old friend, Dr. Peter's from the county hospital working there. This guy was showing up in my life again when I needed him again.

We talked about it, and he directed me where to go with what I was witnessing. I sent a letter to the director of the State. I figured this would be the end of my job, but I did not care. I was not going to just sit there and watch this abuse. If you are not part of the solution, you are part of the problem.

> *"He who passively accepts evil is as much involved in it as he who helps to perpetrate it. He who accepts evil without protesting against it, is really cooperating with it." – Martin Luther King Jr.*

To my surprise, not only did he respond to me, but I was invited up to talk to him. Then after we met, we started to meet over and over again. He listened to me and he wanted to hear the truth, and he also wanted to change things.

We looked over all the statistics and went about it the right way and most accurately. The staff would say the patients are unruly, however, one staff member would restrain someone 25-percent of the time they were working, while another staff would never use a restraint for the exact same patients.

The ones who were using restraints were the same ones describing these patients as "dangerous" and then going on the news stations and notifying the public about the treacherous work conditions they face each day. Yet, the truth is that eighty-percent of the time they were on the computer or drinking coffee and not interacting with the patients. They would fake injuries and tell everyone that if they went to the hospital it would be reported as an OSHA injury. None of them even spent time with the patients or made any effort to communicate with them. While I was working there, these same staff members were caught drunk at work or sleeping while on the job. They needed no training to be there, just an attitude to abuse power.

If the patients actually did stand up for themselves, or complained about their mistreatment, they would certainly be punished.

I started to bring these complaints and slowly things started to change. People began to know it was me who was talking to the director which was bringing about changes. We went from 25 restraints one month to zero, all in a time span of just three months. I felt proud. I was helping change things. However, people did not like being forced to take classes on trauma, learn about the diagnosis, and getting to know patients and alternative methods.

This is the frightening part about this place and this industry. Not the patients, but the staff and the entire attitude. Imagine if this was any other area of healthcare and the staff was so completely uninformed and ignorant about the people they treat – there would be an outrage.

There was one instance in which a patient with developmental disabilities was not allowed to be restrained; yet, despite this condition the patient was held in a chair for eight hours! Another example was a 65-year-old woman being held down as if she was a danger. Restraints were supposed to be used only as a last resort.

It had now been 20 years since I was committed to this place, and here I am watching this unfold before my eyes. There was a lot of pushback as I was trying to help create change. These people had been abusing patients for 25 years and they all know each other. They were all part of their own little "good ole boys club." There was major resistance and eventually the director of the hospital was removed.

As hard as I tried, I was not being heard and the restraints increased once again and nobody was listening. I could not take it anymore and left the facility. Devastated that I could not give the patients what they needed, what they deserved, and allowing the corruption to continue.

However, about nine months after I left, someone had noticed. Not only did they notice, but they documented the corruption and brought it to the public.

A series of undercover investigations brought change. A staff member had secretly photographed the abuse. The result was 177 million dollars in new funding, new beds, and the termination of most of the administration.

> *"I am not going to change the world. But I guarantee I am going to spark the brain that will change the world." – Tupac Shakur*

CHAPTER XXVI

Taking the Mask Off

Chapter 26
Taking the Mask Off

Along the coast of a small village in West Africa, a 16-year-old girl is abducted from her family, taken into captivity by authorities without any explanations. Her innocence gone, lives forever changed, and she knows this is the last time she will see her family.

Near the sea, she spends a week in a dark, secure facility with about a thousand others from various tribes uncertain of the crime they have committed or where their future lies. Eventually they are brought to the surface only to be stripped naked, inspected, and branded with hot iron on their skin with an unfamiliar marking. An enormous ship is docked along the shore awaiting the human cargo.

Aboard the ship, there is an unbearable stench of death immediately creating nausea and vomiting. The prisoners are crammed into tiny docks about three feet high, forced to sit between each other's legs, with no chance of lying down or even changing positions. The ship crams nearly 600 people into the docks like sardines with little breathable air, forced to sit in feces, and take on the scorching sub-tropic sun.

After a few months of these deplorable conditions, the ship docks in New Orleans at an auction house for white savages. Again inspected carefully, one-by-one they are sold as property, given new names, and sent to their slave master's plantation.

This girl is renamed Elizabeth and she is sent to live with Christian Hoover, a plantation owner in rural Mississippi.

In the early 1800s, this is one of the final Transatlantic Slave Trade shipments as the trade was finally made illegal in 1807. In all, more than 54,000 journeys have taken place stealing nearly 12 million Africans from their home and put into the trade. But this is just the number that survived. It is estimated that more than 20 million, like Elizabeth, were abducted in West Africa during this time.

It was a worldwide three-part system. The Europeans would trade guns, rum, and clothing to African kings for slaves. At first, the kings would send criminals, or prisoners from war, but the demand from the Europeans was too great. This led to African kingdoms starting war, with the new guns they were purchasing, and hunting down slaves to keep the movement alive.

The middle passage was the horrendous transatlantic voyage described above putting the slaves into the fields for free manual labor. The essence of colonization is conquering an undeveloped country, strip them of their natural resources, to produce cheaper products to increase profits. In the Americas the raw materials were tobacco, sugar, rice, and cotton – all of which were labor intensive. In order for the colonies to succeed and America to prosper, they needed cheap labor, and the slave trade made this newfound nation an economic super power.

In elementary school, we all learn the famous line written by Thomas Jefferson in the Declaration of Independence, *"We hold these truths to be self-evident, that all men are created equal, that they are endowed by their Creator with certain unalienable Rights; that among these are Life, Liberty and the pursuit of Happiness."*

Less known, or told in school, is that Jefferson owned more than 600 slaves throughout his lifetime to help build his estate. Later, in a message to a friend, Jefferson then wrote:

> *"If there is a just God, we are going to pay for this."*

Stealing land from Native Americans for more room to grow and using stolen Africans to do the work, America soon became the leading exporter of cotton. In the 1800s, cotton was king just as oil has been since the 1900s. And America was exporting 75-percent of the world's greatest cash crop.

On the Hoover plantation, Christian was married and had 11 children. It was not uncommon at this time for the women to be giving birth on a yearly basis. It was also common for select slave women to serve as "bed warmers" while the wife was pregnant, sleeping with their master.

Elizabeth served as a bed warmer for Christian and gave birth to a light-skinned daughter named Elizabeth Ann. Although born with light skin, any slave child was considered black and was granted no rights – giving these children the most undesirable of situations being excluded by both blacks and whites.

From here, the Hoover family tree gets tangled which was typical on slave plantations. They are even more difficult to keep track of due to no records being kept of slave births in most states.

- 1814 - Christian Hoover has a daughter with his slave, Elizabeth. They also name her Elizabeth Ann.
    - 1830 – Christian Hoover has a daughter with Elizabeth Ann (also his daughter) and they name her Emily Allen – making Christian both the father and grandfather of Emily.
        - 1859 – Emily Allen goes on to have many children with all of her half-brothers. Her oldest son is named Ivery Hoover. This makes Christian both the maternal and paternal grandfather of Ivery.

- 1834 – Elizabeth Ann then passes for white, moves to Washington, D.C., and marries William Hoover. They have one son, John Hoover.
  - 1857 - John Hoover then marries a woman and they have three children. The oldest is Dickenson Naylor Hoover.
    - After Dickenson Naylor Hoover marries Anna Marie he is put into an insane asylum.
    - While in the asylum, Anna Marie moves back to Mississippi and has an affair with Dickenson's cousin, Ivery Hoover. She becomes pregnant and gives birth to John Edgar Hoover (J. Edgar Hoover) on January 1, 1895.

Dickenson was aware that J. Edgar was not his child and he was abused and neglected throughout his childhood. The embarrassment and shame of having a slave child was too much for the family to bear and this became the dark secret of the Hoover family for decades.

Growing up, Hoover likely considered himself to be white until the secret was finally exposed to him in which he kept with him to his grave – in fact, he did everything he could to don his mask as a white man. And it was not the only mask Hoover wore.

At age 29, Hoover rose to the director of the Federal Bureau of Investigations (F.B.I.). Crime in America had been steadily rising and Hoover was the man to make the change. He gained prominence with his efforts for chasing down radicalism and communists with his landmark case of deporting Marcus Garvey.

Garvey was a pioneer in the black civil rights movement. Hoover, part-black himself, often targeted black activists and viewed their beliefs as radical. Perhaps this was his way of hiding his true identity – because if it were ever discovered his heritage he would have never been allowed to prosper in racist America in the early 1900s.

Garvey was born in Jamaica and traveled throughout the Americas and recognized everywhere he went that blacks were on the lower end of society. His vision was to improve their quality of life, self-determination, and repatriation to Africa. Hoover brought him down by hiring insiders to find dirt on Garvey and eventually got him arrested and deported on charges of mail fraud.

Although some of Garvey's views were controversial, he did trigger the remarkable leaders such as Malcolm X and Martin Luther King, Jr. who spread his message in the 1960s. Not coincidentally, both were also premier targets of Hoover in his prime.

Knowing the foundations of the African people in America, imagine all the good Hoover could have done for the civil rights movement with his passion, intelligence, and determination. Instead, he focused on shutting it down to protect his true identity. This is the danger of growing attached to our psychological masks.

Although crime was rising, the Alcohol industry likes to blame this strictly on Prohibition as the sole contributor. In reality, organized crime was on the rise and prohibition just opened up a new industry for the mafia – bring a product (alcohol) to a population that had a high demand and their supply taken out from under their feet.

In 1929, the stock market crashed. This was followed by banks failing, leading to fewer loans, less spending, fewer wages, no jobs, reduced trading, and a global economic collapse – also known as the

Great Depression. Not too much different than what we experienced in 2008.

One out of every four citizens was unemployed, people waited in bread lines for food, or headed out west in hopes of finding work. Criminals like John Dillinger, "Baby Face" Nelson, "Pretty Boy" Floyd, and Bonnie and Clyde weren't necessarily viewed as criminals, but more like Robin Hood. They destroyed mortgage papers at the banks they hit.

Harry Pierpoint explained, "I stole from the banks who stole from the people."

Dillinger became the most famous of all with lotteries putting up odds as to when he would be arrested next. More money was spent on trying to catch Dillinger than the actual money he stole from banks.

This was Hoover's next prized possession. And cleverly enough, Hoover created a public relations campaign of his own – making the cops the new heroes. The name Hoover was synonymous with the FBI and soon people were cheering for the cops instead of the robbers.

With all his amazing capabilities to fight crime, capture secrets, and change the perception of America – it's too bad his mask led him down a path of greater crime than that of the criminals he exposed.

And it is not just that Hoover did not like black progressive leaders, he abused his power in a hell-bent effort to bring them down. Hoover's used phrase such as "Neutralize black-nationalist groups," or "Prevent the rise of the black messiah."

But it wasn't just blacks that Hoover was after, he was out to expose and eliminate the homosexual community. Hoover's reasoning was that Communists would blackmail U.S. Citizens – specifically those involved in government agencies – to gather secrets. His claim was that no one had more at risk of being exposed than the homosexual population.

This was known as the "Lavender Scare," which Hoover was focused on removing any and all homosexuals from office and exposing them to light. During the time of the Cold War, rise of the American Mafia, and all other events going on during this time, it makes one question why targeting homosexuality was a priority.

Although never openly admitted, Hoover was incredibly involved with his number-two man at the Bureau, Clyde Tolson. While there is plenty of evidence to support they had a romantic or sexual relationship, that is not the point of this article and more in-depths documents have been revealed. The point is that that, much like the Larry Craig incident in the Minneapolis restroom, Hoover's anti-gay rhetoric was clearly a cover-up to prevent himself from being exposed. In fact, nearly the entire Hoover estate was willed over to Tolson at his death in 1972.

So, here you have the best cop in the world, in charge of the greatest police force in the world – yet we have a rise of the American Mafia?

Hoover adamantly downplayed the rise of the mafia or their existence. It baffled people inside and outside the organization as it was a glaringly obvious problem, which Hoover refused to acknowledge.

Well, Hoover had another vice which connected him to the mafia. He was a gambling addict. At the time, horse racing was king in the United States. The mafia set up gambling rings, set lines on the races, betting wires, and even fixed the races. Hoover was highly invested in this system, connecting him to the mafia, and if he were ever to try to go after the mafia – all his secrets, or mask, would be exposed.

On November 22, 1963, the president of the United States is killed in Dallas, Texas. This is in the height of the Cold War and you would expect the most thorough investigation in the history of the world to take place. But instead, Hoover was at the race track the next day. Again, it is well-documented that he frequented such places as the Del Mar race track and that every town Hoover went, you would find him at the local track.

But in testifying to the Senate in 1951, Hoover states, *"The gambling problem must be viewed as a phase of the entire crime picture. Organized gambling is a vicious evil. It corrupts our youth and wipes the lives of our adults. It becomes a springboard for other crimes such as embezzlement, robbery, and even murder."*

The man who held the most secrets on others, held the most secrets about himself. It was all just another ploy to protect his mask.

It was a real-life game of Spy-vs.-Spy. The Mafia likely had secrets on Hoover and it was in his best interest to stay away from being exposed. Again, his mask prevented him from doing his work and corrupting a nation.

Regarding the killing of Kennedy, another highly unknown nugget is that Lyndon Baines Johnson hired Hoover to do his own investigation. His 500-page report alleged that Lee Harvey Oswald acted as the lone gunman. Rather than the Warren Commission doing their own diligence, they relied heavily on Hoover's report and agreed that Oswald was the "lone nut."

Even at the time of release, only 56-percent of American's believed Oswald acted alone. Today less than one out of 10 people believe the government's official story that stemmed from Hoover's "investigation." In the 888-page Warren Commission mockery of an investigation, it never gives a motive for Oswald killing the president. Just a lone nut.

Whether or not Hoover was directly involved in the assassination, it is clear he played a role in the cover up. Not only this protected Hoover directly, there is a more indirect protection here. The lone-nut theory, clears the mafia from any alleged involvement – protecting Hoover's secrets from being exposed by his friends in the organized crime business.

On May 2, 1972, Hoover passed away and his body was found by his chauffeur (or possibly his live-in cook). His cook then contacted Tolson, who in turn contacted Hoover's secretary Helen Gandy. At this time, Gandy went to work shredding all of Hoover's most secretive files as one final attempt to keep Hoover's corruption and illegal activity in the darkness.

Since his death, Hoover's legacy has been tarnished due to the uncovering of some of his illegal activities of wiretapping, break-ins, bugs, confiscating mail, and blackmail. Hoover was discriminatory, racist, contradicting, and viewed everyone as the enemy. He rose to power by punishing those who shared characteristics of himself – African-Americans, homosexuals, and addicts.

Stigma about race, about sexual orientation, and disease of compulsion turned Hoover into a monster. What if he were to unmask himself and join the fight for equality and empower people like Garvey or King? What if the most powerful man in the world told us he was a homosexual, what would that have done to propel the gay rights movement? And what if he sought help for his addiction and freed himself from his allegiance to the mafia?

A six-page pamphlet written by Hoover in 1957, entitled, "If I Had a Son," speaks candidly about activities boys should be involved when in their youth. A strikingly odd title for a man who never wanted a son, nor did he ever want a wife. Indirectly, Hoover unmasks himself in this little-known document. In the booklet, Hoover writes:

> *"If I had a son, I'd do one thing. I'd tell him the truth. I'd never let him catch me in a lie. And in return, I'd insist that he tell the truth. When children go astray, it isn't the fault of the children but of their parents…I'd try to understand my son. For if I didn't, I'd be a failure as a Dad!"*

Taking the Mask Off

The opening story of the final chapter of the book is a true story about a very notorious figure in American History. It is told her to show how a mask is created, why it is we cling to the mask, and the damage it does not only to us personally, but to those around us, and to our society.

Yet, the premise of this book is quite simple but so effective. We have created a psychological mask for our protection and we are terrified to go about living without it. However, it has entrapped us and our only way to freedom is to remove the mask. Each one of us, one at a time, and all together at once. To live again as free, pure, innocent souls just as we did when we were children. To love freely, to live together, and in harmony with all that is.

This brings me to today. In the opening chapter about Jim, I told you that I attempted suicide and failed. Today, I am telling you that

I did succeed in killing my false self and only have my true self to show the world. In that true self, I am making strides at being a part of the revolution. Not to be part of the revolution so I can show the world because that is ego based, but to do so because it is the right thing to do and what my heart and soul is guiding me.

I am looking at life with a more open mind and seeing that everything is a symbol, a sign, and a synchronicity. I am no longer angry at religions, it is man that has interpreted religions for their own desires. All religions teach the same thing, but the irony is that it cannot teach us anything that we do not already know.

We all hold the truth within. There is nothing that I can write in this book that you do not already know at some deeper level. Because we are all interconnected as the science, philosophies, and prophets have always known. There are no "good" or "bad" people because all of us are one. Each person is God that is experiencing the universe subjectively. When we can go about our day and seeking ourselves, or God, within each other living creature you will instantly bring about a sense of inner peace and remembering our divinity.

It has been quite a journey. To think, over twenty years ago I was committed to this same state hospital as mentally ill and unable to care for myself to becoming a charge nurse at the same hospital. Throughout this journey, I have come to believe that the fix is quite simple, but we complicate it unintentionally.

The first thing we must do is become healthy ourselves. Even if we want to be the healer, we cannot fix others if we are not well. We must be whole in body, mind, and spirit. This will allow for us to have an open mind, be non-judgmental, and offer an attitude of compassion. And finally, we must not try to guide others' lives. They are on their own journey and we are just a passenger with the roadmap but everyone has the answers within.

Then we can begin to make a difference.

It is also important to remember to be patient and that we are not going to change someone's world in one interaction. It starts with just saying "hello" and finding a way to connect. Be open, and approachable, and give people time and when they are ready they will let you know. Show true love, compassion, and genuine concern for the person and their journey. Give them meaningful compliments and take time to get to know about them and their life, dreams, and desires. Do not have preconceived notions about them, go into each interaction as if you know nothing about them, but also looking for yourself, or God, in their eyes and in their stories.

Be ready to walk through hell, which is only the mind running wild and believing it to be true. Be well equipped, knowledgeable, and study. Study the things in which you have an opposing view to help gain perspective. If you are against medication, study about medication. If you are against religion, study more about religion. Find out about those who have different ideas and opinions and listen to them. Take lessons from everything, ever person, and every interaction.

Finally, be willing to fight for people that cannot fight for themselves. Figure out how to deliver the message in the most appropriate way to reach the right people. Don't worry about the outcomes, they are always out of your control. Only focus on what you can control, which is your action. Do your best in those actions. Don't ignore your instincts that is your soul guiding you.

Be a teacher, find positives in everyone and pull them out. Do not see anyone as a bad person. When you see them struggling, take the extra time to help them out. If not you, then who else is going to do this?

Power of Love

> *"If you want people to love you for who you are, take off the mask." -- unknown*

I remember one time a woman was struggling with identifying her higher power for many weeks. Finally, one day she approached me and told me she figured it out.

"Love," she said smiling, "Love is my higher power."

Everyone around was silent. It was interesting looking around the group and seeing everyone nod their heads but really not know what to say. At the time, I did not realize how accurate she was in defining her higher power. People often explain that the higher power is a portal in which love enters. So, her thought was that love could be a portal through which life flows.

You can't see love, it is a feeling. It is like God or Buddha. It is there at any moment to tap into. That is our free will to connect at any time and allow love to flow.

Now, I am not cured. I am going to have moments and I am going to learn a lot more. I am certainly no expert and I cannot tell you how to find the way. Anyone who claims they can show you the way, has more learning to do than the person who is asking.

Each of our journeys are unique with different lessons to learn. That is why there are so many ways into heaven or nirvana. This just happens to be my story. It is my way of finding peace, being present, and freeing my soul. This is my message and what I have learned.

I wish there was a simple answer that would end all the pain and suffering but that is not the case. However, what I do know that every moment we have an opportunity to give it all we have and it will build a ripple effect. In every moment we can give love and replenish what we need. That is all we can do, yet, it is the only way to change the world. One moment at a time. Each moment is an opportunity to be guided by love or fear.

In my final words, I'll quote Riley as I was leaving my job at the psychiatric rehab facility and telling her how much I learned from her. We loved psychoanalyzing everything and getting into the roots of everyone's issues. I said to her,

"This was great learning about all the inner workings of the mind and how this happens."

"Yeah but you know what?" She responded, "All this talk, there is a cure for all mental health problems. Jung figured it out, Erikson, all expert analysis all comes down to one thing that can cure every problem."

"And what is that?" I asked.

"Love." Again, she was right.

Made in the USA
Columbia, SC
31 May 2019